Macromedia Flash™ MX ActionScript:
The Complete Reference

About the Author

Dr. William B. Sanders is a professor of Interactive Information Technology at the University of Hartford. He has written four previous books on Flash and more than 40 computer-related books covering everything from assembly language to JavaScript. Macromedia Flash MX plays a key role in the courses he teaches on developing interactive elements to be merged into the quickly expanding world of the Internet. His research is currently focused on the changing nature of human interaction over the Internet and the interfaces to facilitate that interaction.

Macromedia Flash™ MX ActionScript: The Complete Reference

William Sanders

McGraw-Hill/Osborne

New York   Chicago   San Francisco
Lisbon   London   Madrid   Mexico City
Milan   New Delhi   San Juan
Seoul   Singapore   Sydney   Toronto

The **McGraw·Hill** Companies

McGraw-Hill/Osborne
2600 Tenth Street
Berkeley, California 94710
U.S.A.

To arrange bulk purchase discounts for sales promotions, premiums, or fund-raisers, please contact **McGraw-Hill/Osborne** at the above address. For information on translations or book distributors outside the U.S.A., please see the International Contact Information page immediately following the index of this book.

Macromedia Flash™ MX ActionScript: The Complete Reference

1234567890 DOC DOC 0198765432

ISBN 0-07-222643-9

Publisher
  Brandon A. Nordin

Vice President & Associate Publisher
  Scott Rogers

Acquisitions Editor
  Nancy Maragioglio

Project Editor
  Jody McKenzie

Acquisitions Coordinator
  Athena Honore

Technical Editor
  Dave Emberton

Copy Editor
  Lunaea Weatherstone

Proofreader
  Susan Carlson Greene

Indexer
  David Heiret

Computer Designers
  George Toma Charbak
  Tara A. Davis

Illustrators
  Melinda Moore Lytle
  Michael Mueller
  Lyssa Wald

Series Design
  Peter F. Hancik

This book was composed with Corel VENTURA™ Publisher.

This book is dedicated to my wonderful wife, Delia.

Contents at a Glance

Part III ActionScript Objects

Part IV ActionScript User Interface Components

Contents

Part I

Introducing Macromedia Flash MX ActionScript

Part II

Fundamental ActionScript

Part III

ActionScript Objects

Part IV

ActionScript User Interface Components

Acknowledgements

Several people were generous with their time, advice, and help in creating this book. The people at Macromedia provided valuable assistance: Henriette Cohn, Eric Wittman, Michael Williams, Jennipher Tchejeyan, Jeremy Allaire, and Matt Wobensmith. Along with other developers who worked with this group, I was most grateful for the help they always provided.

The Flash community is another important group connected with the success of Macromedia Flash MX in the early days of its existence. In going over my e-mails I was surprised to find the number of others working with Flash MX in a professional capacity who had been so helpful. Included in that group are Robert Penner, Helen Triolo, Sudhir Kumar, aYo Binitie, Bill Drol, Derek Franklin, Jon Warren Lentz, Brian Lesser, Robert M. Hall, Jeroen Steenbeek, Claus Wahlers, Cortlandt Winters, Samuel Wan, Matt Hampton, Ric Ewing, Todd Marks, Michael Hurwicz, Ian Chia, Robert Reinhardt, and Navneet Nair. Many of this group went on to publish books and chapters about Macromedia Flash MX themselves, but none were stingy with their knowledge and willingness to share. To me, this made their assistance all that more valuable.

My colleagues in the University of Hartford's Interactive Information Technology (IIT) were supportive as always, along with others with whom I shared an interest in Macromedia Flash. John Gray and Steve Misovich were most supportive. Also, the

IIT students are always pushing the edge of the envelope in Internet and Web technology, and without their enthusiasm and expectations, my own would not be as high.

The people at McGraw-Hill/Osborne were constantly supportive, from the initial work with Tim Madrid and Jim Schachterle to finishing up with Athena Honore, Jody McKenzie, and Nancy Maragioglio. I am also grateful to Margo Hutchinson for making it possible to work with McGraw-Hill/Osborne. Perhaps the greatest asset provided by the publisher was providing me with the genius of David Emberton as a technical editor. Never have I worked with a more knowledgeable, tactful, and helpful technical editor, and I have worked with some of the best. Any flaws in this book are solely due to my taking the perilous path of not heeding David's good advice.

To express a kind word to one's spouse is expected. However, my wife, Delia, represents *douceur de vivre* to me and her support was a balm. Our Greater Swiss Mountain Dog, WillDe, was a welcomed daily distraction from work as he hauled me off on our daily two-mile hike.

Introduction

This book is structured and written so that it will be useful to and used by Macromedia Flash MX developers and designers. It is a general-purpose ActionScript MX book in that it is designed to serve many purposes. The first chapter is a transition to ActionScript MX from other languages such as JavaScript, Visual Basic, C++, Java, and earlier versions of ActionScript. Those familiar with JavaScript will find that ActionScript MX is designed around the ECMA-262 standards and should have no trouble picking up the syntax and structure quickly. (ECMA standards are developed by the European Computer Manufacturer's Association, and the 262 standards are those for Internet scripting languages such as JavaScript and ActionScript.) Likewise, those familiar with other scripting or programming languages will find familiar structures.

However, if this is your first venture into ActionScript, spend a little time with the first chapter to see how Flash MX ActionScript is written in the Actions panel. You should be able to see the differences between ActionScript and other languages quickly. If you are learning ActionScript as your first programming or scripting language, you will want to spend time carefully going over Chapters 1 and 2. Under any circumstances, before tackling ActionScript, you should be familiar with Flash MX.

Whatever your background and orientation to programming, this book is one to be used sitting right next to your computer. Use your own system of bookmarks, dog ears, colored tags, marking pens, or any other reference system you choose to flag those parts you have to keep looking up. Everything possible was done to make this book highly usable. You should be able to quickly find everything you need for any programming task with Flash MX, with both explanations and examples. You will find all of the major examples online at http://www.osborne.com/ and at http://www.sandlight.com/ in a format that you can download. The files contain the source code in FLA files.

Who Is this Book For?

This book is written for the Flash user who wants to have a thorough grounding in ActionScript MX. The level ranges from beginner in the first part to advanced in the latter parts of the book. A novice who goes through the book from cover to cover will not be a novice at the end, and an advanced user should find useful information in the very first chapter about what changes have been made in the language since Flash 5. However, the focus of the book is not set to be any particular level so much as it is an attempt to provide a thorough coverage of ActionScript in Flash MX.

When you're creating a Flash MX movie, this book should be available to quickly look up what you need for any term in the ActionScript lexicon. The examples accompanying the terms are designed to illustrate the concept within the term. Sometimes an abstract example is used if it best reveals exactly what the term does, and at other times a very concrete example is used to do the same thing. Most of the examples are fairly short, taking up no more than a few lines. Other examples, though, required a more elaborate script to show how terms work in some context. For example, to show how the XML object in ActionScript works, it was necessary to use an actual XML file and a script that parses the XML so that text nodes appear as information on the screen. A few back-end examples required a little PHP to serve as illustrative examples to accompany an explanation of an ActionScript term. Likewise, to understand and use XML socket objects, you need to use an open socket server, and so the sample movie shows where to get an open socket server (free!) and how to use it with Macromedia Flash MX ActionScript XML open socket objects.

However, even the longest examples are not very long as far as coded materials are concerned. They are just long enough to clearly explain what is going on. The goal is to provide the reader with good clear examples and not indulge the author in showing off slick code. All of the longer examples are provided online in FLA files so you do not have to spend a lot of time typing in code. The code is part of the book and, seen in the context of the book, should be clear. You can look at the code and the explanation and then go ahead and write your own ActionScript to get done what you need to accomplish.

Wherever possible and sensible, the book follows the ActionScript standards suggested by Macromedia. The standards, as you will see later in this introduction, are really a set of best practices and not strictures. So if some of the code is a little different from what you may be used to seeing in ActionScript, it may be due to adherence to standards. However, if the standards got in the way of clearly showing how a term in ActionScript operates, the standards were not artificially and unnecessarily imposed in the examples. This was generally the case in the shorter examples.

The image kept in mind while writing this book was that of someone working on a Flash MX project using ActionScript and needing to look up something fast. More than anything else, this book is a practical guide to learning and using ActionScript MX thoroughly.

How this Book Is Organized

In deciding the best way to organize the different ActionScript terms, it seemed that a natural way to link the different terms in the Actions toolbox would be to use toolbox organization. The highest level folders in the toolbox are organized in the following sequence:

- Actions
- Operators
- Functions
- Constants
- Properties
- Objects
- Deprecated
- Flash UI Components

As you open the folders you will find both ActionScript terms and subfolders. By following this organization in the book, it should be very easy to find what you need. However, not all of the folders are equal in size or scope. The top-level Constants folder has very few terms, while the Objects folder has enough terms to take up half the book. Also, the Deprecated terms, while important for some applications, were assigned to an Appendix where they are both available and out of the way at the same time. So, in looking at the overall organization of the book, you will find that it closely follows the organization of the Actions toolbox.

The book is divided into four parts. Part I, "Introducing Macromedia Flash MX ActionScript," is an introduction to scripting in Flash MX whether transitioning from another language or from earlier versions of Macromedia Flash ActionScript. The two chapters in this part explain what you need to know about getting started using scripts in Flash MX. Even if you're familiar with Flash 5 ActionScript, you are likely to want to go over these two chapters to see what is new about Flash MX ActionScript. Flash MX ActionScript is about twice as big as the previous version, so you will find a good deal of new material. Also, the tools and panels in Flash MX are significantly different from earlier versions, including Flash 5.

Part II, "Fundamental ActionScript," contains the core actions in ActionScript, and most of these are similar, if not identical to, Flash 5 ActionScript. Two chapters, "Basic Actions I" and "Basic Actions II," cover ActionScript's statements (called actions). "Basic Actions I" covers Movie Control, Browser/Network, Movie Clip Control, and the Variables folders, and "Basic Actions II" examines the Conditions/Loops, Printing, User-Defined Functions, and Miscellaneous Actions folders. The remaining three chapters in Part II look at Operators, Functions, Properties, and Constants.

Part III, "ActionScript Objects," is the very soul of Flash MX ActionScript. While some of the objects in Flash MX originated in earlier versions of Flash, the majority of the different terms in this part are new. Besides having methods and properties, some of the objects now have their own events and listeners. These new elements make a difference in the way objects can be controlled with ActionScript. Chapters 8 and 9 cover the Core objects. While most of the objects in the Core folder will be familiar from earlier versions of Flash, some of the methods are new to Flash MX. For example, the sortOn() method of the Array object is new in Flash MX. Chapters 10 through 12 examine the Movie folder objects. In these chapters, most of the objects are new to Flash MX, such as Button, Stage, System, TextField, and TextFormat, among others. Also, you will find that the familiar Key and Mouse objects now have listeners that you can use to find out what their most recent state is. Chapter 13 covers Client/Server and Authoring objects. Included in this chapter is the new and very important LoadVars() object that will be replacing most uses of loadVariables() and loadVariablesNum(). The object is key to passing variables between Flash MX and backends. You will also find the XML and XML socket objects in Chapter 13 as well as the new CustomActions object.

Part IV, "ActionScript User Interface Components," is all about the new UI Components in Flash MX. The chapters in this part are especially important for designers because they show how to apply formats to the different components available for user interfaces. By having the ability to format the component instances, designers can incorporate the components seamlessly into an overall design. Chapters 14 through 20 examine individual components and their related methods. Chapter 21 shows how to use the FStyleFormat object and its methods and properties to style component instances on the stage. Designers will be able to populate a movie with as many components as they want and then, using a defined style format, apply the format to all of the different types of components.

For those used to Flash 5 ActionScript, the appendix is a quick review of the terms in the Deprecated folder, showing the terms in table format and what they have been replaced with. The appendix also shows which terms will be needed for scripting in Flash 5 for devices. (At this writing, most devices such as cell phones and PDAs only run the Flash 5 player.)

ActionScript Standards

In March 2002, Macromedia published a white paper entitled "ActionScript Coding Standards," by Michael Williams, available at http://www.macromedia.com/desdev/mx/flash/whitepapers/actionscript_standards.pdf.

The paper lays out a set of important guidelines that were generally followed in this book. As noted previously, the standards are best understood as a set of best practices and some programming style tips, not as guidelines to make scripting difficult for you. Following the standards will make your scripts perform better.

The rest of this section touches on some of the standards you should think about in preparing your code. However, you should read the Williams white paper to get a full understanding of why the standards were adopted and what they mean.

Style

Williams describes three style elements. First, regarding naming guidelines, you should name functions, variables, and objects so that their meaning is clear. Sometimes variable names like "x" or "i" and similarly vague identifiers are used out of habit and convenience. For example, you will see the "i" variable used in loops because it has been favored as an "increment" name from the early days of programming. Sometimes a short variable name is used because it is an index variable in a loop with the sole purpose of generating numbers to identify elements in an array or some similar sequential task. In these circumstances, the name is not as crucial. However, when you have a program with lots of identifiers, the clearer they are, the easier it is to deal with them. When developing the script and later when you want to edit your script, you will have a better idea of what the names identify.

Two general styles of writing identifiers are used. One style uses underscores to tie words together. The following shows how this convention looks:

```
var blue_car = 33;
```

A second, newer convention uses intercase terms like this:

```
var blueCar = 33;
```

Either system works fine, and you can use the one you like best. Some suggest that you pick one style or the other and stick with it, but it is far more important to have clearly understood identifiers. As long as it is clear, there should not be a problem with using mixed styles, but it is less confusing if you use a single style.

A second style element is the clear naming of layers. Leaving names like Layer 1 and Layer 12 in your timeline is pretty unclear. Use good descriptive names. Also, the top layer should be used for ActionScript. In just about every example in the book, that is where you will find the ActionScript. You can use your top layer for other purposes as well, but the first frame ought to be where you put your ActionScript.

Finally, adding comments to your code is always important. You will find that the examples in this book have commented code, but not as much as would be used in a typical script. The big advantage of having code in a book is that all of the comments can be made in the text. So while you will see comments in the examples, fewer than normal are placed there because it sometimes got in the way of clearly seeing the sequence of the code and the process taking place in the script.

Scope

The scope of a variable in Flash is unique in that not only can it be local or global, but it can also be on different timelines. However, in line with ECMA-262 standards, the Flash 6 player has a stricter scope than Flash 5. The scope hierarchy is

- Global object
- Enclosing MovieClip object
- Local variables

The use of _root is discouraged in favor of _global. While it's important to adopt the conventions of the new standard, this book uses _root in several examples because it has a certain clarity of purpose for the transition from Flash 5 to Flash MX—namely the root level from which any object can be addressed. However, as you proceed, you will see a gradual transition from using _root to _level0 because each level has its own root level.

ActionScript Conventions

Williams includes several conventions, but I only want to comment on a few here. First, and probably the most important for Flash MX, is keeping actions together. Beginners like the little scripts that can be placed with buttons and movie clips because they are short and clear. However, with more complex movies, finding and debugging can be a real headache with scripts scattered all over the place. As a result, you will see very few examples, including the longer ones, that have more than a single frame with an associated script.

Related to keeping actions together is a convention of avoiding attaching code to movie clips or buttons. This represents a radical departure for Flash 5 ActionScript users, but in order to keep code together, it should not be associated with MCs and buttons. As a result, the code you see will have fewer examples like this:

```
on(release) {
    gotoAndPlay(5);
}
```

and more examples like this:

```
someButton.onPress = function() {
    gotoAndPlay(5);
};
```

As much as possible, this book adheres to these standards recommended by Macromedia. Some of the standards, such as creating external files to store ActionScript and then using the #include action to load the ActionScript, really do not make sense in a book with the primary goal of explaining how to use different ActionScript terms. However, the practice of using the #include action and external .as files is encouraged (like all of the others in the standards) when developing Flash MX movies. Likewise, creating prototypes of objects and some of the other standards would get in the way of explaining how to use specific actions, objects, methods, properties, functions, events, and listeners. Nevertheless, the standards should be used in general scripting, and you are again encouraged to download the PDF file containing these standards. Treat the standards not as strictures, but as a guide to creating the best scripts possible.

Online Code

You will find all of the major examples online at http://www.osborne.com/ and at http://www.sandlight.com/ in a format that you can download. The files contain the source code in FLA files. The supporting text and example sound files are available as well at the same URLs.

Conclusion

Macromedia Flash MX ActionScript has many new features, and the best way to learn how to use them—whether for the first time or as an upgrade to former skills—is to jump right in and start using it. You can start at the beginning and sequentially go to the end of the book, or you can hop around to those sections that you find most useful and interesting. Above all, though, this book is designed to be used sitting next to your computer. Take the examples and configure them for your own use, change, experiment, and enjoy this wonderful scripting language from Macromedia.

The Complete Reference

ActionScript

Part I

Introducing Macromedia Flash MX ActionScript

The Complete Reference

Chapter 1

Working in ActionScript

This first chapter provides the basic bedrock of information you need to work with Macromedia Flash MX ActionScript. As noted in the introduction, the purpose of this book is to give intermediate and advanced level developers a quick way to get up and running in ActionScript. All of the ActionScript terms and structures are intentionally close to JavaScript, so if you know JavaScript, you'll be treading in very familiar territory. If your background is in Basic—including Visual Basic—you will find similar structures. However, the structures are handled in a different manner than you might be used to in Basic, so in the discussions of loops and conditionals, you will want to take a close look at the format. C++ and Java programmers will find many similar-looking structures in ActionScript, but ActionScript is a weakly typed language and interpreted, not compiled. Be sure to take a close look at the characteristics of ActionScript as a scripting language and be assured that they're less work than either C++ or Java.

The most important feature addressed in this chapter is the way ActionScript is entered in the Actions panel in conjunction with the new Properties panel. The new Properties panel introduced in Macromedia Flash MX provides the window to enter instance names for movie clip objects and text field variable names, and you'll need to understand how that works in conjunction with the code you enter. So even if you're familiar with earlier versions of Flash, go over the way the Properties panel works with the Actions panel for coordinating the different parts of a movie.

Unlike most languages that are whipped up in a text editor, Macromedia Flash MX provides a dual editor in the Actions panel with a Normal Mode and an Expert Mode. For most readers, the Expert Mode will probably be the easiest, because it's pretty much like a text editor in which you can merrily enter code without the click-and-drag environment of the Normal Mode. Both modes have advantages and disadvantages, and, unless you're familiar with Flash 5 ActionScript, you'll need to spend a little time working with them.

For readers with a grip on Flash 5 ActionScript, you will find Macromedia Flash MX ActionScript has a good deal more built-in objects. The new objects, along with associated properties, methods, events, and listeners, make up the bulk of the new ActionScript terms added to the lexicon. Also, you will find that the new set of user interface (UI) components have some interesting connected ActionScript formats you might not be readily familiar with.

Background of ActionScript

ActionScript had its embryonic stages in Flash 2, came into limited but active use in Flash 4, and blossomed in Flash 5 into an honest-to-goodness scripting language. Flash 5 introduced the dot syntax that could be used in conjunction with the older slash syntax used exclusively in Flash 4 and moved to being an object-based scripting language. In Macromedia Flash MX, refinements bring the language more in line with JavaScript EMCA standards.

The unique aspect of ActionScript compared to other languages is that it is tied to a particular application—Flash. The scripts tend to be modular and small, and they are associated with particular Flash elements, such as buttons, movie clips (MCs), and frames. ActionScript also has the unique characteristic of working with multiple timelines and target paths related to the timelines. However, after you get used to the idea of the language being connected closely to Flash and particular actions (statements) that address elements in Flash (for example, statements that go to a particular frame in a Flash movie), you will find that the language shares characteristics with most other programming and scripting languages.

What's New in ActionScript MX?

Macromedia has launched an "MX" strategy with their line of Internet-related products, and the overall strategy is reflected in the new ActionScript. For those familiar with Flash 5, the new elements primarily are in the form of new built-in objects and a whole set of UI objects. Equally important is the new panel set. Many of the old panels found in Flash 5 remain, but a new context-sensitive panel called the Properties panel replaces some of the older panels. The next few sections summarize the new elements as well as deprecated or eliminated elements in Macromedia Flash MX that directly affect ActionScript.

New ActionScript Terms

In the area of coding, you will find the bulk of the new ActionScript terms in the Objects folder in the Actions toolbox. They include the following general areas in Toolbox order:

- Objects | Core | arguments
- Objects | Core | Array
- Objects | Core | Boolean
- Objects | Core | Date
- Objects | Core | Functions
- Objects | Core | _global
- Objects | Core | Math
- Objects | Core | Number
- Objects | Core | Object
- Objects | Core | String
- Objects | Core | _super
- Objects | Core | _this

- Objects | Movie | Accessibility
- Objects | Movie | Button
- Objects | Movie | Capabilities
- Objects | Movie | Color
- Objects | Movie | Key
- Objects | Movie | _level
- Objects | Movie | Mouse
- Objects | Movie | MovieClip
- Objects | Movie | _parent
- Objects | Movie | _root
- Objects | Movie | Selection
- Objects | Movie | Sound
- Objects | Movie | Stage
- Objects | Movie | System
- Objects | Movie | TextField
- Objects | Movie | TextFormat
- Objects | Client/Server | LoadVars
- Objects | Client/Server | XML
- Objects | Client/Server | XMLSocket
- Objects | Authoring
- Flash UI Components

The list of new elements might seem small, but consider that each of the preceding categories includes a subset of properties, methods, and events. For example, in the Movie | Button folder, you will see

- Methods
- getDepth
- Properties
- enabled
- tabEnabled
- tabIndex
- trackAsMenu
- useHandCursor

- Events
- onDragOut
- onDragOver
- onKillFocus
- onPress
- onRelease
- onReleaseOutside
- onRollOut
- onRollOver
- onSetFocus

Also, you will find several other new terms in ActionScript throughout the Actions toolbox.

Tip *All of the new terms introduced in Flash MX that do not work with the Flash 5 player are highlighted in yellow when you set your publishing parameters to Flash 5. To do this, select File | Publish Settings. Click the Flash tab, and in the Version pop-up menu, select Flash Player 5. Backward compatible additions such as switch or strict equality (===) are not highlighted.*

A fundamentally important addition to ActionScript is the inclusion of methods, properties, and events to more objects than movie clips—text fields, for example. So not only are the new additions to ActionScript quantitatively different, they are qualitatively different as well.

Macromedia Flash MX UI

The new UI in Macromedia Flash MX has some key panel changes. Table 1-1 shows the panels that have been deleted and integrated into the new Properties panel and the new panels.

In the discussion later in this chapter on how to add scripts to Flash, you will learn more about the new Properties panel and how it works with the Actions panel when you enter your script.

Deprecated Elements

Macromedia Flash MX retains many of the elements that were deprecated in Flash 5. All of the old string operators are retained as deprecated, as are some favored functions, such as int and random. Newly deprecated elements include scroll and maxscroll, because they have been replaced by new properties of text field objects (which can now be addressed and changed dynamically). Conveniently, all of the deprecated terms are now in a single folder in the Actions toolbox.

Deleted Panels from Flash 5 (Integrated into Properties panel)	New Panels in Macromedia Flash MX
Fill	Property inspector
Stroke	Answers panel
Character	Components panel
Paragraph	Reference panel
Text Options	Accessibility panel
Instance	
Effect	
Frame	
Sound	

Table 1-1.   *New and Deleted Panels in Macromedia Flash MX*

Writing ActionScript

The ActionScript editing tool in Macromedia Flash MX is called the Actions panel. The panel is broken into two columns, or panes. The left pane is the Actions toolbox, and the right pane is the Script pane, sometimes called the ActionScript editor. To open the Actions panel, press the F2 key or select Window | Actions on the menu bar. A new feature in Macromedia Flash MX is the context-sensitive button on the right side of the Properties panel that will open the Actions panel if a scriptable element in Flash is selected.

To accompany the Actions panel in Macromedia Flash MX, you need the Properties panel. The Properties panel is a context-sensitive tool that changes depending on the task you're currently working on. If you select a movie clip, you will see a set of options associated with an MC, but if you select a button, text field, or frame, you will see a different set of objects. In the Properties panel, shown in Figure 1-1, you must enter the all-important instance name of different objects on the stage and variable names for text fields. Open the Properties panel by selecting Window | Properties on the menu bar or by pressing CTRL-F3 (Windows) or CMD-F3 (Macintosh).

The Actions panel shows whether you have a button, MC, or frame selected to enter code. You enter your code in the Script pane (the right pane). You can open the window by selecting Window | Actions on the menu bar, pressing the F2 key, or using the toggle button on the Properties panel. To enter code, you must select an object or frame and enter the script using any of the following methods:

- **Drag and drop**   Select the script you want, and drag it from the Actions toolbox to the Script pane.

- **Double-click**   Double-click a script element from the Actions toolbox, and it appears in the Script pane.

- **Menu method**   Click the plus (+) sign above the Script pane, and select an item from a pop-up menu.

- **Type in**   Type in the code with or without help from Flash tools. This approach accommodates people who like the free range of a text editor and come from a programming background. The Expert Mode might be best suited for this style.

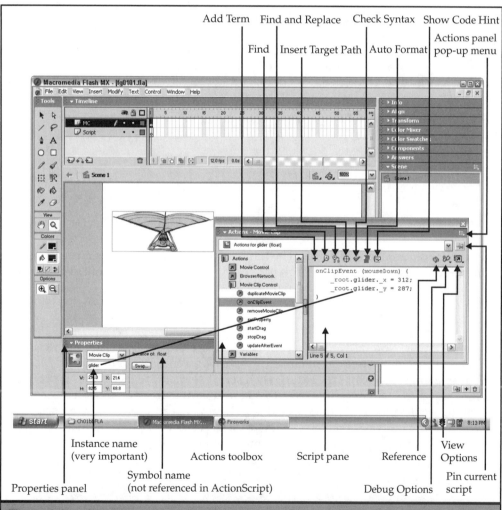

Figure 1-1.   *The Properties panel is context sensitive to the current selection, changing depending on what is currently selected.*

- **Shortcut keys**   Use ESC-*code* to enter script. To see a full list of the Escape key shortcuts, open the Actions panel pop-up menu, and select View Esc Shortcut Keys.

- **Combination**   Use any of the preceding combinations in Expert Mode. Macromedia Flash MX provides the best of all worlds for entering ActionScript.

If you're not familiar with entering script using Flash, spend a little time familiarizing yourself with the different ways it can be done. Then select the one that you're most comfortable with.

Expert Mode

By selecting Expert Mode, you basically enter a wide-open text editor. (Figure 1-1 shows script entered in Expert Mode.) If you're an experienced programmer, you will find this mode easier to use than Normal Mode. If you turn the Code Hints on, the Expert Mode offers assistance in Macromedia Flash MX syntax. You can toggle Code Hints on and off by clicking the Code Hints button. With the Code Hints on when you enter ActionScript from the Script pane, you will get a hint regarding what to do next. For example, if you have a simple gotoAndPlay action, with the Code Hints turned on, you will see a little bar below the script showing

```
gotoAndPlay ( frame );
```

or

```
gotoAndPlay ( scene, frame )
```

in a small hint bar below the cursor. The hint lets you know that you must enter some frame and/or scene and frame information, but it does not put labels in quotes or provide other information about the parameters.

Normal Mode

Entering script in Normal Mode is recommended if you're less familiar with coding and the kind of syntax used in ActionScript. When you enter script in Normal Mode, the parameters are clearly laid out for each script element, whether it's an action, function, operator, property, or object. If you are entering script for either a movie clip or button, event handlers for the selected object automatically surround your script. For example, if you select a movie clip and then select a property to put in a script, the property is put into a "container" beginning with:

```
OnClipEvent(load) {
```

and terminating with the closing curly brace:

```
}
```

Not only does the preceding save you some typing, but it helps you get started on the right foot if you're not familiar with ActionScript. Later in this chapter, you can work through an example that shows how to enter script in Normal Mode. You can easily move between the two modes by clicking the View Options button.

Action Panel Options

Macromedia Flash MX provides several options to help you create scripts in the Action panel. The following sets are available on one or both of the modes (see Figure 1-1, shown earlier in this chapter):

- **Add (+)** Adds ActionScript from a pop-up menu when selected.
- **Auto Format** (Expert Mode only) Automatically formats script.
- **Check Syntax** (Expert Mode only) Checks syntax for errors.
- **Debug Options: Set Breakpoint, Remove Breakpoint, and Remove All Breakpoints** A breakpoint is a position in the script that stops the Flash player and lets you step through the script.
- **Delete (-)** Deletes selected script from the Script pane.
- **Find and Replace** Finds and replaces selected script with replacement script.
- **Find** Finds terms in the script.
- **Insert a Target Path (Bulls Eye)** Opens the Insert Target Path dialog box showing available targets.
- **Pin Current Script** Keeps the current script in the Script pane while other objects are selected. Don't overlook this feature! When you're checking the instance name of an object you want to enter into a script, by pinning the current script, you can select different objects to check their names in the Properties panel.
- **Reference** Opens the Reference panel for the selected term. You will find this panel helpful for getting to know the various ActionScript terms. You can toggle this panel on and off to keep it out of the way.
- **Show Code Hint (Expert Mode only)** Displays options for the currently selected term. This feature is very helpful without being intrusive.
- **View options** Switches between Normal Mode and Expert Mode, and displays line numbers in script.

With all of the new helpful features now in Macromedia Flash MX, be sure to spend a little time with each one. They will save a lot of time in both debugging and creating ActionScripts.

 When writing scripts in the Expert Mode, I found that if you click the Auto-Format button, you will get an error message if there's a bug in your code. It won't format it for you if you have a coding error.

Places Where ActionScript Goes

One of the most important and fundamental concepts in ActionScript and Flash is the connection of ActionScript to a frame, movie clip, or button. Scripts in frames fire when the playhead moves over the frame, and event handlers fire scripts in movie clips and buttons. If you select an object that will not accept ActionScript, you will see a notice in the Script pane stating, "Current selection cannot have actions applied to it." When you select a frame, button, or MC, the Actions panel indicates which is currently selected, and the Properties panel shows the appropriate object in its top-left pop-up menu.

Frames

When you select a frame, the script you enter into the Script pane fires whenever the playhead passes through the frame. If the movie is continuously in a loop, the script fires repeatedly. The context-sensitive Properties panel shows the options available to set when the frame is selected. The Frame Label eases the process of targeting the correct frame by providing a descriptive and unique label. For example, a label of "wink" in a frame could be used to describe a winking action that takes place when the playhead moves to the frame. Alternatively, as shown in the following illustration, it could signal a starting point with the label, "startHere."

An important new feature of ActionScript is the ability to use button methods, primarily event methods, with movie clips. This allows more direct event involvement with movie clips and removes many of the limitations inherent in using the onClipEvent() function. When onClipEvent() is used with a movie clip, any event on the stage will trigger the event. For example, onClipEvent(mouseDown) triggers a mouse press anywhere on the stage, while on(press) only triggers an event when the event is associated with the button containing the script. Now you can write all of the event handlers for movie clips (and buttons) in frames rather than solely by selecting the object and writing the script in the Objects Action panel. For example, to trigger a movie clip to be dragged, you can create a script associated with a frame like the following (where "wagon" is the instance name of a movie clip):

```
_root.wagon.onPress = function() {
    this.startDrag();
}
_root.wagon.onRelease = function() {
    stopDrag()
}
```

In Flash 5, multiple dragable objects had to be accomplished using buttons and movie clips, but with Macromedia Flash MX, you can write event handlers by selecting a keyframe and start writing the object event–related script.

Buttons

All buttons need to begin their script with event handlers in the following format:

```
on (event) {
    actions
}
```

Possible events you can use for launching scripts associated with buttons include the following:

- Drag out
- Drag over
- Key press
- Press
- Release
- Release outside
- Roll out
- Roll over

When selected, buttons have a unique set of options available in the Properties panel, as shown below. The most significant new feature in Macromedia Flash MX is the instance name for buttons. As discussed in the next section, any object with an instance name can be changed dynamically in a Macromedia Flash MX movie. For example, the following illustration shows the Properties panel with the word "launcher" used as the instance name:

Movie Clips

Beginning with Flash 5, scripts could be associated with movie clips. Like buttons, MCs have their own set of events to fire them in the following format:

```
onClipEvent (event) {
    actions}
```

The events you can use to fire MC scripts are

- Data
- Enter frame
- Key down
- Key up
- Load
- Mouse down
- Mouse move
- Mouse up
- Unload

Unlike button events that require a user to place the mouse over the button to fire a script, clip events monitor the entire stage. Thus, if you have an MC script with a mouseDown event to fire a script and a button with a release event to fire another script, as soon as you click the button, both scripts would be launched! So, unless you plan to fire multiple scripts with a mouse click, be aware that movie clip events cover the whole stage. Likewise, no two MCs should be on the stage at the same time with identical events firing scripts. While, there is no technical limitation to the number of movie clips and events occupying the stage at the same, it's easy to get your events and MCs working at cross-purposes if you do. New options, including listeners, are now available so that you can build objects that help you organize the events your movie clips respond to.

In the Properties panel, the most important task for a developer is to enter an instance name for the MC. Without an instance name, a script cannot address a movie clip and, therefore, cannot make dynamic changes in a movie. (The name of the MC symbol is float, but that name has no effect other than to differentiate it from other MCs in the movie.) As you can see in the next illustration, the Movie Clip is an Instance of "float" but the instance name is "glider."

Dynamic Changes and ActionScript

For the most part, scripts in Flash have been used to direct a movie to different frames, change MCs dynamically, handle input and output in text fields, and control external communications (such as load movies, fire a PHP script, and so forth). Of these tasks allocated to ActionScript, by far the most important is changing movie clips dynamically.

In Macromedia Flash MX, dynamic change is no longer restricted to movie clips, even though dynamically changing MCs is likely to remain the key dynamic change developers will be making. Any object—including buttons, text fields, sounds, and other objects identified with an instance name—can now be targets of ActionScript programs that induce dynamic change.

One of the more interesting objects where instance names can now be applied is the text field. Text fields in previous versions of Flash have had an optional association with variables, and a variable's value would appear in any text field associated with it. For example, the following script would send the string "Work with me" to any text field associated with the variable named work:

```
_root.work="Work with me";
```

In the Properties panel, by entering a variable name in the Variable text box, a selected text field shows the current value of the variable.

In Macromedia Flash MX, a text field with an instance name can be referenced by both the instance name and the variable name. So, not only can the contents of the text field be dynamically changed, so can the text field itself. (See Chapter 12 for detailed descriptions of the TextField object and its methods, properties, events and listeners along with examples of how to use this new Macromedia Flash MX object.) Figure 1-2 shows both the instance name and variable name applied to a text field.

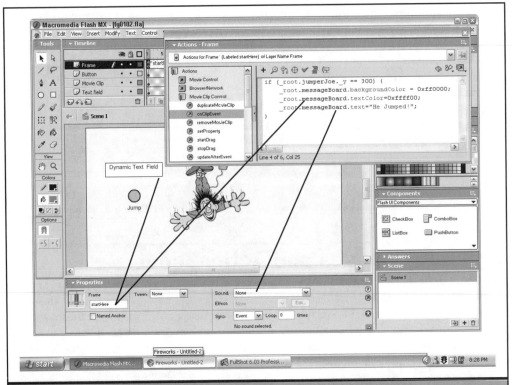

Figure 1-2. *While a text field can have both an instance name and variable associated with it, generally the instance name is used with one of the TextField properties, such as "text" to place data into a Dynamic text field.*

Note *In Figure 1-2, the script shown in the Script pane is not "in" the text field that is selected. Rather, the script is associated with the frame labeled startHere (partially visible in the first frame of the top layer). To display an object or frame other than the one associated with a script, first select the frame or object associated with the script, and then click the Pin Current Script button. When other objects or frames are selected, the pinned script stays on the screen, and no other script appears until the script is unpinned by clicking the pin button again to toggle it off. (See Figure 1-1 for the location of the Pin Current Script button.)*

Test Drive the Actions Panel

To familiarize yourself with the Actions panel, there's no substitute for experience. The following steps walk you through the process of entering script using the example in Figure 1-2 (you can substitute any movie clip you want for the bungee jumper image):

1. Open a new Macromedia Flash MX movie, and add four layers named Frame, Button, Movie Clip, and Text field. Be sure that the Properties panel is visible on the stage along with the toolbox. Add seven frames to each layer.

2. In the Movie Clip layer, create an MC to serve as the bungee jumper. (You can use a simple rectangle if you want.)

3. Place the MC near the top of the stage.

4. With the MC selected, enter the instance name **jumperJoe** in the Instance Name field below the Movie Clip pop-up menu on the Properties panel.

5. Using the Text tool, click the stage next to the MC. The Properties panel recognizes that the object is a text field, and the pop-up menu defaults to the last type of text field created.

6. In the pop-up menu where the type of text field appears, change the type to Dynamic Text if it is not already. Then type **Dynamic Text Field** in the field. (See Figure 1-2.)

7. Beneath the text field, create a button in the Button layer.

8. Click the Show Border Around Text button, and type **output** in the variable window (the one labeled Var) and **messageBoard** in the Instance Name field. (See Figure 1-2.)

9. Select the button, and click the little arrow button on the right side of the Properties panel to open the Actions panel.

10. Enter the following script in the Script pane:

```
on (release) {
    _root.jumperJoe._y = 300;
}
```

The script first addresses the main timeline (_root). It then addresses the instance name of the MC (jumperJoe), and then the vertical position on the stage (_y). The value of the MC's vertical position is set to 300 (the higher the number, the lower the MC appears on the stage). The MC moves toward the bottom of the stage when the button is clicked.

11. Finally, select the first frame, and enter the following script:

```
if (_root.jumperJoe._y == 300) {
    _root.messageBoard.backgroundColor = 0xff0000;
    _root.messageBoard.textColor=0xffff00;
    _root.messageBoard.text="He Jumped!";
}
```

After the MC instance (jumperJoe) has moved to the 300 Y position on the stage, the frame script fires. New in ActionScript MX are (among others) the backgroundColor and textColor properties of text fields. Using the format 0x + six-digit hexadecimal number, both the background color and the text color of the text field are assigned color values. The object is referenced by its instance name (jumperJoe) in the same way that movie clips are. Finally, the text property of the text field object is assigned the value "He Jumped!"

The new object references in ActionScript MX add far more control and options over objects on the stage. With far more properties and methods available for various aspects of Flash, you will find this current version of ActionScript more robust than previous versions with a lot more opportunities to experiment with motion graphics.

Conclusion

Working with ActionScript provides both ease and power. Writing scripts in either the Normal or Expert modes is done with a good deal of aid from the Actions panel. The ActionScript toolbox puts the entire language at your fingertips. On the other hand, ActionScript is coming into its own as a powerful language with the structures found in the ECMA-262 standards set for JavaScript. About half the terms in Flash MX ActionScript were not in Flash 5, making the language twice as robust as before.

In Chapter 2, you will find all of the data types used by Flash MX ActionScript and an in-depth discussion of how ActionScript handles variables. As you will see, the variables in ActionScript are very "smart" in that they can tell when they contain different types of data. This relieves the developer from the task of declaring different types of variables for different types of data. However, the variables handle the data just as well as "strongly typed" languages where you have to specify different data "types." Thus, you will continue to find the both the ease of use and power of ActionScript in Chapter 2.

The
Complete
Reference

Chapter 2

Variables and Data Types

This chapter looks at the use of variables and the types of data they can hold in Macromedia Flash MX ActionScript. For those new to programming, this chapter holds critical information for storing and passing information in a script. All of the objects, statements, and other components of ActionScript do something with variables or are affected by variables and the data they contain. The good news is that the data used in ActionScript variables are "weakly" typed, which means you can put different types of data into variables and ActionScript is smart enough to figure out what kind of data you have. If you're familiar with JavaScript, VBScript, or just about any other language, you will find the use of variables in Flash to be familiar. The one key difference is that Flash scripts commonly have variables on different timelines associated with frames, movie clips, and buttons and not a part of a single script source. So whether you're familiar with programming or new to scripting code, you will find the information in this chapter will get you off on the right foot with ActionScript variables.

Variables in Macromedia Flash MX ActionScript

One of the fundamental components of any kind of programming is the variable. As the name implies, variables change—they vary. Probably the best way to think of a variable is as a box of different things. In programming, variables store different types of data with different values. For example, container cargo ships carry large shipping containers. Each container has different crates. Some crates may have perishable food and others may have hardware like nuts and bolts. Also, the crates can have different quantities. One crate may contain 250 lamps and another crate 100 lamps. The crates with perishable food can have carrots in one, oranges in another, and apples in still another. So you can think of variables like the containers with different kinds of materials and different quantities. The quantities refer to the different *values*, while the qualities refer to different *types*. Likewise, variables have different quantities and different qualities.

For programmers, an important characteristic of Macromedia Flash MX ActionScript is the contextual nature of variables. Languages such as C++ have strongly typed characteristics that require declaring not only a variable, but also the type of variable. Is the variable going to store text, integers, or floating point numbers? ActionScript, like virtually all scripted languages, does not require such declarations. ActionScript automatically deals with different types of data stored in variables.

Naming and Assigning Variables

The name you select for a variable should give a clue to what the variable does. Names such as VariableA, VariableB, and so forth are essentially useless. Names such as ItemCost and Tax, however, tell you what the variable contains and make the variables easy to find, remember, and use accordingly. If you use shortcuts when naming variables in longer scripts or complex movies and call them "a," "b," and "c," always go back and provide descriptive names before you start working on other parts of your ActionScript.

In Flash, clear variable naming is even more important because the scripts are short (generally) and scattered all over the place. For example, you may want to find or change the value of a variable that resides in a frame that is part of a movie clip embedded in another movie clip. You think you're going to remember what the variable "k" does in that maze? Probably not.

Variable names or identifiers must be a single string of connected characters, with no spaces between the words. Variable names such as "final bill" or "Billy the Kid" are not acceptable; however, finalBill, Final_Bill, or finalbill are—just keep the spaces out. Moreover, ActionScript is not case sensitive. If a variable is named FinalBill, you can use FINALBILL or finalbill to call the variable's current value. However, Final_Bill will not be recognized as the same variable as FinalBill because it contains an extra character, the underscore. This lack of case sensitivity makes it easier when you want to call a variable by name, but make sure that you don't use names such as BIGSTORE and bigstore for your variables in the same button or frame. You may think they are different, but ActionScript won't.

Another naming convention you need to consider in naming variables is the use of reserved words or keywords. The keywords in the ActionScript vocabulary cannot be used as labels, variable names, or function names. These 20 keywords are as follows:

break	instanceof
case	new
continue	return
default	switch
delete	this
else	typeof
for	var
function	void
if	while
in	with

Two more terms—true and false—are Boolean literals, which also cannot be used. Names of actions, built-in functions, and other terms that you may confuse with scripting words should be avoided as well.

Declaring and Assigning Values to Variables

In order for a variable to be recognized as such, it must be declared. Usually, variables are declared by the simple expedient of assigning a name a value using the equal (=) assign operator. Thus, the line:

```
mySweetVariable=365;
```

assigns the value 365 to and declares the variable named mySweetVariable. You may also declare a variable with no value assigned at all, using the var keyword. For example:

```
var expendedFuel;
```

might be a variable you will want to assign a value to at a later time but declare as part of organizing your variables.

In this chapter, you will learn about the different data types that can be assigned to variables with further examples. Also, you will learn about the scope of variables and how to declare variables with different scopes.

A second, older method to declare a variable is with the set variable action. Use the format:

```
set(myOldVariable, "Horsefeathers");
```

This sets a string value (Horsefeathers) to a variable named myOldVariable. Throughout the book, you will find virtually all variables assigned with the assign operator as shown in the first example. If you are writing a script for older versions of Flash, you can use the old method, and it is still built into the Actions panel. Generally, it should be avoided.

Identifiers

When naming a variable, you do so with an identifier. The first character of an identifier must be a letter, underscore (_), or dollar sign ($). Also, since ActionScript is case insensitive, identifiers can be either letter case, but remember that the variable name looseScrew is the same as LOOSEscrew or LoOsEsCrEw. Identifiers are also used in naming objects, properties, functions, and methods, and follow the same naming rules.

I tend to avoid using dollar signs as a first character when naming identifiers. In some languages like PHP, all variables begin with dollar signs, and in other languages, the dollar sign means that the variable is a string. Also, some calculations are monetary ones that you will want to use with a dollar sign when displaying output. So, while it's perfectly legal to begin variable names with dollar signs, it can lead to confusion.

Literals

With apologies to Sam Spade, literals are the stuff that variables are made of. Literals are the raw data that you can put into variables. For example, "cow" is a string literal, and 23.45 is a numeric literal. Boolean literals are either true or false. In the next section, on data types, you will learn more about the kinds of literals you can put into variables.

Function Literals

Function literals are a special kind of literal for creating functions. Generally, functions begin with the function statement and an identifier. However, function literals are created as a statement and assign the value generated in the function to the variable. Chapter 6 examines functions in detail, but the following shows what a function literal looks like relative to the contents of a variable:

```
var seekJoeMC = function () { return [_root.joe._x,_root.joe._y]; };
```

In Macromedia Flash MX, you will find extended uses for function literals. As noted in Chapter 1, movie clips can use button events, and as a result, you will find more opportunities to incorporate function literals using movie clips and other objects. For example, the following is a typical use of a movie clip incorporating a function literal:

```
_root.cloakingAct.onPress = function() {
this._alpha=(this._alpha -10);
}
```

One of the more useful aspects of function literals regarding buttons and movie clips is that the scripts can be placed together associated with a frame. If the code is well commented, when it comes time to debug the code, instead of having to look at scripts in several different movie clips and buttons, you have all of the scripts in one place.

Expressions

Expressions are considered compound because they contain more than a single element. They are any combination of ActionScript terms that are legally combined with an operator. In ActionScript, a simple logical expression looks like the following:

```
var total = 7 + 5;
```

The value of total is 12. The expression is compound (the 7 and 5 make it compound), but the value of total is 12 because it is not broken down into its component properties. However, why type "7 + 5" when you know it's 12? Programmers generally do not enter such a simple expression. The concept of expressions begins to make more sense if you look at the following:

```
var total = ItemCost + Tax;
```

The variable total is the total value of two other variables. You may not know the value of the variables because they are variables. Variables change. Rather than having to keep track of what's in the variable, ActionScript does it for you and calculates the total. For example, consider the following script using variables and expressions:

```
var ItemCost = 12;
var Tax = ItemCost * .08;
var Sum = ItemCost + Tax;
```

The first variable, ItemCost, is defined with a literal having the value 12. The second variable, Tax, is an expression using the value of the first variable multiplied by .08. (The .08 represents an 8 percent sales tax rate.) The third variable, Sum, uses another expression that is the total of the first two variables.

The terminology of expressions is relatively simple, made up of operators and operands. The operators are the symbols for different calculations, and the operands are the values manipulated by the operators. For example, in the expression:

```
Sum = ItemCost * .08 + ShippingCost;
```

the operators are * and + and the operands are ItemCost, .08, and ShippingCost.

Data Types in ActionScript

The sets of values and operations performed on the values are data types. Primitive data types have a constant value, and reference data types refer to an object that has values that can change even though the reference is constant. (Null and Undefined are special cases with a single constant value.) Table 2-1 shows ActionScript's different data types and whether they are primitive or reference.

Strings

The easiest way to think of strings, initially, is just as words or text. In programming, you will often see strings used as messages. For example, a string in a variable can be:

```
doggy = "Greater Swiss Mountain Dog"
```

The variable is doggy, and the string literal is "Greater Swiss Mountain Dog." A literal is the raw data that goes into a variable. The type of doggy can change, but a Greater Swiss Mountain Dog is always going to be a Greater Swiss Mountain Dog—the literal. Sometimes a string can be a numeral, such as:

```
StreetNumber = "521"
```

Data Type	Value Type
Strings	Primitive
Number	Primitive
Boolean	Primitive
Object	Reference
Movie clip	Reference
Null	Special
Undefined	Special

Table 2-1. *Data and Value Types*

The value "521" is just another string literal that consists of numeric characters. In fact, just about any alphanumeric string of characters is a string. The phrase "string of characters" means that it can contain most punctuation marks and spaces as well as alphabetic characters and numbers. (Note that "Greater Swiss Mountain Dog" includes spaces.) Characters and numbers can be used in any combination. Strings, such as the following, have to make sense only to the designer and Flash; the user doesn't see them or have to understand them:

```
Combo = "121 Elm Street"
```

An important fact to keep in mind about strings is that they are not numbers. You can spot a string because it has quotation marks around it. In the earlier StreetNumber example, the number "521" is in quotation marks. If "521" were added to "521," the result would be "521521," not "1042." Quotation marks around a literal usually mean that it's a string literal.

String Concatenation

When two or more strings are joined together, the process is known as concatenation. All concatenations are treated as expressions. In ActionScript, the add operator, +, is used to join strings:

```
Generations = "Old" + "New";
```

results in "OldNew." The value of the variable Generations becomes "OldNew." Concatenation is very useful when putting together strings that go together, such as first and last names. You've probably filled out forms in which you entered your first name in one field and your last name in another. Using concatenation, the names can be joined. Because a space is needed between the first and last names, the concatenation has to add a space, as shown here:

```
firstLast = "David" + " " + "Miller";
```

Two plus (+) signs are needed. The first one joins "David" and the space (two quotation marks with a space between them), and the second joins "Miller." The output is then "David Miller" instead of "DavidMiller."

A Space Variable

If you're using spaces a lot in formatting your scripts, you might as well put them in a variable. In that way when you read your code you'll know exactly how much space you have put in and what it is. Just define it as:

```
var space=" ";
```

and then when you write your script you can use the space variable to more clearly see what the script does:

```
var wayCool = "ActionScript" + space + "is" + space + "way cool.";
```

Additional operators used with strings are discussed in Chapter 9.

Boolean Expressions

Boolean expressions can also be used in ActionScript. The results of a Boolean expression in Flash are 0 (No, false) or 1 (Yes, true). Named after George Boole, a brilliant British mathematician, Boolean expressions are extremely useful in conditional statements. (See Chapters 5, 6, and 8 for more on Boolean expressions.) For example, the following variable, Bigger, declares that 10 is greater than 15. Because that's not true, the variable Bigger is false.

```
Bigger = 10 > 15;
```

The assigned value is the expression "10 > 15," not 0 or 1. Programmers are well aware of the value of Boolean expressions. Nonprogrammers may see little value in such expressions initially, but they will come to appreciate them.

Boolean Objects

Boolean literals are very smart. If you assign a Boolean value to a variable such as:

```
BooVar= 9 < 10;
```

the result is true, but it can also be interpreted as a 1. For example, if you type:

```
BooVar= 9 < 10;
Total=BooVar + 20;
```

your variable Total is 21. To control your Boolean results to specify a value or a string, you may use the Boolean objects. The Boolean object acts as a container for the Boolean properties. A Boolean constructor and two methods are available in ActionScript:

- **new Boolean()**   Constructor for the Boolean property
- **toString()**   Method converts Boolean literal to string "true" or "false"
- **valueOf()**   Method returns the Boolean primitive

The following script uses the Boolean constructor and its two methods:

1. The variable booVar provides a name for the Boolean object with the contents of the Boolean literal true or 1 because 8 is greater than 7.
2. The variable s then stores the string literal of booVar, which is true.
3. The variable v stores the primitive value of booVar, which again is the Boolean literal of true or 1.
4. The variable textVal uses the plus sign (+), which works like add for concatenation. Because adding a string to anything else returns the string and the number as a string, the outcome should be "true2".
5. When the Boolean literal is treated as a value, the results should be 3 (1 + 2 = 3) and stored in the variable realVal.

```
booVar = new Boolean( 8 > 7);
 s=booVar.toString();
 v=booVar.valueOf();
 textVal=s + 2;
 realVal=v + 2;
 output=textVal + newline + realVal;
```

The variable output is a text field so that the results show on the screen. The newline function serves to add a carriage return so the results are sorted out and clear in the text field.

```
true2
3
```

For nonprogrammers, Boolean expressions may not seem very useful; as you begin using them, however, you will discover their value. At the end of this chapter, the learning utility uses a Boolean to change the automatic rounding down in the integer function that truncates any decimals in a number. (See also the "Integers" section in this chapter.)

Numbers

Numbers include positive and negative integers and floating point numbers. These numbers are actual numeric values in that you can perform math operations with them:

```
costWithDiscount = -5 + 15;
```

or

```
deficitSpending = -5 + -15 + 3;
```

Integers

Integers are simply whole numbers with any decimals lopped off. In creating variables, you do not have to declare what type of variable you are using (integer or floating point). To create integers, however, you must tell the variable that the numbers are to be treated as integers. An integer is declared as such by using the integer function. For example, to create an integer, you may write:

```
whole = parseInt(Inventory / Parts);
```

The expression "Inventory / Parts" means that the variable Inventory is being divided by a variable named Parts. No matter what the outcome of the expression, the function turns the results into an integer with the decimals deleted. Thus, a value of 17.9 is rounded down to 17. If you had 17.84563, it also would be rounded to 17. The number of decimals after an integer has no effect on rounding. (Using the Math object, you can round up or down, or you can use a round method. See Chapter 8 for details.)

In a Flash movie, you frequently use integers when you script loops. (See Chapter 4 for a full discussion of loops.) Because loops are generally stepped in single units, some designers make sure that all of the steps are integers. Likewise, frame numbers are integers (there's no Frame 7.5). If you use calculated values with frame numbers, turning the outcomes into integers assures the correct frame.

Real Numbers (Floating Point)

To avoid losing those added decimals and to have greater accuracy, most programmers use real—or floating point—numbers. The default character of numbers in ActionScript is floating point. Also, unless an integer function is used, integers return to floating point values when further calculations are made. The following shows an example:

```
avKids = numChildren / numFamilies;
```

The variable numChildren represents the number of children. and the variable numFamilies represents the number of families—a good bet that these values will be integers. To find the average number of children per family, the first variable is divided by the second. Supposing there are 20 families and 50 kids, the average is 2.5 children per family. So even though the values in the variables are integers, the value in the variable, avKids, is floating point.

Constants

Constants are values that do not change. ActionScript contains three types of constants. Global constants are found throughout scripts and are not associated with a Math or Number object. The other two types of constants are Math and Number. Table 2-2 shows all of the constants and their categories.

While not all constants are numeric values, most are. Even true and false will automatically convert to 1 or 0 if put into a context where a number is required. The constant newline is the same as a carriage return (pressing ENTER or RETURN on the keyboard), and null and undefined are discussed below. Otherwise, all of the other constants return some kind of numeric value.

Global	Math	Number
false	E	MAX_VALUE
newline	LN10	MIN_VALUE
null	LN2	NaN
true	LOG10E	NEGATIVE_INFINITY
undefined	PI	POSITIVE_INFINITY
SQRT1_2		
SQRT2		

Table 2-2.   *Constants*

Objects

Objects are elements considered to be collections of properties and methods in ActionScript. You can create your own objects, or you can use built-in objects. All properties have a name and a value. For example, _rotation is the name of a property that can have a positive or negative value between 0 and 360. Objects may also have methods—or functions—to perform a calculation or create a transformation. For example, previously you saw that the Boolean object Boolean.toString() contained a method that transformed a Boolean literal into a string. In Part II, you will find a full discussion of objects, and different objects are introduced throughout the book as appropriate.

One of the key new features you will find in Macromedia Flash MX compared to Flash 5 is the addition of several new built-in objects. Besides the Core objects such as Array, Boolean, Date, and Math, Macromedia Flash MX has a complete set of Movie, Client/Server and Authoring objects. Chapters 7 through 9 closely examine these objects. Keeping in mind that objects reference data types, it's important to understand how the reference works.

Suppose you have a movie clip with the instance name of slip, which includes a script that allows the user to drag it around the screen. You want to keep track of the horizontal position of the MC instance slip on the screen. To do this, you define a variable as the horizontal (x) position of the MC as the following:

```
var output = _root.slip._x;
```

The property _x is the horizontal position of slip on the screen. However, because the MC is being dragged around the screen, the _x value in the object named slip keeps changing. Because the variable output gets its value by a reference to the object slip, the variable's value is by reference instead of a primitive.

Before going on to the next data type (movie clips), arrays, an object that shares many characteristics with variables, should be introduced here so you can see how they are used in a similar way to variables.

Arrays

Arrays are objects containing several properties or elements. For the general use of arrays, you can think of them as numbered variables. Each element of the array is a property with its value being the string, Boolean literal, or number equated with the array element. Each element in an array is numbered from 0 to the length of the array minus 1. A six-element array may look like the following:

```
dogs[0]="German Shepherd";
dogs[1]="English Springer Spaniel";
dogs[2]="Australian Shepherd";
```

```
dogs[3]="Greater Swiss Mountain Dog";
dogs[4]="St. Bernard";
dogs[5]="Mutt";
```

To create an array, use the Array object. For example, the preceding array, dogs, could be created with the constructor new Array in either of the following formats:

```
dogs=new Array("German Shepherd", "English Springer Spaniel")
dogs.push("Australian Shepherd", "Greater Swiss Mountain Dog")
dogs.push("St. Bernard", "Mutt");
```

Alternatively, the array could have been created by typing:

```
dogs=new Array(6);
```

and then designating each element as before, beginning with:

```
dogs[0]="German Shepherd";
dogs[1]="English Springer Spaniel";
....
```

The real value of arrays is appreciated when you use a loop to enter or send data. Chapter 8 contains examples that show you how loops and arrays work together.

Movie Clips

The most important data type in ActionScript is the movie clip. It is the primary graphic object that can be changed dynamically by ActionScript. (In Macromedia Flash MX, buttons, text fields, and the new UI Components can be changed dynamically, but the movie clip remains the primary graphic object that designers target.) Like objects, movie clips (MCs) have their own methods that can be used with the MovieClip object. In later chapters, as various concepts are introduced, more MovieClip objects will be introduced. MCs can be both the target of another object's action commands or the source for issuing an action command to another object. MCs can issue actions to the main timeline, other MCs, or go to a specific frame. The following are examples of MovieClip objects. In these examples, the instance name flame is a reference of the MC:

```
flame.gotoAndStop( 8 );
flame.gotoAndPlay(6);
flame.play();
```

```
flame.stop();
flame.nextFrame();
```

The most important thing to keep in mind with movie clips is their instance name. When you initially create an MC, the name you provide is the symbol name, not the object name. Once you construct an MC symbol and have an instance of that symbol on the stage, the first thing you should do is give it a name in the Properties panel. The following shows where the Instance name "raceCar" is placed in the Properties panel.

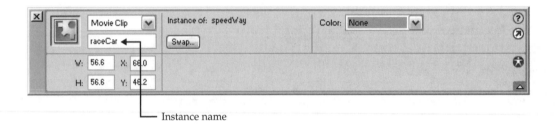

Instance name

Null and Undefined

As data types, null and undefined are often used interchangeably. However, they are different. A variable can be given a value of null, and in some cases your script may be looking for null. An undefined variable simply means that a variable has not yet been defined. An undefined variable does not necessarily mean your script has an error. For example, put the following script in the first frame of a new movie:

```
var alpha =null;
if (alpha == 20) {
    var beta = 49;
}
trace(alpha);
trace(beta);
```

The script essentially defines a variable named alpha as being null. Then a statement asks if alpha equals 20, but since its value is null, a Boolean false is generated. Because the condition is false, no value is placed in the variable beta, and so it remains undefined. Also, because both null and undefined are valid data types, you can define any variable as either null or undefined. (You would create a paradox by defining a variable as undefined, but it's a legal paradox.)

Text Fields and Variables

One of the big changes in Macromedia Flash MX is how variables are associated with text fields. Text fields in Flash have both instance names and variable names. If you give a dynamic or input text field a variable name, the value of a particular variable appears in the text field with the associated variable name. Likewise, that same text field can be given an instance name to dynamically change a characteristic of the text field when the movie runs. The newer reference format for addressing a variable in a text field is

```
TextFieldInstanceName.text=someValue;
```

The value can be a literal or a variable, and whatever is assigned to .text shows up in a dynamic or input text field.

For example, if you have an online calculator in ActionScript, the viewer can see the calculated outcome in a text field, and the field itself can be changed as well. Figure 2-1 shows a calculator in development and the connections between a script and instance names of text fields.

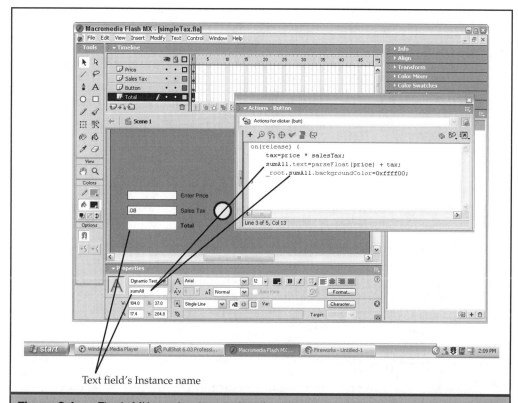

Text field's Instance name

Figure 2-1. *Flash MX emphasizes using the Instance name and the text property reference rather than a variable name.*

To see exactly how text fields are associated with variables and can be acted on as objects, the following steps through the process of creating a little movie that uses ActionScript to link text fields with variable names. The movie also uses ActionScript to dynamically change the text field itself by giving it a new background color. Figure 2-1 shows what it looks like.

1. Create a new page in Flash and add three layers to the existing layer for a total of four layers.

2. From top to bottom, rename the layers: Price, Sales Tax, Button, and Total.

3. In the Price layer, use the Text tool to create an input text field by clicking on the stage, and then select Input Text from the Text type pop-up menu in the upper-left corner of the Properties panel. In the Instance Name window, type **InitialPrice** and in the Var text window, type **output**.

4. In the Sales Tax layer, create a second text field, but make it a dynamic text field. Type **.08** in the field, and give it an instance name of **tax** and a variable name of **salesTax**.

5. In the Total layer, add a third text field. Make the field dynamic, and add the instance name **sumAll**.

6. In the Button layer, draw a button and then convert it to a button symbol by pressing the F8 key and selecting the Button option. In the Properties panel, type **clicker** in the instance name field. (You don't have to give it an instance name, but it's a good habit to develop.)

7. Select the Button object and enter the following script:

```
on(release) {
    tax=price * salesTax;
    sumAll.text=parseFloat(price) + tax;
    _root.sumAll.backgroundColor=0xffff00;
}
```

8. Use the Text tool to label the top field **Enter Price**, the second field **Sales Tax**, and the bottom field **Total** in bold. Be sure that when you type in the labels you set the text field to Static Text in the Properties panel.

9. Test the movie by pressing CTRL-ENTER or CMD-RETURN, or select Control | Test Movie from the menu bar. When the movie appears, type a number in the field labeled Enter Price, and click the button. You should see a new value in the Total field with a yellow background. The new value represents the initial value with an 8 percent tax added to it.

Examining the Results

For those who are new to programming, one of the most frustrating experiences is forgetting to put in some little character or adding the wrong character so that the program doesn't run as expected. Typos are killers in coding, so be very careful and proofread your scripts. (Experienced programmers get the same little "bugs," but they seem to do so in much more complex programs and with more ingenuity than beginners. Just remember, people are smarter than computers. However, computers are always smarter than programmers.)

Tip   *One of the best debugging devices in Macromedia Flash MX is the color of the different ActionScript terms. If you are using an ActionScript term, it should turn a specific color. If you put in code like gotoAndPlay(5), it should turn the color reserved for actions. (See Edit | Preferences for the different color codes you can assign.) However, if you type gotoandPlay(5), your code will not turn to the actions color because you did not capitalize the "a" in the statement.*

First, see if you can figure out what should appear on your screen. Here's how to break it down:

- **Line 1**   The top line is an event handler for the button. It waits for the button to be pressed down and then released before firing the script. (It's virtually the same as a mouse click, but in some cases when a mouse button is pressed or released it can fire different scripts.)

- **Line 2**   Using the variable names from the first (price) and second (salesTax) text fields, a new variable, tax, is created. The variable tax does another important task besides multiplying the first value by the second. When the ActionScript interpreter encounters a math operation other than addition, it assumes that numeric characters are numbers and transforms them from text strings to numbers. All data in text fields, including numbers, are initially treated as strings (text).

- **Line 3**   This next operation involves adding the value of the price variable to the tax variable. However, because a plus sign (+) works to both to concatenate strings and to add in math, it needs to know that both values are numbers. The tax variable became a number because it is the result of a mathematical expression in the previous line. Because Flash thinks that the price variable is a string because it came from a text field, it needs to be changed into a number. The key functions, parseFloat( ) and parseInt( ), transform strings into real (floating point) or integers respectively. Thus, the script, parseFloat(price) turns price into a floating point number that is added to the value of the variable tax. Finally, the resulting sum is placed into the text area of the object named sumAll. Because the name sumAll is the dynamic text field's instance name, any values you place in sumAll.text will appear in the dynamic text field.

- **Line 4**   One of the new Macromedia Flash MX properties available for text fields is backgroundColor. The hexadecimal value ffff00 (expressed as 0xffff00) translates as yellow. Thus, not only do the contents of the last text field change because a value is placed in the variable name associated with the field, but so too do the field's characteristics (its background color) because the object property has been changed.

Variables and Scope

Macromedia Flash MX ActionScript variables are one of three scopes:

- Global
- Local
- Timeline

A variable's scope refers to where and how a variable and reference to it may be used in a program, what assignments change a variable's value, and how the variable can be addressed. Flash is unique in that variables can belong to different timelines, so the timeline scope is one to consider in addition to variables that are global and local in scope.

Global Variables

A variable whose scope encompasses the entire movie is global in scope. Global variables can be referenced and assigned from any script, in any timeline, in any object, or in any frame. Global variables are handy for any movie-wide dimensions that you wish your movie to track. For example, if you make an interactive game that awards points for actions occurring in different movie clips, generated by different buttons and frames, a global variable could keep track of points awarded or deleted.

All timelines share global variables without a reference to the variable's path. A global variable buried in a button script three levels down in a hierarchy of movie clips has the same status as one in the first frame on the main timeline. Every object can affect and be affected by the changes in a global variable. When you need to coordinate several objects with information from a single variable, global variables can be very helpful. When you use the same variable name in different places, however, you can get confused about which value has been assigned the same variable. For example, a common loop variable is "i" because it has conventionally been shorthand for "increment." If the same loop variable is used in two different scripts inside the same timeline, the value of the variable may have been changed in one loop, yet it affects another loop. So, although global variables have important uses, they can also be a problem.

Macromedia Flash MX has a new identifier to declare global variables, _global. Precede the variable declaration using the identifier as the following shows:

```
_global.scoreKeeper = 0;
```

Local Variables

Local variables are ones declared using the var statement inside of a script. When a variable is declared using var between the curly braces { } of a function script, only changes within that function affect the variable's value. For example, you might have a function in MC that keeps track of the MC's "fuel." With several MCs that have a common fuel capacity, the same local variable (in fact, the same script) could be used in each of the MCs without affecting the others. For example, the following function and local variables could be placed in several MCs that use fuel and none would affect the variables of the other MCs' variables because other than the variable called fuelSupply they're all local. The fuelSupply variable would affect all of the MCs.

```
function checkFuel() {
var fuel= 20;
if (move == true) {
fuelSupply -= 1;
        if(tank > fuel) {
            var empty = true;
        }
  }
}
```

Several MCs can use the same function and any changes in the local variables affect only the variables within the same function within the MC.

Timeline Variables

The last category of variables are what might be called "regular" variables in the context of Flash. These variables are declared simply by assigning them a value. The reason they're called timeline variables is because they must be addressed through the path to the timeline they are on. A global variable can be referenced anywhere in the movie without a reference to a target path, but timeline variables are unique to a target path. Suppose you have an MC named car, and within the car MC, you have an engine MC, and within the engine MC you have a spark variable with Boolean values of true or false. To reference the timeline variable, spark, you would have to follow the path:

```
_root.car.engine.spark=false;
```

Any timeline variable in a movie can be referenced by any other timeline as long as the correct target path is followed. Another MC may have a variable named spark as well, but because MC instance names must be unique, the reference to the path would be different. For example:

```
_root.emergencySupplies.flint.spark=true;
```

uses the same variable name of spark, but the target path is different and so would not affect the spark value of the variable part of the car and engine MCs. Figure 2-2 shows

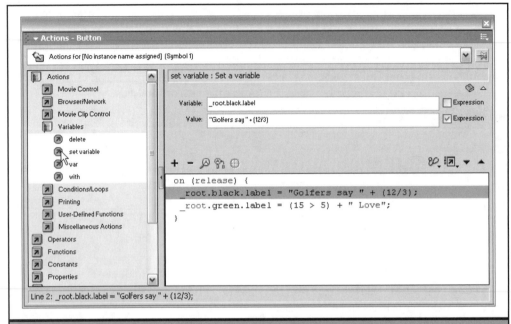

Figure 2-2. *Though it's not recommended, the same variable name can be used on different variables on different timelines without one canceling the other.*

the Actions panel with a script addressing two different timeline variables sharing the variable name label.

Changing Variables with Button Scripts

In a Flash movie, when a button is pressed and/or released, a script is launched, and depending on the data type, you will see different results, either in the state of an object or as output in a dynamic or input text field. To better understand how to use variables with the different data types, the following movie is a "test bench" for different types of data shown. Figure 2-3 shows the frames and objects laid out with one of the button scripts in the Actions panel. Figure 2-4 shows output with two floating point values entered. The following steps show how to create the test bench. The purpose of the test bench is to show the different types of data that can be generated from data entered into an input text field.

Note   *While this example movie uses separate scripts associated with the different buttons, as you progress in the book, you will see more and more scripts written for buttons using function literals (unnamed functions). Macromedia recommends using the button's instance name and an event associated with the button as part of a single script associated with the first frame in the main timeline. In this way, rather than hunting all over the movie for the right script, all of the scripts are in one place and much easier to debug.*

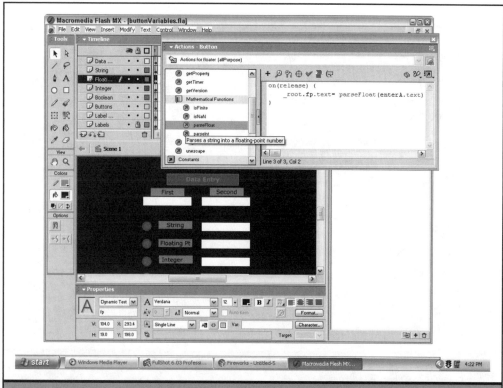

Figure 2-3. *The script uses instance names and the text property interactively with dynamic text fields.*

1. First, create seven layers with the following names and objects:
   - **Data Entry**   Two input text fields
   - **String**   One dynamic text field
   - **Floating Point**   One dynamic text field
   - **Integer**   One dynamic text field
   - **Boolean**   One dynamic text field
   - **Buttons**   Four button instances
   - **Label Text**   Text to label objects (static text fields)
   - **Label**   Background images for text labels
2. Next, use Table 2-3 to assign variable names to the text fields. Be sure to click the Show Border Around Text button. Use Figures 2-3 and 2-4 as rough guides to where to place your text field.

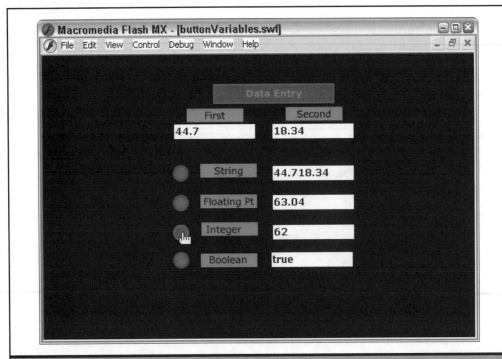

Figure 2-4. *Depending on the data type, the output varies even though the values used may be identical.*

3. Place the two input text fields on the Data Entry layer side by side, with the enterA variable on the left and enterB on the right. Then arrange the other four dynamic text fields in a single column in the following order from top to bottom: string, fp, integer, boole.

Layer	Object
Data Entry	Input text field
Data Entry	Input text field
String	Dynamic text field
Floating Point	Dynamic text field
Integer	Dynamic text field
Boolean	Dynamic text field

Table 2-3. *Layers and Text Fields*

4. Once all of the text fields are in place, select the Buttons layer, create a button, and make four instances of the button. Place one next to each of the four text fields, as shown in Figures 2-3 and 2-4.

5. Once the buttons are in place, use the following scripts in each, respectively:

String button:

```
on(release) {
    _root.string.text= enterA.text + enterB.text;
}
```

Floating Point button:

```
on(release) {
    _root.fp.text= parseFloat(enterA.text) + parseFloat(enterB.text);
}
```

Integer button:

```
on(release) {
    _root.integer.text= parseInt(enterA.text) + parseInt(enterB.text);
}
```

Boolean button:

```
on(release) {
    boole.text=enterA.text > enterB.text
}
```

6. The final step is to add layer backgrounds and labels using Figures 2-3 and 2-4 as guides. Use light colored rectangles in the Label layer, lock the layer, and then put the labels on top of them in the Label Text layer.

Once you've got everything in place, give it a test drive by pressing CTRL-ENTER or CMD-RETURN. Try putting in different data—text and numbers, whole numbers, and numbers with decimal places. As you can see in Figure 2-4, the two floating point values placed in the two input text fields had different outputs when the two were added together in the scripts. When treated as strings, the two values were concatenated. The floating point data added all of the values, including the fractions, and the integer value dropped the fractions. (Remember that difference when working with financial figures!) The only exception to using the plus (+) operator was in the script for the Boolean comparison. The Boolean operator (>) compared the first to the second values from the two input data fields. If the value on the left was greater than the value on the right, the output indicates true, otherwise it shows false. With numbers, it's fairly obvious that a 5 is greater than a 4, but what about strings? The following section explains string Boolean comparisons.

String Booleans

Because Boolean expressions are one of the fundamental data types, you should learn a little more about using strings with Boolean expressions. In the previous example, the Boolean expression used the greater-than (>) operator to compare data. The lines:

```
"Alaska" > "Texas"
```

states that the value of the string "Alaska" is greater than the string "Texas". Because the value of strings in Boolean expressions is based on the position of the first letter of the string in the alphabet (A = 1 and Z = 26), the string "Alaska" is not greater than the string "Texas". Therefore, the expression returns a value of false, as you will see if you place Alaska in the left window of the test bench movie and Texas in the right.

Generating Variable Changes in Frames

Flash movies have a unique way of changing variables in frames. Because movies loop, each time a frame comes up, any script in that frame fires. If a variable is in a frame loop, the variable can get changed a good deal. In a frame with three frames (all keyframes), a variable declaration could begin in the first frame, be incremented in the second frame, while the third frame sends the movie back to the second frame so that the declaration value is not reset.

```
Frame 1:  myVariable = 1;      //declare variable

Frame 2:  myVariable += 1;      //increment by 1

Frame 3:  gotoAndPlay(2);      //send the playhead back to frame 2
```

Variables generated in frames on one timeline can address variables on another timeline. For example, in a movie clip with its own timeline, it could increment a variable on the main timeline. Likewise, a movie frame on the main timeline could affect variables in a movie clip.

```
From Main to MC:  _root.mcInstance.mcVariable +=3;      //increment by 3

From MC to Main:  _parent.mainVariable -= .5 //decrement by .5
```

Like any other script variable, scripts residing in frames have the same ways of dealing with variables as those in buttons. Whether a script is fired because another script has issued a command to go to the frame and play it or it's part of a looping action caused by the movie repeating itself, each time a frame script containing a variable is encountered, the variable can be affected and affect other parts of the movie. Scripts associated with buttons tend to be event-driven and will occur only when a given event is triggered.

Conclusion

At the heart of any language is the manner in which it uses variables and data. ActionScript has "smart" variables in that they can tell what type of data they contain. Unlike some languages, the variables need not be defined as a certain type that can only contain one data type. Flash MX ActionScript not only automatically differentiates between data types, it also automatically changes them as needed.

In Chapter 3, we begin to look at the basic actions of ActionScript. As you will see, actions are actually another name for "statements." However ActionScript actions contain certain terms such as nextScene and gotoAndPlay that are unique to ActionScript. That is because these statements are designed to address Flash's unique timelines, and while other languages, such as JavaScript, may share many of Flash MX ActionScript's characteristics, one characteristic they do not share is the ability (or necessity) to address different timelines connected to actions on a stage. The variables and data covered in this chapter are used extensively with the different actions discussed in the next.

The
Complete
Reference

ActionScript

Part II

Fundamental
ActionScript

The Complete Reference

ActionScript

Chapter 3

Basic Actions I

In this and the following chapters, the different language elements are arranged in the same order as they are in the ActionScript toolbox. This decision is based on the unique way that Macromedia Flash MX handles scripts and is preferable to a straight alphabetical listing or a more traditional arrangement used for covering other languages that do not have the Flash-like scripting considerations. The first two chapters covered the nitty-gritty tools used in Flash, and they will be referenced in this and future chapters but not revisited in any detail. (For example, instance names are placed in the Properties panel, and while reminders of that fact are appropriate, you'll have to go back to the first two chapters to see what the Properties panel looks like.)

Action Categories

Actions in ActionScript are equivalent to statements in other languages. The references to actions and statements mean the same thing and the terms will be used interchangeably. Actions are divided into eight categories:

- Movie Control
- Browser/Network
- Movie Clip Control
- Variables
- Conditions/Loops
- Printing
- User-defined Functions
- Miscellaneous Actions

A short introduction to each of these eight subcategories gives you a broad view of what the actions in the categories do. Most are very logical groupings—a compliment to Macromedia since I'm using the order they have—but some of the statements seem to be a little misplaced. Rather than arguing they belong elsewhere, the focus is on explaining what they do and providing an example of their doing so. This chapter examines the first four categories, and the next chapter, the second group.

Actions and Methods

Further on in the book, you will be meeting up with the same set of actions as methods of movie clip objects. Fortunately, the actions and functions perform almost identically except for the arrangement of target paths.

■ Movie Control Actions

For the most part, movie control actions direct the playhead to move to a frame or start or stop the movie. These statements are uniquely a part of the Macromedia Flash MX environment and may not have an equivalent in most other computer languages.

gotoAndPlay

gotoAndPlay("Scene", frame): Action

The reference points in a Flash movie are contained in frame numbers or frame labels or a combination of scene names and a frame reference. Frames in Flash are sequential through different scenes. A reference to Scene 2, Frame 15, could also be referenced as Frame 35 if Scene 1 has 20 frames. For example, the following three scripts would arrive at the identical frame in a timeline:

```
gotoAndPlay("Scene 2", 7);
//Scene 2, Frame 7 has the frame label "buzz."
gotoAndPlay("Scene 2", "buzz");
gotoAndPlay(27); //Scene 1 has 20 frames.
```

All frame labels in the scene must be unique, and a reference to any frame name assumes the current scene unless the scene name has been specified.

Clip events and buttons require different types of information when issuing a location to move the playhead. In a clip event, if you do not specify a path, the MC's own timeline is assumed as the target. For example, the following shows the correct syntax for a movie clip event using gotoAndPlay() action:

```
onClipEvent(mouseDown) {
    _root.gotoAndPlay("frameName");
}
```

However, button scripts do not require the path if the target is on the same timeline as the button as illustrated in the following example, which effectively does the same thing as the script associated with the movie clip:

```
on (release) {
    gotoAndPlay("frameName");
}
gotoAndPlay("Scene", frame);
```

Flash provides an action to move the playhead to a specified frame and then keep playing the movie beyond the frame. It executes any script in the target frame, and unless it encounters a stop() action, it will keep on playing the movie. The play() action is not playing the script in the frame. That will be executed simply because the playhead has moved into the frame. Rather, the play() action forces the playhead to keep on moving beyond the target frame unless the frame contains a stop() action.

The reference to the scene is optional, and all scene references are written as string literals (for example, "Scene 1", "myScene") and all frame numbers as integers. Frames with labels can be addressed as strings (for example, "score", "start"). The following examples provide the formats typically found:

To frame number, no scene reference. Will go across scenes.

```
gotoAndPlay(55);
```

To frame label, no scene reference. Will go to named frame in current scene.

```
gotoAndPlay("myFavoriteFrame");
```

To scene and frame number relative to the first frame of the scene.

```
gotoAndPlay("Scene 4", 18);
```

To scene name and frame label.

```
gotoAndPlay("Three Bears", "Mama");
```

If an error occurs in targeting a frame, the movie goes to the end and stops. If a value less than 1 is issued, the movie stops in the first frame.

Originated in: Flash 2

gotoAndStop

gotoAndStop("Scene", frame): Action

The gotoAndStop() action moves the playhead to the specified frame and stops the movie. The stopping frame does not need to be a keyframe, and if you issue the command to stop the playhead at a frame in the middle of a tween, it will.

When the playhead arrives at the frame, the script is launched. If no script is in the frame, the movie simply stops. However, if a play() or some other movie control action other than stop() is associated with the target frame, the movie will keep playing until it encounters script that instructs it to do otherwise.

To frame number, no scene reference. Will go across scenes.

```
gotoAndStop(43);
```

To frame label, no scene reference. Will go to named frame in current scene.

```
gotoAndStop("liveAction");
```

To scene and frame number relative to the first frame of the scene.

```
gotoAndStop("Fred", 22);
```

To scene name and frame label.

```
gotoAndStop("Southside", "franchise");
```

If an error occurs in targeting a frame, the movie goes to the end and stops. If a value less than 1 is issued, the movie stops in the first frame.

Originated in: Flash 2

nextFrame

nextFrame(): Action

This statement moves the playhead to the next frame and stops. At the last frame on a timeline, the action will not cause the playhead to cycle back to the first frame, but rather, the playhead stops. The action has no arguments (parameters).

If the next frame the playhead moves to has a movie control script to play the movie, instead of stopping, the control will be passed to the new script. The following examples show the main forms of the action:

```
onClipEvent(mouseUp) {
    _root.nextFrame(); //must include some path information with clip event.
}
```

```
on(release) {
    nextFrame(); // button event
}
```

Originated in: Flash 2

nextScene()

This statement moves the playhead to the first frame of the next scene and stops. At the last scene on a timeline, the action will not cause the playhead to cycle back to the first scene, but keeps it in the current frame. The action has no arguments (parameters).

If the next frame the playhead moves to has a movie control script to play the movie, instead of stopping, the control will be passed to the new script. The following example shows the main form of the action:

```
on(release) {
    nextScene(); // button event
}
```

The action is not available for clip events or timelines, even using a target path.

Originated in: Flash 2

on(event)

The on() action is the event handler for the button object. The action can read different mouse and keyboard events and release the script bounded by the action's container with the following format:

```
on(event) {
    ActionScript to be launched
}
```

The following eight formats are employed:

- **on(press)**   Pointer is on button and mouse button is held down.
- **on(release)**   Pointer is on button and mouse button is pressed and released.
- **on(releaseOutside)**   Pointer is on button and mouse button is pressed and then released with pointer outside of button hit area.
- **on(rollOut)**   Pointer first rolls over button and then fires on roll out.
- **on(rollOver)**   Pointer rolls over button hit area.
- **on(dragOut)**   Pointer is on button and mouse button is pressed and held while mouse is moved from hit area.
- **on(dragOver)**   Pointer is on button and mouse button is pressed and held while mouse is moved from hit area and then moved back over button. (Drag mouse off of button and then drag it on again.)

■ **on(keyPress " key")**   This event has two different formats. The first format specifies the key in quotes (for example, "A", "a", "r", "V"). The second syntax uses a tag format for specialized keys with the form <KeyName>. The following keys tags are available:

<Left>	<Enter>
<Right>	<Up>
<Home>	<PageUp>
<End>	<PageDown>
<Insert>	<Tab>
<Delete>	<Escape>
<Backspace>	<Space>

The following shows typical examples of using the button event handler:

```
on(dragOut) {
gotoAndPlay(15);
}
```

```
on(keyPress "B") {
    _root.output.text="Baltimore";
}
```

```
on(keyPress "<Left>") {
    _root.ship._x = (_root.ship._x) - 2;
}
```

While the keyPress event relies on keyboard events, it must reside in a button instance. You cannot place an on(event) event handler in a frame. One way to accomplish this task is to create an invisible button and put the script in the invisible button. To create an invisible button, select Insert | New Symbol from the menu bar. Then in the Symbol Editing mode, place no images on the stage and click the Scene button to return to the main timeline. Create an "invisible button" layer, and then drag the Button object from the library to the desktop with the invisible button layer selected. (The invisible button should be the only object on the layer.) Because the button is invisible, all you will be able to see is a little circle icon in the upper-left corner of the stage. If you cannot find the button, one trick is to toggle the visibility of the layer on and off. Whatever appears when you toggle visibility on is the button icon to select so that you can enter script related to the button.

Once you run the movie, you will find that you must click the mouse on the stage once before you can use the keys. Then you can use any and all of the keys you have defined and need not click the stage again. Using the Key object (see Chapter 10) provides more control and no dependence on invisible buttons and special stage clicking.

Originated in: Flash 2

play

play(): Action

The play() action restarts a stopped movie. The action has no parameters and can be placed in frames and objects. Movie clip events require a minimal target path like the other movie control actions unless they are acting on themselves.

The following shows the format for a frame:

```
play();
```

The following shows the format for a button:

```
on(release) {
play();
}
```

The following shows the format for a movie clip:

```
onClipEvent(mouseUp) {
_root.play();
}
```

Originated in: Flash 2

prevFrame

prevFrame(): Action

This statement moves the playhead to the previous frame and stops. At the first frame on a timeline, the action will not cause the playhead to cycle back to the last frame, but rather, the playhead stops. The action has no arguments (parameters).

If the previous frame the playhead moves to has a movie control script to play the movie, instead of stopping, the control will be passed to the new script. The following examples show the main forms of the action:

```
onClipEvent(mouseDown){
    _root.prevFrame(); //must include some path information with clip event.
}

on(keyPress "<Backspace>") {
    prevFrame(); // button event
}
```

Originated in: Flash 2

prevScene

prevScene(): Action

This statement moves the playhead to the first frame of the previous scene and stops. At the first scene on a timeline, the action will not cause the playhead to cycle back to the last scene on the timeline, but rather, the playhead remains in the current frame. The action has no arguments (parameters).

If the previous frame the playhead moves to has a movie control script to play the movie, instead of stopping, the control will be passed to the new script. The following example shows the main form of the action:

```
on(dragOver) {
    prevScene(); // button event
}
```

The action is not available for clip events, even using a target path or from within a clip timeline.

Originated in: Flash 2

stop

stop(): Action

The stop() action stops a movie. The action has no parameters and can be placed in frames and objects. Movie clip events require a minimal target path like the other movie control actions.

The following shows the format for a frame:

```
stop();
```

The following shows the format for a button:

```
on(release) {
stop();
}
```

The following shows the format for a movie clip:

```
onClipEvent(mouseUp) {
_root.stop();
}
```

Originated in: Flash 2

stopAllSounds

stopAllSounds(): Action

This global function, while grouped with actions works more like a function than statement. It has no parameters and will stop all current sounds from playing. However, if new sounds are launched, it will not prevent them from being played. The function can be launched from a frame or button script or a movie clip script. Because the function is global, no path is required in a clip event script as shown in the following excerpt:

```
onClipEvent(mouseUp) {
stopAllSounds();
}
```

Originated in: Flash 3

Browser/Network

This next set of actions is for communicating with the browser and files on Web servers. Macromedia Flash MX has many of the actions in this section working as methods in movie clip objects, but they are still important for scripts on the main timeline. Perhaps the most important use of this set of actions is in calling up server-side middleware such as PHP, CGI/Perl, and ASP scripts. Flash has proven to be a very stable cross-browser platform for connections to middleware and databases, as well as passing variables back and forth between the Flash movie and sever-side scripts.

fscommand

fscommand(command, parameters): Action

This global function has the purpose of communicating with scripting languages like JavaScript, sending commands to a standalone player, and communicating with Lingo in a Director movie. Of these functions, the most general is a set of parameters associated with controlling the standalone player, and it will be discussed first.

Standalone Player

Using the fscommand() with the standalone player allows the developer to have some level of control over Macromedia Flash MX movies played in a standalone player. Table 3-1 shows the different commands available.

The fscommand() format expects a command and a parameter, except when using the quit command where no argument is required. For example, the command to create a full screen appears as follows:

```
fscommand("fullscreen", "true");
```

Command	Parameters	Actions
fullscreen	true/false	Maximizes screen to full size
allowscale	true/false	A true condition allows player to rescale movie to screen size shape, while a false condition maintains the original scale
showmenu	true/false	Allows the menu items in player to be available or not
trapallkeys	true/false	Controls whether all keystrokes will be sent to Flash movie (true)
exe	path + application name	Launches external application using the format path/application.exe (for example, D:/games/marbles.exe)
quit	none	Quits player

Table 3-1. *fscommand() Commands, Parameters, and Actions*

FUNDAMENTAL ACTIONSCRIPT

The other commands related to the standalone player are similar. However, keep in mind that the standalone player commands do not apply to movies running in browsers.

Communicating with Browsers and Director

Using the fscommand() for a general Internet audience can be problematic. The fscommand() function cannot be used with Internet Explorer on the Macintosh or with Netscape Navigator 6+ at all. Furthermore, what can be accomplished is of dubious utility. A better and more useful way of communicating with JavaScript or VBScript is to use getURL().

As for Director, the preferred way of communicating between Flash and Director is to use the getURL() action (see the following section) with either event: or lingo: syntax.

Originated in: Flash 3

getURL

getURL(url, window, method): Action

This global function serves as a linking one (loading a page), but it also launches server-side script, JavaScript, and other protocols. The function has the following general format:

```
getURL("URL", "_window", "method");
```

For example, the following line would launch a PHP file in a new blank page, using the POST method to send timeline variables to script:

```
on (release) {
    getURL("http://www.sandlight.com/talker.php", "_blank", "POST");
}
```

URL

The URL specifies the path to the document using either absolute or relative addressing. It uses the same format as an HTML link. The following shows both relative and absolute addressing:

```
getURL("http://www.omh.com/books.html); //Absolute address
getURL("bank/newMov.html"); //Relative address
```

Window

The target window can be one of five types:

■ **userDefined**   The user-defined frame name. Any named frame in the target URL is acceptable.

```
getURL("http://www.macromedia.com", "flashHere");
```

- **_self**   Current frame from which the SWF file called the URL.

  ```
  getURL("http://www.werehere.com", "_self");
  ```

- **_blank**   New window with the called URL, with the current movie on the screen in a separate browser window.

  ```
  getURL("http://www.flashkit.com", "_blank");
  ```

- **_parent**   Frameset containing the movie is replaced with the called URL.

  ```
  getURL("http://www.flashmagazine.com", "_parent");
  ```

- **_top**   URL target is sent to the top frame replacing all framesets in the window.

  ```
  getURL("http://www.amazon.com", "_top");
  ```

Method

Only GET or POST is used to send variables in this optional parameter. Using the GET method, variables are appended to the URL and are generally used when only a small number of variables are being sent. When larger numbers of variables are sent, POST places the variables in a separate HTTP header.

Other Protocols

The other protocols besides HTTP include ones for Director (event: and lingo:), for files (file: and ftp:), for printing (print:), and scripting languages (javascript: and vbscript:). To invoke one of the other protocols, the protocol name is placed in the URL section of the function followed by a colon and the name of the command, event, or target. For example, if you have a JavaScript function called setUp() in the same HTML page as your Flash SWF file, the following line would launch the specified function:

```
getURL("javascript: setUp()");
```

If your HTML page has several JavaScript functions embedded in it, the JavaScript protocol could be used to fire off any or all of them.

Originated in: Flash 2, added method in Flash 4

loadMovie

loadMovie("url", "level/MC" [method]): Action

The loadMovie() action loads an external SWF file into a specified movie clip, taking on the instance name of the named clip. This allows you to create a single movie clip and load different movies into the clip. Whatever movie is moved into the clip inherits the clip's reference. For example, if you have a movie clip with the instance name "first" and you load a SWF file named bounce.swf, when the SWF file is loaded you can refer to it by the instance name of the movie it was loaded into. The following script shows a SWF file loaded into a movie clip. Then, using the instance name of the original MC, the new movie is moved on the stage and rotated.

```
on(release) {
    loadMovie("bounce.swf",_root.first);
    _root.first._x=150;
    _root.first._y=-100;
    _root.first._rotation=50;
}
```

Alternatively, you can enter a level number stated as number (such as 0, 43, 129), or use _level and a value (for example, _level0, _level44) instead of an instance name.

```
loadMovie("jump.swf", 0)
loadMovie("jump.swf", _level8)
loadMovie("jump.swf", "_level0")
```

If you load a movie into the level of the calling timeline, the current timeline is replaced with the loaded movie. Generally, a string is used to express the level because if the level you are calling does not exist (that is, it currently contains no movie), the movie will be loaded into the level of the calling movie. The most effective use of this global function is to load SWF files into movie clips using the movie clip instance name as a target.

The optional methods are GET and POST for sending timeline variables from the current movie clip.

Originated in: Flash 4

loadMovieNum

loadMovieNum("url", level, method): Action

The main difference between loadMovie() and loadMovieNum() is that the latter does not accept instance names of movie clips and requires a number for a level. The number used can be any legal level number. If the same level number is used as the current movie, the current movie will be replaced by the loading movie. Most often, this will happen with level0. For example, the following will replace the current movie with the named SWF file:

```
loadMovieNum("whisky.swf",0);
```

Generally, loadMovieNum() is preferred when several movies need to be loaded to different levels. The following script is typical of one using concatenation to load sequentially named movies into level 0. In order not to remove the current movie, the loop begins with an index value of 1 instead of 0.

```
for (var count=1; count < 24; count++) {
    loadMovieNum("lemming" + count + ".swf", count);
}
```

The optional methods are GET and POST for sending timeline variables from the current movie clip.

Originated in: Flash 3 as Load Movie, developed into current state in Flash 5

loadVariables("url", "MC", [method])

The loadVariables() global function is used to receive and send variables. Variables can be loaded from text files on the server, or can pass variables to and receive data from middleware such as PHP, Perl, Cold Fusion, and ASP. The variables loaded into Macromedia Flash MX have the following format:

```
variableName=string of words
```

Multiple variables are separated by ampersands with each new variable following the previous ampersand. The following shows how you would assign three variables:

```
firstVar=lots of text&secondVar=less text&thirdVar=1234 Elm Street
```

Using loadVariables() you can direct variables to be loaded into an MC. For example, the following button script instructs Flash to load a file named var.txt into an MC with the instance name of texHouse:

```
on(release) {
    loadVariables("var.txt","texHouse");
}
```

The data loaded into the texHouse instance can be directed to a text field in the MC. For example, the following script is the absolute address to the text field with the instance name mcText. The variable name alpha is from the text field loaded.

```
_root.texHouse.mcText.text=alpha;
```

The GET and POST methods can be used to send variables from the current timeline to middleware that can use the variable values as data for a database or in some other way. For example, in an application, suppose you are using PHP for a mail agent. If you have a variable containing an e-mail address in Macromedia Flash MX, when you issue an instruction like this:

```
loadVariables("target.php","emailMC","POST")
```

and if the timeline from which that instruction is issued contains a variable, myEmail, that variable can be passed to the PHP script using the same name. Thus, in the PHP script, the variable:

```
$myEmail;
```

now contains the value in the variable myEmail that originated in Flash. (PHP variables are identified by preceding dollar signs [$].)

Originated in: Flash 4

loadVariablesNum

loadVariablesNum("url", num, [method]): Action

This global function is similar to loadVariables() except that it must have a level value as a number instead of a string, and it cannot be used to load variables directly to movie clip instances. All variables from the current timeline will be sent to a specified URL using the GET or POST methods. It has the format:

```
loadVariablesNum("targetPath.file", 0, "POST/GET");
```

For example, to pass variables to and from a PHP script, the following button script would get any PHP variables and send the Macromedia Flash MX variables from the current timeline:

```
on(release) {
loadVariablesNum("php2msql.php", 0, "POST");
}
```

For loading and sending variables from movies with different levels, loadVariablesNum() could be set up in a loop with the level number being the current index value in a loop. Consider a movie with three levels, 0–2:

```
on (release) {
    for (var count = 0; count<3; count++) {
        loadVariablesNum("lots.php", count);
    }
}
```

Originated in: Flash 5

Macromedia Flash MX now has a new object, LoadVars(), that should be used as an alternative to both loadVariablesNum() and loadVariables() whenever possible. (See Chapter 12.)

unloadMovie("MC/_level")

The unloadMovie() function removes a specified movie clip or an unspecified movie at a level, expressed as a string. No variables are passed, and because only a single movie can be at a given level, level specification is enough to remove any movie, including its accompanying movie clips. For example, the following script removes whatever movie happens to be at level 7:

```
on(release) {
unloadMovie("_level7");
}
```

A nice feature of unloadMovie() is that it allows you to remove the contents from a movie clip instance from within a movie. However, rather than removing the movie clip instance itself, the instance stays in the movie as an empty movie clip, and using loadMovie(), you can add different contents to the MC. For example, the following script removes the contents from the movie clip instance rabbit and replaces it with the contents of the SWF file hare.swf:

```
on(release) {
unloadMovie("_root.rabbit");
loadMovie("hare.swf", _root.rabbit);
}
```

The function is useful for keeping a minimum number of movies and movie clip contents in memory at any one time.

Originated in: Flash 4

unloadMovieNum(number)

The unloadMovieNum() function works like unloadMovie() except that rather than putting a string argument to specify a movie clip instance or a string for the level number, all the function requires is a level number. For instance:

```
onClipEvent (load) {
    unloadMovieNum(3);
}
```

Using unLoadMovieNum(), movies from sequential layers can be removed using a loop. For example, the following script could be used to remove movies from levels 250 to 255:

```
on (release) {

    for (var count = 250; count<256; count++) {
    unloadMovieNum(count);
    }
}
```

Originated in: Flash 3 as Unload Movie, introduced in current format in Flash 5

Movie Clip Control

Movie clip controls are a set of actions that manipulate movie clips beyond setting properties, but including setting properties. The setProperty() function is an older, less desirable way to set a movie clip property and is included in case the need arises to create a movie that can be run on a Flash 4 player.

duplicateMovieClip

duplicateMovieClip("MC", "dupMC", depth): Action

Duplicating movie clips dynamically in Macromedia Flash MX is done with this function. Each duplicated movie clip is set at a unique depth. Those assigned a lower depth value are covered by those assigned a higher depth value. The basic format for the action is

```
duplicateMovieClip("originalMCinstanceName", "newInstanceName", depth number)
```

For example, a movie clip with the instance name alpha is duplicated to one named beta with a depth of 15 in the following example:

```
duplicateMovieClip("alpha", "beta", 15);
```

Unless stated otherwise, duplicated movies are placed directly on top of the duplicated movies. Therefore, in most applications, a new position is generated for the new movie clip as well. For example, if the existing MC instance is located at x = 50, y = 125, the following script would ensure that the new instance would be placed elsewhere:

```
on(release) {
    duplicateMovieClip("cat", "kitten", 4);
_root.kitten._x=100;
_root.kitten._y=200;
}
```

Multiple movie clips can be generated in loops. The names of the new instances must be unique and can be made so by concatenating as a loop index value with a string (for example, "mcName" + index), as shown in the following script:

```
on (release) {
    for (var count = 22; count<25; count++) {
        duplicateMovieClip("bb","bBlock" + count,count);
        _root["bBlock"+count]._x=Math.random()*300 + 100;
        _root["bBlock"+count]._y=Math.random()*200 + 100;
    }
}
```

Note that the script generates new positions for each of the new instances.

Note   *You can use the reference returned by duplicateMovieClip in a variable. Thus, if you assigned a variable duplicateMovieClip("origN", "newN", level), you could then assign property values to the variable that would affect the MC.*

Originated in: Flash 4

onClipEvent

onClipEvent(event): Action

Beginning with Flash 5, the onClipEvent() action allowed developers to include scripts associated with movie clip instances in addition to buttons and frames. The event handler, onClipEvent(), has a different character than the button handler, on(). Not only are different events included, such as load, but mouse events need not occur while the mouse is over the MC instance. Nine different events are associated with onClipEvent(), as shown in Table 3-2.

Event	Description
load	Loading the movie clip triggers the event
unload	Unloading the movie clip triggers the event
enterFrame	Movie's frame rate triggers the event continuously
mouseMove	Any movement of the mouse pointer triggers the event
mouseDown	Left mouse key clicked anywhere on stage triggers the event
mouseUp	Left mouse key released after being clicked triggers the event
keyDown	Pressing a keyboard key triggers the event
keyUp	Pressing and releasing a keyboard key triggers the event
data	Linked to loadVariables() or loadMovie() events, occurring once with loadVariables() and repeatedly with loadMovie() as data in different parts of the movie come out

Table 3-2.   *Events for onClipEvent()*

The general format of the event handler is as follows:

```
onClipEvent(event) {
script here launches when event occurs;
}
```

load and unload

The load and unload events are related solely to the placement or removal of the movie clip. Any movie clip instance using a load event will trigger the related script as soon the movie with the movie clip loads. The unload event is related to the unloadMovie() action. For example, if a button has the following script:

```
on (release) {
    unloadMovie("bb");
}
```

and the movie clip named bb had this script:

```
onClipEvent (unload) {
    _root.message.text="Gone!"
}
```

as soon as the button script fired, the movie clip would be unloaded, but it would still launch any script within the event container. Thus, the text field with the instance name message would contain the text "Gone!".

Mouse Actions

The mouse actions recognized as events by the onClipEvent() action are relatively uncomplicated. The only important caveat is that the action need not take place while the mouse pointer is over the movie clip. For this reason, be careful about having more than a single movie clip with an associated mouse action. For example, the following script's event handler would launch it plus any other MC using the mouseDown event:

```
onClipEvent(mouseDown) {
    _root.message.text="Right";
}
```

Problems occur when contradictory scripts from different movie clip instances are fired at the same time. For example, if one clip has a script to put the message "Right" and another one has a script to put the message "Wrong" in the same text field, with both using a mouseDown event, only one message will appear. The resulting message may not be the one intended by the designer.

Key Actions

Key actions are based on keys being up or down, and in order to trap a specific key, you will need to use the Key object and the getCode method associated with the Key object. The action of any key will fire the script, but with conditional statements to find a specific key, you can nullify any key press that is not the target key. For example, the following script uses the PAGE UP and PAGE DOWN keys with a keyDown event:

```
onClipEvent (keyDown) {
    if (Key.getCode() == Key.PGUP) {
        _root.star._y = (_root.star._y)-8;
    } else if (Key.getCode() == Key.PGDN) {
        _root.star_y = (_root.star._y)+8;
    }
}
```

As with mouse actions, be careful about having contradicting actions fired by the same key event.

Data

The loadVariables() and loadMovie() actions are both data events. From within a movie clip, some event first loads the data, and then the data fires the script. The important aspect is arranging the MC to invoke the loadVariables() or loadMovie() action from inside the MC. To illustrate how this works, look at the following three scripts.

The first script represents an external PHP script:

```php
<?php
$alpha="message=Hello from PHP."; //Formatted for Flash variable
echo $alpha;
?>
```

The second script is a button script inside of a movie clip with the instance name "dClip":

```
on(release) {
    _root.dClip.loadVariables("message.php");
}
```

This third script is associated with "dClip":

```
onClipEvent (data) {
    _root.output.text=message;
}
```

The only difference between using loadVariables() and loadMovie() is that the data in the latter is retrieved at different points while the movie runs with each new piece of data firing the script.

Originated in: Flash 4

removeMovieClip

removeMovieClip(target): Action

Movie clips created using duplicateMovieClip() or attachMovie() can be removed using the removeMovieClip() action. The only parameter is the instance name of the movie clip and its path. For example, a movie clip created inside another movie clip would have two instance names to identify, as shown in the following script:

```
on (release) {
    removeMovieClip(_root.body.tonsils);
}
```

Originated in: Flash 4

setProperty

setProperty(target, property, value): Action

This older method of assigning a value to a movie clip persists seemingly for no other reason than to provide a way to create scripts for Flash 4 players. The target is a movie clip instance name, and the property and value are legitimate properties and related values for movie clips. For example, the following changes the rotation angle of a MC with the instance name titanic:

```
setProperty("titanic", _rotation, 90);
```

Since Flash 5, and continuing in Macromedia Flash MX, the same property setting is done using dot syntax:

```
_root.titanic._rotation=90;
```

Originated in: Flash 4

startDrag

startDrag(target, lock, left, top, right, bottom): Action

The startDrag() action allows for the scripting of a draggable movie clip. Only a single clip can be dragged at one time. The target is the MC instance name, and lock is a Boolean value to lock (true) the cursor's center to that of the MC. The script need not be in a movie clip, but can be initiated in a button or frame script as well. The following shows an example of how to use this action with a movie clip:

```
onClipEvent(load) {
    startDrag(this,true);
}
```

To restrict the movie clip movement, set the left, top, right, and bottom parameters to screen position values. Top left is 0,0 and right bottom depends on the size of the stage. For example, a stage measuring 500 by 250 would have a right bottom value of 500,250. Movement restriction is useful in creating levers, or area-restricted moves (for example, movie clips of animals in a cage that can be dragged within the confines of the cage). The following shows the setup for horizontal and vertical levers:

```
startDrag(_root.leverH,true, 50,250,350,250); //Horizontal lever
startDrag(_root.leverV, true,250,10,250,300); //Vertical lever
```

Usually, the startDrag() action is used in conjunction with stopDrag(), described in the next section.

Originated in: Flash 4

stopDrag

stopDrag(): Action

To disconnect the mouse pointer from a movie clip and stop dragging the clip, use stopDrag(). The action has no parameters and will stop drag actions working as a global function. For example, the following script initiates a dragging action for the movie clip with the instance name boat. As soon as the mouse is clicked (mouseUp), the dragging action stops and the mouse pointer is freed from the movie clip.

```
onClipEvent(load) {
    startDrag(_root.boat,true);
}
onClipEvent(mouseUp) {
    stopDrag();
}
```

Originated in: Flash 4

updateAfterEvent

updateAfterEvent(): Action

To update the display screen, use updateAfterEvent() from within a clip event. It also can be used as part of a method or function passed to setInterval(), but if used outside of either context, the Flash player ignores the action.

A typical use of the action is when an object is being dragged around the screen, as shown in the following script:

```
onClipEvent (mouseMove) {
    startDrag(_root.mover, true);
    _root.showX.text = _root.mover._x;
    _root.showY.text = _root.mover._y;
    updateAfterEvent();
}
```

Because of the constant movement and change of images, the updateAfterEvent() action helps keep the flicker down and display a smoother movie.

Originated in: Flash 5

Variables

Only four actions are associated with variables. Three are used for variable and property assignment and declaration, and one for removing variables and objects.

delete

delete: Action

The delete operator is an interesting one because it not only deletes objects and variables, it returns a Boolean value. The syntax is simple, using the following form:

```
delete varName; //Or objName
```

When a variable or object is deleted, memory is freed for other objects and variables, and given a large enough file, deleting unused variables and objects could improve the movie's performance.

One of the interesting aspects of delete is that while it is an operator, in many ways it acts like an action. When a variable has been deleted, a Boolean true returns. For example, the following script will return a true because the variable is deleted. (alpha is deleted, and beta stores the Boolean literal generated.)

```
alpha=5;
beta=delete alpha;
trace(beta);
```

If you attempt to delete an undeclared variable, the delete operator returns a Boolean false. Likewise, built-in objects and properties cannot be deleted nor can variables declared using var.

Originated in: Flash 5

set variable

set(var, exp): Action

This statement is an older way of setting a variable's value, and while not deprecated, its primary value lies in creating scripts for Flash 4 players. The format is

```
set (variable, expression)
```

For example, the following sets a variable goodHealth to a Boolean true:

```
set(goodHealth,true);
```

The dot syntax introduced in Flash 5 and used in Macromedia Flash MX is much clearer. The same declaration could be made using the following:

```
goodHealth=true;
```

Unless you absolutely need script to run in Flash 4 players, there is no advantage or reason to use this statement.

Originated in: Flash 4

var

var: Action

The var action is used to declare local variables. You can declare the variable with or without assigning a value, and you can declare and/or assign multiple variables on the same line. For example, the following are all legitimate declarations and assignments:

```
var peaches = "fruit"; //declared and assigned
var oranges; //declared but not assigned
//multiple declarations and assignments
var cost="5.95", tax=.06, total= cost += tax;
```

If the variables declared using var are not within a function launched with a call action or inside of a block (typically in an event handler), the variable is not local.

Originated in: Flash 5

with

with(): Action

Using the with statement allows multiple statements to be included in assigning actions and values to movie clips and other objects. The with statement replaces the deprecated tell target action. The general format is

```
with (object) {
Statement 1
Statement 2
Etc.
}
```

For example, the following assigns the movie clip properties with only a single statement of the clip:

```
with(_root.underGroundTrain) {
    _x=232;
    _y=73;
    _alpha=34;
    _rotation=80;
}
```

Basically, using the with statement saves the amount of typing that has to be done and is clearer, especially when several different movie clips or objects have to have several properties assigned values.

If needed, you can nest with statements by including embedded elements of one object as nested in others. For example, if the parent object is boat, you can change different objects that belong to the boat object. The following example illustrates this nesting:

```
with (_root.boat) {
    with (mast) {
    _rotation=90;
}
    with(anchor) {
    _rotation=40;
    _scale=30;
    }
}
```

The above written in the dot syntax without using with would look like the following:

```
_root.boat.mast._rotation=90;
_root.boat.anchor._rotation=40;
_root.boat.anchor._scale=50;
```

As noted, the major use of with is to save time in coding and clarifying multiple property assignments. The extent to which it does either or both may depend on the context of its use.

Originated in: Flash 5

FUNDAMENTAL ACTIONSCRIPT

Conclusion

The actions in this first set are generally closely associated with Flash movies, especially those that involve movie control. The movie control and browser and network control actions are the key ones used in Macromedia Flash MX navigation. For those familiar with Flash 5 ActionScript, very little has changed with the collection of actions discussed in this chapter. However, as you will see in Chapters 8–13 , many of the actions have become methods associated with objects. This change is especially noticeable with the LoadVars() object, which is supplanting older actions like loadVariables() and loadVariablesNum().

Chapter 4

Basic Actions II

This second set of actions includes the branching and loop actions, which are basic to virtually all programming languages. Anyone familiar with basic structures will not find any surprises in the ways that conditional statements and the different types of loops work in Macromedia Flash MX. One of the nicest additions to Macromedia Flash MX not previously available is the switch...case structure. It will save a lot of if...else statements.

The printing actions are few, as they should be for an application where the main viewed materials will appear on the Web and not a static page. However, some may find printing very helpful during the debugging process, and some applications can set up materials that are best used by allowing the user to print them to paper.

The group of actions associated with user-defined functions are basic function/ return statements along with a previously deprecated action, call. The last group of actions are appropriately grouped as Miscellaneous actions. Here you will find actions associated with several different aspects of Macromedia Flash MX.

Conditions/Loops

Chapter 2 introduced conditional statements and loops in general terms. This section examines all of the statements in ActionScript related to conditional branches and looping. The use of branches allows "decision-making" options using ActionScript in Macromedia Flash MX affecting every element controlled by actions. Additionally, loops can generate multiple iterations of different controls. Some controls are unique to Flash, such as duplicating movie clips, while other looping actions are typical for most other programming languages.

break

break: Action

Essentially, the break statement serves to jump out of either a loop or a block of code and continue with the next statement beyond the block. The break action is problematic for some programmers because it stops a program flow rather than following through to a condition that meets the requirement for ending a program segment. However, in some cases, the break statement works to keep a program from needlessly going through a segment when the condition for stopping has been met. As such, the break statement fires if the condition for stopping the program segment has occurred. The most appropriate use of break is in conjunction with switch and case statements. For example, in this next script, the switch condition is met in the first case, and so the rest of the cases can be skipped by using a break action:

```
on (release) {
    switch ("ready") {
```

```
case 'ready' :
    trace("Prepared");
    break;
case 'set' :
    trace("All set");
    break;
case 'go' :
    trace("They're off!");
  }
}
```

In a situation where your script calls for looking at the position of 50 movie clips, the break action would save having to go through all of the 50 case statements and speed up the process considerably. As you can see in the following illustration, the search was broken off after the first case because the switch parameter and case parameter matched.

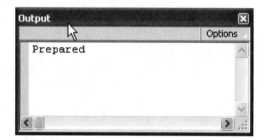

Originated in: Flash 4

case

case: Action

The case statement is used exclusively with the switch action defining conditions for it. See switch later in this section. See also break, in this section.

continue

continue: Action

Like the break action, the continue statement can be a bit problematic because it interrupts the flow of a block of code. The continue statement is used in different types of loops and has different actions depending on the type of loop structure.

FUNDAMENTAL ACTIONSCRIPT

default

default: Action

The default statement is used exclusively with the switch statement and defines the default case for switch. The default case is the one selected if none of the other case statements meet the switch condition. (See switch later in this section.)

Originated in: Macromedia Flash MX

do...while

do...while: Action

The loop begins with the do statement and launches all statements within the loop block until the termination condition set by the while statement. The do while loop tests the condition at the bottom of the loop and so the first time through the loop all statements will be executed, even if the first condition is false. For example, the output in the following script would be 12 because the increment operator (++) increases the value of the test variable (alpha) before the program reaches the while termination condition:

```
on (release) {
    alpha = 11;
    do {
        alpha++;
    } while (alpha<10);
    trace(alpha);
}
```

Using loops to position objects sequentially is not recommended. For example, the following script would rotate the movie clip "block" so fast that it would appear to barely tilt:

```
on (release) {
    rotAngle = 0;
    do {
        _root.block._rotation = rotAngle;
        rotAngle++;
    } while (rotAngle<360);
}
```

You can use tweening instead, or you can place the same code in an event handler such as enterFrame to achieve the same results. Reserve loops for other kinds of repetitive actions, and do loops for situations where the first iteration of the loop must launch a statement within the loop block.

Originated in: Flash 4

else

else: Action

The else statement is used in conjunction with the if statement. It provides an alternative branch if the initial condition set by the if statement is not met (is false). For example, the following script checks an MC's position with an alternative where the initial if condition is false:

```
if (_root.myMC._x == 240) {
    gotoAndPlay("Scene 4", "Port");
} else {
    _root.myMC._x += (_root.myMC._x)+2;
}
```

Originated in: Flash 4

else if

else if: Action

Where several different conditions need to be checked, the else if statement provides several alternatives within the context of an if statement. When the original if statement is evaluated to be false, the script proceeds to the first else if statement and evaluates it. If it is true, it executes any statements within its curly braces and exits the set of conditions. If it is false, it goes on to the next else if. If there are no others, it exits the conditional block. For example, the following script evaluates the first if condition as false and the first else if statement as true. However, it then exits the block even though the next else if statement is also true.

```
on (release) {
    alpha = 11;
    beta=12;
    gamma=22;
    if(alpha==40) {
        trace("Alpha is correct");
    } else if (beta==12) {
        trace("Beta is correct"); //Statement executed and exits block
    } else if (gamma==22) {
        trace ("Gamma is correct"); // Statement not executed
    }
}
```

As can be seen from the script, the order of the else if statements is crucial because the first one evaluated to be true is the only one that will execute the statements within its curly braces. Many programmers prefer the switch and case statements for multiple conditional statements. As you can see from the following output, the multiple conditional statements were able to locate the correct match.

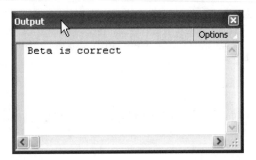

Originated in: Flash 4

for

for: Action

The for() loop begins with three elements: the initial value of the index variable, the exit condition, and the increment/decrement value of the index variable. It has the following format:

```
for(index var = initial value; exit condition; increment/decrement) {
    statements;
} // End of loop
```

For example, the following loop will iterate 10 times (0–9) before termination:

```
on (release) {
    for (var x = 0; x < 10; x++) {
        y=x;
        trace(x);
    }
}
```

To decrement an index value, use the decrement operator (--). For example, by changing the above script slightly, the iteration will be reversed:

```
on (release) {
    for (var x = 10; x>0; x--) {
        trace(x);
    }
}
```

The Output window traces the first value at the top and the last at the bottom, as the following illustration shows:

```
Output                          ⊠
                        Options
    10
    9
    8
    7
    6
    5
    4
    3
    2
    1
```

In addition to using simple increments and decrements, you can use full expressions as well. For example:

```
for (var x= 0; x < 200; x += (counter + Math.sqrt(x+9))){
trace (x);
}
```

The third element in a for() statement is any expression that changes the value of the index variable. If the index variable does not change to the point of meeting the exit condition, you will receive an error message.

Originated in: Flash 5

for...in

for...in: Action

The for...in loop iterates through properties of movie clips and other objects. Each child's path is returned in a movie clip. The format expects a variable name to be used to iterate through the property in the following general format:

```
for (varName in objectName) {
    statements; //In the format of objectName[varName]
}
```

For example, the following script iterates through a movie clip with the instance name block with two child MCs with instance names simple and simon. The variable name is prop.

```
on (release) {
    for (prop in block) {
        trace(block[prop]);
    }
}
```

The script generates the following output:

```
_level0.block.simon
_level0.block.simple
```

Using the for...in loop in conjunction with movie clips allows the development of scripts that can address all of the child properties in a given MC with only the instance name of the target MC.

Other objects are equally open to use with the for...in statement. The following script iterates through an array object:

```
on (release) {
    ark = new Array("zebra","gorilla", "puppy dog");
    for (guest in ark) {
        trace(ark[guest]);
    }
}
```

The output will be in the order listed from right to left, appearing from top to bottom, as shown here:

Originated in: Flash 5

switch

switch: Action

As a well-ordered alternative to the else if statement, the switch statement contains an expression and a series of cases. If a case matches the expression, the statements associated with the case are executed. Also associated with case is the default statement. If none of the case statements meet the switch expression, the statement associated with the default statement executes. The conventional arrangement of a switch statement is the following:

```
switch (exp) {
case 'exp1' :
    statements;
    break;
case 'exp2' :
    statements;
    break;
default :
    statements;
}
```

As soon as a case name matches the switch expression, the statements in the case are launched. Generally, a break statement follows all statements associated with a given case so that it can exit the switch block as soon as a match is made and the statements launched. The following shows a simple example:

```
term = "second";
switch (term) {
case 'first' :
    trace("First one");
    break;
case 'second' :
    trace("Second one");
    break;
default :
    trace("None of the above");
}
```

The output will be "Second one." If no break statement was in the second case, after the first output, both "Second one" and "None of the above" would appear in the output. While it does not have to be in the position of the last case, the default statement typically is put in that position.

Originated in: Macromedia Flash MX

while

while: Action

The while loop has its test condition at the top of the script and loops until the condition is met. If the condition is met in the first iteration, unlike a do while loop, none of the expressions in the loop are launched. It has the following general format:

```
while (condition) {
statements;
} //End of loop block
```

Figure 4-1 shows a while loop set up to duplicate a movie clip.
The following script shows a while loop used to duplicate movie clips:

```
_root.boatButton.onPress = function() {
    delta = 10;
```

```
while (delta>0) {
    duplicateMovieClip(_root.ship, "ship"+delta, delta+1);
    _root["ship"+delta]._x = Math.random()*400;
    _root["ship"+delta]._y = Math.random()*300;
    delta--;
}
};
```

Using the while loop prevents statements from being executed if they do not meet the loop condition on the first iteration of the loop. Figure 4-2 shows the movie before the button is clicked and Figure 4-3 shows the movie after the while loop has generated duplicate copies.

Originated in: Flash 4

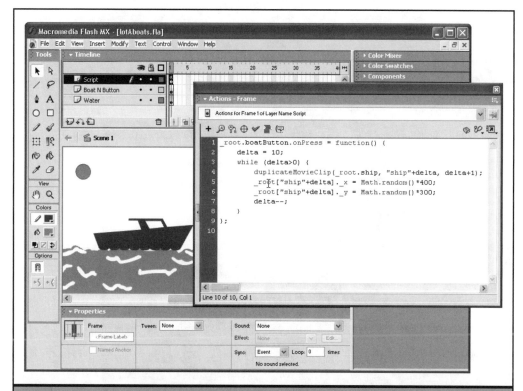

Figure 4-1.   *The while loop can be used in a number of repetitive actions, including duplicating instances of movie clips.*

Figure 4-2. *The button, which looks like a moon high over the horizon, fires the while loop.*

Figure 4-3. *The while loop generates multiple copies of the object, randomly dispersing them on the stage.*

Printing

Given the nature of Flash as a motion graphics tool, printing may not be the most practical application for it. However, under certain conditions, providing users with the ability to print out a portion of a movie (such as a coupon) can be a very useful application. This section examines what happens when a print action is executed and how to set the parameters to get what you want.

In the Normal Mode of editing in the Actions panel, you will see that the Actions toolbox displays only print in the Actions/Print folders. When editing in the ActionScript pane, you can select either Level or Target in the Location drop-down menu. If you select Level, it automatically changes the action to printNum() or printAsBitMapNum(), while if you select Target, it will change to either print() or printAsBitMap(). In the Print parameter in the Normal Mode, the drop-down menu provides a selection of either As Vectors or As Bitmap. The action will change to print() or printNum() if As Vectors is selected, and to printAsBitMap() or printAsBitMapNum() if As Bitmap is selected. In the Expert Mode, all four print functions are listed in the Actions toolbox.

print

print("target", "bounding box"): Action

The print() statement in Macromedia Flash MX has parameters for either a target or level and an optional bounding box. The target can be either a movie referenced by the timeline, such as "_root" or a movie clip referenced by its instance name.

Each frame in Flash is treated as a separate page, and when a print() statement is issued for a movie, each frame in the movie is printed as a separate page. If you want to print only a limited number of pages, label the keyframes you want printed using the #P designator. (Flash accepts #P as duplicate frame labels, but they can wreak havoc on your navigation to labeled frames.)

The bounding box argument has three different possibilities:

- **bmovie**   Specifies a frame to use as the cropping area. Place the label "#b" in the frame to be used as the bounding box (crop) area.

- **bmax**   Creates a bounding box to accommodate all print-designated frames using the frame's scale relative to other objects.

- **bframe**   Scales each frame to fit the printed page. Printed objects are not accurate relative to the movie, so if in the movie you have a tiny object in one frame and a large object in another, both will appear to be the same size on the printed page.

FUNDAMENTAL ACTIONSCRIPT

The format depends on whether you use a level or target name. In the Normal Mode in the Actions panel, if you select a level instead of a target name, print() automatically changes to printNum(), as shown below. To designate a level as a target, use "_levelN" where "N" is the level number, keeping the quotation marks. The following shows some different designations using print():

```
print("myMC","bmovie");
printNum(0,"bmax"); //Note printNum() is used
print("_level0", "bmax");//Same as previous example
print("myMC");
print("_root"); //Prints movie on current timeline
```

Originated in: Flash 4.2

printAsBitmap

printAsBitMap("target","bounding box"): Action

The printAsBitmap() function has the same parameters as print, but instead of printing vector graphics, it prints bitmapped graphics. Besides the more obvious reason for printing bitmapped graphics used in a Flash movie, it can be used to print transparency effects (alpha), gradient fills, and other effects that can be difficult to print using the print or printNum actions. Otherwise, all targeting and bounding box information is the same as print. Non-PostScript printers, which includes all inkjet printers, print output as bitmapped.

Originated in: Flash 4.2

printAsBitmapNum

printAsBitmapNum(level,"bounding box"): Action

This works the same as printAsBitmap() except that a level number instead of string is used to describe the print target.

Originated in: Flash 4.2

printNum

printNum(level,"bounding box"): Action

The printNum() function uses a level number instead of target string, but otherwise works the same as print().

Originated in: Flash 4.2

User-Defined Functions

The user-defined functions contain actions associated with functions that the user defines. In other words, these are functions other than the many built-in functions in Macromedia Flash MX. Of the three actions in this folder, one is formerly deprecated, and the other two are crucial.

call

call(): Action

This function is oddly listed in the Actions toolbox. Originating in Flash 4, it was deprecated in Flash 5, but it was not placed with the other deprecated terms in the Deprecated folder. It functions to execute the code associated with a frame using the syntax:

```
call(frameNumber/Name);
```

You can use either a frame label or number. For example, the following two examples show how to use it where the call is made to the same timeline:

```
call(44);
call("MaeWest");
```

To direct a call to a frame on another timeline, you need to invoke another deprecated term, tellTarget(). For example, the following script will fire the script in frame 7 of a movie clip with the instance name of moonRock:

```
tellTarget("moonRock") {
    call(7)
}
```

When you do use call(), the script is launched without the playhead moving to the frame associated with the script. After the script executes, no local variables will exist because the script is called and executed in the scope of the calling movie clip. Use function() as an alternative to call().

Originated in: Flash 4

FUNDAMENTAL ACTIONSCRIPT

function

function(arg): Action

A function bundles a set of statements that can be launched from different locations in the movie. Its parameters (arguments) are optional, and any legitimate statements can reside within a function's boundaries. It has the following format:

```
function functionName (arguments) {
statements;
}
```

The arguments or parameters in a function are used in the statements within the function. Values for the arguments are then provided when the function is placed in a script where it will be launched. For example, the following function provides arguments for horizontal and vertical movement of a movie clip:

```
function moveBoat(posX,posY) {
    _root.slowBoat._x=posX;
    _root.slowBoat._y=posY;
}
```

When launched, the script would need to include literal values or variables as illustrated in the following two examples:

```
//literal values in arguments
moveBoat(231,59);
```

```
//variables used in arguments
var goHoriz = 89;
var goVert = _root.slowBoat._y + 15;
moveBoat(goHoriz,goVert);
```

When creating a function where the argument is an MC, you need to put the argument into brackets. For example, the following function expects an embedded movie clip's instance name:

```
function spinner(mcPath) {
    _root.mcBlock[mcPath]._rotation = 40;
}
```

The path to the movie clip is partially laid out with _root.mcBlock (the name of the host MC) and then any MC within the host MC can be called and rotated.

Another use of function() that is particularly relevant to Macromedia Flash MX is the function used as a literal. For example, when creating scripts for buttons and button movie clips, you can save time by placing all of the scripts for a set of buttons or button MCs in a frame association using the following format:

```
instanceName.onEvent = function() {
      //actions;
}
```

For example, if you have a button with the instance name of launchCretins, you could put in the following script:

```
_root.launchCretins.onPress = function() {
      _root.Cretins.play();
}
```

Originated in: Flash 5

return

return: Action

Used with function, the return action provides a way to pass data generated in a function to a variable. The expression following the return statement effectively sends out the contents of the expression to a variable assigned the value of the function. For example, consider the following two scripts, one with and one without return.

Without return:

```
function findMcPos() {
     var alpha= _root.airplane._x;
}
var gamma=findMcPos();
trace(gamma);
```

Because nothing is returned in the function, the variable gamma is undefined, as seen in the following output.

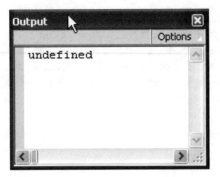

With return:

```
function findMcPos() {
    var alpha=_root.airplane._x;
    return alpha;
}
var gamma=findMcPos();
trace(gamma);
```

Once return has been added to the function, the variable gamma now has legitimate content that can be passed as the variable's value as shown in the following Output window:

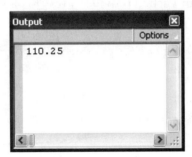

In the above examples, the first function places the horizontal position (x) of the MC named airplane into a local variable called alpha. However, while the local variable within the function contains the movie clip's position, it cannot be passed to gamma because the function returns nothing. However, by adding the return statement, any variable assigned the function findMcPos() will have the value. In fact, the step of placing the value of the MC's position into a variable was unnecessary in the second script because the return statement expects an expression and so it would have been correct to write it as:

```
function findMcPos() {
    return _root.airplane._x;
}
gamma =findMcPos();
trace(gammma);
```

As soon as a function's script encounters a return statement, it terminates parsing any other statements in the function. Therefore, only one return value is allowed per function, and unless it is the last statement in a function, those statements following it will not be executed.

Originated in: Flash 5

Miscellaneous Actions

This last set of actions makes up a residual category.

#endinitclip

#endinitclip: Action

The #endinitclip statement is used to terminate a block of component initialization actions. It is used with #initclip to form a container for component initialization. (See #initclip below.)

Originated in: Macromedia Flash MX

#include

#include: Action

This statement is used to pull in ActionScript from an external file. The general format is

```
#include "fileName.as"
```

The .as extension is the preferred convention for any file containing external ActionScript code. When using the #include action, no semi-colons are used in the line where you put the #include statement, but lines before or after the #include statement may have optional semi-colons. The following illustrates a script associated with a button using #include correctly:

```
on (release) {
    #include "test.as"
    _root.name.text="Samantha";
}
```

When the movie with the #include statement is first tested and/or published, the resulting SWF file contains the script from the script (.as) file. If you change the script file's contents, the changes will not be reflected in any new execution of the SWF file. In other words, once the #include statement has brought in the external file, that file stays that way until changes have been made in reconstituting the SWF file—usually by republishing the contents of the FLA file.

If you have event handlers in the #include file, be sure you do not duplicate them in the script using #include. For example, if you have the following script file, you would not put event handlers in the script associated with the button that fires the script:

```
//file saved as "showOff.as"
on(release) {
var alpha="From out of Flash..."
_root.dyna.text=alpha;
}
```

The script associated with the button would be as follows, using no event handlers or semi-colons:

```
#include "showoff.as"
```

Originated in: Flash 5

#initclip

#initclip: Action

The #initclip statement is used to initiate a block of component initialization actions. It is used with #endinitclip to form a container for component initialization. (See #endinitclip above.) The general container is made up of the beginning and ending container statement with the initialization statements in between as follows:

```
#initclip
     //UI Component initialization statements;
#endinitclip
```

The initialization statements used for components are actions, like class definition and registration. Where you see the prototype object of a component being assigned values represents a typical initialization process.

Originated in: Macromedia Flash MX

clearInterval

clearInterval(in): Function

The clearInterval() function only works in conjunction with setInterval() (see below in this section). It clears and effectively halts the interval that was set. The syntax is

```
clearInterval (intervalName)
```

In order to use the clearInterval() function, you need to provide an identifier for the setInterval() process. By assigning the setInterval() code to a variable name, this can be accomplished quite simply. For example, the following provides the setInterval() function with a variable name and shows how clearInterval() clears the interval setting:

```
on (release) {
    function announce() {
        trace("Follow this.");
    }
    var whozit = setInterval(announce, 250);
}
//
//
//elsewhere in the movie
clearInterval(whozit);
```

Originated in: Macromedia Flash MX

comment

comment: Delimiter

The comment delimiters in Macromedia Flash MX are two forward slashes (//). All comments, by default, are tinted a light gray in the Actions panel. The comment delimiters can be placed on separate lines from other code or on the same lines. The following examples show both:

```
_root.locomotive.gotoAndPlay(44); // Goes to the station;
//All other locations use frame labels.
```

The comment delimiters begin at the double slashes and end at the end-of-line. For longer comments, a second type of comment delimiter is /*. Comments can be multiple lines and are treated as comments until the */ symbol.

```
/* All code in this section needs to reference the script in Frame 343
It shows all of the variables associated with this next block of code */
```

Originated in: Flash 1 (///) and Flash 5 (/)*

setInterval

setInterval(function, interval [,arg1, arg2...,argN]): Action

The setInterval() function works like a timer using milliseconds to set the time of the intervals for firing scripts. With 1,000 milliseconds to a second, you can have very good precision for any timed behavior. The most basic format is as follows:

```
setInterval( function, interval in milliseconds, [arguments])
```

The arguments are optional, but can be used when needed. The following script shows an example of a script that rotates an MC every quarter second using a function literal:

```
on (release) {
    setInterval(function () {
        _root.mcBlock._rotation = _root.mcBlock._rotation + 3;
    }, 250);
}
```

By changing the interval value from 250 to greater (slows) or less (speeds), you can adjust the timing precisely. Showing the hands of an analog clock moving could be done using setInterval() to show the accurate time.

You can add arguments as you normally would to a function. The data for the arguments is then placed in the arguments section of the setInterval() function, right after the interval. In this next example, a dynamic text field is made into a flashing sign. The first function uses no arguments and the second uses two.

```
on (release) {
    function setTxBg() {
        _root.dyna.backgroundColor = 0x00ff00;
    }
    function setTxMsg(ohsay,hue) {
        _root.dyna.textColor = hue;
        _root.dyna.text = ohsay;
        _root.dyna.backgroundColor = 0xff0000;
    }
    setInterval(setTxBg, 500);
    setInterval(setTxMsg, 333, "Look here", 0xffff00);
}
```

Using different intervals (500 and 333) generates a disjointed flashing effect—the uncertain flicker-flash of a neon sign with a short. Note in the second use of setInterval() the function arguments were a string literal ("Look here") and a hexadecimal value for the color of the text (0xffff00). The following illustration shows what appears on the screen after the interval:

FUNDAMENTAL
ACTIONSCRIPT

A final way that setInterval() can be used in ActionScript is with an object's method. The method is executed at the specified interval using the syntax:

```
setInterval(object, method, interval)
```

The following shows a simple implementation:

```
on (release) {
    getThis = new Array("Alpha", "Beta", "Gamma", "Delta");
    getThis.popIt = function() {
        _root.dyna.text = getThis.pop();
    };
    setInterval(getThis, "popIt", 1000);
}
```

Originated in: Macromedia Flash MX

trace

trace(exp): Action

The trace() function displays expressions in the Output window. Used as a key debugging device, it allows developers to see what their code is doing. It has the following format:

```
trace (expression)
```

For example, the following script placed into a frame in a looping timeline will continuously update the x position of the mouse:

```
var mousey = _xmouse;
trace(mousey);
```

Throughout this book, you will see numerous examples of the trace() function, and it is a key debugging statement in Flash.

Originated in: Flash 4

Conclusion

This chapter wraps up the actions (or statements) available in Macromedia Flash MX. For the most part, the structural makeup is almost identical to JavaScript, and certainly much more so than previous versions of Flash ActionScript. For those familiar with programming in general and JavaScript in particular, there should be very few surprises in this second group of actions. However, like all ActionScript, it does exist in (and is intended for use with) Macromedia Flash MX. As a result, you need to keep in mind that Flash has different timelines as well as frame and scene references. Likewise, actions can be associated with different objects in ways unique to Flash.

The
Complete
Reference

ActionScript

Chapter 5

Operators

Operators are the connecting links in scripts. They assign values, compute arithmetic calculations, compare values, and generally tie together the different components that make up a script. In the Macromedia Flash MX environment, the scripts associated with movie clips, frames, buttons, and other objects use operators in exactly the same way. This chapter looks at the different ways in which operators are used in Macromedia Flash MX ActionScript. In previous chapters, operators have been used extensively, and so much of this chapter will cover materials introduced earlier. However, that only goes to show the ubiquitous nature of operators.

Operator Categories

Macromedia Flash MX has divided operators into six folders, leaving two operators in the General operator folder with no category assignment. (I've assigned these three "orphan" operators to a General category.) The following operator categories are used in Macromedia Flash MX and in this book:

- General
- Arithmetic
- Assignment
- Bitwise
- Comparison
- Logical
- Miscellaneous

The Arithmetic operators are those used in mathematical computations. Assignment operators are used in assigning values to variables, objects, and properties, and include both standard and bitwise assignments. The Bitwise operators are actually a subset of all of the Bitwise operators minus the bitwise Assignment operators. Comparison operators are those used extensively in branching and loop statements where one or more values are compared. The Logical operators include AND, OR, and NOT which are used in both multiple comparisons and strictly logical operations. The Miscellaneous operator category is well named because it is made up of several operators that fit into none of the other categories.

The organizational component of the operators that may be confusing is the inclusion of bitwise Assignment operators in the Assignment category. Most programmers do not use bitwise operations in higher level languages, and some included in the Assignment folder may lead to accidentally choosing the wrong operator. Finally, a set of string operators, along with other deprecated terms, have been placed in a Deprecated folder outside of the Operators main folder. The string operators were last required for Flash 4 for string comparisons, and so they have been listed in Appendix A along with the other deprecated terms where they are available but out of the way. String operators such as "eq" (equate) have been replaced by the General comparison operators, such as "==" and have reduced confusion because the Macromedia Flash MX variables are weakly typed and change with context.

Precedence

Precedence refers to the order in which operations are executed in a script and the direction of the operation (left to right or right to left). For example, all multiplication operations are executed before all addition operations, and so the line:

```
10 + 5 * 2 //Result=20
```

would result in 20 instead of 30 (2 times 5 equals 10 plus 10 equals 20). Using parentheses, the order of precedence can be changed, because all operations in parentheses are executed before multiplication. Hence the line:

```
(10 + 5) * 2 //Result=30
```

would result in 30 (10 plus 5 equals 15 times 2 equals 30). So while a standard precedence is in place, changing precedence to meet requirements is not difficult.

Table 5-1 shows the different operators in their order of precedence. Those higher on the list have precedence over those operators lower on the list. The Associativity column refers to the precedence order on a line, beginning on the right and moving left (RL) or beginning on the left and moving right (LR). Bitwise operators are not included on this list to reduce the number of entries and because they are not often needed in higher level operation. However, their precedence is discussed in the section "Bitwise Operators."

Operator	Description	Associativity
+	Positive number	RL
-	Negative number	RL
!	Logical NOT	RL

Table 5-1. *Operators, Use, and Associativity*

Operator	Description	Associativity
++	Post-increment	LR
--	Post-decrement	LR
( )	Function argument/grouping to change precedence	LR
[ ]	Array access	LR
.	Structure member	LR
++	Pre-increment	RL
--	Pre-decrement	RL
New	Allocate object	RL
Delete	Deallocate object	RL
instanceof	Object belongs to specific class	RL
typeof	Type of object	RL
void	Notice of undefined value	RL
*	Multiply	LR
/	Divide	LR
%	Modulus	LR
+	Add	LR
-	Subtract	LR
<	Less than	LR
<=	Less than or equal	LR
>	Greater than	LR
>=	Greater than or equal	LR
==	Equal	LR
===	Strict equality	LR

Table 5-1. *Operators, Use, and Associativity* (continued)

Operator	Description	Associativity
!=	Not equal	LR
!==	Strict inequality	LR
&&	Logical AND	LR
||	Logical OR	LR
?:	Ternary	RL
=	Assignment	RL
All compound assignments[1] (%=, &=, |=, *=, -=, +=, /=, <<=, >>=, >>>=, ^=)	Assignment	RL
,	Multiple evaluation	LR

[1] Includes both standard and bitwise compound assignments.

Table 5-1. *Operators, Use, and Associativity* (continued)

Operators

Most of the operators are consistent with and derived from both scientific and commonsense reasoning. As a result, they tend to be relatively easy to grasp, and with a few exceptions, examples will use the trace() statement to illustrate their use. Some operators are demonstrated in a bit more detail so that their use can be understood in the context of a Flash movie.

General

The General operators in Flash are the double/single set of quote marks, parentheses, and curly braces, shown in Table 5-2.

Quotation Marks

The sets of double quotes and single quotes are used interchangeably. Both are used to assign string variables, demarcating the beginning and end of the string. If single

Operator	Description
"" [' ']	String demarcation
()	Grouping arguments, statements, parameters
{}	Grouping statements

Table 5-2.   *General Operators*

quotes are within a set of double quotes, they will be shown as single quotes. For example, the following script:

```
trace("This looks 'funny' on me.")
```

would show

```
This looks 'funny' on me.
```

By the same token, the script:

```
trace('This looks "funny" on me.')
```

would show

```
This looks "funny" on me.
```

Parentheses

Parentheses are employed for grouping operations of different types ranging from mathematical operations to parameters in functions. They may be nested, with one set of parentheses inside another. For example, the following script uses three sets of parentheses:

```
trace((54 + 10) * (20-11));
```

When using nested parentheses, each parenthesis mark must be linked with an opposite facing one, and one set cannot close outside of one it began in. For example, if the second parenthesis in trace() was closed after the multiplication operator (*), the script would fail, as illustrated in the following:

```
trace((54 + 10) * ) (20-11);
```

In the debugging process, always look for misplaced parentheses.

Curly Braces

The curly braces are used with event handlers, as object initializers, in function groupings and other groupings where multiple statements are issued such as loops and conditional statements. They are not included in the Operators folder in the Actions toolbox, but are automatically included at the beginning of a script when a button or movie clip is selected and the Normal Mode of editing is being used. The following are some examples.

With event handlers:

```
onClipEvent(enterFrame) {
statements;
}
```

With functions:

```
function doSomething() {
statements;
}
```

With function literals:

```
var jumpUp = function() {

    statements;

};
```

Note *When using function literals, a semi-colon follows the second curly brace by convention. It also helps identify where function literals are used in the script.*

With object initializer:

```
myObject = {};
```

This is the same as:

```
myObject = new Object();
```

You can add as many elements as needed using a set of curly braces as an object initializer. For example, the following object generates four properties for the object along with values:

```
doggy = { breed: "Greater Swiss Mountain Dog",
 gender: "Male",
 age: "10 months",
 event: "Obedience" };
```

The equivalent object could also be written as:

```
doggy= new Object();
doggy.breed="Greater Swiss Mountain Dog";
doggy.gender="male";
doggy.age="10 months";
doggy.event="Obedience";
```

To some extent you can save time using curly braces over conventional object definitions. In some ways, the conventional object definitions are a bit clearer because the foundation Object object is invoked.

Arithmetic Operators

Five operators make up the Arithmetic folder, as shown in Table 5-3.

Of all the operators, these are the most familiar, with the possible exception of modulo (%). Also, the plus (+) operator serves a dual role.

Operator	Description
%	Modulo
*	Multiply
+	Add/concatenate/positive value
-	Subtract/negative value
/	Divide

Table 5-3. *Arithmetic Operators*

Modulo

The modulo (%) operator returns the remainder in a division. Hence, the following returns 3:

```
trace(7 % 4)
```

(7 divided by 4 is 1 with a remainder of 3.) The modulo can be useful in rounding off numbers. For example, the following script truncates any added fractions in working with dollars and cents:

```
total = 55.0856; //Use any number with fractions beyond 2 places.
dollars = Math.floor(total);
cents = Math.round(total*100)%100;
if (cents<10) {
    cents = "0" + cents;
}
trace("$"+dollars+"." + cents);
```

Other uses include keeping track of units that are not parts of wholes. For example, an inventory program might want to keep track of partially filled bins based on the whole number of units in each bin (each bin holds 35 bolts, and you have 80 bolts in three bins).

Add and Concatenate

The plus (+) operator works to add values and to concatenate strings. If used with a number and a string, the operator returns a string. To work as a math addition operator, both operands must be numbers or Boolean literals. (Boolean literals are valued as 0 and 1 for false and true, respectively.) The following show different results:

```
//Two numbers
trace (6 + 29); //returns 35

//Number and Boolean
var zooWise = "zebras" > "apes";
trace(zooWise + 33); //returns 34

//Two strings
trace("Happy" + " Go Lucky"); // returns Happy Go Lucky

//Number and string
trace( 55 + "88"); // returns 5588;
```

Remember that the plus (+) operator is context sensitive and all numbers concatenated with strings, become strings. The same plus (+) symbol is used with positive numbers as well.

Multiplication, Division, and Subtraction

The multiply (*), divide (/), and subtract (-) operators are consistently used to do arithmetic. The minus symbol (-) is also used to assign negative values to numbers. The following examples illustrate different uses. Remember to pay strict attention to precedence.

```
var gamma = 8 * -5 +20 //Multiply negative number
trace(gamma); //  Outcome = -20 (8 times -5=-40) + 20 = -20
var delta = -7 + -14 - (-22) //Subtract a negative number
trace(delta); // Outcome =1 When subtracting a negative
//number, the negative number must be in parentheses.
var zeta = 2/ -345 // Divide by negative number
trace(zeta); // Outcome =-.005797101449
```

Assignment

Assignment operators really have three groupings. The single equal (=) sign assigns values to variables, objects, and their properties. The compound operators perform a mathematical operation and assign a value. Finally, the Bitwise operators generate various register shifts. Table 5-4 shows the different Macromedia Flash MX Assignment operators.

Simple Assignment

The Assignment operator equates one expression with another. The expression on the left is given the value of the expression on the right. Any identifier, variable, property, or object can be assigned some kind of value with the Assignment operator. The following are some examples:

```
var beta = "Greek letter";
var delta = 565;
_root.myHotRod._x = 233;
_parent.curtain._alpha = 35;
var boo_lee_ann = true;
```

A variable can be defined initially as a string, number, or Boolean and later changed to a different type of variable. Thus, a variable can initially be assigned a numeric value, then a string value, and later on another numeric value.

Operator	Description
%=	Compound assign modulo
&=	Compound bitwise assign AND
|=	Compound bitwise assign OR
*=	Compound assign multiply
-=	Compound assign subtract
+=	Compound assign add
/=	Compound assign divide
<<=	Compound bitwise assign signed shift left
>>=	Compound bitwise assign signed shift right
>>>=	Compound bitwise assign unsigned shift right
^=	Compound bitwise assign XOR
=	Assign value

Table 5-4.   *Assignment Operators*

Compound Assignments

Compound assignment essentially uses one expression's initial value to change the same expression's value. The expression on the left must be a variable of some kind. For example, the following expression:

```
beta += 5;
```

is the same as:

```
beta = beta + 5;
```

The other compound expressions work the same way. The following expression pairs show the compound expressions with their simple assignment equivalents:

```
beta *= 5;
beta = beta * 5;
```

```
beta /= 5;
beta = beta / 5;

beta -= 5;
beta = beta - 5;

beta %= 5;
beta = beta % 5;
```

The main purpose of compound assignments is to save some time and space.

Bitwise Compound Assignments

To understand Bitwise operators, brush up on your binary math. Like non-bitwise compound assignments, bitwise compound assignments perform the operation using the expression on the left with itself and the value on the right. For example, the following script uses the compound bitwise assignment AND:

```
//Returns 1
alpha = 5;
trace(alpha &= 3);
```

To see how the bitwise compound assignment works, look at a standard assignment configuration:

```
alpha = alpha & 3
```

This gives you 5 logical AND 3. To see how it works, break each number into a binary value:

```
0011 =3
0101 =5
```

The bitwise logical AND is true only if both integers in the same column are set. In looking at the binary equivalent of 3 and 5, you can see that the bits are set only in the far right column:

```
0011
0101
0001    Logical AND
```

By setting the bit in the far right column, you arrive at 0001 or decimal 1. Hence, the logical AND between 5 and 3 is 1. If the operator is changed to the compound assignment of |= (logical OR), the result is 7. That's because if at least one bit is set in either of the two expressions, the bit in the result is set. Thus, logical OR would result in the following between 5 and 3:

```
0011
0101
0111    Logical OR
```

In column 1 (far right) the bit is set in both operands. In column 2, the expression in one number is set, so that results in setting another bit in the result, and the same is true in column 3, resulting in 0111 or the decimal value 7. The final logical bitwise compound assignment is ^= (XOR). If one operand has a bit set and the other does not, the result is set. Looking at 5 and 3 again, the XOR compound assignment would result in the following:

```
0011
0101
0110    Logical XOR
```

The resulting value is 0110 or decimal 6.

Macromedia Flash MX also has three compound operators for shifting registers. The shifts in binary numbers can result in significant differences. When a shift occurs, the binary values shift to the left or right and a 0 is placed in the column shifted away from, as the following examples illustrate:

```
alpha =5
alpha >>= 2; //Shift two to the right
00101    binary 5
00001    binary 1

alpha = 5
alpha <<=2 ; //Shift two to the left
00101    binary 5
10100    binary 20
```

In the first example, the first set bit is shifted to the first column and the second is shifted off the register, leaving a single set bit in the first column for a decimal value of 1. In the second case, the numbers are shifted to the left two columns. The column on the far right is changed to 0, the set bit in the first column is moved to the third column, and the set bit in the third column is shifted to the right two places to the fifth column. The result is 10100 or decimal 20.

 A shift by 1 to the right will have a decimal value rounding down to the nearest whole, and a shift by 1 to the left will double it. Thus, if beta=17, beta <<= 1 will result in decimal 34.

The final shift is an unsigned right shift. Because it is unsigned, it can move between negative and positive values. However, because negative values are one bit beyond positive numbers, a very low negative number shifted once becomes a very high positive number. For example, the following compound bitwise assignment results in a value over 2 billion with a single unsigned shift! (2,147,483,647, to be exact.)

```
alpha = -2
trace( alpha >>>= 1)
```

So unless you're used to counting in 32-bit binary numbers, take care when using the unsigned shift and negative values. The unsigned right shift works the same as the signed right shift when using positive values.

Bitwise Operators

Macromedia Flash MX has seven operators in the Bitwise folder, as shown in Table 5-5.

All of these operators were discussed in detail in the previous section on compound bitwise operators with the exception of logical NOT (~). The logical NOT changes the sign on a number and subtracts 1. Thus ~8 becomes -9. The process involves turning the value into a 32-bit integer and reversing the bit settings. For example, the NOT 8

Operator	Description
&	Logical AND
~	Logical NOT
|	Logical OR
<<	Signed left shift
>>	Signed right shift
>>>	Unsigned right shift
^	Logical XOR

Table 5-5. *Bitwise Operators*

begins with 8 (1000), changes it to a 32-bit integer and reverses the bits (0111). However, all of the other bits in the 32-bit integer are reversed as well. Thus, the process looks like the following:

```
00000000000000000000000000001000    +8
11111111111111111111111111110111    -9 // Result of ~8
```

Again, it is important to emphasize that most programmers go through life happily not having to use bitwise operators. However, should you have occasion to use them, you now know something about them.

Comparison Operators

Operators used to compare expressions generate Boolean results. Typically, their use is found in conditional statements (see Chapter 3) and other statements waiting for a condition to be true or false, such as while loops. The eight operators found in the Comparison Operators folder in the Actions toolbox are shown in Table 5-6.

Equality and Inequality Tests

Of the four operators used to test for equality and inequality, two are new to Macromedia Flash MX. The standard equality (==) and inequality (!=) operators only look to see if the values are equal. Thus, the following statement returns a value of true:

```
alpha=8, beta="8";
trace(alpha==beta);
```

Operator	Description
!=	Not equal
!==	Strict inequality
<	Less than
<=	Less than or equal to
==	Equal to
===	Strict equality
>	Greater than
>=	Greater than or equal to

Table 5-6.   *Comparison Operators*

Standard tests for equality do not differentiate between the types of variables (numeric, string, Boolean), and so if a number and string happen to be the same, Boolean true returns. Because Boolean values return both true/false and 1/0, a numeric variable can be found to equal a Boolean 1, as the following shows using the inequality operator:

```
alpha=new Boolean(true);
beta=1;
gamma=5 != 4;
trace(alpha!=beta); //False -- they are equal
trace(alpha!=gamma); //False -- they are equal
```

In conditional statements, the operators generate a Boolean outcome as well. For example, consider the following statement:

```
alpha=15, beta =20
if (alpha == beta) {
  gotoAndPlay("depot");
}
```

Because the values of alpha and beta are different, the statement generates a Boolean false, and the statement inside the conditional statement does not launch. However, by changing the operator, as in the following, the Boolean generates a true because the values are unequal:

```
alpha=15, beta =20
if (alpha != beta) {
  gotoAndPlay("depot");
}
```

In Flash 4, the Assignment operator and numeric equality test were both the single equal sign (=). Strings were evaluated using the eq operator, now deprecated. However, with Flash 5 and continuing with Macromedia Flash MX, the equality operator is now == for all variable types.

Strict Equality and Inequality

New to Macromedia Flash MX is the strict equality === and inequality !== operators. They differ from the standard equality and inequality operators in that they do compare the type of data. A test for strict equality === will be false if two different data types are used, such as strings and numbers. For instance, consider the following slight revision of the script used above:

```
alpha=8, beta="8";
trace(alpha===beta);
```

Because the alpha variable is a number and the beta variable is a string, the two variables are found to be unequal using the strict equality operator. Otherwise, the strict equality operators act like the standard Comparison operators.

Greater and Lesser Comparisons

To compare elements of unequal value, Macromedia Flash MX provides four operators. The greater than (>) and greater than or equal to (>=) operators generate true if the left operand is greater than (or equal to using the latter operator) the right operand. Thus, the following statement would generate a Boolean true:

```
alpha=55, beta=24;
trace(alpha > beta);
```

The operators also compare strings. Letters higher in the alphabet (assuming a=1, z=26) are considered as greater than letters lower in the alphabet. Thus, the following would generate a Boolean true:

```
alpha = "Joy", beta = "Avarice";
trace(alpha >= beta);
```

However, the string comparisons are case sensitive, and uppercase letters are lower in a comparative statement. For instance, changing the case of "Avarice" to "avarice" generates a Boolean false:

```
alpha = "Joy", beta = "avarice";
trace(alpha >= beta);
```

When the equal sign (=) is added to either the greater than (>) or less than (<) operators, the combined operator checks for both unequal and equal values.

Logical Operators

Flash has three standard (non-bitwise) Logical operators, shown in Table 5-7.

Operator	Description
!	Logical NOT
&&	Logical AND
||	Logical OR

Table 5-7.   *Logical Operators*

Used in conditional statements, you can add multiple conditions or look for the negative case to generate a Boolean true.

Logical NOT

The logical NOT (!) reverses a conditional test. You can test for the presence of a variable having been declared in a movie by using the logical NOT in a conditional statement, as shown in the following:

```
if (!beta) {
    trace("No beta:");
}
```

You can also test for expressions not matching one another, but usually it makes more sense to use a NOT comparison such as !=.

Logical AND

For the logical AND (&&) to be true, all of the expressions must be true. The logical AND is used extensively where more than one condition must be checked and found to be true. For example, the following uses several logical AND operators:

```
if (gamma <= delta && ship1._x < ship2._x && score >= 5000) {
    trace("You won!)
}
```

Using logical AND, if any of the conditions are false, the entire grouping is false and generates a Boolean false.

Logical OR

The logical OR (| |) is employed when more than a single condition can generate a Boolean true. As long as a single expression in a grouping is true, the grouping is true. For example, the following generates a Boolean true:

```
alpha = 5;
beta = 6;
delta = 57;
if (alpha<beta || beta>delta || delta>alpha) {
    trace("This alone is true.");
}
```

With two false statements and only one true statement, the result is true and so the conditional statement is launched.

Miscellaneous Operators

The Miscellaneous operators are well named because they seem to defy classification. However, they include some widely used and important operators. Table 5-8 shows the "orphans" of the operators.

For purposes of explanation, this set of operators has been grouped into increment and decrement, instanceof and typeof, with ternary and void operators treated separately.

Increment and Decrement

The increment (++) and decrement (--) operators are usually associated with loop statements where the index variable is incremented or decremented. The operators either add or subtract 1 from the related variable. For example, the following loop typifies the use of these operators:

```
for (var x = 0; x<20; x++) {
    trace(x);
}
```

Each time through the loop, the variable x is incremented by 1 as long as the termination condition is not met.

These operators are also used in the course of a program outside of a loop, and they certainly could be used in scripts associated with frames where multiple passes are made. Both have a pre- and post-increment format. The alpha variable uses the post-decrement format so that it will not decrement until the next pass, while the

Operator	Description
++	Increment
--	Decrement
?:	Ternary
instanceof	Test for class
typeof	Test for data type
void	Discard expression value

Table 5-8. *Miscellaneous Operators*

FUNDAMENTAL ACTIONSCRIPT

gamma variable uses the pre-decrement format, and so its value is decremented immediately, resulting in a lower value for delta than beta.

```
alpha = 5;
gamma = 5;
beta = alpha--; //Post-increment
delta = --gamma; //Pre-increment
trace("beta =" + beta + newline + "delta=" + delta);
```

In some respects, the increment and decrement operators work like compound assignment variables in that a variable's value is changed based on its current value plus or minus 1.

instanceof and typeof

Each of these operators can be used to find the category an expression belongs to. The typeof operator determines the data type of an expression. It has the following results:

- string
- movieclip
- object (button, text field, or object)
- number
- boolean
- function

For example, the following script would result in movieclip where tclip is the instance name of a movie clip:

```
trace(typeof(tclip));
```

The typeof operator is useful in debugging scripts.

New to Macromedia Flash MX, the instanceof operator returns a Boolean true if an object is an instance of class; otherwise it returns false. In this context, a class refers to a constructor object. For example, the following returns a Boolean true:

```
alpha = new String("a classy expression") instanceof String;
trace(alpha);
```

With more complex classes, the instanceof operator can help determine which objects belong to classes.

The Ternary Operator (Conditional)

The ternary operator (?:) is actually a shorthand version of an if/else statement. It has the format:

```
(test condition) ? true statement : else statement;
```

For example:

```
alpha = ("bears">"tigers") ? trace("Big Bears") : trace("Tough
Tigers");
```

is the same as writing this:

```
if ("bears">"tigers") {
    trace("Big Bears");
} else {
    trace("Tough Tigers");
}
```

The key advantage to the ternary operator is that it is far more concise than a standard if/else statement.

The void Operator

To get rid of a variable's value and essentially create an undefined variable, use the void operator. It also can be used in conditional statements to test for undefined variables. For example the following would return "undefined":

```
alpha="This is defined";
beta=void(alpha);
trace(beta);
```

This operator currently has few uses in ActionScript.

Conclusion

Using operators is so essential for creating good ActionScript that it's one of the few areas that should be reviewed on a regular basis. By understanding fully what operators can do in a script, you are in a position to create better scripts. Most operators are fairly simple, but programmers can get in the habit of using the same script segments again and again. They may forget (or never learn of) new operators that can do the same job with less code and just as efficiently, if not more so. This is especially true with compound operators or little-used ones like modulo. Be on the lookout for other creative uses of coding with different operators, and return to this chapter on a regular basis to see if you can find a better way to solve a scripting problem using operators in creative ways.

ActionScript

Chapter 6

Functions

The general functions built into Flash MX have two general categories. First, you will find conversion functions. These functions are used to convert data into a certain data type, such as Array, Boolean, and Number data. The second type of function returns information about some aspect of the data in the script, such as getTimer() thats get the number of milliseconds since the SWF file began playing.

Besides looking at built-in functions, this chapter also examines user functions. These are the functions the developer creates to "package" a number of statements to be executed when the function is called. Both the built-in and user functions can use arguments or parameters. The parameters can represent different types of data that must be entered when the function is employed in a script.

Built-in Functions in Macromedia Flash

Macromedia Flash MX has fewer general functions than previous versions of Macromedia Flash. Most of the built-in functions have been transferred to methods associated with different objects. However, several types of general functions are still extant. Table 6-1 summarizes different general functions in Macromedia Flash MX ActionScript organized as you will find them in the Actions panel.

Function	Use
Array	Defines array object.
Boolean	Converts arguments to Boolean string or primitive value type.
Number	Converts arguments to numeric value or primitive value type.
Object	Converts arguments to an Object object.
String	Converts arguments to Boolean string or primitive value type.
escape()	Converts string to URL encoded format.
eval()	Evaluates an expression and returns the calculated results.
getProperty(target, property)	Generates the immediate state of a movie clip's property.

Table 6-1.   *Built-in Functions*

Function	Use
getTimer()	Milliseconds since SWF (Shockwave Flash) file began playing.
getVersion()	Returns the version of the Macromedia Flash player that is playing the movie.
Mathematical Functions	
isFinite()	Boolean value for finite (true) or non-finite (false) number.
isNaN()	Evaluates argument to be a number (false) or not (true).
parseFloat(string)	Takes string argument and converts it into floating point number.
parseInt(string)	Converts expression into integer.
targetPath()	Converts the target path to a string that can be used with the dot operator to issue commands.
unescape()	Decodes string from URL format. Reverses escape function.

Table 6-1.   *Built-in Functions* (continued)

Conversion Functions

Working with the built-in functions depends on the nature of the function. Many of the conversion functions have been replaced by the object constructors and methods associated with different objects. As a result, the conversion functions are somewhat redundant. However, others will come in handy.

The general format of the conversion functions is

```
newVariable=functionName(variable);
```

Basically, the variable is converted into the new variable. The conversion is a type conversion. In looking at the different types, you can clearly see how they operate to convert variables into objects they were not.

Array

Array(): Function

The Array function converts variables into array objects. Generally, you would begin by creating an array object and then assign the object different properties and methods. However, some ActionScript may begin life as a variable and then be converted so that the same name can be used for a set of values. For example, the following script begins with one variable assigned a string literal (cat), and then it is converted to an array element. The first element of an array is 0, so after the conversion, pets[0] has the same value as the variable that was converted to an array. The output is shown in the following illustration.

```
var pet = "cat";
var pets = Array(pet);
pets[1] = "doggy";
trace(pets[0]+newline+pets[1]);
```

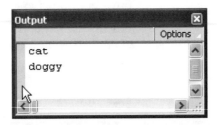

For more information about arrays, see the Chapter 8 discussion of array objects.

Originated in: Flash 5

Boolean

Boolean(): Function

A Boolean conversion function changes a value into a true or false value. All positive or negative numbers other than 0 are parsed as true. Both -0 and +0 return false. All strings return false. The following example shows how a variable assigned an expression (4-3) and then turned into a Boolean value can be used to test a conditional expression. Because the expression results in a positive value (1), the Boolean function turns it into a true value. When tested in the conditional statement, the results return true and so the first condition is displayed. Create a movie with a dynamic text field with the instance name tester. Place the following script in the first frame of a movie and execute it:

```
var simSub = 4-3;
var nuBoo = Boolean(simSub);
```

```
if (nuBoo) {
    _root.tester.text = "hooray!";
} else {
    _root.tester.text = "rats!";
}
```

Try the above script using different values in the variable simSub. Depending on the results you can quickly tell whether the assigned value or expression is a Boolean true or false. For more information about Booleans, see the Chapter 8 discussion of Boolean objects.

Originated in: Flash 5

Number

Number(): Function

The Number function converts a string with a numeric value into a real number. The function does not round the value up or down. The following example shows how the string "55.2" is converted into a real number resulting in the sum of 110.

```
var myString = "55.2";
var nowNum = Number(myString);
trace(nowNum+54.8);
```

Try different values or expressions in myString to see what happens. For more information about numbers, see the Chapter 9 discussion of Number objects.

Originated in: Flash 4

Object

Object(): Function

The Object function converts a literal or variable into an object. Because objects can have both properties and methods, you can test an object by seeing if it can have properties with assigned values. The following shows how a variable is converted into an object, with the output shown in the following illustration:

```
var someVar = "I'm a variable";
var nowObj = Object(someVar);
nowObj.someProp = "A property.";
trace(nowObj.someProp);
```

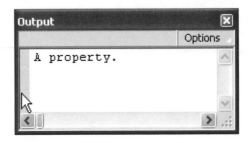

For more information about the Object function, see the Chapter 9 discussion of Object objects.

Originated in: Flash 5

String

String(): Function

Converting numbers to strings can be accomplished using the String() function. Far more can be accomplished using the String object and its many properties and methods. However, for a simple conversion from a non-string to a string variable, use the String() function. The following example shows how to accomplish this conversion and illustrates the different outcomes when using strings and numbers in addition and concatenation:

```
var alpha=44.5;
var beta=33.2;
var sum=alpha+beta;
var sum2=String(alpha);
var sum3=String(beta);
var sum4=sum2+sum3
trace(sum4+newline+sum);
```

Strings and using strings are essential for formatting output, searches, and other string-related activities in Macromedia Flash MX. For more information about using strings, see the Chapter 9 discussion of String objects, their properties, and methods.

Originated in: Flash 4

Math Functions

The math functions, in some respects, are a residue of older versions of Macromedia Flash. Several former math functions have become part of the Math object, such as the random() function which is now deprecated. However, two of the handiest functions are those that convert text (strings) into floating point and integer numbers. This set of functions can be very useful for converting numbers (e.g., 8, 23) from text to floating point or integer numbers (all values stored in dynamic text fields are treated as text). However, even if a number is stored in a text field, some of the functions can tell whether they are numbers or not. Also, you will find these math functions invaluable for testing values to find whether they are text or numbers.

isFinite

isFinite(val): Function

The isFinite() function determines whether a value is a finite number, and returns a Boolean true if it is. Otherwise, it returns a Boolean false. The function is the logical opposite of isNaN() in that isFinite() returns a Boolean true for numbers and a Boolean false for non-numbers. For example, the following script might be found in a form-entry checker:

```
alpha = "Total bill";
if (isFinite(alpha)) {
    trace("Thank you");
} else {
    trace("Please enter numbers only");
}
```

One of the main benefits of the isFinite() function is that even when a value is in a text field, it can determine whether it is a number or not. For example, the following script requires a button with the instance name of tester, an input text field with an instance name of inHere, and a dynamic text field with the instance name out. (The script should be placed in association with the first frame.)

```
tester.onPress = function() {
    alpha = _level0.inHere.text;
    if (isFinite(alpha)) {
        _level0.out.text = "Yes, it's a number.";
    } else {
        _level0.out.text = "Nope, not a number.";
    }
};
```

When the script is tested, you can see that placing numbers, including scientific notations, in the input field returns a true Boolean showing as "Yes, it's a number." However, any string that is made up of something other than numbers, or numbers with the letter "e" (scientific notation), generates a Boolean false.

Originated in: Flash 5

isNaN

isNaN(): Function

This function tests to determine whether a value is a number or not. It returns a Boolean true for anything other than a number and false for a number. It represents the Boolean opposite of the isFinite() function. Even if the number is zero (0), this function recognizes it as a number. For example, the following returns a false—a value is tested to be not a number and found to be a number. A double negative can be found in this logic, and this example:

```
alpha = 0;
if (isNaN(alpha)) {
    trace("Nope");
} else {
    trace("Yes, it's a number");
}
```

This kind of function can be extremely helpful in setting up a form to make sure that the user enters a number instead of a string. For example, most credit card numbers are made up of number-only series. By including the isNaN() function, you can check for characters other than numbers.

Originated in: Flash 5

parseFloat

parseFloat(): Function

The parseFloat() function transforms text or strings into floating point numbers. The most important implementation of this function is where you need to have real (floating point) numbers in text fields. You can divide, multiply, and subtract numbers in text fields without a problem. However, when you attempt to add numbers in text fields, Macromedia Flash MX concatenates the values instead. For example, try the following script where tester is the instance name of a button, inHere and inHere2 are two instance names for input text fields, and out is the dynamic text field used for output:

```
tester.onPress = function() {
    alpha = _root.inHere.text;
    delta = _root.inHere2.text;
    beta = alpha+delta;
    _root.out.text = beta;
};
```

When you run the script, all numbers are concatenated. So 23 plus 32 results in 2332. Now change it to:

```
tester.onPress = function() {
    alpha = _root.inHere.text;
    delta = _root.inHere2.text;
    beta = alpha-delta; // Change to a minus (-) sign.
    _root.out.text = beta;
};
```

On this second try, you will find that the values in the text fields handle mathematical subtraction. To fix the script so that it will handle addition, use the parseFloat() function. The following script shows the conversion:

```
tester.onPress = function() {
    alpha = parseFloat(_root.inHere.text);
    delta = parseFloat(_root.inHere2.text);
    beta = alpha+delta;
    _root.out.text = beta;
};
```

Keep in mind that while the isFinite() and isNaN() functions can determine whether a value in a text field is a number or not, you need to convert numbers in text fields for addition. Otherwise, attempts at adding numbers result in concatenation.

Originated in: Flash 5

parseInt

parseInt(val): Function

The parseInt() function converts string numbers into integers and real numbers into numbers with no decimal points. If a number has any decimal points, even .999, the decimal is dropped, leaving the integer. For instance, the following script drops the decimal and returns a value of 22:

```
real = 22.999;
integer = parseInt(real);
trace(integer);
```

You can use the parseInt() and parseFloat() functions together if you need an integer and real number in the same calculation. For example, suppose that two text fields with instance names of first and second need to calculate a multiplication result that goes into a dynamic text field with the instance name of third. Add a button, and enter the following script for the button:

```
on(release) {
    alpha=parseFloat(_root.first.text);
    beta=parseInt(_root.second.text);
    _root.third.text=alpha * beta;
}
```

The text in the first input window is converted into a real (floating point) number, and the text in the second input window is converted into an integer. First, the script is associated with the button by selecting the button and placing the script in the Actions panel (see Figure 6-1). The dynamic text field then displays the calculated results and displays them on the screen (see Figure 6-2).

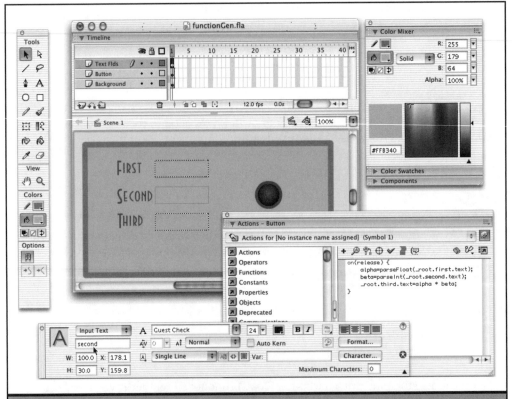

Figure 6-1.   *Two conversion functions, one integer and the other floating point, are used in the script.*

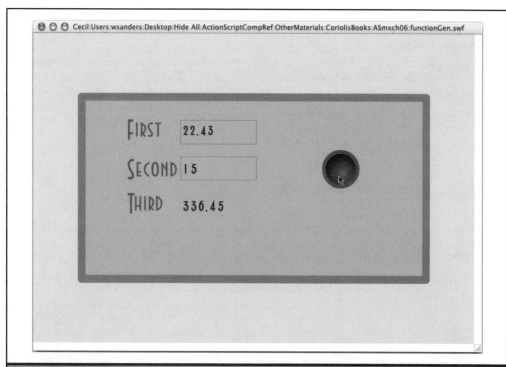

Figure 6-2. *When an integer is multiplied by a floating point number, the results will be floating point.*

FUNDAMENTAL
ACTIONSCRIPT

Note *Using multiplication with text fields does not require the translation of the text field values to numbers. However, whenever dealing with text fields and calculations in general, making conversions to real numbers or integers is a good practice. In that way, when two numbers need to be added, you will get the results you expect and not a surprising concatenation.*

Originated in: Flash 5

General Functions

The general functions in Macromedia Flash MX have a number of different applications as can be seen from the preceding summary. Some of these functions are left over from earlier versions of Macromedia Flash but still have useful purposes. For example, the eval() function in Macromedia Flash 4 was used to simulate array-like structures. It was used to evaluate an expression as a full variable.

escape

escape(exp): Function

The escape() function prepares strings for URL encoding. Wherever a non-digit or other character is not an unaccented letter between a and z or A and Z, it is replaced by a hexadecimal value representing the character. The format is a percent sign followed by the hex value. For example, a space is %20 and a period is %2E. The following script places escape code in the URL, www.sandlight.com/dog house/myPup.swf:

```
var myURL = "www.sandlight.com/dog house/myPup.swf";
var readyURL = escape(myURL);
trace(readyURL);
```

The output in the following illustration shows clearly where the characters have been replaced by the hexadecimal values.

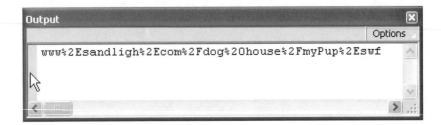

eval

eval(exp): Function

The eval() function examines an expression as a variable name. This function is very useful for generating a series of variable names when you need unique names for each variable. For Macromedia Flash MX, eval() can still be used as such and may be useful for generating variable names made up of a string and a number. The following example illustrates this process:

```
var alpha5 = "three little pigs";
var beta = 5;
delta = eval("alpha" + beta);
trace(delta);
```

The name of the variable, alpha5, can be interpreted to be a variable made up of two or more of its parts. In the script, beta is assigned 5 and delta is assigned the eval()

function of the string "alpha" plus beta. Now delta has the same value as alpha5. Instead of using the eval() function, try the same script using a standard variable:

```
var alpha5 = "three little pigs";
var beta = 5;
delta = "alpha" + beta;
trace(delta);
```

Because the eval() function can derive the value of a concatenated variable from an expression, it has uses for duplicating movie clips and other tasks involving variables made up of numbers and strings. However, most of those tasks are handled by arrays.

Originated in: Flash 4

getProperty

getProperty(inst, prop): Function

Other than writing ActionScript for older versions (Macromedia Flash 3) of Macromedia Flash, the getProperty() function has little use. The function returns the property value of a specified object instance, such as a movie clip instance. It uses the format:

```
getProperty(instance, property);
```

Ever since Macromedia Flash 5 introduced the dot syntax, a property's value has been returned using the format:

```
instance.property
```

So the following two lines are identical as far as returning an instance's property value, but the latter is shorter and simpler:

```
var gamma=getProperty(myMc, _x);
var gamma = myMc._x;
```

However, if you need ActionScript for Macromedia Flash 4 users, the following will work fine with Macromedia Flash 4, 5, and 6 players:

```
var gamma = getProperty(tester, _x);
var beta = getProperty(tester, _y);
var sigma = getProperty(tester, _alpha);
```

```
var delta = getProperty(tester, _name);
var cr = newline;
trace(gamma+cr+beta+cr+sigma+cr+delta);
```

The following illustration shows the output based on the position, transparency, and the name of the instance "tester."

The term "tester" is the instance name of an object. In Macromedia Flash MX, you will find more elements, such as buttons and text fields, can also be objects. Even though they're much newer than the getProperty() function, their properties can be gleaned from it.

 The constant, newline, is placed in the variable cr in the previous script because cr is shorter and just as easy to remember. Chapter 7 discusses all of the constants and their uses.

Originated in: Flash 3

getTimer

getTimer(): Function

The getTimer() global function returns the time in milliseconds between the beginning of the running of the movie and the current time. The timing depends on the playback speed of the movie, and the getTimer() function is not affected by the clock speed. For example, the following script samples 10 values of the getTimer() function:

```
for (var x = 0; x<10; x++) {
    var sinceStart = getTimer();
    trace("Milliseconds since started playing = "+sinceStart);
}
```

In comparing the speeds of an 863 MHz computer and a 400 MHz computer, the output from the script shows the difference due to processing speed. The top illustration shows output from the 863 MHz processor, and the bottom one shows output from the 400 MHz processor.

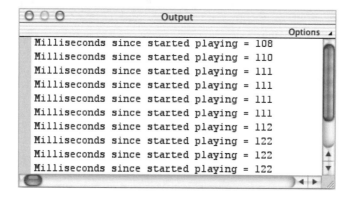

Originated in: Flash 4

getVersion

getVersion: Function

The getVersion() global function returns the version of the player being used to play the movie. The standard Publish in Macromedia Flash MX generates HTML that automatically calls up a URL to upgrade to the Macromedia Flash 6 player when running movies for the Macromedia Flash 6 player (default). However, if sidetracked to www.macromedia.com, some users may opt to go to another site. By having an initial movie in Macromedia Flash 4 or 5, you can find the player in use, and then call up the appropriate Macromedia Flash movie for the version of the Macromedia Flash player the user has. At the end of the movie you can always suggest that the user upgrade his player to Macromedia Flash 6. The following script shows how the function gets and returns data:

```
var beta=getVersion();
trace(beta);
```

The returns indicate the platform and version. For example, a Windows XP might return this:

```
WIN 6,0,30,42
```

and a Macintosh, this:

```
MAC 6,0,21,0
```

The important character to trap is the first one after the platform type. In the example, both are different versions of the Macromedia Flash 6 player. The following script shows one way to do this:

```
var thisVersion = getVersion();
var stringVer = String(thisVersion);
var playerVer = stringVer.charAt(4);
if (playerVer != 6) {
    getURL("http://www.macromedia.com/downloads");
}
```

Originated in: Flash 5

targetPath

The targetPath() function returns the complete path to a named target. However, the information that you need to provide assumes you already know a good deal about the object's path to begin with. If you are seeking one movie clip within another, for example, you need to indicate both the parent object and the child object. The following shows an example where a movie clip with the instance name ball2 is part of the ball1 object. When you trace the inner movie clip, you have to specify the path from the parent movie clip as follows:

```
trace(targetPath(ball1.ball2));
```

The output is the following:

```
_level0.ball1.ball2;
```

Because the only information missing from the function's argument is the level and because you have already laid out the path in the argument, essentially all you get is the level. However, in cases where you have multiple objects on the stage and you need to use the same objects on different levels, the level number can be the only information you will actually use. In loading multiple movies, any information about levels is equally important.

Another use for this function is with variables whose values are object references. If a root variable stores the path of a movie clip three nesting levels deep, the targetPath() function can return the full path.

Originated in: Flash 5

unescape

The unescape() function strips the hexadecimal values and the accompanying percent (%) symbols. When moving data between Macromedia Flash and server-side scripts or URLs where hexadecimal values will be employed, using unescape() will put everything back in order. For instance, taking the escape() example from earlier in the chapter and adding another line, you can see output that first puts in the hexadecimal value and then removes it:

```
var myURL = "www.sandlight.com/dog house/myPup.swf";
var readyURL = escape(myURL);
var readReady = unescape(readyURL);
trace(readyURL+newline+readReady);
```

The top line in the output shows the address with the escape characters and the bottom shows the more readable text after the unescape() function is used, as shown here.

Originated in: Flash 5

User-Defined Functions

Functions that the developer creates on his own are user-defined functions. They are like built-in functions except they perform a set of actions that the developer wants to happen. They have the following format:

```
function titleOfFunction (arguments) {
 statements;
 statements;
 etc...;
}
```

The arguments are simply parameters. The arguments can be a literal, string, number, Boolean, or object. Between the name of the function and the closing curly brace, you just add statements that do something you want. The following function, for example, calculates the cubic feet in a container. The function requires three arguments: height, width, and depth. (Note that the parameter name is "high" because "height" is a property name.)

```
function container(high, width, depth) {
    cubicFeet = high * width * depth;
    return cubicFeet;
}
trace(container(5,5,7));
```

The return action evaluates the expression parameter. (It sends it out, so to speak.) Then, when you launch the function, the value generated in the function is sent out. The trace() action illustrates how the function is launched with all of the parameters (arguments) set.

In a more practical example, an e-business may need to reuse a function that enters an item's price and then calculates the sales tax and adds shipping charges. Shipping charges are a constant ($6.99, for instance), and the tax is 8 percent (.08). The price is variable, so price can be used as an argument. Also, using a Math function (described in the next chapter), you can format the data to two decimal points:

```
function ringUp(price) {
    var total = price * 1.08 + 6.99;
    var dollars = Math.floor(total); //Rounds down to nearest whole
    var cents = Math.round(total*100)%100; //Gets remaining decimal points
    if (cents<10) {
        cents = "0"+cents;
    }
```

FUNDAMENTAL
ACTIONSCRIPT

```
    var remit = "$"+dollars+"."+cents;
    return remit;
}
trace(ringUp(24.33));
```

The script first uses the argument (price) and calculates the combined total by working out the sales tax (price * 1.08) and then adds the shipping cost. It then separates out dollars and cents using Math functions. Then, using a conditional statement, it finds if the cents are less than 10, and if so, it adds a leading zero ("0"). Finally, it formats dollars and cents into a string named "remit" which is then sent out with a return statement. The trace() statement simply shows how to format the function and see the results in the Output window. To fire the function, simply place it in a context where it will be parsed (interpreted) in Macromedia Flash, such as in a button script as shown in the following:

```
on (release) {
 ringUp(14.95);
}
```

In fact, you could put that function (or any other function) on any frame, button, or MC script by simply writing the function and data for the argument. This next movie shows how this function works. (See hamburgerMenu.fla at the book's web site, www.osborne.com.) The function script is in the first frame, and each button script uses the function (see Figure 6-3).

Use the following layers in the listed order:

- Text Fields
- Buttons
- Script
- Background

Follow this set of steps to create the movie:

1. In the Background layer, place text labels for hamburgers, French fries, soda, onion rings, and price using the illustrations as guides. You can also add backdrop rectangles. Lock the Background layer.

2. In the Script layer, click on the first frame, open the Actions panel and add the following script:

```
function ringUp(price) {
    var total = price * 1.08;
    var dollars = Math.floor(total); //Rounds down to nearest whole
```

```
var cents = Math.round(total*100)%100; //Gets remaining decimal points
if (cents<10) {
    cents = "0"+cents;
}
var remit = "$"+dollars+"."+cents;
return remit;
}
```

This is the same function described previously except the shipping amount ($6.99) and trace() action are removed. It will be used in all of the button scripts. Lock the Script layer.

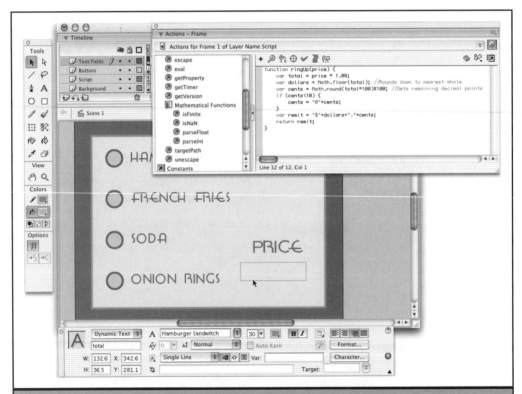

Figure 6-3. *Different Math function methods are used to round off fractions created when tax is added to purchases.*

3. Create a button and place four instances of the button on the stage next to each of the four labels (hamburger, French fries, soda, and onion rings.) Use the following scripts for the respective buttons:

Hamburger button script:

```
on(release) {
    _root.total.text = ringUp(1.25)
}
```

French fries button script:

```
on(release) {
    _root.total.text = ringUp(1.10)
}
```

Soda button script:

```
on(release) {
    _root.total.text = ringUp(1.35)
}
```

Onion rings button script:

```
on(release) {
    _root.total.text = ringUp(1.75)
}
```

Note *All of the scripts use the same function, with the only difference being the value in the argument. When you have all of the buttons in place and the scripts written, lock the Button layer.*

4. The last step is to create a dynamic text field. Place the text field directly under the Price label and in the Instance name window in the Properties panel, type the word **total**. In the button scripts, the reference to _root.total.text is to this text field. That's it, you're all finished. As seen in the following illustration, all of the fractions after the last cent have been dropped.

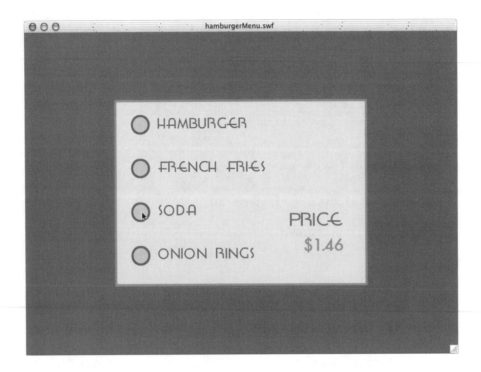

Conclusion

While much of what functions have done in the past has been taken over by methods associated with objects, functions still play an important role in Macromedia Flash MX. Some older functions such as random() have been deprecated and replaced by the Math.random object method. Others are still key functions that you will use in Macromedia Flash MX and most likely in future versions of Macromedia Flash.

User functions and function literals are as important as ever. With changes in the ability to address objects such as buttons and text fields with instance names, function literals can work just like event handlers have in buttons and movie clips in past versions of Macromedia Flash. In fact, using function literals, you can trap button events using movie clip objects.

Most of the work done by functions in this chapter have dealt with changing variables, reading variables, and using variables in conditional statements. The next chapter examines constants and properties. Both the constants and properties are the global ones that apply to different objects on the stage in Macromedia Flash MX. Constants have a single value that does not change but can be used as values in variables. Properties have values that can be placed into variables as well, but more important, properties are changed to change associated objects. In many ways properties are variables in that their values change, but unlike variables, a property is always associated with an object.

The
Complete
Reference

Chapter 7

Properties
and Constants

Constants and properties make up two separate folders in the Actions toolbox. However, they are examined here in a single chapter because they constitute an interesting juxtaposition between the fluid and the unchangeable. Properties are a type of variable in that their values change; constants are unchanging values. For example, the value of _alpha can change from 0-100 and any intermediate values in between. However, global constants like "undefined" and "newline" will mean the same under different circumstances. Moreover, some constants can be assigned to properties. For example, the constant true can be a value of the property _visible.

In one of the few places in this book where the order of folders is not in the same order as in the Actions toolbox, properties and constants are switched in order. This was done to look at the properties that may possibly contain constants and see the context in which they would be used.

Properties

The properties listed in the Properties folder are Flash 4-era properties. They are listed separately because they are the only ones that work with the legacy getProperty()/setProperty() functions. Unlike the properties linked to particular objects, such as TextField.scroll or Stage.height, the properties in the Properties folder all contain the underscore, a residue from the properties in Flash 4 ActionScript. However, these properties are as important as ever, and you will be using them regularly and often in Flash MX.

What Is a Property?

A property is an element, state, or condition of an object. Just as people have characteristics—or properties—so do objects in a Flash movie. For example, a person can be described by name, height, weight, appearance, address, accomplishments, and relationship. You can describe Nancy as being five and a half feet tall, 125 pounds, smooth complexioned, living in El Paso, a college graduate, and married. Nancy can change. She may move from El Paso to Omaha, lose or gain weight, and change her marital status. Certain conditions or properties will remain the same, however. She will continue to be a woman, a college graduate, and the same height (at least until she is very old).

Flash operates the same way. Some objects can be changed, and others remain constant. Although you can find out what an object's properties are, you may not always be able to change them. For example, _currentframe can be used to read a movie clip's current frame, it cannot be used to change it. On the other hand, the _x property is an object's horizontal position on the screen and can be both read and changed.

Variables and Properties

In many respects, properties are like variables. Both are assigned values using unary (=) and compound (+=) assignment operators, and the same kind of data types are used. However, unlike variables, properties have restricted types of data that can be assigned to them. For example, the _rotation property can only have realistic values from 0–360 assigned (any value over 359 starts at 0, and 361 is the same as 1). Other properties, such as _visible, can only accept Boolean values of true or false.

The with Shortcut and Assigning Property Values

When defining an object's properties, you may find yourself with a long list of properties to define. For example, the following is a typical assignment of property values:

```
_root.block._alpha=80;
_root.block._rotation=44;
_root.block._x=300;
```

Rather than having to repeat the name of the object and path with every line, using the with statement, you can save time as shown in the following:

```
with(_root.block) {
    _alpha=80;
    _rotation=44;
    _x=300;
}
```

Not only can you save time by not retyping the object name, but the properties stick out more and it's easier to debug your scripts. Once you begin routinely adding several properties to objects, you will be glad you have the with function. This next movie will give you a better idea of all of the different properties you may encounter in defining an object:

1. Open a new movie and add a layer. Name the top layer Text Fields and the bottom Background.

2. Add four dynamic text fields using the following labels and instance names: customer, account, region, and rep.

3. Click on the first frame and add the following script:

```
with (customer) {
 text="ActionScript"
 background=true;
 border=true;
 borderColor=0xff0000;
 backgroundColor=0x000000;
 textColor=0x00ff00;
 selectable=true;
}
```

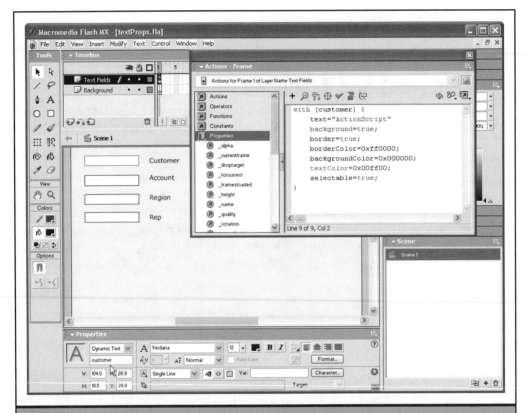

Figure 7-1. *When developing script in movies where multiple objects must be defined, using the with variable saves time.*

Each of the other three text fields will need a similar definition for unique properties, and using the with variable, you can save a great deal of time. Figure 7-1 shows the movie under development.

Table 7-1 lists the Macromedia Flash MX properties in the Properties folder. Each is accompanied by a brief description and whether the property is read only or read and set.

Term	Description	Read/Set or Read Only
_alpha	Transparency in percent (0 = fully transparent, 100 = fully opaque)	Read/Set
_currentframe	Number of current frame	Read only

Table 7-1. *Property Characteristics*

FUNDAMENTAL
ACTIONSCRIPT

Term	Description	Read/Set or Read Only
_droptarget	Slash syntax of target path	Read only
_focusrect	Specifies whether object has yellow rectangle around it	Read only
_framesloaded	Returns the current number of frames of a movie loaded	Read only
_height	Object's height in pixels	Read/Set
_name	Object's name	Read/Set
_quality	Global quality with LOW, MEDIUM, HIGH, and BEST values	Read/Set
_rotation	Number of degrees an object is rotated	Read/Set
_soundbuftime	Global property to establish number of seconds to prebuffer sound	Read/Set
_target	Returns target path	Read only
_totalframes	Total number of frames in movie	Read only
_url	URL of the SWF file from which movie clip was downloaded	Read only
_visible	Boolean value for an object's visibility	Read/Set
_width	Object's width in pixels	Read/Set
_x	Object's horizontal position on the screen	Read/Set
_xmouse	Current horizontal position of mouse cursor in relation to the stage	Read only
_xscale	Relative scale of object's width	Read/Set
_y	Object's vertical position on the screen	Read/Set

Table 7-1.   *Property Characteristics* (continued)

Term	Description	Read/Set or Read Only
_ymouse	Current vertical position of mouse cursor in relation to the stage	Read only
_yscale	Relative scale of object's height	Read/Set

Table 7-1.   *Property Characteristics* (continued)

Working with Properties

Generally, you will be working with properties connected to different objects. In previous chapters, you have seen several examples where an object's properties were changed. Here, you will see some generic examples of using properties so that you can begin working with them. However, for the most part, properties are considered as part of an object such as a movie clip, a sound, or the stage, and not the whole movie. Global properties are an exception, and no matter where they are used in a movie, they affect all elements of the movie.

Global Properties

The general syntax for setting a property is to name the property, generally attached to an instance, and assign it a value. For example, draw a circle on the stage and try the following script in the first frame:

```
_quality="LOW";
```

The circle will appear with ragged edges when you test the movie. Any drawing will appear with the low quality because the property is global. Likewise, all symbols and other drawings will look ragged, even in different scenes.

Object Properties

Property values associated with objects only affect the objects themselves and will not affect the other objects, even if the other objects are instances of the same symbol. For example, create a button and drag two instances of the button on the stage. Select one button and give it the instance name of jack. The Instance Name window in the Properties panel is where you type in the instance name for buttons, movie clips, and text fields. Name the other button instance on the stage jill. Finally, type the following in the first frame:

```
_root.jack._alpha=50;
```

When you test the script, you will see that the button named jack appears transparent on the screen, and the instance of the same button symbol, jill, does not. That's because the change in property was a local one linked to a specific instance of an object.

Read-Only Properties

Read-only properties give information, but they cannot be changed. For example, _xmouse and _ymouse are the positions of the cursor, and while they can be changed by dragging the mouse on the screen, they cannot be changed by assigning them new values using ActionScript. However, they can be passed to other objects. For example, to display the current position of the mouse on the screen, try the following:

1. Create two dynamic text fields. In the Instance Name window in the Properties panel, name one mouseX and the other mouseY.

2. Label the mouseX field "Mouse X position" and the mouseY field, "Mouse Y position."

3. Add a second frame to the first layer and then select the first frame. In the Actions panel, type the following script:

```
_root.mouseX.text=_xmouse;
_root.mouseY.text=_ymouse;
```

When you test the movie, you will be able to see the current position of both the _xmouse and _ymouse properties (read only), and at the same time, your script will constantly update variable values using the read-only properties. The following illustration shows what you will see.

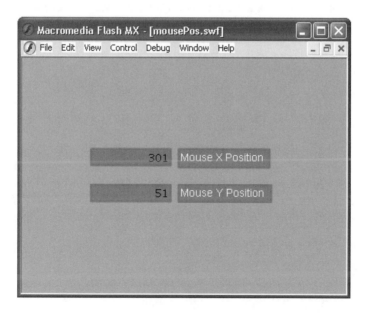

Throughout the rest of the book, you will be seeing the properties discussed in this chapter used with a number of different objects. Most of the time, you will be seeing the property in specific references to a set of properties belonging to a specific object. For example, the TextField object has 28 different properties assigned to it. Figure 7-1 showed a script for a text field with the instance name customer.

Property Parameters

The properties listed in the Properties folder in the ActionScript toolbox are global ones. Other properties in the ActionScript toolbox are in subfolders associated with objects in the main folders. However, the global properties can be assigned to an object with its own subset of properties. For example, the Button object has five properties listed in the subfolder with the Button object. However, you can change global properties in the button. To see how this works, follow these steps:

1. Create an oval on the stage using a dark color and select it.
2. Convert it to a button by pressing F8 and selecting Button for Behavior in the Convert to Symbol dialog box.
3. Type in the name NewButton and click OK.
4. Give the new button the instance name testMe in the Properties panel.
5. Click the first frame and add the following script:

```
_root.testMe._alpha=33;
```

You can use the same script on movie clips, text fields, and any other object that has some degree of transparency. Math objects and Sound objects would not be included among those objects where the global property _alpha would apply. So, while a property can be global, it does not necessarily mean it can be applied to all objects. The properties in this section are global ones that can apply to all objects or only certain ones, depending on the nature of the property itself.

_alpha

Units: Percent

Range: 0–100

The _alpha property adds opaqueness to an object. Conversely, lowering the value of the _alpha property increases an object's transparency. Objects behind (on lower layers than) an object that has less than 100 percent _alpha can be viewed. The following example uses two layers:

1. Open a new movie and add a layer.
2. Place a small orange square on the bottom layer.
3. On the top layer, place a large dark-yellow rectangle movie clip with the instance name blockHigh that fully covers the square.

4. Also on the top layer, on top of the rectangle, place a white round button with a black stroke.

5. Use the Align panel to center everything vertically and horizontally with one another.

6. Add the following script to the first frame:

```
_root.changer.onPress = function() {
    _root.blockHigh._alpha = 30;
    this._alpha = 40;
};
```

Both the rectangle and the button will turn transparent (see image on the left), and you will be able to see the square beneath (on the right).

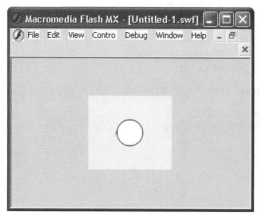 

_currentframe

Units: Integers (frame number)

Range: 1 to number of frames in the movie

The _currentframe property returns the frame number where the playhead currently resides in a movie. When creating movies where you want to trap information at a particular frame, the _currentframe property can come in handy. To see how it works, recreate the following movie:

1. Open a new movie and add about 30 frames.

2. Add a button with the instance name of changer.

3. Add a dynamic text field with the instance name of showMe.

4. Click in the first frame and add the following script in the Actions panel:

```
stop();
_root.changer.onPress = function() {
    nextFrame();
```

```
        stop();
        _root.showMe.text = _currentframe;
    };
```

When you run the script, you can see that all frames (not just keyframes) return a value for the _currentframe property.

_droptarget

Units: String

Range: Path of object

This read-only property returns the path to the movie clip on which the movie clip was dropped. The dropped movie clip *is not* the path returned, but rather, the movie clip path on which the other movie was dropped is returned. To translate the path to the dot format, use the eval function. Follow these steps for a simple demonstration:

1. Open a new movie and add a layer.

2. Select the first frame of the top layer and create a movie clip on the stage, and give it the instance name frog in the Properties panel.

3. Select the first frame of the bottom layer and create a second movie clip and give it the instance name lilyPad.

4. Open the Actions panel, click the first frame of the top layer, and enter the following script:

```
_root.frog.onPress = function() {
    this.startDrag();
};
_root.frog.onRelease = function() {
    stopDrag();
    trace(this._droptarget);
    trace(eval(this._droptarget));
};
```

You will see the top of the Output window showing the slash syntax (/lilyPad) and the second row of the output in dot syntax (level0.lilyPad).

_focusrect

Units: Boolean

Range: true, false

The _focusrect property is a global one that can be invoked to create a yellow rectangle around buttons set up for sequential selection by tabbing. If a script includes assigning _focusrect a Boolean true value, whenever a tab to a button is made, the button will have a yellow rectangle around it. For example, try the following:

1. Open a new movie and place an input text field on the stage.

2. Add two buttons with the instance names b1 and b2.

3. Click on the first frame and add the following script:

```
b1.onPress = function() {
    _focusrect = true;
};
b2.onRelease = function() {
    _focusrect = false;
};
```

FUNDAMENTAL
ACTIONSCRIPT

You won't find too many examples of this property, but it has promising future as a Web usability feature! The feature was added around the time Microsoft's WebTV started supporting Flash content, because WebTV users do not have a mouse to point with. So it's a usability enhancement that has particular benefit for TV users.

The following two illustrations show how the focus changes from the text field to the button on the left. As soon as the user presses that Tab key, the button on the left is surrounded by a rectangle showing its selection.

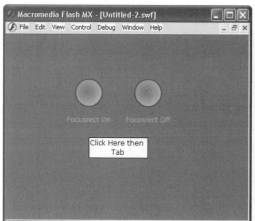 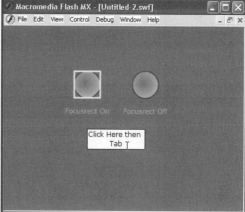

_framesloaded

Units: Integers

Range: 1 to total number of frames in a movie

The _framesloaded property is an important one for creating preloaders in Macromedia Flash MX. It returns an integer with the current number of frames loaded in a movie. Generally used in conjunction with _totalframes, a comparison between _framesloaded and _totalframes makes up most preloaders. The following is an example of the kind of script you will find in most ActionScript preloaders:

```
var loadNow = _root._framesloaded;
var loadTotal = _root._totalframes;
if (loadNow == loadTotal) {
    gotoAndPlay("Scene 2", 1);
}
```

Other than while loading a movie, _framesloaded is not used.

_height

Units: Pixels

Range: 0 to screen resolution

The _height property reads or sets the height of a movie clip, button, or text field object. You can assign real numbers as values or treat the property as a value for other properties or variables. The following script matches the height of a text field with a movie clip:

```
_root.clipper.onPress = function() {
    tTall = _root.message._height;
    this._height = tTall;
};
```

The movie clip's instance name is clipper, and the text field's instance name is message.

_name

Units: String

Range: Instance names in movie

The _name property returns or assigns the instance name for a movie clip. For example, in a game, a movie clip character object may be assigned a different name if it is moved to a different level of "experience." For example, the following script looks at a score variable, and changes the name of a movie clip if the score is at or above a certain level.

```
if (score>=200) {
    _root.novice._name = "intermediate";
}
```

_quality

Units: String

Range: LOW, MEDIUM, HIGH, or BEST

The _quality property is a global one that controls the rendered quality of a movie. The _quality property has four values:

- **LOW**   Graphics are not anti-aliased, bitmaps are not smoothed.

- **MEDIUM**   Bitmaps are not smoothed, and graphics have medium (2×2 pixel grid) anti-aliasing.

- **HIGH**   Bitmaps are smoothed if movie is static, and graphics have high (4×4 pixel grid) anti-aliasing (Flash default).

- **BEST**   Bitmaps always smoothed, and graphics have high (4×4 pixel grid) anti-aliasing.

Whether the property is associated with an object or is assigned a value independent of an object, the effects of changes are global. For example, if you associate _quality with a movie clip's property:

```
specificMC._quality = "MEDIUM";
```

both the movie clip and every other affected object (movie clips, buttons, and text fields) will be rendered at a medium quality. To see how it works, try the following:

1. In a new movie, create a rectangle movie clip with the instance name looker.

2. Create an oval button object with the instance name lookerB.

3. Create a dynamic text field with "Look at this" typed in the text area.

4. Click on the first frame and type the following script in the Actions panel:

```
looker.onPress = function() {
    testText._quality = "LOW";
};
looker.onRelease = function() {
    testText._quality = "BEST";
};
```

Even though the only object addressed by the property is the dynamic text field, when you press down on the movie clip, you can see the changes in all of the objects on the stage. Now add the following script to the first frame. Test the movie and this time click the button instead of the movie clip.

```
lookerB.onPress = function() {
    _quality = "LOW";
```

```
};
lookerB.onRelease = function() {
    _quality = "BEST";
};
```

You will see identical results. Essentially what you see is a global property applied globally whether acting as a property of a single object or assigned independent of any object.

_rotation

Units: Degrees
Range: –0 to 360

The _rotation property changes an object's angle with 0 being its original position. All instances of symbols are embedded in a 0-degree positioned rectangle. So even a shape in a symbol at 45 degrees is within a rectangle whose top and bottom sides are parallel with the top and bottom of the stage. Positive values rotate clockwise, and negative values rotate counter-clockwise. For a simple demonstration of how rotation works, create a square movie clip and give it an instance name of block. Place it in a movie with two frames and put the following script in the first frame:

```
beta -= 1;
block._rotation=beta;
```

When you play the movie, the movie clip turns counter-clockwise. Change the script to:

```
beta += 1;
block._rotation=beta;
```

and it rotates clockwise.

_soundbuftime

Units: Seconds (integer)
Range: Greater than 0

The _soundbuftime property specifies the number of seconds a sound prebuffers before it starts playing. The _soundbuftime can be used to help ensure that all of a sound has loaded into a buffer before streaming to avoid the sound breaking up. For example, the following prebuffers the sound for five seconds prior to streaming:

```
_soundbuftime=5;
```

_target

Units: String

Range: Path of object

The _target property returns, in slash format, that path to a button, movie clip, or text field. The _target property can be set up and addressed using the dot syntax, but it returns the path in the Flash 4 syntax using slashes. To see how it works, follow these steps:

1. On a new page, create a movie clip and give it the instance name topDog.

2. Double-click the movie clip to enter the Symbol Editing Mode, and create a button and assign it the instance name insideBtn.

3. Add the following script to the first keyframe:

```
var beta =topDog.insideBtn._target;
trace(beta;)
```

You will see the output:

```
/topDog/insideBtn
```

If for some reason you need to rewrite a script to include Flash 4 functionality, you can use the _target property to check on syntax.

_totalframes

Units: Integers

Range: The number of frames in a movie

Used with _framesloaded, the _totalframes global property is used to create preloaders. (See an example earlier in this chapter, in the discussion of _framesloaded.) However, you can use the _totalframes property in any other way you want. For example, the following script uses _totalframes to set up a loop:

```
for (var counter = 0; counter<_totalframes; counter += 5) {
    trace(counter+newline);
}
```

Like any other global property, _totalframes can have many uses, but generally you only see it used with preloaders.

_url

Units: String
Range: Path to SWF file

This read-only property contains the address of the current movie. The format is URL encoded where all non-alphanumeric characters are escaped using the hexadecimal format preceded with the percent (%) sign. Thus, when being read, _url is usually used in conjunction with the unescape function. The following illustrates this property's use:

```
var beta = _url;
var clearIt = unescape(beta);
trace(clearIt);
```

The following output window shows what you will see when the URL is your desktop:

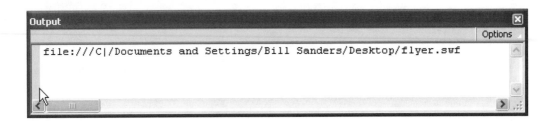

```
Output                                                    [X]
                                                   Options
  file:///C|/Documents and Settings/Bill Sanders/Desktop/flyer.swf
```

_visible

Units: Boolean
Range: true, false

The _visible property has two functions. First, if _visible is set to false, the object associated with it disappears from view. Second, when _visible is false, the object is disabled with some events. That is, setting _visible to false not only removes the visibility, it turns off some of its functionality. To best see how the property works, set up the following movie:

1. In a new movie, draw a rectangle with a 3.5 stroke and no fill with dimensions of W = 145 and H = 120.

2. In the center of the rectangle, draw a large circle that fills the center of the rectangle.

3. Select the circle and convert it to a button by pressing F8. In the Properties panel, give it the instance name nowUsee.

4. Above the rectangle, draw a smaller circle, convert it to a button, and give it the instance name appear in the Properties panel.

5. Click on the first frame and enter the following script:

```
_root.nowUsee.onPress = function() {
    this._visible = false;
    _root.appear._x = (_root.appear._x+10);
};
_root.appear.onPress = function() {
    _root.nowUsee._visible = true;
    _root.appear._x = (_root.appear._x-10);
};
```

When you test the movie, click the large button in the middle of the rectangle. When you click it, the button becomes invisible and the little button jumps 10 pixels to the right (see the following illustrations). Now, click where the large button is again. It's already invisible, but you know it's in the rectangle so it shouldn't be hard to click. Watch the small button. It does not jump. That's because the invisible state of the large button has rendered it inoperable for onPress events. When you click the small button, the large one returns, and you can now use it to make it disappear and move the little button.

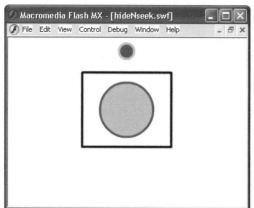
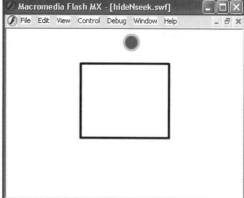

_width

Units: Pixels

Range: 0 to width of object

The _width property sets and retrieves the width of an object. Any instance (excluding non-symbols) that can be addressed by ActionScript, including movie clips, buttons, and text fields, can add _width to an instance name to find or reset the object's width. If _width is called without an object reference, it retrieves that widest element on the stage, including drawings. It does not, however, take its value from the stage dimensions. For example, try the following:

1. Draw a circle on the stage with a diameter of 50.

2. Draw a line with a width of 300 and stroke of 3.5 centered below the circle.

3. Enter the following script in the first frame:

```
trace(_width);
```

Because the line is longer than the circle is wide, its width is returned with the size of the stroke added. So, instead of returning 300, you will see 303.5.

_X

Units: Pixels

Range: 0 to width of movie

The _x property represents an object's horizontal position from the left side of the stage measured in pixels. The object is measured from its own center to determine the _x value. (If you change the registration to the upper-left corner when you create the symbol, this too will affect the _x value.) You can use the Free Transform tool to move the center of an object to the side, but the measure will still be to the center as defined by the position of the crosshairs in the middle of movie clips and buttons. So the measurement of an instance is actually to the center as defined by the crosshair position on the object.

In using the _x property, it can be self-referent—that is, you can use the current horizontal position to change the position. To see how this works, place a movie clip with the instance name clipee on the stage, add a frame to the layer, click on the first frame, and place the following script in the Actions panel:

```
clipee._x += 10;
counter += 1;
if (counter>20) {
    clipee._x = 20;
    counter = 0;
}
```

The movie clip keeps adding 10 to its current position until the counter reaches 20 and then it starts over again.

_xmouse

Units: Pixels

Range: 0 to width of screen

The _xmouse property is a read-only global property that retrieves the current horizontal position of the mouse. It can be used in many different ways in a Macromedia Flash MX movie. One simple use of the _xmouse property is to create a "following" movie clip that will move to the left or right of the mouse pointer's horizontal position. For example, the following script places a movie clip with the instance name follower 60 pixels to the left of the horizontal mouse position:

```
_root.follower._x=_xmouse-60;
```

Generally, you would not use the _xmouse to drag a movie clip across the stage, but doing so is a quick and visual way to observe what the _xmouse property does.

_xscale

Units: Percent

Range: 0–100

The _xscale property retrieves or sets the horizontal scale of addressable objects or retrieves horizontal scale values. An object's default _xscale value is 100, representing 100 percent of its size. Increase and decrease in the _xscale value will make the object wider or narrower. (An interesting effect is to use negative values to flip the object on the X axis.)

```
var beta;
_root.bellows._xscale = beta+100;
if (beta != 100 && flag != 1) {
    beta += 10;
} else {
    flag = 1;
}
if (flag == 1 && beta>-150) {
    beta -= 10;
} else {
    flag = 0;
}
```

_y

Units: Pixels

Range: 0 to width of movie

The _y property can be used to set the vertical position of an object and to retrieve that same position. It has the same characteristics as the _x property discussed above except that it uses the vertical axis instead of the horizontal axis. The following shows a simple example using a movie clip with the instance name climber:

```
steps++;
_root.climber._y = steps+30;
_root.climber._alpha = (100-steps);
if (steps>=100) {
    steps = 1;
}
```

FUNDAMENTAL
ACTIONSCRIPT

One of the characteristics of the _y property is that it behaves in the opposite of a Y value of an X/Y axis. On a typical X/Y axis, the height of the position is directly related to the value of Y. In Macromedia Flash MX, the relationship between the value of the _y property and the height of the object on the stage is an inverse one.

_ymouse

Units: Pixels
Range: 0 to height of movie

The _ymouse property is a read-only global property that retrieves the current vertical position of the mouse. It operates in the same way as the _xmouse except that it retrieves the vertical instead of horizontal position of the mouse pointer. The following script should be used with a dynamic text field object in the two-frame movie. Use the instance name showMe with the text field. Select the first frame and type the following script in the Actions panel:

```
showMe.text=_ymouse;
```

As you move the mouse around the stage, you will see the current vertical position of the mouse. When the mouse indicates a negative value, it indicates that the mouse is off the stage. The top edge of the stage is the zero point and so anything above the stage is treated as a negative value.

_yscale

Units: Percent
Range: 0–100

The _yscale property retrieves or sets the horizontal scale of addressable objects or retrieves horizontal scale values. An object's default _yscale vertical value is 100, representing 100 percent of its size. Increase and decrease in the _yscale value will make the object taller or shorter. If you have a need to create bar charts, the _yscale property is very handy. Follow these steps to make one:

1. On a new page, use the rectangle tool to create two rectangles 300 pixels high and 50 pixels wide.

2. Select one of the rectangles and convert it to a movie clip symbol.

3. Double-click it and in the Symbol Editing Mode, select the rectangle, and move it so that the crosshair is at the bottom of the rectangle.

4. Return to the main timeline and use the Free Transform tool to move the rectangle's center point to the bottom of the rectangle.

5. Repeat steps 2 through 4 with the second rectangle.

6. In the Instance Name window in the Properties panel, name one rectangle bar1 and the other bar2.

7. Create two dynamic text fields, giving one the instance name data1 and the other data2.

8. Create a button and give it the name makeChart.

9. Select the first frame, open the Actions panel and enter the following script:

```
_root.bar1._yscale = 0;
_root.bar2._yscale = 0;
_root.makeChart.onPress = function() {
    _root.bar1._yscale = _root.data1.text;
    _root.bar2._yscale = _root.data2.text;
};
```

Because this is a simple demonstration of using the _yscale property, you will have to keep the data values between 0 and 100. However, you can see how _yscale works to first reduce the two bars to hairlines on the screen, and then generate charts for comparative measures. Figure 7-2 shows the bar chart at work.

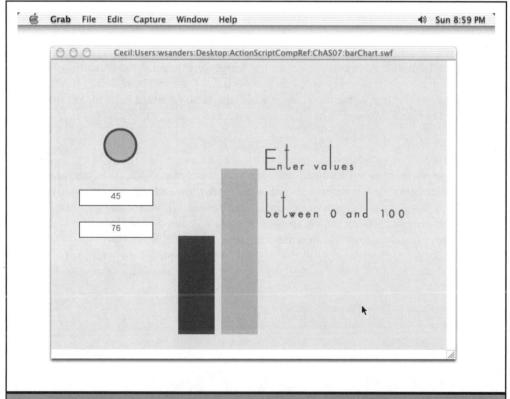

Figure 7-2.   *Using the _yscale property and moving the centers to the bottom of the bar movie clips, making dynamic bar charts is easy.*

Constants

Unlike variables and properties, constants have a single, unchanging value. Macromedia Flash MX has five constants, three of which you have employed in examples so far in this book. Both true and false have been used with Booleans, and newline has been used to format output.

false

The false constant is one of two Boolean states. A Boolean variable can be assigned a false value, but usually a false is generated in a conditional statement where the evaluated condition has not been met. The false is implied but not seen in the script. For example, the following script would generate the output, "This is false."

```
var test = 50;
if (test == 20) {
    trace("This is true.");
} else {
    trace("This is false.");
}
```

The constant false does not appear in the script, but because the condition is only possible because of a false outcome, it is implied. For the most part, when not used as assigned values for properties such as _visible, the false constant is implied and not present in a script. However, it has the same effect as being in the script.

newline

The newline constant is not found in JavaScript and is not an EMCA 262 standard term. However, newline is an extremely useful constant for formatting output to a dynamic text field because it places a carriage return in a stream of data. Data coming from a database or generated in an action or function usually needs a series of new lines to clearly display the data, and that is where newline comes in. To see how it works, create a multiline dynamic text field with the instance name viewWindow and type in the following script:

```
var message = "newline";
message = String(message);
for (counter=0; counter<message.length; counter++) {
    _root.viewWindow.text+= message.charAt(counter)+newline;
}
```

By adding the newline constant, you are able to take the horizontal string "newline" and display it as a vertical line.

null

The null constant is an odd bird. It can be assigned to a variable or used in a conditional statement, but otherwise, it is a constant worth nothing—or null. However, it is good for turning things off. For instance, suppose you have a button that you want to turn on and off connected to a certain function literal. The following script simply makes the movie clip named block invisible using an unnamed function associated with pressing a button with the instance name zapper:

```
zapper.onPress=function() {
     block._visible=false;
};
```

Further on in your script, you want the button to be turned off under some circumstances, such as the user having achieved a certain level of points in a game. Now try the following script:

```
zapper.onPress=function() {
     block._visible=false;
};
zapper.onPress=null;
```

The assignment of the null value to the button's onPress event handler renders the handler inoperable. Unlike the first script, which worked fine for making the movie clip disappear, the second one has no effect on the MC's visibility.

However, null is not the same thing as zero. Try the following:

```
var que=0;
if(que==null) {
    trace("This is null");
} else {
    trace("Que is not null, it is zero!");
}
```

As you will see when you execute the code, null is not the same as zero, either. So in cases where you might want to add a variable to your script dynamically, you can test for null and then assign the variable a value if the results indicate a null.

true

Like the false constant, the true constant is more likely to be implied than seen in a script. The Boolean true is derived from a statement assigning a Boolean value to a variable, a conditional statement, or a literal assignment of the true constant. For example, the following statement assigns a Boolean true to the variable beta:

```
var beta = 10 > 8;
```

The following script:

```
var beta = 10>8;
if (beta) {
    trace("That is true.");
}
```

is identical to the script where you actually see the true constant:

```
var beta = 10>8;
if (beta==true) {
    trace("That is true.");
}
```

While you can see the true constant as a Boolean value assigned to properties such as _visible, like the false constant, it is often implied but not actually present as a term in a script.

undefined

Undefined is the actual value of a variable that either has not been defined or has been declared and not assigned a value. It is very similar to null, and if null and undefined are compared, they return a Boolean true. The actual retrieved value of a declared but unassigned variable is "undefined" as shown in the following:

```
var beta;
trace(beta);
```

When undefined is converted to a string, you get an empty string instead of the string literal "undefined". For example, the following script uses two undefined variables, but when they are concatenated in output with the newline constant, they are converted to strings rendering them invisible.

```
var beta;
trace(beta+newline+jupiter);
```

If you attempt to find the difference between the null constant and the undefined constant, you won't have any luck there either, because they are treated as the same, as you will see in the following script:

```
var compare = (null == undefined);
if (compare) {
    trace("Null and undefined are treated as the same!");
}
```

The key difference—and it's not much of a difference—between null and undefined is that when undefined converts to a string it translates to an empty string, and null still displays "null".

Conclusion

The properties examined in this chapter provide objects and the movie in general with dynamic possibilities for change. Like variables, properties can change their values, but unlike variables, properties are limited to the data types they can handle, while variables have a far wider range. In many ways, properties are the "variables of objects" in that when a property's value changes, so too does the object. Also like variables, properties can derive their values from literals, variables, or other properties.

Most of the global properties are actually associated with some limited set of objects such as movie clips, buttons, or text fields. Others have very specific tasks such as prebuffering sound or keeping track of the numbers of frames a movie has. With Macromedia Flash MX, you will begin to find many objects with their own specialized properties that address the unique characteristics of the objects. In the next chapter, you will leave the world of the old Flash ActionScript and enter into the more elegant world of the new Flash. Many more objects along with their own unique properties, methods, events, constants, and listeners can now be found in ActionScript. With the new objects and their associated elements, you will find a far richer ActionScript.

The Complete Reference

ActionScript

Part III

ActionScript Objects

The Complete Reference

ActionScript

Chapter 8

Core Objects I

ctionScript MX has come into its own as an object-oriented programming (OOP) language. Over the last several years, both JavaScript and ActionScript have had many—if not most—of the features that characterize true OOP in the sense that you can create object-oriented programs. Some programmers distinguish between "real" OOP languages like C++ and Java on the one hand and JavaScript and ActionScript on the other, but I think they may be missing the essential point that OOP is an approach more than something hard-wired into the language itself. You can use C++ and Java and not really attend to OOP principles. At the same time, you can follow OOP principles in languages like ActionScript and create object-oriented programs that behave exactly like OOP programs in other languages.

Object-oriented programming needs to be understood as an approach with advantages rather than a way to straitjacket your mind into a certain narrow path. So, if you want to make your programs follow the lines of OOP, do it to make better programs and make yourself a better programmer.

The two major approaches to programming are procedural and object-oriented. The procedural approach contains data structures represented as a network of interacting associated structures. Procedures are a network of interacting routines that call one another. Older languages have this more procedural or linear approach to programming. The OOP approach can be understood as a collection of discrete modules or objects that have their own data structures and behavior. The objects are associated with each other in a single network.

Simply put, an object is a collection of properties and methods. In Flash MX, in addition to properties and methods associated with objects, you also have listeners and events. The listeners are new and are explained in Chapter 10. However, by thinking of familiar Flash elements such as movie clips and buttons as objects, you can assign them events associated with other objects. For example, in previous chapters, you have seen scripts like the following:

```
_root.myClip.onPress = function() {
    //some actions here;
};
```

The importance of this script is that the event onPress is assigned to the object myClip, which you can assume is a movie clip instance. However, if you try a script like the following, associated with a movie clip instance, you will receive an error message:

```
on(press) {
    //some actions here;
}
```

By treating movie clips, both concrete (a movie clip on the stage) and abstract (a constructor-defined object) elements in Flash, as objects, you can find a more consistent set of events, properties, and methods. Chapter 9 examines the concept of class and inheritance. At the end of this chapter, you will see how to use constructor functions and the prototype property.

OOP has two essential advantages: complex designs are easier to develop, and the modules can be used to build other components. A prefabricated house is an example that follows OOP principles. Instead of starting from scratch, you begin with modules that serve as building blocks. The prefab house has prebuilt attics, rooms, fireplaces, kitchens, bathrooms, and other components that make up a house. The modules can be used in several different houses, and you don't have to reinvent the wheel each time you build a house. In the same way that you use modules to build houses, you can use objects to build programs. This chapter introduces the first part of the core objects in ActionScript. As you look at them, begin thinking about self-contained objects as little data structures or systems that are the building blocks to larger and more complex systems.

Arguments

Arguments: Object

An array that has the values passed as arguments (parameters) in a function, the Arguments object is created each time a script calls a function. You need not construct the Arguments object, as it is automatically constructed when you create a function. The following example shows a function with two arguments, and you can find the content of the arguments in the arguments' array elements:

```
function rectangle(s1, s2) {
    trace(s1*s2);
    trace(arguments[0]);
    trace(arguments[1]);
}
rectangle(5, 6);
```

When the script executes, the values of the arguments appear in the two argument elements along with the computation of the area of the rectangle.

callee

arguments.callee(): Property

The callee property is a self-referral within a recursive function. For a standard function where you name the function, you'll rarely need this property because you have the name of the function. However, for use with functional literals where a recursive function is at work, the name is anonymous, so you can use arguments.callee() as shown in the following example (viewer is the instance name of a movie clip):

```
_root.viewer.onPress = function() {
    extract++;
    var goodies = new Array("Optical Mouse", "USB Hub");
    goodies.push("WebCam", "Headphones", "Microphone");
    trace(goodies[extract-1]);
    if (extract<goodies.length) {
        arguments.callee();
    }
};
```

The script checks to see if all of the elements in the array have been extracted. If they have not, the function literal calls itself using the only name it has—arguments.callee().

caller

arguments.caller: Property

The caller property refers to the Arguments object of the calling function.

length

arguments.length: Property

The length property contains the number of arguments (parameters) that were passed in the function call. The following script uses two arguments, s1 and s2, so the length of the argument object should be 2:

```
function rectangle (s1,s2) {
    trace(s1*s2)
    trace(arguments.length);
}
rectangle(5,6)
```

When the function is called, it displays the results of multiplying 5 and 6 (30) and the correct number of arguments (2) in the function itself.

Array

The array is a multi-element object. Within the array, you can store the same kinds of data that you can in variables and properties. By using and treating the array as an object, instead of only entering and extracting elements, you have several options in the form of methods and a single property.

new Array()

Array(): Constructor

The keyword Array() is a constructor object used to create an array object. You can optionally add an argument for the size of the array. The following example shows declaring and assigning a five-element array. (The first line is unnecessary, but it is included to show how you can assign an array length in the construction of the array.)

```
var herd = new Array(5); //Five elements would be numbered 0-4
var herd = new Array("Buffalo", "Horses", "Elephants", "Zebras", "Shoppers")
```

Alternatively, the array could be assigned values using the element values:

```
var herd = new Array(5);
herd[0] = "Buffalo";
herd[1] = "Horses";
herd[2] = "Elephants";
herd[3] = "Zebras";
herd[4] = "Shoppers";
```

Array elements are frequently assigned values using loops. The following example shows how one loop first assigns values and the second loop extracts the values in the elements:

```
manyMcs = new Array();
for (var counter = 1; counter<11; counter++) {
    manyMcs[counter] = "CoolMC"+counter;
}
for (var outtie = 1; outtie<11; outtie++) {
    trace(manyMcs[outtie]);
}
```

The output shows that each element has been assigned a unique value.

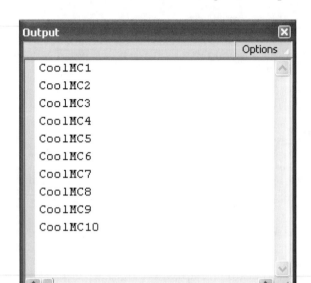

Essentially, the constructor creates an object that can be used with both the properties and methods associated with the Array object. Once an Array object has been declared, the same object need not be declared again.

Methods

The Array object has twelve methods. Most of the methods are used to format the contents of the different elements that make up arrays. However, other methods, such as push() and pop() add or subtract elements to or from arrays. You will find a good deal of functionality in the methods associated with arrays, and these methods provide the developer with a very nice set of options to work with in arrays.

concat()
array.concat(): Method

The concat() method ties together or concatenates two or more arrays. Use the format:

```
array3=array1.concat(array2)
```

or:

```
array1=array1.concat(array2)
```

You can use the same or different arrays to make a third or combine two into one of the original arrays. For example, the following creates a third array from two existing arrays:

```
guys = new Array("Tom", "Dick", "Harry");
gals = new Array("Suzy", "Nancy", "Barbara");
guysNgals = guys.concat(gals);
for (var extract = 0; extract<6; extract++) {
    trace(guysNgals[extract]);
}
```

The new array, guysNgals, did not involve a constructor to create the Array object. So, even though creating the Array object with the Array constructor is recommended so that you can see what kind of object it is, doing so is not required. While less descriptive, the same results can be generated by the following script:

```
guys = new Array("Tom", "Dick", "Harry");
gals = new Array("Suzy", "Nancy", "Barbara");
guys = guys.concat(gals);
for (var extract = 0; extract<6; extract++) {
    trace(guys[extract]);
}
```

which simply concatenates the second array to the first.

ACTIONSCRIPT OBJECTS

join

array.join(): Method

Elements in an array are made into a single concatenated string with an optional separator. The separator can be any set of characters you want. For example, the following revives an old rock group:

```
var oddCombo = new Array("Guns", "Roses")
trace(oddCombo.join(" & "))
//Returns Guns & Roses
```

While at first, the join() method may appear to be the same as the concat() method with the added optional separator, it is not. The join() method joins the elements into a single string within a single array, while concat() concatenates two or more arrays, leaving the elements alone.

pop

array.pop(): Method

The pop() method returns the last element in an array and removes it from the array. If you are familiar with the stack in programming or languages like FORTH or PostScript, you will be familiar with this LIFO (Last In First Out) process. This process is often compared with a stack of trays in a spring-loaded carrier. The last tray placed on the top will be the first one removed. The pop() method works the same way.

To see one application of using the pop() method with an array, the array is built on the main timeline, and then the pop() method is applied on a movie clip's timeline. Figure 8-1 shows the script associated with the main timeline and Figure 8-2 shows the script in the MC's timeline.

The script in the first frame of the main timeline needs to construct the Array object and place data into its elements:

```
//Make 3 copies of MC
for (x=1; x < 4; x++) {
    _root.ball.duplicateMovieClip("ball" + x, x);
}
stack = new Array("100", "100", "200", "200", "300", "300");
```

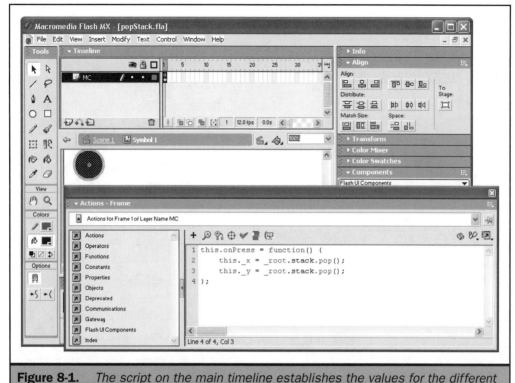

Figure 8-1. *The script on the main timeline establishes the values for the different elements of the array needed to position the object that actually uses the values in the array.*

Next, using the movie clip's timeline, a function literal is used to pop the information from the elements (beginning with 300, 300) and then work its way to the bottom of the array named stack:

```
//All duplicated MCs are in the same place
//The pop() method provides data for a new location.
this.onPress = function() {
    this._x = _root.stack.pop();
    this._y = _root.stack.pop();
};
```

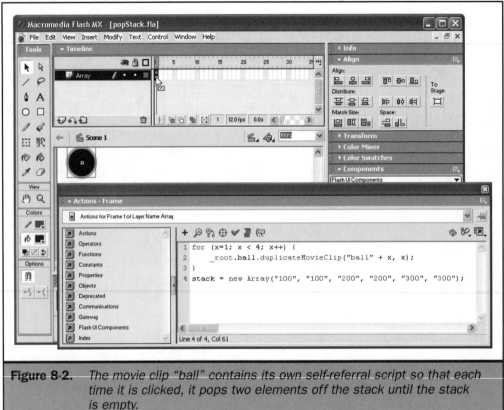

Figure 8-2.   The movie clip "ball" contains its own self-referral script so that each time it is clicked, it pops two elements off the stack until the stack is empty.

Figure 8-3 shows where the movie clip is positioned with the data from the array.

push

array.push(): Method

To add a new element value to an array, use the push() method to add it to the top level. Like the stacking trays used in explaining the pop() method, the push() method adds a tray on the top of the stack. Therefore, when the pop() method removes and returns the

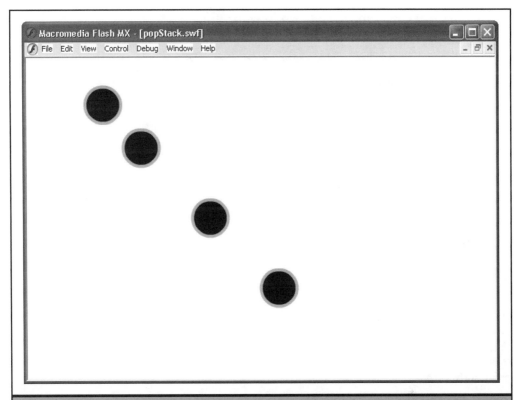

Figure 8-3.   *The array initially duplicates the movie clip, and each click repositions the movie clip.*

value of the top element in an array, it's always the one last pushed on the array. The following example shows how data is pushed onto a stack and then "popped" off:

```
stack = new Array("up", "down");
stack.push("sideways");
var beta = stack.pop();
trace(beta);
```

As you can see, "last in, first off" works with push() and pop().

reverse
array.reverse(): Method

The reverse() method simply reverses the order of the elements in an array. The top element is sent to the bottom and everything in between is reversed in its order. The following is a simple example:

```
var bigStates = new Array("New York", "Texas", "California");
trace(bigStates.reverse());
//Output = California,Texas,New York
```

shift
array.shift(): Method

The shift() method is like the pop() method, except rather than returning and removing the top item in the array, it does so with the bottom item. If you used array.reverse() and then array.pop(), you could do what array.shift() does in a single method. The following example uses the shift() method twice to show which elements are removed from the array.

```
var lineUp =new Array("Anderson", "Smith", "Jones", "Patterson");
trace(lineUp.shift());
trace(lineUp.shift());
```

The results show that the leftmost two elements are removed and displayed.

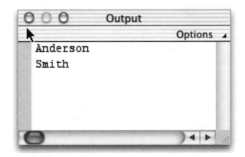

slice

array.slice(): Method

The slice() method requires two arguments, the starting and ending elements, in the following format:

```
arrayName.slice(s,e)
```

where a segment of array beginning with *s* and ending with *e* is extracted. However, unlike pop() and shift(), the original array is left unchanged. The following example shows how to select elements from the middle of an array:

```
var comSites = new Array ("Kerala", "London", "Boston", "Bloomfield");
var talkTo = comSites.slice(1,3);
trace(talkTo)
```

The outcome shows which elements are plucked from the array. The second parameter is 3, and one would conclude that would mean that Bloomfield would be included in the slice. However, the last index value is not inclusive, and so only London and Boston appear.

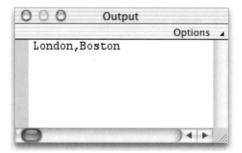

sort

array.sort(): Method

The sort() method arranges the elements in alphabetical order. You can sort the elements and then use the shift() method to open and display the elements in ascending order. (You could also use the reverse() method and then pop() the elements off the array alphabetically.) The following shows an orderly arrangement of ice cream flavors:

```
var favFlavors = new Array ("Chocolate","Strawberry");
favFlavors.push("Watermelon", "Peach");
var lineEmUp = favFlavors.sort();
trace(lineEmUp);
```

The outcome is quite predictable as you can see:

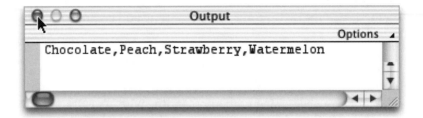

If you mix words beginning with upper- and lowercase letters, the lowercase letters have a higher value and so show up later in the sort. For example, the strings "chocolate", "Chocolate", and "Czech" would be sorted", Chocolate", "Czech", "chocolate".

sortOn

array.sortOn(): Method

The sortOn() method is new to Macromedia Flash MX. It works only with a special type of array broken down into elements containing several fields with the following format:

```
arrayEl[0]={cat1: "value", cat2: "value", catN: "value"};
arrayEl[1]={cat1: "value", cat2: "value", catN: "value"};
arrayEl[N]={cat1: "value", cat2: "value", catN: "value"};
```

The sortOn() method allows you to specify the category on which you want to sort your data. The statement has the following format:

```
arrayName.sortOn("categoryName");
```

The important feature of the statement is that the category for sorting must be in quotation marks. So while the categories in assigning element values are not in quotation marks, when an argument is placed in the sortOn() method, it must be. The following example shows a simple two-category array and how sortOn() works to sort by either method:

```
dogShow = new Array();
dogShow.push({breed:"German Shepherd", title:"Fuzz"});
dogShow.push({breed:"Gr Swiss Mt. Dog", title:"WillDe"});
dogShow.push({breed:"Collie", title:"Lassie"});
dogShow.push({breed:"Border Collie", title:"Nerves"});
dogShow.push({breed:"Great Dane", title:"Babe"});
```

```
dogShow.push({breed:"Saint Bernard", title:"Brandy"});
//Sort it out
function heel(category) {
    dogShow.sortOn(category);
    breed = title="";
 var cr=newline;
    for (i=0; i<dogShow.length; i++) {
        doggyType.text = breed += dogShow[i]["breed"]+cr;
        pupName.text = title += dogShow[i]["title"]+cr;
    }
}
//Button Scripts
_root.pupWho.onPress = function() {
    heel("title");
};
_root.pupWhat.onPress = function() {
    heel("breed");
};
```

Figure 8-4 shows the sorting on the category breed and Figure 8-5 shows sorting on the category title.

splice

array.splice(): Method

For adding or deleting elements to the middle of an array, you can use the splice() method. The general format requires up to three arguments:

```
splice(indexStart, delete #, newValues1, newValues2..)
```

The indexStart is the position in the array (the first element is 0) where you want to begin deleting elements or adding new values. Suppose you want to delete items 3 and 4 in an array with five elements. Because the third item is index 2, the first parameter you enter would be two, and you want the third and fourth items deleted, a total of two elements, so you would put in 2 for the second parameter as well. The following script shows this:

```
var alphabetChomp = new Array("a","b","c","d","e");
alphabetChomp.splice(2,2);
trace(alphabetChomp);
```

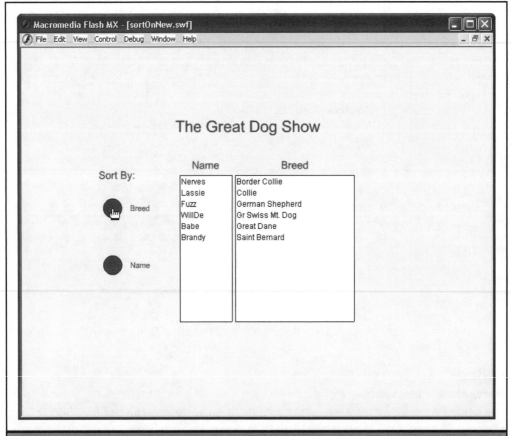

Figure 8-4.   *When the Breed button is clicked, the items in both columns are sorted on the type of breed.*

If you want to insert new values and delete nothing, you would place a 0 where the number to delete goes. Then you would simply add the new values separated by commas. The following shows how to splice() up a salad:

```
var salad = new Array("lettuce", "onions");
salad.push("tomatoes", "bell peppers");
salad.splice(2, 0, "cucumbers");
for (var counter = 0; counter<salad.length; counter++) {
    trace(salad[counter]);
}
```

As you can see, the output shows that the cucumbers went right in the middle of the salad.

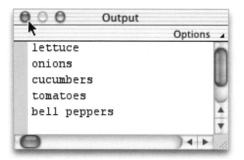

Figure 8-5. *When the Name button is clicked, the items in both columns are sorted on the dog's name.*

toString
array.toString(): Method

When you want an entire array converted to a string, use the toString() method. The element values are still separated by commas in the new string, but instead of being in separate elements, the values are fused into a single unit. The following script shows how an array is placed into a single variable:

```
var computerStore = new Array ("Computers", "Monitors");
computerStore.push("WebCams", "Software")
var I_want_it_all = computerStore.toString();
trace("Here's what I want:" + newline + I_want_it_all);
```

You will see in the outcome that all of the values are separated by commas.

unshift
array.unshift(): Method

The unshift() method adds elements to the beginning of an array. It is the opposite of the shift() method, which extracts and removes elements from the beginning of an array, hence the name unshift(). The following array adds two elements to the beginning of an array.

```
var RRmodels = new Array("Silver Spirit", "Silver Spur");
RRmodels.push("Silver Ghost", "Silver Shadow");
RRmodels.unshift("Silver Cloud", "Silver Wraith");
for (var spirit = 0; spirit<RRmodels.length; spirit++) {
    trace(RRmodels[spirit]);
}
```

The output shows six Rolls-Royce models, with the Silver Cloud and Silver Wraith added at the beginning.

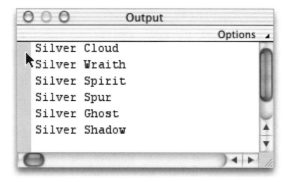

Properties

While the Array object has several methods, it has a single property. However, you will find that the property, length, is one that has many uses.

length
array.length: Property

The only property of the Array object is its length. The length is a property that contains an integer with the number of elements in the array. The length property value can be assigned during declaration by providing a value in the parameters. For example, the following would return a value of 7:

```
var stockPortfolio = new Array(7);
trace(stockPortfolio.length)
```

However, if you add new elements to the array, unspecified elements remain as part of the array's length. The following example sets the array length to 7 and then pushes three more elements into the array. The three elements do not fill up the first three of the unspecified elements with values in the original seven, but instead, they add to the total number of elements:

```
var stockPortfolio = new Array(7);
trace("Original constructor value="+stockPortfolio.length);
stockPortfolio.push("Macromedia", "Dell", "Apple");
trace("With 3 added elements="+stockPortfolio.length);
```

The outcome shows the number of the original and added elements:

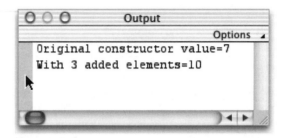

One of the most common and useful applications of the length property is as a loop limit in extracting information from an array. Rather than having to guess or set a break action using an unknown loop limit, the length of the array -1 provides the element values beginning with 0. The following script shows how the length property is used in this manner:

```
var salesRegions = new Array("West Coast", "Mountain");
salesRegions.push("South", "Central", "New England");
for (var extract = 0; extract<salesRegions.length; extract++) {
    trace(salesRegions[extract]);
}
```

The example shows that no matter how many new elements are pushed into the array, it maintains the correct number. The problem that may arise using the length of the array as a loop limit is when the array has been assigned a number of elements during its construction. Thus, in Macromedia Flash MX ActionScript, when you declare a new array, generally there is no good reason to specify the number of elements to reserve, because doing so may throw off the actual number of assigned elements in the array. However, with no "element reservation" in the construction of the array, the length property can keep an accurate count of the number of elements in the array, as the output for the example shows.

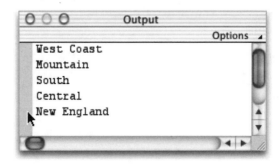

Boolean

The Boolean object has a constructor and two methods. To create a Boolean object that can use the methods, you need to do so with the Boolean constructor. The Boolean object is used to retrieve either the data type or string representation of a Boolean object.

new Boolean

new Boolean(): Constructor

Use the Boolean constructor to create a Boolean object that can be *used as an* object with the two methods available to it. An optional argument can be inserted following the Boolean logic as to its outcome. If no argument is used in the construction, the default value is false. The following script shows several different ways to construct a Boolean with an argument and what Boolean value is placed.

```
var Boole = new Boolean();
trace("empty="+Boole);
var Boole = new Boolean(3);
trace("3="+Boole);
var Boole = new Boolean(0);
trace("0="+Boole);
var Boole = new Boolean(true);
trace("true="+Boole);
var Boole = new Boolean("true");
trace("\"true\"="+Boole);
var Boole = new Boolean(null);
trace("null="+Boole);
```

You can see from the results that non-zero values (positive and negative) are interpreted as true, but strings are false, as are empty, zero, and null values.

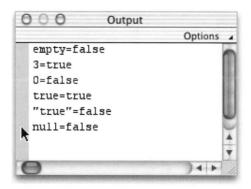

Methods

The two methods return either a string representation or a primitive value type. The string does not have Boolean characteristics, but is strictly a string object.

toString
Boolean.toString(): Method

When a Boolean object's value is converted to a string, it no longer has the characteristics of a Boolean value. It is strictly a string with all of a string's characteristics. The following script shows how converting a Boolean value into a string results in a false condition even though the original Boolean value is true:

```
var George = new Boolean();
George = 5>2;
trace("George is "+George);
var GeorgeString = George.toString();
if (GeorgeString) {
    trace("This is true Boole.");
} else {
    trace("This is only a string.");
}
```

As you can see from the outcome, the string transformation did not lead to a conditional finding of "true".

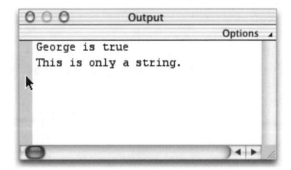

valueOf
Boolean.valueOf(): Method

The valueOf() method returns the primitive value type, true or false, of the Boolean object. Unlike the Boolean.toString() method that removes the Boolean characteristic of the value, the valueOf() method retains it. The following script is identical to the one above with the important difference that the valueOf() method replaces the toString() method.

```
var George = new Boolean();
George = 5>2;
trace("George is "+George);
var GeorgeString = George.valueOf();
if (GeorgeString) {
    trace("This is true Boole");
} else {
    trace("This is only a string.");
}
```

The following illustration shows how a Boolean object can be used to generate different outcomes.

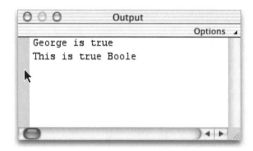

Date

To fully understand the Date object, you need to understand how the Date object gets its time and date. The time is either set up for UTC (Coordinated Universal Time) or local time based on your computer's clock. Actually, both UTC and local time depend on your computer's clock, but one is offset to UTC and the other is not. (For more on UTC, see the section "UTC" later in this chapter.) Different operating systems deal with the clock in slightly different ways, and they need to be examined prior to continuing.

- Windows allows the Date object to adjust automatically to Daylight Saving Time (DST). The only problem is that when you calculate future and past dates, DST stays in effect, which can throw off calculations.

- Macintosh OS 8 and OS 9 use the current DST without regard for the date or time in a calculation that may occur when the time is not DST. A July calculation made during Standard Time for the month of February (which is not in DST) in New York, for example, will miscalculate.

- Macintosh OS X is more like Windows in handling DST and automatically adjusts to it. Mac OS X contains a time zone database used to calculate the correct date and time.

When looking at the Date object and its many methods, try to think of it as more than a fancy clock. Macromedia Flash MX has many different uses for timing devices and comparing different times that may never appear in a clock in the traditional sense.

new Date

new Date(): Constructor

The Date constructor object is identical to other constructors used in ActionScript. The importance of constructing a Date object is to make an object that can be used with the many Date methods. For example, the following script will fail because a Date object has not been constructed:

```
var beta = timeEnough.getDay();
trace(beta);
```

The results are "undefined." However, if you add the constructor, the same script works fine.

```
timeEnough = new Date();
var beta = timeEnough.getDay();
trace(beta);
```

The output will be the day of the week code with the first being 0 for Sunday.

Methods

Prior to using any of the methods, the Date object must first be constructed. The Date methods are divided into categories: get() and set(). The get() methods retrieve values from Date objects, and the set() methods assign values to Date objects.

getDate()

Date.getDate(): Method

The getDate() method returns the day of the month as a number between 1 and 31. Note that the value range begins with 1 instead of 0, so you need not use an offset to display the correct date number.

```
var useDate=new Date();
trace("The day of the month is now "+ useDate.getDate()+".");
```

The output shows the exact day of the month. (When you try this, the odds are about 1 in 30 you will see the same output on the day you try it out.)

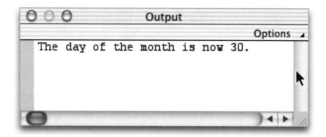

getDay()

Date.getDay(): Method

The getDay() method returns the day of the week expressed as a value between 0 and 6, with Sunday = 0. A simple array can translate the output into text versions of the day of the week:

```
var today = new Array("Sunday", "Monday", "Tuesday");
today.push("Wednesday", "Thursday", "Friday", "Saturday");
var useDate = new Date();
trace("Today is "+today[useDate.getDay()]+".");
```

By using text representations, you are less likely to confuse the starting point as 0 instead of 1 as shown in the output.

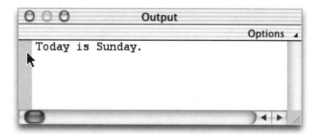

getFullYear()

Date.getFullYear(): Method

The getFullYear() method returns the current year in clear text, so you don't have to reformat the output:

```
var useDate = new Date();
var myYear = "The year is now: ";
trace(myYear+useDate.getFullYear());
//Depending on when you run this script
//your year will vary.
```

The output, as you can see, uses the common format without abbreviations or the need for conversions.

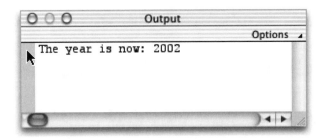

getHours()

Date.getHours(): Method

The getHours() method needs adjustment just about every time you develop an application that uses it. First, it returns 24 hours from 0 to 23 (Midnight = 0) which you may want converted into A.M. and P.M. formats. Second, you have to adjust for Daylight Saving Time. A simple script will return your 24-hour clock without any additional coding:

```
var useDate=new Date();
trace(useDate.getHours());
```

You just get an integer. For example at 7:59 A.M., you will get a 7. Nothing is rounded up or down because all the script requests is the hour, and all it returns is an integer between 0–23. The following script is a little fancier because it converts the time into A.M. and P.M.:

```
var useDate = new Date();
var timeNow = useDate.getHours();
if (timeNow == 0) {
    timeNow = 12;
}
if (timeNow>12) {
    timeNow = (timeNow-12)+" pm";
} else {
    timeNow += " am";
}
trace(timeNow);
```

For formatting non-military time, you get a clear result. Because most people are used to looking at analog clocks, the conversion saves them from doing the conversion.

getMilliseconds()
Date.getMilliseconds(): Method

The getMilliseconds() method returns 0–999 in milliseconds. (A millisecond is 1/1000 of a second, not to be confused with a microsecond, which is 1/1,000,000 of a second.) Generally you will not be using milliseconds for a visible clock on the stage, but rather for timing events. You can add delays between one time and another and then create variables you can compare. One way to set up a delay is to add a loop to hold up execution of the next action until the loop is complete. Then by adding another variable, you can get another time in milliseconds and compare the two variables. The following script shows how this might be done:

```
var useDate = new Date();
var now = useDate.getMilliseconds();
_root.viewer.text = now;
//Delay loop
for (x=0; x<1000; x++) {
}
//Comparison variable
var thenDate = new Date();
var then = thenDate.getMilliseconds();
_root.viewer2.text = then;
trace(then-now);
```

Setting up the now and then variables to have two different values requires a delay loop. The longer the loop, the more time between the first and the second reading of the current number of milliseconds. You can see the difference in the output window and the actual values in the two text fields.

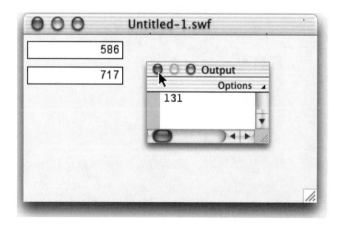

Using a loop as a delay mechanism is only for demonstration purposes. A more typical application of timing would be in setting up a preloader. When the preloader starts, put in the beginning code. Then, when it ends, put in the ending code to give you an exact reading of how long the loading takes.

getMinutes()
Date.getMinutes(): Method

The getMinutes() method returns the current minute of the hour in an integer between 0 and 59. The one characteristic of this method that requires a little extra scripting is the fact that no leading 0 precedes minutes below 10. So if you set up an hours and minutes clock, you have to remember to concatenate a leading 0 to not end up with an ambiguous time like 4:7 instead of 4:07. The following script should take care of that:

```
var useDate=new Date();
var now = useDate.getMinutes()
if (now<10) {
    now="0"+now;
}
trace(now);
```

To make a clock for hours and minutes, just add the hour component using the Date.getHours() method to the one getting minutes and you can easily add a clock to your movies. Here's how the combined script would look:

```
var useDate = new Date();
var pm = new Boolean();
var timeNow = useDate.getHours();
if (timeNow == 0) {
    timeNow = 12;
}
if (timeNow>12) {
    timeNow = timeNow-12;
    pm = true;
} else {
    pm = false;
}
var now = useDate.getMinutes();
if (now<10) {
    now = "0"+now;
}
```

```
function FlashClock() {
    if (pm) {
        clock = timeNow+":"+now+" pm";
    } else {
        clock = timeNow+":"+now+" am";
    }
    return clock;
}
trace(FlashClock());
```

Now whenever you need a clock, you can add the FlashClock() function and get a formatted A.M./P.M. clock as shown in the output.

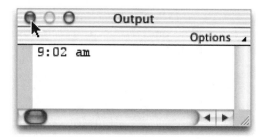

getMonth()
Date.getMonth(): Method

The getMonth() method gets the current month from 0 to 11, with January = 0. Like the days of the week, placing the words for the months instead of a value is done with an array. The following script shows a simple example that adds both the day of the month and the full year.

```
var useDate = new Date();
var monthNow = useDate.getMonth();
var textMonth = new Array("January", "February", "March");
textMonth.push("April", "May", "June");
textMonth.push("July", "August", "September");
textMonth.push("October", "November", "December");
today=useDate.getDate();
year=useDate.getFullYear();
todayIs=textMonth[monthNow]+ " "+today+", "+year;
trace(todayIs);
```

The output shows the current date, day, and year.

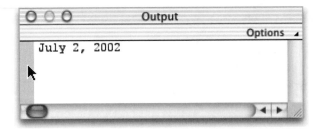

getSeconds()

Date.getSeconds(): Method

The getSeconds() method returns the current seconds between 0–59. Like hours and minutes, the seconds are considered to be an actual time and not simply timed intervals. Therefore, when you get a current second, it reflects the seconds on your computer's clock and not the number of seconds since the movie has been launched.

```
var useDate=new Date();
var now = useDate.getSeconds()
trace(now);
```

getTime()

Date.getTime(): Method

The getTime() method returns the number of milliseconds between Date() value and midnight January 1, 1970 GMC. This is a useful method for comparing two times in milliseconds. First, use the following script to see the number of milliseconds between the current time and midnight January 1, 1970:

```
var useDate=new Date();
var now = useDate.getTime()
trace(now);
```

Now, to do something useful with the number you get, you can make a little game using the timer. The movie uses 12 frames in the default 12 FPS so that each iteration takes one second. A timer will see if you can click the start button and stop it before the playhead reaches the end. Use the following steps to set it up:

1. Open a new movie and add two layers to the existing layer naming them Buttons, Text Field, and Labels, from top to bottom.

2. Select the first frame of the Buttons layer, and create a button symbol and drag three instances of it to the stage.

3. Position the three buttons as shown in Figure 8-6 and use the instance names beginTime, endTime, and replay.

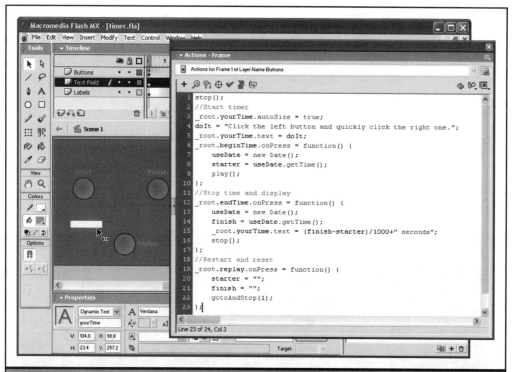

Figure 8-6. *By placing all of the script in the first frame, you will find that the script is easier to debug than looking for individual scripts in each of the buttons instances.*

4. Select the first frame in the Text Field layer and add a dynamic text field with the name yourTime.

5. Select the first frame in the Labels layer and label the buttons as shown in Figure 8-7.

6. Select the first frame in the Buttons layer and add the following script.

```
stop();
//Start timer
_root.yourTime.autoSize = true;
doIt = "Click the left button and quickly click the right one.";
_root.yourTime.text = doIt;
_root.beginTime.onPress = function() {
    useDate = new Date();
    starter = useDate.getTime();
    play();
};
//Stop time and display
```

```
_root.endTime.onPress = function() {
    useDate = new Date();
    finish = useDate.getTime();
    _root.yourTime.text = (finish-starter)/1000+" seconds";
    stop();
};
//Restart and reset
_root.replay.onPress = function() {
    starter = 0;
    finish = 0;
    gotoAndStop(1);
};
```

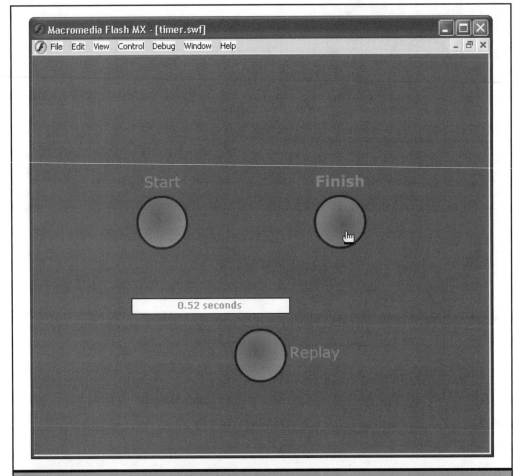

Figure 8-7. *By using the getTime() method, you can time changes from one event to another.*

getTimezoneOffset()
Date.getTimezoneOffset(): Method

The getTimezoneOffset() method calculates the difference in minutes between local time and UTC (Coordinated Universal Time, formerly known as Greenwich Mean Time, or GMT).

```
var useDate = new Date();
GMT = useDate.getTimezoneOffset();
trace(GMT/60+":"+GMT%60);
```

The final outcome can be read in hours if you divide the total by 60. Some places, such as India, have fractional hour differences. To accommodate those, you can use the modulo operator to get the number of odd minutes with the offset.

UTC

This next set of get() methods, and further on, several set() methods, employ UTC, an abbreviation for Coordinated Universal Time. The time is based on the time at 0 longitude in Greenwich, England. (People often still use the term "Greenwich Mean Time" or "GMT" to refer to UTC.) The longitude position (Z for zero) is sometimes used in the time reference to UTC (for example, 1134Z), and for this reason, pilots refer to UTC as Zulu time because Z in the pilot's phonetic alphabet is Zulu. Flight advisories are given in Zulu time rather than local time because flights frequently go from one time zone to another, and rather than schedule flight coordination around different time zones, it's easier to use UTC. In a world that gets smaller by the year, UTC is an important concept to understand in the Date object. Fortunately, the only difference between UTC and other time elements is that UTC begins at the zero position for standard time in Greenwich, England.

getUTCDate()
Date.getUTCDate(): Method

The getUTCDate() method returns the UTC day of the month (1–31). Essentially, the method is same as getDate() except that it uses UTC.

```
var useDate=new Date();
var now = useDate.getUTCDate()
//Returns day of the month.
```

ACTIONSCRIPT
OBJECTS

getUTCDay()
Date.getUTCDay(): Method

The getUTCDay() returns the UTC day of the week (0–6). Essentially, the method is same as getDay() except that it uses UTC.

```
var useDate = new Date();
var today = new Array("Sunday", "Monday", "Tuesday");
today.push("Wednesday", "Thursday", "Friday", "Saturday");
var now = useDate.getUTCDay();
trace(today[now]);
```

getUTCFullYear()
Date.getUTCFullYear(): Method

The getUTCFullYear() returns the UTC year (such as 2003). Essentially, the method is same as getFullYear() except that it uses UTC. (This will be different from getFullYear() for only 23 hours and 59 minutes.)

```
var useDate=new Date();
var now = useDate.getUTCFullYear();
trace(now);
//Returns full year
```

getUTCHours()
Date.getUTCHours(): Method

The getUTCHours() returns the UTC hours (0–23). Essentially, the method is same as getHours() except that it uses UTC.

```
var useDate=new Date();
var now = useDate.getUTCHours();
```

getUTCMilliseconds()
Date.getUTCMilliseconds(): Method

The getUTCMilliseconds() returns milliseconds of a UTC date. Essentially, the method is same as getMilliseconds() except that it uses UTC.

```
var useDate=new Date();
var now = useDate.getUTCMilliseconds();
trace(now);
//Returns current milliseconds 0-999.
```

getUTCMinutes()

Date.getUTCMinutes(): Method

The getUTCMinutes() returns UTC minutes (0–59). Essentially, the method is same as getMinutes() except that it uses UTC.

```
var useDate=new Date();
var now = useDate.getUTCHours();
trace(now);
//Returns integer between 0-59
```

getUTCMonth()

Date.getUTCMonth(): Method

The getUTCMonth() method returns the UTC month (0–11). Essentially, the method is same as getMonth() except that it uses UTC. The following example shows the text dates along with the other UTC Date methods for a UTC calendar.

```
var useDate = new Date();
var monthNow = useDate.getUTCMonth();
var textMonth = new Array("January", "February", "March");
textMonth.push("April", "May", "June");
textMonth.push("July", "August", "September");
textMonth.push("October", "November", "December");
today=useDate.getUTCDate();
year=useDate.getUTCFullYear();
todayIs=textMonth[monthNow]+ " "+today+", "+year;
trace("UTC date is: "+todayIs);
```

If you live in London, you will find this to be always accurate!

getUTCSeconds

Date.getUTCSeconds(): Method

The getUTCSeconds() returns UTC seconds (0–59). Essentially, the method is same as getSeconds() except that it uses UTC.

```
var useDate=new Date();
var now = useDate.getUTCSeconds();
trace(now);
//Returns integer between 0-59.
```

ACTIONSCRIPT
OBJECTS

getYear()

Date.getYear(): Method

The getYear() method is an unusual one. The year is based on 1900, and the current year is presented as the difference between 1900 and the current year. Thus, 2004 is 104.

```
var nowDate = new Date();
yr=nowDate.getYear();
trace("This year is "+yr+ " years after 1900");
```

The following illustration shows the output generated for the year 2002.

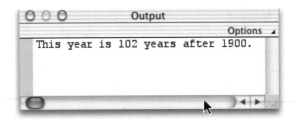

Set Methods

Setting the Date object is the reverse of getting Date information using the different get methods. In using the set methods, you need to be aware of the different values that each method uses with the Date object. Some values, like using 1-31 for the setDate() method and 0-6 for the setDay() method, have different beginning points. So keep your book handy while learning to use the many different values involved.

setDate

Date.setDate(): Method

The setDate() method is used to set the day of the month between 1–31. (It does not change your computer's internal clock.)

```
var useDate=new Date();
useDate.setDate(12);
var myTime=useDate.getDate();
//myTime = 12 no matter what the day is
```

setFullYear

Date.setFullYear(): Method

The setFullYear() method is used to set the year to the specified year using the format YYYY (for example, 2004):

```
var useDate=new Date();
var now=useDate.getFullYear();
useDate.setFullYear(1984);
trace("That was " + (now - useDate.getFullYear()) + " years ago." );
//Returns the time between the current year and 1984.
```

setHours
Date.setHours(): Method

The setHours() method is used to set the hours of the day using integers ranging from 0–23:

```
var useDate=new Date();
useDate.setHours(13);
trace(useDate.getHours());
//Sets the time to 1300 hours or 1pm.
```

While changing the hours in a script will affect the hours within that script, it does not change the actual time on your computer's clock.

setMilliseconds
date.setMilliseconds(): Method

The setMilliseconds() method is used to set the number of current milliseconds to an integer between 0 and 999. (Values over 999 reduced to the three rightmost values—for instance, 5432 reverts to 432.)

```
var useDate=new Date();
useDate.setMilliseconds(740);
trace(useDate.getMilliseconds());
//Returns 740
```

setMinutes
date.setMinutes(): Method

The setMinutes() method is used to set minutes between 0 and 59:

```
var useDate=new Date();
useDate.setMinutes(58);
trace(useDate.getMinutes());
//Returns 58
```

setMonth
date.setMonth(): method

The setMonth() method is used to set months between 0 and 11. January is 0 and December is 11.

```
var useDate=new Date();
var textMonth = new Array("January", "February", "March");
textMonth.push("April", "May", "June");
textMonth.push("July", "August", "September");
textMonth.push("October", "November", "December");
useDate.setMonth(10); //Sets November
trace(textMonth[useDate.getMonth()]);
//Returns November
```

setSeconds
date.setSeconds(): Method

The setSeconds() method is used to set seconds between 0 and 59:

```
var useDate=new Date();
useDate.setSeconds(22);
trace(useDate.getSeconds());
//Returns 22.
```

setTime
date.setTime(): Method

The setTime() method is used to set time in milliseconds relative to January 1, 1970. You can set precise dates using this method. For example, the following sets the date to July 5, 2003.

```
var useDate = new Date();
var textMonth = new Array("January", "February", "March");
textMonth.push("April", "May", "June");
textMonth.push("July", "August", "September");
textMonth.push("October", "November", "December");
useDate.setTime(1057318567576);
var nowDay = useDate.getDay();
var nowMonth = useDate.getMonth();
var nowYear = useDate.getFullYear();
trace("Date: "+textMonth[nowMonth]+" "+nowDay+", "+nowYear);
```

Obviously, setting the date using the setDate(), setDay(), and setFullYear() methods would be a good deal easier, but if you ever have need for very precise date setting, you can use the setTime() method. The following results are output:

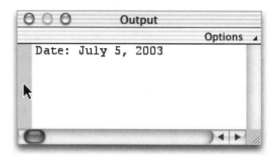

setUTCDate
date.setUTCDate(): Method

The setUTCDate() method is used to set the UTC day of the month (1–31):

```
var useDate=new Date();
useDate.setUTCDate(22);
trace(useDate.getUTCDate());
//Returns 22
```

setUTCFullYear
date.setUTCFullYear(): Method

The setUTCFullYear() method is used to set the UTC full year (such as 2020). It works like SetFullYear() except it starts at 0 longitude rather than the local longitude.

```
var useDate=new Date();
useDate.setUTCFullYear(2002);
//Returns 2002
```

setUTCHours
date.setUTCHours(): Method

The setUTCHours() method is used to set UTC hours (0–23):

```
var useDate=new Date();
useDate.setUTCHours(17)
//Sets time to 5pm
```

setUTCMilliseconds
date.setUTCMilliseconds(): Method

The setUTCMilliseconds() method is used to set UTC milliseconds (0–999):

```
var useDate=new Date();
useDate.setUTCMilliseconds(674);
trace(useDate.getUTCMilliseconds());
//Returns 674
```

setUTCMinutes
date.setUTCMinutes(): Method

The setUTCMinutes() method is used to set UTC minutes from 0–59.

```
var useDate=new Date();
useDate.setUTCMinutes(45);
//Returns 45
```

setUTCMonth
date.setUTCMonth(): Method

The setUTCMonth() method is used to set UTC months from 0–11. Like any of the other methods that deal with months where January is 0, using a text representation of the month clarifies the output. The following example illustrates that point:

```
var useDate = new Date();
useDate.setUTCMonth(5);
var textMonth = new Array("January", "February", "March");
textMonth.push("April", "May", "June");
textMonth.push("July", "August", "September");
textMonth.push("October", "November", "December");
var myMonth = useDate.getMonth();
trace("The UTC Month set to: " +textMonth[myMonth]);
```

The output for UTC set months is the same as any of the others.

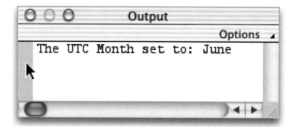

setUTCSeconds

date.setUTCSeconds(): Method

The setUTCSeconds() method is used to set UTC seconds from 0–59:

```
var useDate=new Date();
useDate.setUTCSeconds(30);
var justAsecond=useDate.getUTCSeconds(30);
trace(justAsecond);
//Returns 30
```

setYear

date.setYear(): Method

The setYear() method can either take an integer between 0–99 to add to the date 1900, or you can use it to set dates after 1999 simply by entering the whole year value. For example, the following script returns 1944:

```
var useDate = new Date();
var whatzUp=useDate.setYear(44);
var timezFly=useDate.getFullYear();
trace(timezFly);
```

However, if you put "2004" in the same script, it would return 2004. It really is a residual method left over from pre-Y2K concerns when most dates were entered as two-digit values in the 20th century. (I expect newer versions will simply accept any full date, such as 1778 or 2021.)

toString
date.toString(): Method

The toString() method coverts a date to a string. It is the easiest way to format a Date object so that it is clear and readable.

```
var useDate=new Date();
var stringTime=useDate.toString();
trace(stringTime);
```

If you don't mind the format, this is an easy way to generate a full readable date. The following output shows what the string looks like.

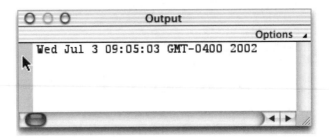

One of the undocumented methods is toLocaleString(). This method is part of the ECMA 262 standard that ActionScript attempts to follow. For example, the following script shows one use of it setting up a date object to output a clear date:

```
if (!Date.prototype.toLocaleString) {
    Date.prototype.toLocaleString = Date.prototype.toString;
}
rightNow = new Date(1970, 0, 1, 0, 0, 1031449600);
trace(rightNow);
```

UTC
date.UTC(): Method

The UTC() method is distinguished by the number of parameters it has as well as by its creation as part of the Date constructor. By using the UTC() method, the Date object is grounded in UTC time rather than local time. All of the parameters except two are optional in setting up a UTC() method constructor. The following arguments can be a part of the method:

- Year (required) four-digit integer using YYYY format (such as 2003)
- Month (required) integer from 0 (January) to 11 (December)

- Date (optional) integer from 1 to 31

- Hour (optional) integer from 0 (midnight) to 23 (11 P.M.)

- Minute (optional) integer from 0 to 59

- Second (optional) integer from 0 to 59

- Millisecond (optional) integer from 0 to 999

You must consider the time of day in setting the date parameter. In setting up the date July 4, 1776, I found that I had to put in an hour that would not put my time and UTC on different days. Midnight in London is one day, and in the United States it is the previous day. By adding the optional time as 12 noon, both the U.S. and UTC share the same day.

```
var independence = new Date(Date.UTC(1776, 6, 4, 12));
trace(independence);
//Returns- Thu Jul 4 07:00:00 GMT-0500 1776
```

Function

The Function object is actually any function, built-in or user, in an ActionScript program. Like other objects, the function can have methods and properties. However, functions are often used as methods themselves, so having functions with their own functions may seem redundant. However, the two methods available for Function objects help in launching the function. The one property of Function objects is the prototype used in creating them as a class.

Function.apply

Function.apply(): Method

The apply() method of the Function object has two parameters. First, it has an object parameter that specifies the object that the function applies to. The second parameter is the Function object along with its arguments. ActionScript code can call a function using the apply() method. Moreover, all functions are considered function objects. Both built-in and user functions are Function objects and can use the methods and property that apply to Function objects. For example, the following function simply gets the square feet of a shed wall, and then is invoked using the apply() method:

```
function shed(h, w) {
    return (h*w);
}
trace(shed.apply(this,[5,6]));
//Return 30
```

As you can see from the script, the parameters are specified as an Array object. Up to 10 parameters can be passed in this manner. The self-referent "this" is employed, but since no other object needs to be specified, the keyword "null" could have been used as well.

Function.call

function.call(): Method

The call() method can be used to launch a function. Generally, a function is fired by the simple format:

```
functionName(parValues);
```

or as a method for an object:

```
objectName.functionName(parValues);
```

However, with the call() method, you can specify the object you want to call as a method using the following format:

```
thisFunction.call(anyObject, parValues);
```

The following script shows how the Function object is first created and then called:

```
function circusArea(r) {
    return Math.PI * (r*r);
}
trace(circusArea.call(this, 7));
```

As you can see from the output, the results are no different than simply naming the function and providing values. By simply substituting another object's instance name, it is possible to fire the function for another object.

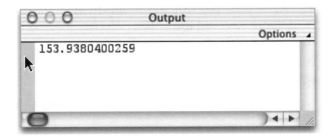

Function.prototype

function.prototype: Property

The prototype property is the only function property. Some confusion may accompany the concept of a function prototype because it is sometimes used synonymously with the function constructor. However, in ActionScript MX, the property is a reference to an object that is the prototype of the constructed class.

The following example shows how the depth function builds upon the shed function and then uses it as part of a new prototype:

```
function shed(h, w) {
    return (h*w);
}
function depth(h, w, d) {
    beta = shed.apply(shed, arguments);
    return beta*d;
}
depth.prototype = new shed();
billzShed = depth(5, 6, 10);
trace(billzShed);
//Return 300
```

You will get the same results whether or not you use the prototype property. What the prototype property accomplishes is to give the entire hierarchy of the object to the new instance so that only a single copy of the function exists in memory. Using prototype makes your script more efficient.

_global

_global.object/variable/class: Identifier

One of the more valuable additions to ActionScript MX is the _global identifier. Rather than being referenced to a timeline or locally declared variables and functions, the value of a globally defined variable or function is that they can be accessed from any timeline in the movie. For example, the following script is from a button inside a movie clip in Scene 1:

```
on(release) {
    _global.CusUser=_root.uname.text;
    _root.play();
}
```

ACTIONSCRIPT OBJECTS

In Scene 2, without reference to a path, the value of the variable is passed to a text field object (cusName):

```
cusName.text = CusUser;
```

It would not have been especially difficult to use the path back to the button in the first scene, but using the _global identifier, the process is made much easier.

Conclusion

This chapter presents the new object-oriented style that Macromedia Flash MX has adopted. While most of the objects in this chapter originated in earlier versions of Macromedia Flash, the orientation was not quite the same. New key terms like Function.apply and Function.prototype all point to a more robust type of object-oriented programming. The next chapter is a continuation of this chapter in that it covers the rest of the objects in the Core folder. As you will see, they too are primarily updates on previous versions of Macromedia Flash, but with certain key new elements that make them far more object oriented.

The Complete Reference

ActionScript

Chapter 9

Core Objects II

The remaining core ActionScript objects in this chapter dig deeper into the rich assortment of objects available in ActionScript. You will find the Math, Object, and Number objects in this chapter along with the special operator, super, and the keyword, this. The great bulk of information in this chapter, like the previous one, covers using the different methods associated with the objects.

However, the Object object is a special case and is associated with several new methods that add more power to constructs of OOP to ActionScript. Also, if you are not familiar with object hierarchy, now is the time to briefly look at the concept and to introduce object prototypes.

In creating an object, you can first make the object and then assign the object methods and properties. With Macromedia Flash MX, you should consider making and using more elements of creating a custom class. Custom classes are objects formed using a constructor function format. For example, the following creates a Boat class:

```
Boat = function() {
}
```

It defines a function class called Boat and the object Boat.

You can refine your class definition by adding different characteristics to the class definition. The following adds properties to the class called Boat:

```
Boat = function () {
    this.name = "Bloomfield Wavery";
    this.type = "sail";
    this.model = "flatty";
};
```

From a class you can add a subclass or "child" class to the object. The subclass inherits all of the characteristics of the parent class and can then add its own properties. The following example creates a child of Boat named Sail. The instance of the subclass Sail is dinky.

```
_global.Boat = function(shape,age) {
    this.shape=shape;
    this.age=age;
    this.compass=1
}
_global.Sail = function (power) {
    this.power = power;
};
Sail.prototype=new Boat();
```

```
Sail.prototype.feature="floats";
dinky=new Sail();
dinky.shape="tubby";
dinky.age=2;
dinky.power="sail";
trace(dinky.shape)
trace(dinky.feature)
trace(dinky.compass)
trace(dinky.age)
```

The Macromedia set of standards suggests using the prototype when creating classes. The reason for doing so is to minimize the amount of memory used to repeat the process for each new child object created or to recreate the same elements more than once. For example, an object is created like a class, and then prototype properties are added.

```
SampleObject = function () {
};
SampleObject.prototype.someProperty = "";
SampleObject.protototype.setProperty = function(propertyID) {
    this.propertyID = propertyID;
};
```

In looking at the objects in this chapter, keep in mind that you need not create a prototype for built-in methods and properties. However, in the development of more sophisticated structures, especially where objects are reused, adding a prototype will save memory and processing time.

Math

The Math object has 18 methods and 8 constants. Most of the common calculations used for geometry, statistics, trigonometry, and general mathematics are included. Unlike some other objects that require a constructor to create, the Math object does not, and you can use the object by simple assignment.

Methods

The methods in the Math object provide a number of different calculated outcomes. Before developing complex math algorithms, first be sure that what you need does not already exist as a Math method or consider using different Math methods to create the math structures that you need.

abs
Math.abs(): Method

The abs() method converts negative values into positive ones, leaving positive values unchanged. The real value in using the abs() method is in determining the difference between two numbers when one is a negative value. For example, in determining the past using negative values and the future using positive numbers, you will generate a positive value when comparing the two:

```
var past = -17;
var future = 21;
var range = Math.abs(past-future);
trace(range);
//Returns 38
```

You will find that using the abs() method prevents mistakes when finding the difference between a positive and negative value or finding differences based on subtracting one from the other. This can be especially tricky using variables because sometimes you will not know whether the value is positive or negative. For example, the following has a different outcome not using the abs() method:

```
var past = -17;
var future = 21;
var range = (past-future);
trace(range);
//Returns -38
```

You can also convert negative values into positive values using the abs() method:

```
trace(Math.abs(-21))
//Returns 21
```

acos
Math.acos(): Method

The acos() method takes a single argument between -1.0 and 1.0 representing the cosine of an angle. The method returns the arc cosine (the inverse of cosine) by an angle in radians. The following script returns the angle where the cosine of an angle is .25:

```
trace(Math.acos(.25));
//Returns 1.31811607165282
```

To convert radians into degrees, use the script:

```
degrees = radians * 180 /Math.PI;
```

where Math.PI is a Math object constant representing pi (3.14159265358979). By and large, you will not be converting degrees into radians because Flash uses radians instead of degrees in its calculation. However, in some calculations, you may have information about degrees that need to be translated into radians. That formula is

```
radians = degrees * Math.PI/180;
```

asin
Math.asin(): Method

The asin() method accepts an argument from -1.0 to 1.0 and returns the arc sine for the argument in radians. It is the inverse of a sine value. The following script shows how this works by first taking the sine value of an argument and placing it into a variable. Then the variable is used in an argument to return the arc sine and show the results in both radians and degrees.

```
var beta = Math.sin(1.25);
var delta = Math.asin(beta);
degrees = delta*180/Math.PI;
cr = newline;
trace("Radians: "+delta+cr+"Degrees: "+degrees);
```

You can see the relative values in the radians and degrees in the output.

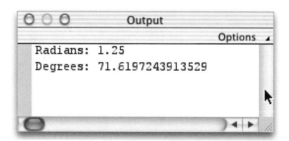

atan
Math.atan(): Method

The atan() method calculates and returns the arc tangent for the number specified in the argument. The arc tangent is the inverse of the tangent of an angle. The arc tangent

takes the tangent value of an angle and returns the angle in radians. The following
script shows first a tangent value extracted from a radian value of 1.38 and then retrieves
that same value using arc tangent displaying the results in radians and degrees:

```
var beta = Math.tan(1.38);
var delta= Math.atan(beta)
degrees = delta*(Math.PI/180);
cr=newline;
trace("Radians: "+delta+cr+"Degrees: " + degrees);
```

atan2
Math.atan2(x,y): Method

The atan2() method takes two arguments, a number specifying the horizontal (x)
coordinate of the point, and a number specifying the vertical (y) coordinate of a point.
The value returned is the arc tangent x/y coordinate in radians. The value represents the
angle opposite the opposite angle of a right triangle where x is the adjacent side length
and y is the opposite side length.

```
x = 300;
y = 200;
var arcTangent2 = Math.atan2(x,y);
degrees = arcTangent2*180/Math.PI;
cr = newline;
trace("Arc Tangent 2: "+arctangent2+cr+"Degrees: "+degrees);
trace("x="+x+" y="+y);
```

All of the relevant values can be seen in the output.

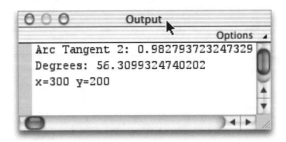

ceil

Math.ceil(): Method

The ceil() function rounds up. This method will round up any fraction to the next whole number. Use this when any fraction must be rounded to the next whole number, as when calculating packaged units, such as a six-pack of soda. For instance, if you are having a party with 20 people and you have to purchase six-packs, you would divide 20 by 6 and get 3.333, which means you would have to get four six-packs. Your party planner would look like this:

```
var partyAnimals = 20;
var sixPacks = 6;
var youNeed = Math.ceil(partyAnimals/sixPacks);
trace("You will have to get "+youNeed+" six packs.");
```

The size of the fraction after the integer is not important, as the following example illustrates:

```
x=4.0001;
y=4.9999;
xC=Math.ceil(x);
yC=Math.ceil(y);
trace("4.001 is now: "+ xC);
trace("4.999 is now: " + yC);
```

As you can see from the output, both values run through Math.ceil() end up the same.

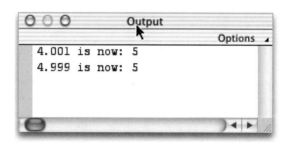

ACTIONSCRIPT OBJECTS

COS

Math.cos(): Method

The cos() method returns the cosine of an angle value provided as an argument. The angle value must be expressed as a radian. To find an x position of a point on the circumference of a circle, you can use the cosine. Using the formula

```
xpos = radius * Math.cos(angle);
```

you can locate the horizontal position by using the trigonometry from a right angle. The radius is the radius of the circle, and the angle refers to the angle opposite both the point on the circle and right angle of a right triangle.

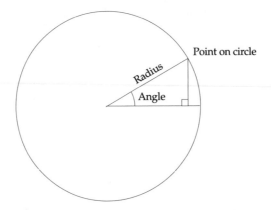

To get the vertical (y) position of a point on a circle, use the formula:

```
xpos = radius * Math.sin(angle);
```

The sine (Math.sin) method (see the sin() method further on in this chapter) combined with the cosine can locate a position on the stage. This next move is a little involved, but it shows an easy way to create a circle using the Math object and cos() method. Figure 9-1 shows the movie clip, its position on the stage, and size.

1. Open a new movie and draw a white circle with no stroke with the dimensions H = 7, W = 7.

2. Select the circle and press F8 to convert it to a movie clip.

3. Position the circle at X = 346 and Y = 200.

4. Give the circle movie clip the instance name disc in the Properties panel.

5. Click on the first frame and enter the following script in the Actions panel:

```
//Circle
for (var p = 0; p<360; p++) {
    xpos = 50*Math.cos(p*Math.PI/180)+300;
    ypos = 50*Math.sin(p*Math.PI/180)+200;
    _root.disc.duplicateMovieClip("disc"+p, p);
    _root["disc"+p]._x = xpos;
    _root["disc"+p]._y = ypos;
}
```

A loop with the index variable "p" generates values from 0 to 359 representing the degrees in a circle. The radius is 50 and the degree values generated by the loop are translated into radians. Both the x and y position values are given offsets to place the circle nearer to the center of the stage.

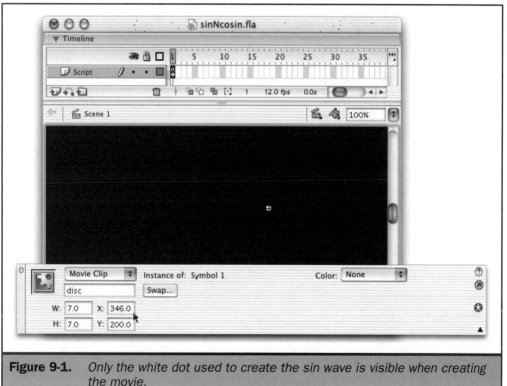

Figure 9-1. *Only the white dot used to create the sin wave is visible when creating the movie.*

The output shows a circle with a seven-point stroke. The original movie clip is hidden as a point on the circle.

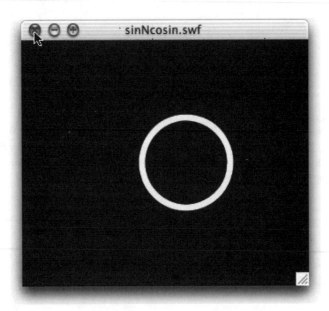

exp

Math.exp(): Method

The exp() method takes a single argument and returns the value of the base of the natural logarithm (*e*), to the power of the exponent specified in the parameter. For example, the following generates the value, 148.413159102577:

```
trace(Math.exp(5));
```

floor

Math.floor(): Method

The floor() method rounds a number down to the nearest whole. It functions the opposite of Math.ceil(), which rounds any fractions up to the next whole number. Compare the following script and outcome with the example in Math.ceil():

```
x=4.0001;
y=4.9999;
xC=Math.floor(x);
yC=Math.floor(y);
trace("4.001 is now: "+ xC);
trace("4.999 is now: " + yC);
```

As can be seen by the output, no matter how close the fraction is to the next higher number, the effect is simply lopping off any fractions.

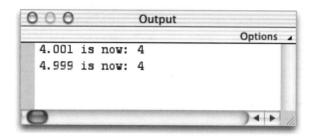

log

Math.log(): Method

The log() method accepts a single argument and returns the natural logarithm of the argument. For example:

```
trace(Math.log(5));
```

returns 1.6094379124341.

max

Math.max(v1,v2): Method

The max() method compares two values and returns the larger of the two. It compares only numbers. For example:

```
trace(Math.max(5,5.00001));
```

returns 5.00001, because the fraction makes the second number larger than the first. Because Boolean values will be interpreted as numbers in a numeric context, they can be used as arguments when using the max() method as shown in the following example:

```
var alpha= new Boolean();
var beta= new Boolean();
alpha = 6 > 4;
beta = 4> 6;
trace(Math.max(alpha,beta));
//Returns 1
```

min
Math.min(v1,v2): Method

The min() method compares two values and returns the smaller of the two. It compares only numbers. It works on the same principle as the Math.max() method except in reverse. For example, the following returns 6.9999 because it is .0001 less than 7:

```
trace(Math.min(7,6.99999));
```

pow
Math.pow(x,y): Method

The pow() method takes the value of the first argument and raises it to the power of the second argument. The second argument essentially instructs the first argument how many times to multiply itself. For example, the following function looks for two input values and applies the Math.pow() method:

```
function bringUp() {
    var beta = _root.value.text;
    var delta = _root.power.text;
    trace(Math.pow(beta, delta));
}
_root.pShot.onPress = function() {
    bringUp();
};
```

You can easily calculate any power of a value using the pow() method, and the values can raise rapidly, as shown by how quickly the value 4 is raised over 1000:

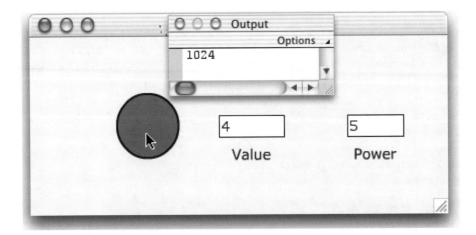

random

Math.random(): Method

The Math.random() function replaces the deprecated random() function. The method generates values from 0 to .9999999. Generally, developers use the value returned by the random() method and multiply it by the upper range of the value they want. Also, because random values are usually employed as integers, the values are rounded off to whole numbers using the floor(), ceil(), or round() Math methods. If you want to exclude the value 0 from the numbers generated, add 1 to the value generated. Using the floor() or ceil() methods, you can absolutely control the upper level of a generated value, and by using round() you can add a bit of range randomness as well.

This next example shows how the _x property of two movie clips can be randomly generated in a "rocket race." Figure 9-2 shows the stage and associated script. Use the following steps to set up the rocket race:

1. Open a new Flash file and add two layers to the existing layer and name them, from top to bottom, Winner, Red Rocket, and Orange Rocket. Add a second frame to each layer.

2. Select the Red Rocket layer, and draw a rocket with a width of about 100 and height of 60. Use a red fill to color it.

3. Select the rocket and press F8 to convert the drawing into a movie clip.

4. Select the Orange Rocket layer, open the Library panel, and drag a second instance of the rocket to the stage.

5. Select the second rocket and open the Advanced option in the Color menu on the Properties panel.

6. Click the Settings button next to the Color menu and change the right column values to R = 255, G = 50, leaving the remainder of the right column at 0 and all of the left column at 100%. You now have an orange rocket.

7. Select the red rocket instance and provide the instance name Blast. Then select the orange rocket instance and give it the instance name Buzz. Select both rockets and left align them with the stage. Position the orange rocket at Y = 125, and the red rocket at Y = 205. If the rockets overlap, move them up and down until they do not.

8. Click the Winner layer and draw a rectangle with dimensions W = 80, H = 22 and the word "Winner!" centered in the middle.

9. Select the rectangle and press the F8 key to convert the image into a movie clip. Drag a second instance of the Winner! movie clip to the stage. Select one of the Winner! clips and provide the instance name winZ, and then select the other and give it the name winT.

10. Position the winZ MC at X = 470, Y = 155, and the winT MC at X = 470, Y = 225. Select both and select Alpha in the Color pop-up menu and set the Alpha value to 0.

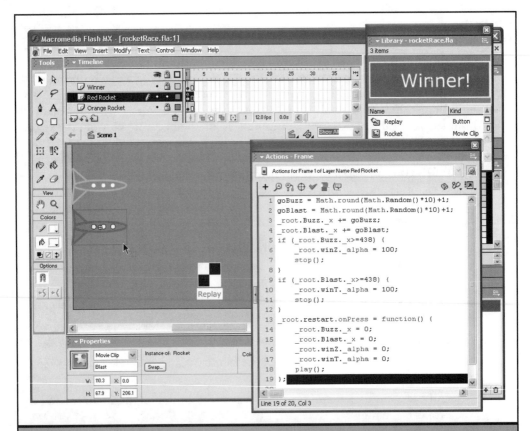

Figure 9-2. *A random assignment of horizontal positions of two movie clips can generate a race with unknown outcomes.*

11. In the Winner layer, draw a white square. In opposite corners of the square, draw two smaller black squares to create a black and white checkered pattern. Select the drawing and press F8 to convert the drawing into a button. Give the button the instance name restart in the Properties panel and then position the button in the middle of the stage beneath the two rockets. Add the label "Replay" below the button, using Figure 9-2 as a guide. Draw a vertical line with a stroke of 1, H = 320, X = 505, and Y = 80.

12. Select the first frame of the Red Rocket layer and add the following script in the Actions panel:

```
goBuzz = Math.round(Math.Random()*10)+1;
goBlast = Math.round(Math.Random()*10)+1;
_root.Buzz._x += goBuzz;
```

```
_root.Blast._x += goBlast;
if (_root.Buzz._x>=438) {
    _root.winZ._alpha = 100;
    stop();
}
if (_root.Blast._x>=438) {
    _root.winT._alpha = 100;
    stop();
}
_root.restart.onPress = function() {
    _root.Buzz._x = 0;
    _root.Blast._x = 0;
    _root.winZ._alpha = 0;
    _root.winT._alpha = 0;
    play();
};
```

The script is set up so that a tie is a possible outcome. Were it not, the rocket with the first-calculated position would have an edge over the one with the second-calculated position. The stop(); action in the conditional statements will stop the playhead, but it will not stop the calculation of either conditional statement's execution. Thus, if both are at the "finish line" (x >=438) at the same time, they both will be declared "Winner!" Figure 9-3 shows what the outcome of the random rocket race looks like.

round
Math.round(): Method

The round() method rounds fractions up or down to the nearest integer. If a decimal value is .5 or greater, the number will be rounded up, while if the decimal is less than .5, it will be rounded down. The following example shows a double use of Math.round() in rounding grades, first as individual scores in an array and then as an overall average to compute a grade:

```
var grades = new Array(76.4, 83.6, 77.2, 84.8, 91.09);
var range = grades.length;
for (counter=0; counter<range; counter++) {
    sigma += Math.round(grades.pop());
}
average = Math.round(sigma/range);
if(average >89) {
    trace("You got an A :"+average)
}
else if(average > 79 && average< 90) {
trace("You got a B :"+average)
```

```
}
else if(average > 69 && average< 80) {
trace("You got a C :"+average)
}
else if(average > 59 && average< 70) {
trace("You got a D :"+average)
}
else {
trace("You got an F Bart :"+average)
}
```

When the script executes, both the grade and rounded average appear. In most such computations, only the final score would be rounded, but double-rounding was used

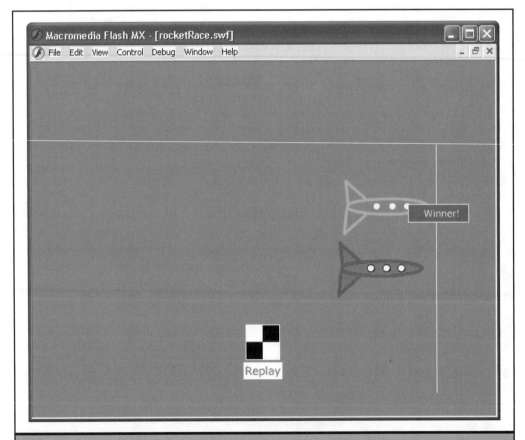

Figure 9-3.   *The Math.random() method generates a horizontal position until one or both reach the "finish line" where the winner is announced.*

in this example to demonstrate the use of the round() method. The results are seen in the output window.

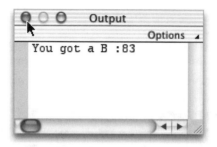

sin

Math.sin(x): Method

The sin() method generates the sine of an angle in radians. Using the sine and cosine you can generate different geometrical shapes in Macromedia Flash MX. The following shows the relationship between the sine, cosine, and angle in the context of a circle:

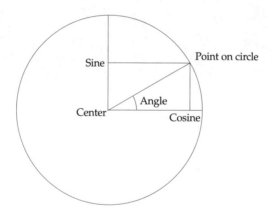

To see a sine wave in Flash, all you have to do is to generate values for angles from 0 to 359 (translated into radians) on the x axis and then position the sine value of the different angles on the y axis. By modifying the script used for creating the circle (see Math.cos() earlier in this chapter) creating the sine wave is simply a matter of removing the cosine calculation from the x position, as shown in the following:

```
//Sine Wave
for (var p = 0; p<360; p++) {
    xpos = (p*Math.PI/180)+100+p;
    ypos = 50*Math.sin(p*Math.PI/180)+200;
    _root.disc.duplicateMovieClip("disc"+p, p);
```

```
    _root["disc"+p]._x = xpos;
    _root["disc"+p]._y = ypos;
}
```

The oscillation generated in the script clearly shows a typical sine wave. (The lone dot marks the 0 point on the Y axis. Values above the line are minus sine.)

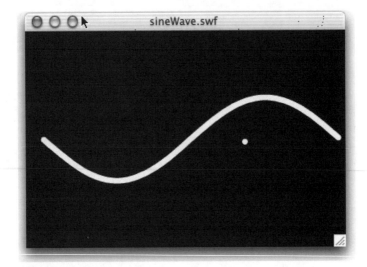

sqrt
Math.sqrt(): Method

The sqrt() method returns the square root of the argument supplied. For example, the following script generates a series of square roots from an array:

```
var Fibonacci = new Array(1, 2, 3, 5, 8, 13, 21, 34, 55, 89, 144, 233);
long=Fibonacci.length;
for (var counter = 0; counter<long; counter++) {
    trace(Math.sqrt(Fibonacci.pop()));
}
```

The Fibonacci series in the array is translated into the square roots of each value in the series.

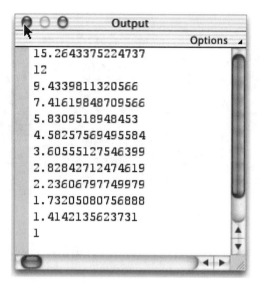

tan
Math.tan(): Method

Like the cos() and sin() methods, the tan() method calculates and returns the tangent of an angle expressed in radians. Among other uses of the tan() method is the generation of different designs. All designs generated are natural mathematical ones and can come up with some interesting effects. For example, if you change the cos() to tan() in the circle example used earlier in explaining how cos() works, you get a different result than a circle:

```
//Tangent Designer
    for (var p = 0; p<360; p++) {
        xpos = 50*Math.tan(p*Math.PI/180)+300;
        ypos = 50*Math.sin(p*Math.PI/180)+200;
        _root.disc.duplicateMovieClip("disc"+p, p);
        _root["disc"+p]._x = xpos;
        _root["disc"+p]._y = ypos;
    }
```

When you launch the script, you will be rewarded with an interesting design. The lone dot is the starting point.

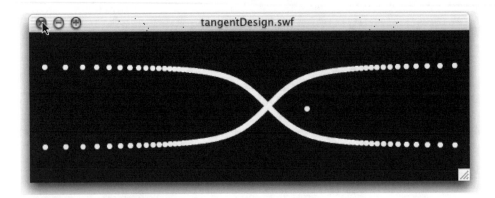

Constants

The Math object has a number of constants. Each of the constants has a single value and can be used as a property or variable assigned value. For example:

```
var beta = Math.LN2;
```

loads the variable beta with the constant of the natural logarithm of 2 or 0.69314718055994528623. Each of the constants needs to be linked to the Math object using the dot syntax. Hence, the assignment:

```
var beta = LN2;
trace(beta);
```

returns undefined instead of the natural logarithm of 2.

E

Math.E: Constant

The Math.E constant is a value for the base of natural logarithms expressed as *e*. The approximate value of *e* is 2.71828.

```
trace(Math.E)
```

LN10

Math.LN10: Constant

The Math.LN10 constant is the mathematical constant for the natural logarithm of 10. Its approximate value is 2.3025850929940459011.

```
trace(Math.LN10);
```

LN2

Math.LN2: Constant

The Math.LN2 constant is a mathematical constant for the natural logarithm of 2. Its approximate value is 0.69314718055994528623.

```
trace(Math.LN2);
```

LOG2E

Math.LOG2E: Constant

The Math.LOG2E constant is a mathematical constant for the base-2 logarithm of Math.E. Its approximate value is 1.442695040888963387.

```
trace(Math.LO62E)
```

LOG10E

Math.LOG10E: Constant

The Math.LOG10E constant is a mathematical constant for the base-10 logarithm of Math.E, with an approximate value of 0.43429448190325181667.

```
trace(Math.LOG10E);
```

PI

Math.PI: Constant

The Math.PI constant is a mathematical constant used to determine the circumference of a circle based on its radius. (PI * r is the value of the circle's circumference.) The value of pi is approximately 3.14159265358979.

```
//Area of a circle
```

```
function circleArea(r) {
    myArea = Math.PI*(r*r);
    trace(myArea);
}
circleArea(7);
//Results 153.9380400259
```

SQRTT1_2

Math.SQRT1_2: Constant

The Math.SQRT1_2 constant is a mathematical constant for the reciprocal of the square root of one half (1/2). Keep in mind that it is the reciprocal and not the square root of 1/2. Its approximate value is 0.707106781186548.

```
trace(Math.SQRT1_2)
```

SQRT2

Math.SQRT2: Constant

The Math.SQRT2 constant is a constant value of the square root of 2 with the approximate value of 1.414213562373.

```
trace(Math.SQRT2)1
```

Number

The Number object in ActionScript is the object for the number data type and now performs better than previous versions of Flash because it has become a native object. All of the properties can be invoked without using the Number constructor, but to invoke the methods, your Number object should be created using the constructor. (Numbers are native objects and, strictly speaking, do not have to be constructed.) For example, the following is the correct way to set up a Number object where the methods can be invoked:

```
var familyFortune = new Number(521);
var houseAddress = familyFortune.toString();
trace(houseAddress.length);
//Returns 3
```

The following script shows the different elements that the parser views depending on whether the value was constructed as a Number object or the transformed object:

```
var anyOldNumber = 521;
var familyFortune = new Number(521);
var houseAddress = familyFortune.toString();
trace(typeof(anyOldNumber));
trace(typeof(familyFortune));
trace(typeof(houseAddress))
```

As you can see from the output, each is distinctive.

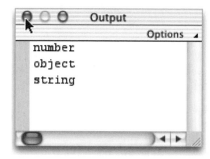

new Number

The Number constructor accepts an argument which then becomes the number object. For example, the following creates an object called longLine with a value of 50:

```
longLine = new Number(50);
```

However, a number variable can be transformed into a Number object. Try the following:

```
var longLine = 50;
trace(typeof(longLine));
longLine = new Number(longLine);
trace(typeof(longLine));
```

The output shows that the variable longLine is initially a number and then becomes an object after it is assigned itself in a Number constructor.

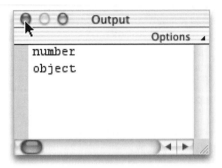

Methods

The Number object has two methods, which are invaluable for translating between decimal and both binary and hexadecimal. All hexadecimal values use the format:

```
0xHHHH
```

where H is a hexadecimal value between 0 and F. If a number is defined as a hexadecimal value, it must be transformed into a string for it to be displayed as a hexadecimal value. Otherwise, it will be displayed as a decimal value. Likewise, binary values must be displayed as strings even though all of the characters are numbers (0 and 1). For example, the following script illustrates a function for those who would like to display their age in a binary value:

```
function binaryAge(age) {
    biAge = new Number(age);
    trace(biAge.toString(2));
}
binaryAge(25);
//Returns 11001
```

Number objects converted to strings can be given any base you want. However, the more common ones associated with computing are base 2 (binary) and base 16 (hexadecimal). This next application converts decimal values into either hexadecimal or binary values using the Number object. The following steps outline the process for developing the movie:

1. Open a new movie, add a layer to the existing layer, and rename the layers Components and Text Fields.

2. Select the Components layer and drag two radio button components to the stage, the first from the Components panel and the second from the Library panel. Arrange them one above the other as shown in Figure 9-4.

3. Select the top of the two radio button components and in the Properties panel, click on the Parameters tab. Rename the label to Hexadecimal and add the name toHex to the Change Handler.

4. Select the bottom of the two radio button components and in the Properties panel, click on the Parameters tab. Rename the label to Binary and add the name toBinary to the Change Handler.

5. Select the Text tool and create an input text field to the right of the Hexadecimal radio button and give the text field the Instance name origNum in the Properties panel.

6. Next to the Binary radio button, add a dynamic text field and give the text field the Instance name convertNum in the Properties panel.

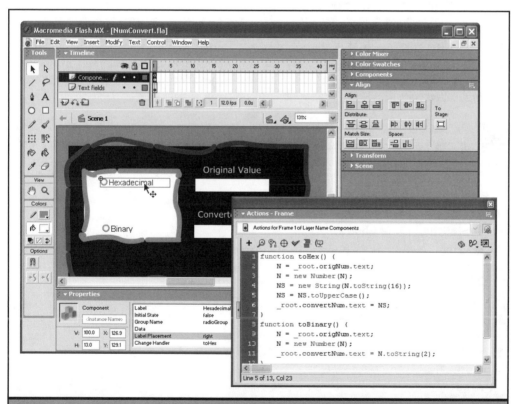

Figure 9-4. Radio button components are used to select between conversion from decimal to hexadecimal and decimal to binary. Each component has a separate function.

7. Click the first frame of the Components layers, open the Actions panel, and enter the following script:

```
function toHex() {
    N = _root.origNum.text;
    N = new Number(N);
    NS = new String(N.toString(16));
    NS = NS.toUpperCase();
    _root.convertNum.text = NS;
}
function toBinary() {
    N = _root.origNum.text;
    N = new Number(N);
    _root.convertNum.text = N.toString(2);
}
```

8. Use the Text tool and static text to label the top text field Original Value and the bottom Converted Value.

When you test the movie, enter a value into the Original Value text field and then click either the Hexadecimal or Binary button. Because both buttons work on an "on change" event handler, whenever you click either button you will see a hex or binary value in the Converted Value text field. Figures 9-5 (hexadecimal) and 9-6 (binary) show the conversion output.

Note *You can add background materials if you like. In the examples in Figures 9-4 to 9-6 you can see background rectangles. They were made using the Custom stroke lines with the values Thickness = 7, Type = Ragged, Pattern = Random, Wave Height = Wild, Wave Length = Long, Sharp Corners = selected. It gives the page a bit of an artistic twist.*

toString

Number.toString(n): Method

The toString() method does more than simply convert a number to a string. It also converts numbers into a base specified in the argument. For example, the following script converts a decimal number into a hexadecimal value.

```
yellow=new Number(16776960);
trace(yellow.toString(16));
//returns FFFF00;
```

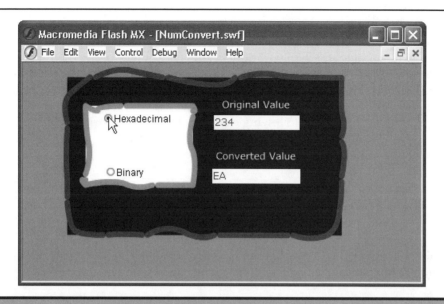

Figure 9-5. *When decimal is converted to hexadecimal the output is converted to all uppercase characters.*

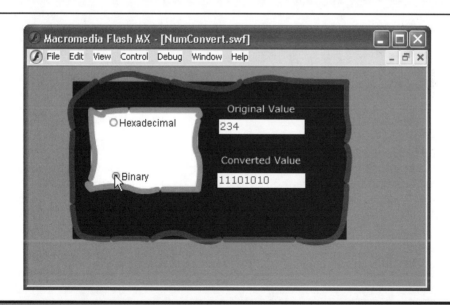

Figure 9-6. *Because the binary output is only going to be values made up of 0s and 1s, you do not need to convert them to uppercase letters.*

valueOf
Number.valueOf(n): Method

The valueOf() method returns the primitive value type of the specified Number object. When dealing with values from text fields, you can use the valueOf() method to convert the values to real numbers to add to other numbers. (You might recall that if you attempt to add values from text fields, they will concatenate with numbers rather than perform a mathematical addition.) The following example shows how a string value is initially used to create a Number object that is then converted to an actual number which is added to another number:

```
var hexy = new Number(0xfd034b);
trace(typeof (hexy));
trace(typeof (hexy.valueOf()));
```

When you execute the script, you will see that when the object is subject to the valueOf() method, it is considered a number, while prior to any method it was an object.

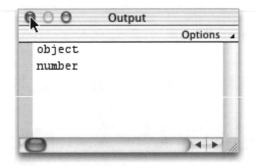

Constants

Number constants, like Math constants, have a single unchanged value. To be invoked, they must be a part of a Number object. The values connected to the Number object are those that represent positive and negative infinity, maximum and minimum values that can be displayed, and a value indicating the value is not a number (NaN). The constants are properties of the Number object and objects themselves. Typically, Number is used as a placeholder for the object and the constant's value is passed to a variable. For example, the following constructs a Number object of beta:

```
var beta = Number.MAX_VALUE;
```

However, instead of returning the type as an object, it is returned as a number. Define beta as a maximum value and then use the following script:

```
trace(typeof(beta));
```

The general use of these constants is error-checking for too large and too small numbers as well as for data that are not numbers at all.

MAX_VALUE

Number.MAX_VALUE: Constant

The MAX_VALUE constant is the largest number that ActionScript can represent. The read-only value is 1.79769313486231e+308. For example, the following script creates a huge number and then checks to see whether it is larger than the maximum value:

```
var huge = Math.pow(2345678, 2345678);
var bigChecker = Number.MAX_VALUE;
if (huge>bigChecker) {
    trace("The value is over the maximum value.");
}
```

Generating too large numbers is very simple using the Math.pow() method. By having such constants as MAX_VALUE, you can prevent lock-up in your computer.

MIN_VALUE

Number.MIN_VALUE: Constant

The MIN_VALUE constant is the smallest number that can be represented in ActionScript. This value is approximately 4.94065645841247e-324.

```
var tiny = Math.pow(2345678, -2345678);
var littleChecker = Number.MIN_VALUE;
if (tiny<littleChecker) {
    trace("The value is below the minimum value.");
}
```

Where a series of divisions occurs in a process, especially a loop, you may want to use this constant so that if the value falls below the minimum, you can trap it in order to stop the process.

NaN

Number.NaN: Constant

The NaN constant is an interesting one because it compares as unequal to any number including itself. Ironically, NaN is a property of a Number object and so will compare unequal to another NaN. For example, try the following script:

```
var Juan = "one";
var noNum = Number.NaN;
var bigMistake= Juan/3;
if(bigMistake != noNum) {
    trace("I'm confused.")
}
```

The variable Juan is a string, "one". Thus, when Juan is divided by 3, the results are NaN. However, when noNum, which is also NaN, is compared with the results of the variable, bigMistake, the results show that they are not equal even though they both are NaN. (You can use the isNan() function instead.)

The use of the Number.NaN constant is best employed as a way to store NaN in a variable and then use it as a global variable for reporting NaN where it is not automatically done in output. However, because it cannot be compared as unequal to generated NaN data, its use is limited.

NEGATIVE_INFINITY

Number.NEGATIVE_INFINITY: Constant

This value is returned when a number larger than -MAX_VALUE is generated in a script. It returns -Infinity rather than a value.

```
var tiny = Math.pow(2345678, -2345678);
var reallySmall = Number.NEGATIVE_INFINITY;
if (reallySmall == tiny) {
    trace("It's infinitely small, Sue");
}
```

POSITIVE_INFINITY

Number.POSITIVE_INFINITY: Constant

Whenever a mathematical operation or function returns a value larger than can be represented, it returns positive infinity. The POSITIVE_INFINITY represents that unrepresented value with the value Infinity. The following script uses the constant to trap such values:

```
var huge = Math.pow(2345678, 2345678);
var reallyBig = Number.POSITIVE_INFINITY;
```

```
if (reallyBig==huge) {
    trace("It's infinite, Jack");
}
```

Object

The core of the ActionScript class hierarchy is the generic ActionScript Object object. Like the built-in objects, the Object object can have properties and methods. However, no built-in characteristics initially accompany the Object object. You have to create them yourself. Once you begin working with objects, you can establish inheritance so that when an object is created, you can add other elements to it that inherit the properties and methods already existing in the object.

new Object

The Object constructor works very much like other object constructors. An identifier is assigned a new object:

```
computer = new Object;
```

Once an object has been constructed, you can then add different components to it. For example, the computer object, once created, can be given properties with values:

```
computer=new Object();
computer.memory="512MB"
computer.monitor="19 inch"
trace (computer.memory);
trace(computer.monitor);
```

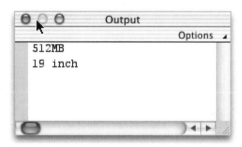

The following example creates a new object from the computer object:

```
computer=new Object();
computer.ports = new Object();
```

```
computer.ports.USB = 5;
computer.ports.IEEE1394 = 2;
trace("USB ports= "+computer.ports.USB);
trace("IEEE 1394 ports= "+computer.ports.IEEE1394);
```

The new object based on the computer object can now have its own properties and values.

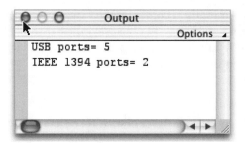

A crucial step in developing objects contained by other objects is putting the sequence of construction in the right order and constructing prior objects in position before attempting to construct a new object. For example, try running the following:

```
computer.ports = new Object();
computer.ports.parallel = 1;
trace(computer.ports.parallel);
```

The results show that the base object (computer) was not constructed.

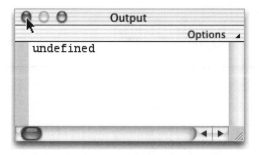

Methods

The methods associated with the Object object have their own unique characteristics. You will see how the getter/setter function works with some of the properties. Because it is a bit more elaborate than what you will see in other properties, you will want to spend some time with the method using the function. However, other methods should prove fairly familiar.

addProperty

Object.addProperty(prop,getFunc,setFunc): Method

The addProperty() method has three parameters. The first parameter is the name of the property you want to add. This name can be any identifier you want to use as a property. The second parameter gets the value for the property and its return value is used as the value of the parameter. The third property is a function that takes one parameter. The parameter is the new value of the property. For example, if the property "computer" has the assignment, computer ="3GHZ", the set function is passed the parameter "3GHZ" of type string. However, the return value of the set function is ignored. The following example shows how a getter/setter function of this type gets its value from the position of a movie clip with the instance name wheel. As the position of the wheel object changes, so too does the value of the computer object.

```
computer = new Object();
function getXpos() {
    var nowX = _root.wheel._x;
    return nowX;
}
function setXpos(n) {
}
computer.addProperty("Xpos", this.getXpos, this.setXpos);
trace(computer.Xpos);
_root.wheel._x += 50;
trace(computer.Xpos);
```

As you can see in the output, the second value is 50 greater than the first value because the movie clip was moved 50 pixels to the right.

Now make a slight change by reassigning the value of computer.Xpos by simple assignment:

```
computer = new Object();
function getXpos() {
    var nowX = _root.wheel._x;
    return nowX;
}
function setXpos(n) {
}
computer.addProperty("Xpos", this.getXpos, this.setXpos);
trace(computer.Xpos);
_root.wheel._x += 50;
trace(computer.Xpos);
computer.Xpos=300;
trace(computer.Xpos);
```

As you can see, the value of computer.Xpos does not change after it has been reassigned a different value.

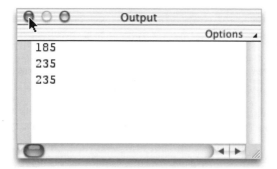

Rather, it keeps the value of the last position of the movie clip. So, once you define an object's property using the addProperty() method, you can only change the property's value by changing the value of the returned value of the "getter" function (first parameter). In the example above, the value is that of a movie clip's horizontal position on the stage.

registerClass
Object.registerClass(): Method

The registerClass() method is a powerful one. With it you can associate a movie clip symbol with an ActionScript object class. As soon as an instance of the specified movie clip symbol is placed on the stage after it has been registered to the specified object class, it is of the object class instead of the class MovieClip. The instance of the movie clip must appear after the symbol, for the instance has been registered as an object class. Thus, if a movie clip is registered in Frame 1 and then the instance of the movie clip appears in Frame 2, it is subject to the object's class. However, if the instance is on the stage at the same time as the instance's symbol is registered, it will not register as the object's class. Likewise, instances created by duplicateMovieClip or attachMovie after a movie has been registered as an object class will be treated as a class of the object rather than a MovieClip class. Also, the linkage properties of the symbol must be set to Export for ActionScript and Export in First Frame.

The general format for this method is

```
Object.registerClass("symbolName", className);
```

The "symbolName" is the name you give the symbol when you create it and in the Linkage Properties dialog box. The className is the class name, set up using the prototype property. To see how this method works, the next example sets up the ActionScript for a symbol on the stage, and then duplicates it so that the new instance can be subject to the registerClass() method. The following steps show how to create the movie:

1. Open a new movie and create a new layer. Name the top layer Actions and the bottom layer Helicopter.

2. In the Helicopter layer, draw a helicopter, select it, and press F8 to open the Convert To Symbol dialog box. Convert it to a movie clip symbol named whirlybird.

3. Drag the helicopter to the top-left corner of the stage, and while still selected, give it the instance name whomp in the Properties panel.

4. Open the Library panel and select the whirlybird name. Right-click (CONTROL-click on Macintosh) and select Linkage from the context menu.

5. Use "whirlybird" for the identifier and select the Export For ActionScript and Export In First Frame Linkage options. Click OK when finished. Figure 9-7 shows the instance on the stage with the Link Properties dialog box open and selected.

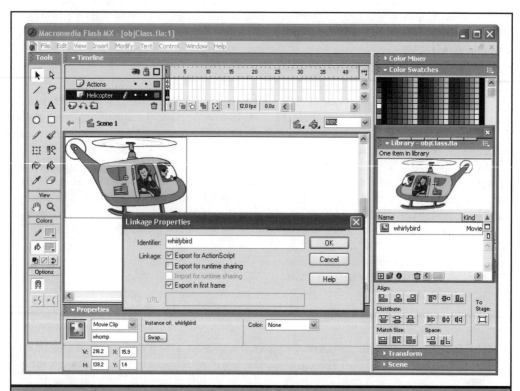

Figure 9-7. *A crucial step in setting up a movie clip to be registered as an object class is setting the correct linkages.*

6. Click the first frame in the Actions layer and type the script shown below and in Figure 9-8.

```
_global.motor = function() {
};
motor.prototype = new MovieClip();
motor.prototype.onPress = function() {
    this._x += 20;
};
Object.registerClass("whirlybird", motor);
duplicateMovieClip(_root.whomp,"whomp2",1);
whomp2._y = whomp._y + 200;
```

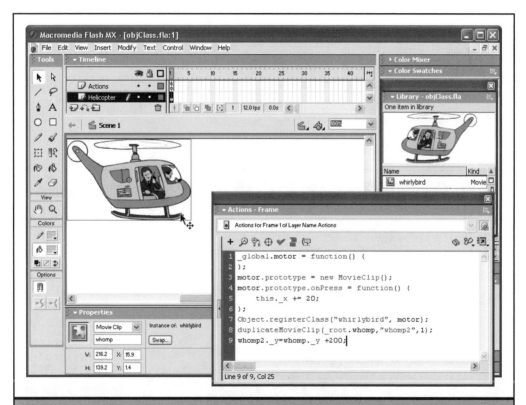

Figure 9-8.   *With only a single frame, it will be necessary to create an instance of the symbol used in the registerClass() method after it has been defined in the script.*

When you initially run the movie, you will see two identical helicopters, one above the other as shown in Figure 9-9. Run the mouse over both, and you will see that the cursor changes only when it is over the bottom helicopter. That is because the instance of the symbol was created after the registration of the symbol as an object class.

If you click the bottom helicopter, it begins moving toward the right with each click (see Figure 9-10). That is because the motor class includes a function that increases the object's horizontal position with each click on the object. You do not have to re-add the MovieClip class back into this mix unless you want to use its methods and properties.

toString

Object.toString(): Method

The toString() method converts an object to a string and returns it. For example:

```
address = new Object();
address=250;
address.toString();
trace(address + " Elm Street");
//Returns 250 Elm Street
```

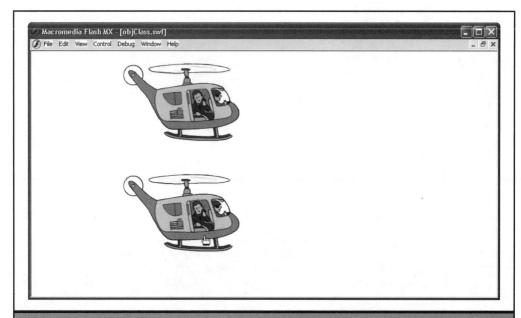

Figure 9-9.   *Only the bottom helicopter indicates that it is a "hotspot" when the cursor passes over it.*

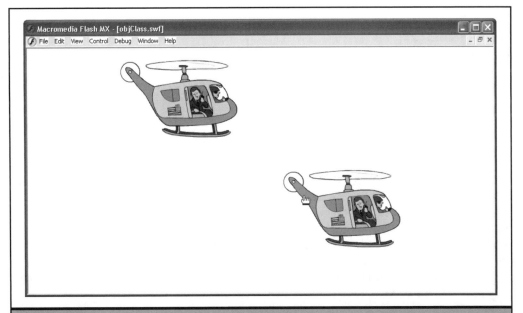

Figure 9-10.   *While the top object (which is part of the MovieClip class) remains immobile, the bottom object that has inherited the method of the class scoots to the right.*

unwatch
Object.unwatch(prop): Method

To appreciate the unwatch() method, you should first look at the Object.watch() method because the unwatch() method removes the watchpoint created by the Object.watch() method. The following shows an example of how the method is applied:

```
_root.stopWatch.onPress = function() {
computer.unwatch("memory");
}
```

If you add the script and a button with the Instance name of stopWatch to the example below explaining how the watch() method works, it will stop the watch() method.

valueOf
Object.valueOf(): Method

The valueOf() method returns the primitive value of an object, or if no primitive value exists, the object itself is returned. For example:

```
address = new Object();
address="Whatzup?";
```

```
var delta =address.valueOf();
trace(delta);
//Displays Whatzup?
```

As can be seen in the example, the value need not be a numeric one. No conversion takes place with the valueOf() method.

watch
Object.watch("prop", func): Method

The watch() method monitors a property associated with an object and fires a function whenever it changes. In movies where you want changes to occur whenever a property changes or reaches a certain level, the watch() method is quite useful. You can use it with either objects constructed with the Object constructor or other objects on the stage, such as movie clips. However, it will not work with either getter/setter properties or built-in ones like _x, _y, _rotation, and _alpha.

The first argument in the watch() method is a string with the name of the property. The property must be defined prior to the watch() method in the script. The second argument is the name of the function that launches when change to the property occurs. The watch function has three arguments:

```
watchFunction(id, oldval, newval)
```

The id is the name of the property. When setting up the watch() method, the id simply takes the first argument, the name of the property. The oldval is the original value of the property, and the newval is the most recently changed value of the property.

The following movie provides a simple illustration of how to use the watch() method. Figure 9-11 shows the initial stage. A drawing of a man and a computer, a dynamic text field, a button, and a simple movie clip set the stage.

Use the following steps to create the movie:

1. Open a new movie and add a single layer. Rename the top layer Actions and the bottom layer Computer.

2. Select the Computer layer and draw a computer.

3. Next to the computer draw a black rectangle and line extending to the computer and type the label Added Memory (static text) above the rectangle. Select the rectangle, line, and label. Press the F8 key to open the Convert To Symbol dialog box, choose Movie Clip as behavior, and click OK. Select the new MC and give it the instance name moreMem in the Properties panel.

4. Use the oval tool to draw a circle, select it, and press F8 to open the Convert To Symbol dialog box. Select Button for behavior and click OK. Provide the button with the instance name dataPump. Above the button add the static text label Data Pump.

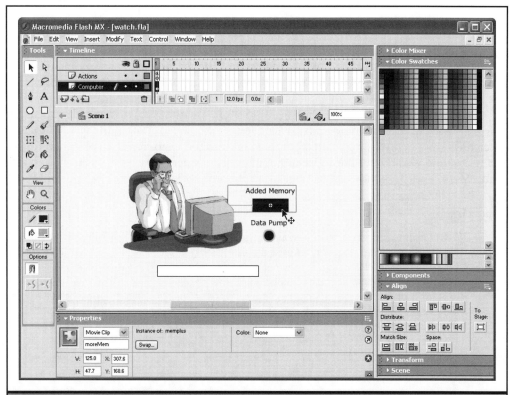

Figure 9-11. *The object property being changed is not on the stage, but will influence those objects on the stage.*

5. Click on the first frame of the Actions layer and enter the following script:

```
computer = new Object();
computer.memory = 1;
_root.moreMem._visible = false;
//Function that executes when change occurs
function watchMem(id, oldval, newval) {
    _root.watchVal.text = id+" "+oldval+"  "+newval+" MB";
    if (newval>50) {
        _root.moreMem._visible = true;
    }
}
//Watch method
computer.watch("memory", watchMem);
//Button script that will change property
_root.dataPump.onPress = function() {
```

```
        moreData += 5;
        computer.memory = moreData;
    };
```

Once you get the script in, you're all set to test the movie. When the movie first runs, click the Data Pump button. You will see the name of the property (memory), the initial value, and the new value, as shown in Figure 9-12.

As you continue to click the Data Pump button, the new values (newval) appear in the text field, but the old value (oldval) is no longer displayed. Within the watch function (watchMem) is a conditional statement that changes the visibility of an object on the main timeline. As soon as the value of the memory property exceeds 50, the MC object (moreMem) appears on the stage as shown in Figure 9-13.

Properties

Ironically, the only property associated with the Object object is only applicable to Flash 5 Player and is not recommended for Flash Player 6.

Figure 9-12. *The Data Pump button changes the memory property, which in turn fires the watch function.*

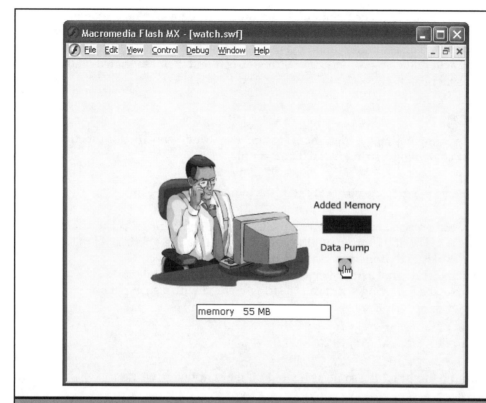

Figure 9-13. *The watch method fires the associated function each time the property changes, so you can trigger conditions within the watch functions that change other properties.*

__proto__

Object.__proto__: Property

The __proto__ property refers to the prototype property of the constructor function that created the object. In certain respects, the __proto__ is the "backward path" to an object's creator. However, __proto__ is not really supported in Flash Player 6 (even though it is in the Macromedia Flash MX ActionScript toolbox). It was originally in Flash 5 and supported by the Flash 5 player, and unless you plan your application for the older player, using __proto__ is not recommended.

String

ActionScript MX has a full component of string methods and properties compliant with ECMA-262 standards. String formatting is essential when using dynamic text fields and for passing string data between external data sources and Macromedia Flash MX.

Typically, external data is not formatted, and unless the data is to be presented as unformatted blocks of text, using and understanding the String object and its methods and properties is an essential skill to master. For those familiar with JavaScript or even Basic, you will find using ActionScript String objects and their associated methods and properties familiar.

new String

To create a String object, the identifier is assigned a String() constructor function, optionally containing a string literal. For example:

```
var beta = new String("All good things.");
```

creates a String object named beta with the value "All good things." (The quotation marks are not part of the string but the period is.) By creating a String object, you can use the methods and properties associated with the String object.

A string literal is not a String object even though string literals call string methods. For example, the following script calls a string method with a string literal:

```
var beta = "Flash";
trace(beta.charAt(3));
```

The output returns "s," the same as it would if the script were written:

```
var beta =new String("Flash");
trace(beta.charAt(3));
```

So what's the difference? If you use a string literal, the string is temporarily transformed into a String object by the ActionScript interpreter and then the String object is discarded after the method is called. The String object can use all of the properties, but the string literal can only use the length property.

Methods

The String object methods perform a number of different functions. The functions center on the position of characters in a string, substrings, and joining and separating strings. Strings include spaces and punctuation characters in addition to alphanumeric characters.

Character positions in strings are zero-based, like arrays. The first character is always 0, the second 1, the third 2, and so forth. However, when a string's length is returned using the length property, the value is the actual number of characters in the string. For example, the word "Flash" is 5 characters with the "F" in the 0 position and the "h" in the 4 position. Phrases like, "Flash MX ActionScript is heavy" follow the same rules as a single word. The following script, for example, returns 30 for the length and "y" for the last character calculated by subtracting 1 from the length:

```
var beta =new String("Flash MX ActionScript is heavy");
trace(beta.length);
trace(beta.charAt(beta.length-1));
```

charAt

String.charAt(x): Method

The charAt() method returns a character in a string at the position specified in the argument minus 1. The zero-position is the first and by adding 1 to the position, you can reinterpret the position to the number of the character in the string. For example, the following script looks for the @ in an e-mail address string:

```
var atSign = new String("bill@sandlight.com");
for (var counter = 0; counter<atSign.length; counter++) {
    if (atSign.charAt(counter) == "@") {
        trace("The @ sign is the "+(counter+1)+"th character.");
    }
}
```

Once the character is found, 1 is added to the index variable to show the adjusted position of the character.

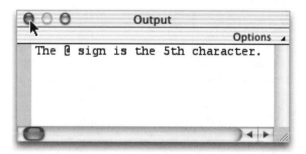

charCodeAt

String.charCodeAt(x): Method

The charCodeAt(x) method returns the ASCII code of the character at position x. It is similar to the charAt() method except rather than returning the actual character, it returns the ASCII code. For example, the following script takes the character in an input text field and puts the ASCII character in a dynamic text field:

```
characterOut.autoSize=true;
_root.asKey.onPress = function() {
    var someCharacter = new String(_root.characterIn.text);
    _root.characterOut.text = someCharacter.charCodeAt(0);
};
```

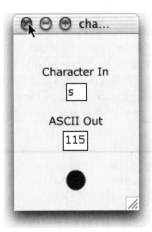

concat
String.concat(s1,s2,..sx): Method

The concat() method concatenates all the strings in the method's argument to a single String object:

```
var myTree = new String("leaf ");
//Note the space between the last letter
//and the quotation marks
var myTree = myTree.concat("branches ","bark ","tree house");
trace(myTree);
```

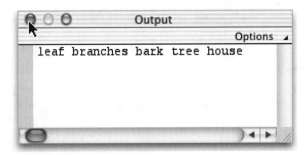

fromCharCode

String.fromCharCode(c1,c2,cx)

The fromCharCode() method works more like a function literal than other methods.
It takes the arguments and creates a string from ASCII or Unicode character values.
For example, the following uses a compound assignment to assign the valentine String
object the value of the character codes concatenated with " U":

```
var valentine= new String("I ");
valentine += String.fromCharCode(76,111,118,101) + " U";
trace(valentine);
//What to tell your sweetie on Valentine's Day.
```

If you attempt the following, it will *not* work:

```
var valentine= new String("I ");
valentine =valentine.fromCharCode(76,111,118,101);
trace(valentine);
//What NOT to tell your sweetie on Valentine's Day!
```

The String object "valentine" does not contain the codes, as it does with the
fromCharCode() method. The fromCharCode() method adds the characters derived
from the code they contain, and not the object using the method.

indexOf

String.indexOf(s,st): Method

The indexOf() method locates the first occurrence of a substring (s) in a string with
an optional start (st) position. In other words, it finds the first character of a substring
within a string using a zero-based index.

```
var delight="I knew you would like it."
var grad = delight.indexOf("like");
trace("She graduated from high school when she was " + grad + ".");
```

You can use the index to insert or delete text, or, as in this example, just use the
value of the position to pass on for any purpose at all.

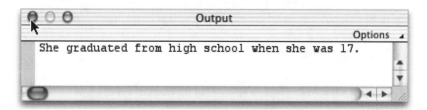

lastIndexOf
String.lastIndexOf(s,st): Method

The lastIndexOf() method searches for the first occurrence of the substring beginning with the last character. Like the indexOf() method, it uses a zero-point index; however, it finds the last occurrence of the substring rather than the first.

```
var quote="The day is for honest men, the night for programmers. --Euripides."
var lastFor = quote.lastIndexOf("for");
trace("The last \"for\" is in position " + lastFor + ".");
//With apologies to Euripides
```

slice
String.slice(s,e): Method

The slice() method creates a substring beginning at the position of the first argument and ending at the position of the second. The position points are both zero-based with the first character at position 0. The following shows how the slice() method is used on a string:

```
var pie = new String("A great big pizza.")
var thanks=pie.slice(12,17);
trace(thanks)
//Returns pizza
```

split
String.split(d): Method

The split() method serves to create an array of a string with breaks at some delimiter assigned by the developer. For example, the following creates a four-element array. The tilde (~) serves as the delimiter for the four elements that will make up the array.

```
var internetStuff=new String("WebCam~DSL~LAN~FlashCom")
var gimme=internetStuff.split("~");
trace(gimme[2]);
//Returns LAN
```

If you define the delimiter as empty quotes (""), each character is treated as a delimiter. For example, the following script breaks down the string into separate elements in an array:

```
var philosopher = new String("Plato");
var oldGuy = philosopher.split("");
```

```
for (x=0; x<oldGuy.length; x++) {
    trace(oldGuy[x]+"=element["+x+"]");
}
```

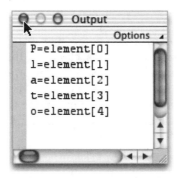

substr
String.substr(b,l): Method

The substr() method returns a substring of a string beginning at the value of the first argument and the length of the second argument. So if the first argument is 4 and the second is 6, it would begin with the fifth character (remember the first is 0) and be six characters long. The following example shows this:

```
var data = new String("Computer parts and television sets");
var tvs = data.substr(19, 15);
trace(tvs);
```

When separating elements from external data, using the substr() method can prove to be very useful.

substring
String.substring(b,e): Method

The substring() method returns a string beginning at the first argument and ending at the second argument. It is very similar to the substr() method, except rather than the second argument being the length of the substring, it is the ending position of the substring in the original string. The following example is identical to the one for substr() except that it uses the substring() method and the second argument contains an argument for the ending position.

```
var data = new String("Computer parts and television sets");
var tvs = data.substring(19, 34);
trace(tvs);
```

ACTIONSCRIPT OBJECTS

As you will see when you run the movie, the output is the same as it was for the example using substr(). However, look at the differences in the second arguments. One reflects the length and the other the position.

toLowerCase
String.toLowerCase(): Method

The toLowerCase() method forces all characters in a string to lowercase. When doing searches for substrings or even entire strings, changing the characters to all lower- or uppercase helps you find what you need. For example, the following creates a little "database" to simulate searching for a term to match. All you need on the stage is a button with the instance name goFind and an input text field with the instance named seeker. Select the first frame and enter the following script in the Actions panel:

```
_root.goFind.onPress = function() {
    var dbNames = new Array("Jane Williams", "Nancy Carter");
    dbNames.push("Jack B. Quick", "June Bug", "Sue M. All");
    dbNames.push("Harold Small", "John Smith", "Collin Cole");
    var search = _root.seeker.text;
    search = search.toLowerCase();
    for (counter=0; counter<dbNames.length; counter++) {
        var dbSearch = dbNames[counter];
        dbSearch = dbSearch.toLowerCase();
        if (dbSearch == search) {
            trace(dbNames[counter] + " is in database.");
        }
    }
};
```

When you launch the movie, you will see that you can put in a name in any case or combination of cases and always find the name if it's in the array:

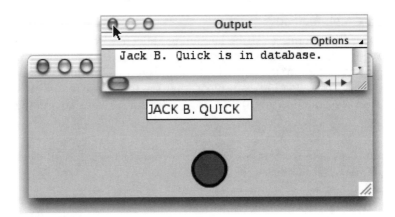

toUpperCase
String.toUpperCase(): Method

The toUpperCase() method forces all characters in a string to uppercase. It serves to take strings in any combination of cases and change them to uppercase. The following example shows how it works:

```
var loCase = new String("i want to shout!");
trace(loCase.toUpperCase());
//Returns I WANT TO SHOUT!
```

Whether you use the toUpperCase() or toLowerCase() method in creating search routines, it's always a good idea to stick with one or the other. Most databases have enough data entry errors to make searches difficult, but one area you can avoid is the misuse of cases in names either in search entry or database entry.

Property

The String object has a single property, length. However, you will find that this single property is one that has many uses.

length
String.length: Property

The only string property is length. It returns the length of a string based on the actual number of characters in the string, including spaces, and not the value of the last character, which is length-1. In several examples in this book, the length property has been used as a termination value in a loop examining string characters, but it can have further uses as well. For example, the following looks at a user name, and if the name is outside of the parameters, it is rejected:

```
var userName = "putz"; //Substitute others as well
if (userName.length>10 || userName.length<5) {
    trace("Your user name must be between 5 and 10 characters.");
    trace("Try another.");
} else {
    trace("Thank you, your user name has been recorded.");
}
```

Substitute the value of the variable userName to see how the length property can be used to detect different lengths.

super

super: Operator

A new Macromedia Flash MX operator, super, invokes the superclass method from within a subclass (child class). It may optionally include arguments from the superclass method. (Superclass refers to the parent class, and the super operator is invoked in the child class only.) The following example shows how super can be put into a child class and invoked from an instance of the child class method:

```
function MainEngine() {
}
MainEngine.prototype.fireUp = function() {
    trace("The main engine is on.");
};
function SupportEngine() {
}
SupportEngine.prototype = new MainEngine();
SupportEngine.prototype.engageSup = function() {
    //Invoke superclass method to perform its original behavior.
    super.fireUp();
    trace("Support Engine now operating.");
};
var engageAll = new SupportEngine();
engageAll.engageSup();
```

When you test the movie, both of the methods, fireUp() and engageSup(), are effectively invoked because within the engageSup() object, the fireUp() method belonging to the parent object was invoked using the super operator.

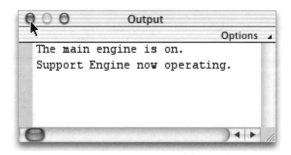

this

this: Keyword

The this keyword can reference an object or instance of a movie clip. Within a script attached to a movie clip, this reference is to the clip instance. For example, the following movie clip button shows one use:

```
_root.moveMyClip.onPress = function() {
    this._x += 10;
};
```

Whenever the movie clip button is clicked, it moves 10 pixels. In the same way, an object can reference itself using this, as the following example shows the myShed object doing:

```
function myShed(wallH, wallW) {
    this.wallH = wallH;
    this.wallW = wallW;
    this.wall = wallH*wallW;
    trace(this.wall);
}
var shed = myShed(8, 8);
//Returns 64
```

Conclusion

This chapter represents the end of the core objects in Flash. As an emerging object-oriented programming language, ActionScript provides a solid base of terms to create good OOP. The built-in core objects represent a wide array of possible uses for creativity in Macromedia Flash MX. However, most of the objects are general ones that can be found in JavaScript compliant with ECMA 262 standards.

The next chapter opens up much more specific, Flash-related objects. The terms in the Movie folder provide objects, methods, events, listeners, and properties that reflect the special characteristics of Flash. To use the Movie objects effectively, you follow the same good programming practices and considerations that you would with the core objects. The only difference is that the objects in the next two chapters focus on more concrete Flash elements.

ACTIONSCRIPT
OBJECTS

Chapter 10

Movie Objects I

The Movie folder contains the bulk of the key objects in Flash MX. To provide sufficient coverage for all of them, they have been divided into three separate chapters. This chapter examines the objects and their related elements within the Accessibility, Button, Capabilities (System Capabilities), Color, Key, and Mouse objects. Chapter 11 covers the MovieClip object, and Chapter 12 examines the objects associated with the Selection, Sound, Stage, System, TextField, and TextFormat objects.

Accessibility

The Accessibility object has a single method that you can employ to create accessible content with ActionScript. This single method is used to detect whether a screen reader is active.

isActive

Accessibility.isActive(): Method

The isActive() method returns a Boolean value indicating whether or not a screen reader program is currently active. This method can be used to guide the movie to a different set of behaviors if the screen reader is active.

```
var beta=Accessibility.isActive()
trace(beta);
//Unless the screen reader is active, returns false
```

Button

The Button object has expanded considerably since Flash 5. It now has 24 properties, 10 events, and a single method. In many ways, the Button object has gained most of the characteristics of a movie clip while retaining its unique characteristics, most notably its unique timeline.

Method

The single method for the Button object is to locate a button's depth relative to other buttons on the stage. It is employed as a read-only method.

getDepth

Button.getDepth(): Method

The getDepth() method checks the depth of a button and returns its depth relative to other buttons on the stage. As noted, an important feature of Macromedia Flash MX is the ability to assign a button an instance name. To find a button's depth, simply attach the getDepth() method to the button's instance name. The second button is assigned a depth 2 greater than the first button. For example, the following script takes three instances of buttons. Two of the buttons are instances of one symbol and the third button is an instance of a different button symbol.

```
var beta = _root.first.getDepth();
var delta = _root.second.getDepth();
var gamma = _root.third.getDepth();
trace("The first button's depth is: "+beta);
trace("The second button's depth is: "+delta);
trace("The third button's depth is: "+gamma);
trace("The difference is always: "+(gamma-delta));
```

The depths begin at -16383 and move toward zero as each new button is added.

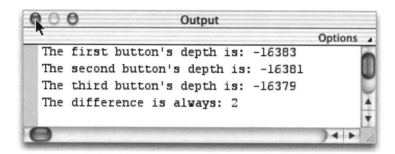

Properties

The Button properties deal with the different button states in Flash MX. These states can be changed to tailor the button to different uses in a Flash movie. For example, the enabled property allows the developer to disable a button under one set of circumstances and then enable it after the user has completed a task. Using the property can add to the usability of the movie by disallowing certain selections by the user under inappropriate circumstances.

enabled
Button.enabled: Property

The enabled property is a Boolean value that can be set. A button's default value is true, but you can disable a button by assigning it a false value. For example, place two buttons on the stage and assign the instance names flash and flow:

```
var beta = _root.flash.enabled;
_root.flow.enabled=false;
```

```
var gamma = _root.flow.enabled;
trace(beta); //Returns the default true
trace(gamma); // Returns false
```

After you run the movie, move the cursor over both buttons. The flash button shows a cursor change, indicating it is enabled, while the flow button does not. If you ever need to dynamically disable and enable buttons in a movie, use the enabled property simply by assigning Boolean values.

tabEnabled

Button.tabEnabled: Property

The tabEnabled property is generally associated with input text fields where users press the TAB key to move sequentially through a set of fields. This property is undefined by default, but you can set a button instance to be tab enabled by assigning it a true value. A true or undefined state of this property is included in custom tab ordering, but if set to false, it is not included. The following shows two buttons, one named larry and the other moe, which can be tab enabled or disabled:

```
_root.larry.tabEnabled = true;
var beta = _root.larry.tabEnabled;
_root.moe.tabEnabled = false;
var gamma = _root.moe.tabEnabled;
trace(beta);
trace(gamma);
```

tabIndex

Button.tabIndex: Property

The tabIndex property allows you to order the TAB sequence of objects in a movie. Undefined by default, you can establish a tabIndex property on a button, movie clip, or text field instance. Generally, tab indexes are associated with input text fields where the user types in information and tabs to the next field. However, buttons can be selected with the TAB key as well and have indexed tabs. The following shows a simple example:

```
_root.larry.tabIndex = 1;
var whaa = _root.larry.tabIndex;
_root.moe.tabIndex = 2;
var grrr = _root.moe.tabIndex;
_root.curly.tabIndex = 3;
var nuknuk = _root.curly.tabIndex;
trace("Larry is "+whaa);
```

```
trace("Moe is "+grrr);
trace("Curly is "+nuknuk);
```

trackAsMenu
Button.trackAsMenu: Property

The trackAsMenu property's value is a Boolean one that indicates whether or not other buttons or movie clips can receive mouse release events. This allows you to create menus. You can set the trackAsMenu property on any button or movie clip object. If the trackAsMenu property does not exist, the default behavior is false.

   You can change the trackAsMenu property at any time; the modified button immediately takes on the new behavior.

```
_root.clothes.trackAsMenu = true;
_root.clothes.onRelease = function() {
    this._alpha = 50;
};
_root.appliances.trackAsMenu = true;
_root.appliances.onRelease = function() {
    this._alpha = 50;
};
_root.toys.trackAsMenu = false;
_root.toys.onRelease = function() {
    this._alpha = 50;
};
_root.mcBut.onRelease = function() {
    this._alpha = 50;
};
```

useHandCursor
Button.useHandCursor: Property

The useHandCursor property allows you to either display the hand cursor when the mouse moves over an active button or not. The default value is true, but if you set it to false, when the cursor passes over an active button, it only shows the arrow cursor. However, both cursors will activate the event associated with the button. For example, the following script assigns a true value to a button with the instance name hand and a false value to a button named arrow:

```
_root.hand.useHandCursor = true;
_root.hand.onRelease = function() {
    this._alpha = 50;
```

```
};
_root.arrow.useHandCursor = false;
_root.arrow.onRelease = function() {
    this._alpha = 50;
};
```

When you test the movie, you will see that while the familiar hand appears over the hand button, it does not over the arrow button. However, both work to fire the script associated with both buttons.

Events

The button events are similar to those discussed extensively elsewhere in this book, and so they have been summarized here in Table 10-1.

Event	Description
BtnInstance.onDragOut	When the drag is off the button after it has been on the button
BtnInstance.onDragOver	Begin dragging inside the button, drag it out and drag it in again
BtnInstance.onKillFocus	Invoked when focus is removed from a button
BtnInstance.onPress	Responds to left mouse button press on target button
BtnInstance.onRelease	Responds when left mouse button press is released on target button
BtnInstance.onReleaseOutside	Responds to left mouse button press over target button and release off of target button
BtnInstance.onRollOut	Responds when mouse pointer begins over target button and rolls out
BtnInstance.onRollOver	Responds on mouse pointer moving over target button
BtnInstance.onSetFocus	Responds when a button has input focus and a key is released

Table 10-1. *Button Events Available for the Button Object in Macromedia Flash MX*

Most of the events have been discussed in Chapter 3, and both the focus-related events are examined in Chapter 12. For the other button events, a single movie has been made to demonstrate how you can use the events. Most of the events in this next movie are self-referring, but some reference other buttons. You may note how similar in behavior the buttons are to movie clips. Because in Macromedia Flash MX buttons can be referenced as objects, their properties can be changed dynamically. Use Table 10-2 for the color mixes and Figure 10-1 and the following steps to reconstruct it:

1. Open a new movie and add three layers to the existing layer. From top to bottom, name them Actions, Buttons, Button Backs, and Background.

2. Use the palette yellow mix for the background color.

3. Lock all layers except the background layer and use a red fill and brown stroke to draw backgrounds for Programmer's Blend, CAFE NADA, and the six cups on the left and right side (use Figure 10-1 for a guide). Also draw a brown 10-point line above the rectangles that will serve as backgrounds for the coffee cups. Lock the background layer.

4. Unlock the Button Backs layer and draw six circles with light tan fills and 3-point stroke using the Oval tool. Draw another, larger, circle in the middle of the 10-point line. Add the text as shown in Figure 10-1.

5. Lock all the layers except the Buttons layer. Draw a coffee cup using brown as a radial fill and the Fill Transformation tool to adjust the radial focus. Select the coffee cup and press the F8 key to open the Convert To Symbol dialog box. Choose Button for the Behavior and click OK. Place the coffee cup button in the larger circle in the middle of the line and give it the instance name mainCup. Drag six more coffee cup buttons from the Library panel and place them over the circles. From top to bottom, use the instance names cup1, cup2, and cup3 for those in the left column. From top to bottom in the right column, use the instance names cup4, cup5, and cup6. Lock the layer.

Name	R	G	B
Yellow	240	213	19
Red	212	0	34
Brown	97	38	30
Light tan	229	223	194

Table 10-2.   *Color Palette*

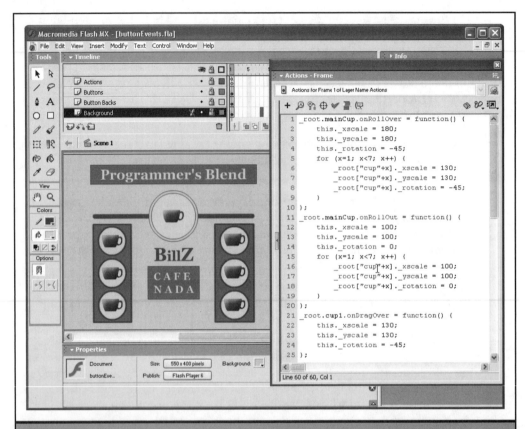

Figure 10-1. *All of the scripts for the buttons are associated with the frame instead of the individual buttons.*

6. Click on the first frame of the Actions layer, and enter the following script in the Actions panel:

```
_root.mainCup.onRollOver = function() {
    this._xscale = 180;
    this._yscale = 180;
    this._rotation = -45;
    for (x=1; x<7; x++) {
        _root["cup"+x]._xscale = 130;
        _root["cup"+x]._yscale = 130;
        _root["cup"+x]._rotation = -45;
    }
};
_root.mainCup.onRollOut = function() {
```

```
    this._xscale = 100;
    this._yscale = 100;
    this._rotation = 0;
    for (x=1; x<7; x++) {
        _root["cup"+x]._xscale = 100;
        _root["cup"+x]._yscale = 100;
        _root["cup"+x]._rotation = 0;
    }
};
_root.cup1.onDragOver = function() {
    this._xscale = 130;
    this._yscale = 130;
    this._rotation = -45;
};
_root.cup1.onDragOut = function() {
    this._xscale = 100;
    this._yscale = 100;
    this._rotation = 0;
};
_root.cup2.onPress = function() {
    this._xscale = 130;
    this._yscale = 130;
    this._rotation = -45;
};
_root.cup2.onRelease = function() {
    this._xscale = 100;
    this._yscale = 100;
    this._rotation = 0;
};
_root.cup3.onPress = function() {
    this._xscale = 130;
    this._yscale = 130;
    this._rotation = -45;
};
_root.cup3.onReleaseOutside = function() {
    this._xscale = 100;
    this._yscale = 100;
    this._rotation = 0;
};
_root.cup4.onRollOver = function() {
    this._rotation = 180;
};
_root.cup5.onRollOver = function() {
```

ACTIONSCRIPT
OBJECTS

```
        this._rotation = 180;
    };
    _root.cup6.onRollOver = function() {
        this._rotation = 180;
    };
```

When you test the movie, you will find that the buttons change depending on the scripted behavior (see Figure 10-2). When you move the mouse over the main cup, it changes all of the other cups as well as changing itself. To change the other cups, it uses a loop, but when you execute the movie, the changes should be too fast to see the sequence of the loop.

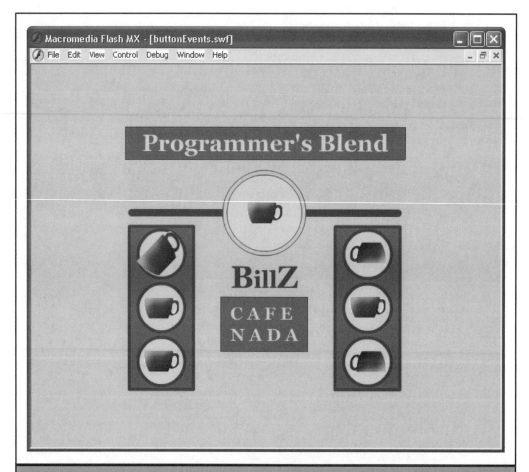

Figure 10-2. *The movie demonstrates most of the button events, and the buttons' actions are all part of the same script in the first frame.*

Capabilities

All of the capabilities refer to *system capabilities*, written as System.capabilities. These are features of the viewer's computer, and they can be very useful in making dynamic changes in a page to configure to the user's computer. In the very near future instead of configuring for a computer, the configuration may be for a device such as a personal digital assistant (PGA) or digital phone.

Properties

Many of the system capability properties return a Boolean value, but others return specific information about the system. Also, some of the properties are not part of the ActionScript toolbox, but they do perform in the same way as those listed properties. The language, manufacturer, OS, and version properties are valid system capability properties, but when you write a script using them, they do not turn to the expected color you have for coding property terms.

Very simple examples accompany the different properties. However, a movie that uses all of the properties in the ActionScript toolbox has been provided at the end of the individual definitions. The movie shows how to use the capabilities of resolution size to make changes to objects on the stage to adapt to the resolution sizes.

hasAccessibility
System.capabilities.hasAccessibility: Property

If the Flash player on the device supports communication between the Flash Player and accessibility aids, the property returns true. However, the default value is false. If special equipment is attached to the device for accessibility, the return should be true.

```
var gotCapability =System.capabilities.hasAccessibility;
trace(gotCapability);
//Returns false
```

hasAudio
System.capabilities.hasAudio: Property

The default Boolean for the hasAudio property is true. It simply indicates whether the player has audio capability:

```
var gotCapability=System.capabilities.hasAudio
trace(gotCapability);
```

ACTIONSCRIPT OBJECTS

hasAudioEncoder

System.capabilities.hasAudioEncoder: Property

The hasAudioEncoder property contains a Boolean value indicating whether the player is capable of decoding different types of audio:

```
var gotCapability=System.capabilities.hasAudioEncoder
trace(gotCapability);
//Default is true
```

hasMP3

System.capabilities.hasMP3: Property

The hasMP3 property contains a Boolean value indicating whether the player is capable of decoding MP3 files:

```
var gotCapability=System.capabilities.hasMP3
trace(gotCapability);
```

hasVideoEncoder

System.capabilities.hasVideoEncoder: Property

The hasVideoEncoder property contains a Boolean value indicating whether the player is capable of decoding video. This capability can be very important when using Flash Communication Server files with streaming video. If the player is older, it will not have that capability and can be tested for it prior to accessing a site that requires it.

```
var gotCapability = System.capabilities.hasVideoEncoder;
if (!gotCapability) {
    trace("You will need to get video encoding to see this page.");
} else {
    trace("You're all set for video.");
}
```

The above script checks for video encoding capability and lets you know if your system can decode video.

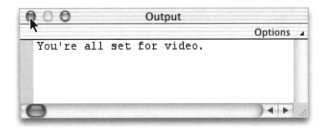

language

System.capabilities.language: Property

The language property returns different types of language capabilities depending on which one the system currently uses. For example, en-US is returned for American English. Others would be returned for British English, French, German, Japanese, and other languages that the system can work with.

```
var gotCapability = System.capabilities.language;
if (gotCapability == "en-US") {
    trace("This system speaks American English.");
} else {
    trace("This system does not speak American English, but");
    trace("it uses " + gotCapability + " instead.");
}
```

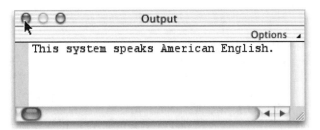

manufacturer

System.capabilities.manufacturer: Property

The language property returns "Macromedia" and the name of the operating system. For example, on a Windows XP OS, the property's value is

```
Macromedia Windows
```

while with any Macintosh, the property value is

```
Macromedia Macintosh
```

os
System.capabilities.os: Property

The os property returns the exact version of your OS. On the Macintosh, it breaks it down to the version number, while on Windows PCs, it returns the version of Windows being used.

```
var gotCapability=System.capabilities.os
trace(gotCapability);
//Example returns are Mac OS 10.1.5, Windows XP
```

pixelAspectRatio
System.capabilities.pixelAspectRatio: Property

The pixelAspectRatio property's value is generally 1. It represents the pixel aspect ratio of the current screen.

```
var gotCapability=System.capabilities.pixelAspectRatio
trace(gotCapability);
```

screenColor
System.capabilities.screenColor: Property

Because most computer monitors are color, the typical value of this property will be color. However, when other devices begin accepting Flash 6, you are more likely to find many are black and white (such as digital phones). Therefore, the information returned becomes more important to use in a script that may have more than a single display—one for color display and another for black and white. The three current values are color, gray, and bw.

```
var gotCapability=System.capabilities.screenColor
trace(gotCapability);
```

screenDPI

System.capabilities.screenDPI: Property

A typical Web page, including a Web page with Flash embedded, is 72 dots per inch (dpi). If the resolution is different on a screen, the designer can opt to have more than 72 dpi displays.

```
var gotCapability=System.capabilities.screenDPI
trace(gotCapability);
//72
```

screenResolutionX

System.capabilities.screenResolutionX: Property

The screenResolutionX property contains the horizontal (x) resolution on a screen. This information can be used to change objects you want to display. (See the following section, "Putting System Capabilities to Work".)

```
var gotCapability=System.capabilities.screenResolutionX
trace(gotCapability);
```

screenResolutionY

System.capabilities.screenResolutionY: Property

The screenResolutionY property contains the vertical (y) resolution on a screen. This information can be used to change objects you want to display.

```
var gotCapability=System.capabilities.screenResolutionY
trace(gotCapability);
```

In the following section, the sample movie demonstrates how to determine both vertical (y) and horizontal (x) screen resolution and then make changes so that no matter what resolution a user has, they will see the design in the correct relationship to their screen.

Putting System Capabilities to Work

In order to see how the capability properties work to determine a system's capabilities and how to use them, this section shows a movie that uses all of the capabilities in the ActionScript toolbox. Figure 10-3 shows the general setup and layers used.

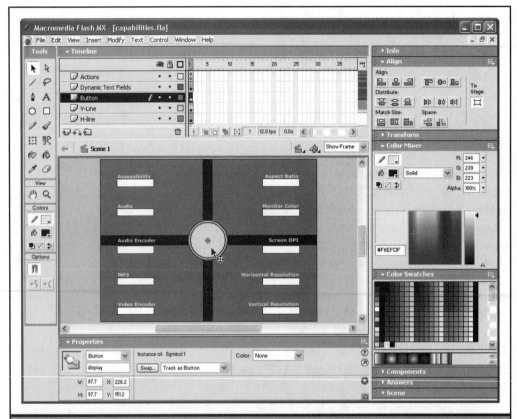

Figure 10-3. *The system capabilities are displayed in dynamic text fields when the large button in the middle is clicked.*

The movie uses the resolution capabilities information to change vertical and horizontal bars to fill the screen, regardless of the user's screen resolution. Because the stage size is 550 by 400 pixels, it uses the stage dimensions as baseline values to divide the horizontal and vertical resolution values returned by the system capabilities properties. Otherwise, the capabilities are simply displayed to show how to access them in a script. Use Table 10-3 for the color values used.

The following steps show how to put it together:

1. Open a new movie and add four layers to the existing layer. Name them from top to bottom, Actions, Dynamic Text Fields, Button, V-Line, H-line.

2. Click on the stage and in the Properties panel select gray for the background color.

Name	R	G	B
Gray	123	114	132
Yellow	255	230	49
Pale tan	246	239	223
Black	0	0	0

Table 10-3. *Color Palette*

3. Select the H-line layer and use the rectangle tool to draw a black borderless rectangle across the horizontal width of the stage (W = 550, H = 25). Select the rectangle and press the F8 key to open the Convert To Symbol dialog box. Select Movie Clip for behavior, and once created, give it the instance name hLine in the Properties panel. Center the rectangle horizontally and vertically with the stage. Lock the layer.

4. Select the V-line layer and use the rectangle tool to draw a black borderless rectangle across the vertical height of the stage (W = 400, H = 25). Select the rectangle and press the F8 key to open the Convert To Symbol dialog box. Select Movie Clip for behavior, and once created, give it the instance name vLine in the Properties panel. Center the rectangle horizontally and vertically with the stage. Lock the layer.

5. Select the Button layer and use the Oval tool to draw a circle with a 98-pixel diameter with a tan fill and 2-point black stroke. Select the circle, copy it, and then paste it in place. In the Transform panel, select 85% with the Constrain option checked. Change the fill color of the interior circle to yellow. Select the combined circles and press the F8 key to open the Convert To Symbol dialog box. Select Button for behavior, and once created, give it the instance name display in the Properties panel. Lock the layer.

6. Select the Dynamic Text Fields layer and create 10 dynamic text fields with five on the left side and five on the right, as shown in Figure 10-3. Select each one and provide instance names for each one, from top to bottom, left column and then right column, c1 to c10. Provide labels for each text field as shown in Figure 10-3. Lock the layer when finished.

7. Select the Actions layer, click on the first frame, and enter the following script:

```
_root.display.onPress = function() {
    _root.c1.text = System.capabilities.hasAccessibility;
    _root.c2.text = System.capabilities.hasAudio;
    _root.c3.text = System.capabilities.hasAudioEncoder;
```

```
_root.c4.text = System.capabilities.hasMP3;
_root.c5.text = System.capabilities.hasVideoEncoder;
_root.c6.text = System.capabilities.pixelAspectRatio;
_root.c7.text = System.capabilities.screenColor;
_root.c8.text = System.capabilities.screenDPI;
var xRes = System.capabilities.screenResolutionX;
_root.c9.text = xRes;
_root.hLine._xscale = (xRes/550)*100;
var yRes = System.capabilities.screenResolutionY;
_root.c10.text = yRes;
_root.vLine._yscale = (xRes/400)*100;
};
```

When you first run the movie, you will see that the vertical and horizontal lines do not extend to the top and bottom and sides of the screen. This will vary depending on the resolution and size of your screen. As seen in Figure 10-4, all of the dynamic text fields are blank as well.

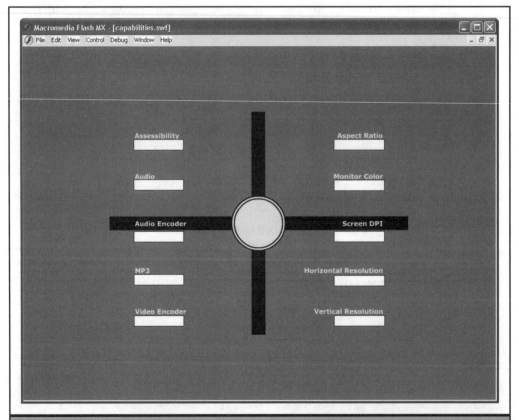

Figure 10-4.   *Before the script is launched, all of the values in the text fields are blank and the horizontal and vertical bars do not extend to the edges.*

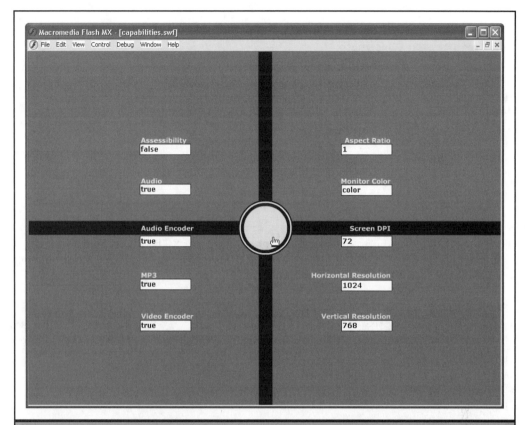

Figure 10-5. *By using the system capabilities in your scripts, you can dynamically change objects to maintain a design with different screen resolutions.*

As soon as you click the button, no matter what the screen resolution, the horizontal and vertical bars extend to the four sides of the screen. Figure 10-5 shows the changes in the lines and the system information about the computer.

Color

The Color object controls what you can do with color dynamically. You are able to target a movie clip and then use either RGB colors or the Advanced (transform) color combinations to change the MC's color. This section has two different movie projects that show how to use both RGB and Advanced colors. The first of the two movies shows how to create RGB sliders to mix colors that change a movie clip, and the second provides input text fields to enter different values to change Advanced colors.

The color object has a constructor and four methods. The methods either get or set RGB or Advanced (transform) colors. However, as you will see, with these few methods you can do a lot with color.

new Color

new Color(*target*): Constructor

The Color constructor creates an instance of the Color object for the movie clip specified by the *target* parameter. Once you have created the Color object, you can dynamically change the color of the MC by using the setRGB() Color method using the format 0xRRGGBB hexadecimal values. For example, the following script creates a Color object for the MC with the instance name canvas:

```
colorClip = new Color(canvas);
colorClip.setRGB(0xabcd45);
```

Methods

The Color object's methods are used to set or get different RGB values. Using base-16 (hexadecimal) values, you can create millions of different colors. In using Color methods, the toString() method is a much-used tool.

getRGB

Color.getRGB(0xRRGGBB): Method

The getRGB() method returns the numeric values set by the last setRGB() call. You must first set the value because the method does not return the original value.

```
colorClip = new Color(canvas);
trace( colorclip.getRGB().toString(16));
colorClip.setRGB(0xabcd45);
trace( colorclip.getRGB().toString(16));
```

As you can see, a 0 is returned for the original color, but the correct color is returned after the setRGB() method is called.

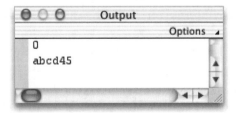

getTransform

Color.getTransform(): Method

The getTransform() method returns the transform value set by the last setTransform call. However, unlike getting color values as you do with getRGB() object information, the getTransform() method has two columns, one with the current offset and the other with the percentage values of the colors. One use is for getting and changing an original setting, as shown in the following, where "canvas" is the instance name of a movie clip:

```
picColor = new Color(canvas);
canvasTransform = new Object();
canvasTransform.ga = 55;
picColor.setTransform(canvasTransform);
canvasTransform = picColor.getTransform();
canvasTransform.aa=30;
picColor.setTransform(canvasTransform);
```

See the section on Color.setTransform() for a full explanation of what the different properties of the transform element mean and what values they have. All settings with the letters "r," "g," or "b" set an RGB (Red Green Blue) value, and settings that begin with "a" set an alpha (transparency) level.

setRGB
Color.setRGB(0xRRGGBB): Method

The setRGB() method sets an RGB color for an instance of the Color object using the format 0xRRGGBB. To get a good feel of how this method can be applied in a movie, the following example uses sliders to change the RGB value of both red, green, and blue movie clips and a movie clip that takes the mixed colors. Table 10-4 shows the color palette used (fairly muted colors) and Figure 10-6 shows the initial stage set up.

Using Figure 10-6 as a guide for placement and Table 10-4 for colors, the following shows how to create the movie:

1. Open a new movie and add three layers for a total of four. Name the layers from top to bottom, Actions, MC, Controls, and Background.

2. Select the Background layer, click on the stage, and choose gray from the palette for the background color.

Name	R	G	B
Muted green	165	178	153
Muted pale green	188	185	154
Gray	213	213	221
Midnight gray	55	60	55

Table 10-4.   *Color Palette*

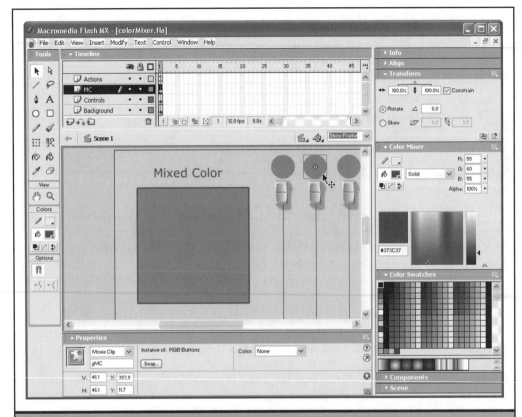

Figure 10-6. *The values of the individual RGB settings are set up to be changed using sliders displaying the decimal values for each color as well as the hexadecimal values for the entire mix.*

3. With the background layer still selected, draw three parallel black vertical 1-point lines 255 pixels in length with Y = 100. Position the first one at X = 342, the second at X = 409, and the third at X = 475. Lock the layer.

4. Create three slider buttons. (I extracted one already drawn from the Buttons Common Library panel and colored the top using the pale muted green with a radial to white.) Select the Controls layer and place the slider buttons at the top of the lines as shown in Figure 10-6. From left to right, give each slider button the instance names, rKnob, gKnob, bKnob. Lock the layer.

5. Select the MC layer and create a circle with a muted green fill color and no stroke with a diameter of 46 pixels. Select the circle and make a movie clip from it. Place an instance of the circle MC above all three sliders as shown in Figure 10-6. From left to right, provide them with the instance names rMC, gMC, and bMC.

6. Draw a square with sides of 225 pixels with a muted green fill and midnight gray border. Select the fill area, press the F8 key, and select Movie Clip for the behavior. Place the movie clip to the left of the three sliders and give it the instance name mainMC. Above the square MC, type in the label Mixed Color as shown in Figure 10-6.

7. Below the square movie clip, place a dynamic text field. Provide it with the instance name main.

8. Beneath the three slider lines, place three dynamic text fields with the instance names, from left to right, rVal, gVal, and bVal. Lock the layer.

9. Select the Actions layer, click on the first frame, and enter the following script:

```
redBall = new Color(rMC);
greenBall = new Color(gMC);
blueBall = new Color(bMC);
mainBlock = new Color(mainMC);
redVal = "0";
greenVal = "0";
blueVal = "0";
_root.rKnob.onPress = function() {
    startDrag(this, false, 340, 85, 340, 340);
};
_root.rKnob.onRelease = function() {
    var red = parseInt((_root.rKnob._y)-85);
    rVal.text = red;
    redVal = red.toString(16);
    if (redVal.length<2) {
        redVal = "0"+redVal;
    }
    if (greenVal.length<2) {
        greenVal = "0"+greenVal;
    }
    if (blueVal.length<2) {
        blueVal = "0"+blueVal;
    }
    redVal2 = "0x"+redVal+"0000";
    redBall.setRGB(redVal2);
    mainOne = "0x"+redVal+greenVal+blueVal;
    main.text = mainOne;
    mainBlock.setRGB(mainOne);
    stopDrag();
};
_root.gKnob.onPress = function() {
    startDrag(this, false, 406, 85, 406, 340);
```

```
    };
    _root.gKnob.onRelease = function() {
        var green = parseInt((_root.gKnob._y)-85);
        gVal.text = green;
        greenVal = green.toString(16);
        if (redVal.length<2) {
            redVal = "0"+redVal;
        }
        if (greenVal.length<2) {
            greenVal = "0"+greenVal;
        }
        if (blueVal.length<2) {
            blueVal = "0"+blueVal;
        }
        greenVal2 = "0x00"+greenVal+"00";
        greenBall.setRGB(greenVal2);
        mainOne = "0x"+redVal+greenVal+blueVal;
        main.text = mainOne;
        mainBlock.setRGB(mainOne);
        stopDrag();
    };
    _root.bKnob.onPress = function() {
        startDrag(this, false, 474, 85, 474, 340);
    };
    _root.bKnob.onRelease = function() {
        var blue = parseInt((_root.bKnob._y)-85);
        bVal.text = blue;
        blueVal = blue.toString(16);
        if (redVal.length<2) {
            redVal = "0"+redVal;
        }
        if (greenVal.length<2) {
            greenVal = "0"+greenVal;
        }
        if (blueVal.length<2) {
            blueVal = "0"+blueVal;
        }
        blueVal2 = "0x0000"+blueVal;
        blueBall.setRGB(blueVal2);
        mainOne = "0x"+redVal+greenVal+blueVal;
```

```
main.text = mainOne;
mainBlock.setRGB(mainOne);
stopDrag();
};
```

When you run the program, you may find that you have to make adjustments to the values so that the red, green, and blue variables range from 0–255. The script uses an offset of 85 because the slider button zero positions were 15 pixels above the top of the lines that had been positioned at Y = 100. Likewise, you might have to fiddle with the X position of the sliders as well. Figure 10-7 shows what you should see when you launch the movie.

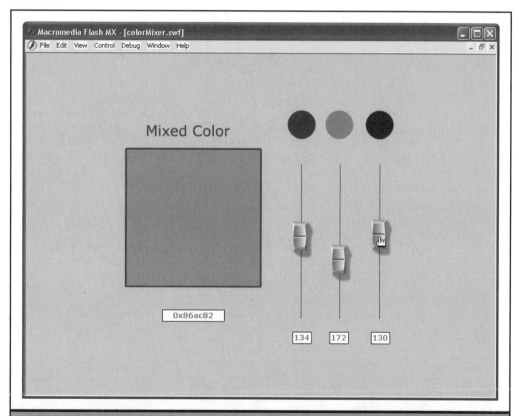

Figure 10-7.   *While the values below the sliders show decimal values, the hexadecimal value below the mixed color object shows the value that actually goes into the setRGB() method.*

setTransform
Color.setTransform(colorTransformObject): Method

Like the advanced color option, the transform color object is more complex than RGB color. Setting the color transform object requires eight different parameters, coded as ra, ga, ba, aa, rb, bb, gb, and ab. The meanings are as follows:

- **ra** Percentage for the red element (-100 to 100)
- **ga** Percentage for the green element (-100 to 100)
- **ba** Percentage for the blue element (-100 to 100)
- **rb** Offset for the red element (-255 to 255)
- **gb** Offset for the green element (-255 to 255)
- **bb** Offset for the blue element (-255 to 255)
- **aa** Percentage for alpha (-100 to 100)
- **ab** Offset for alpha (-255 to 255)

To get an idea of how this works, the following movie lets you enter different values, very much like you would when setting advanced colors in the Properties panel, and see how those colors are applied to a movie clip with the instance name of colorMC. Table 10-5 shows the simple color palette used, and Figure 10-8 shows the stage setup.

1. Open a new movie and set the background color to gray-green.

2. In the middle of the stage, draw a circle with a deep brown fill and an 8-point stroke with a diameter of 155.

3. Select the center of the circle (the deep brown fill only) and press the F8 key to open the Convert To Symbol dialog box. Select Movie Clip for behavior and click OK. Provide the new MC with the instance name colorMC.

Name	R	G	B
Gray-green	165	178	153
Deep brown	76	25	12
Pale, pale green	234	242	224

Table 10-5.   *Color Palette*

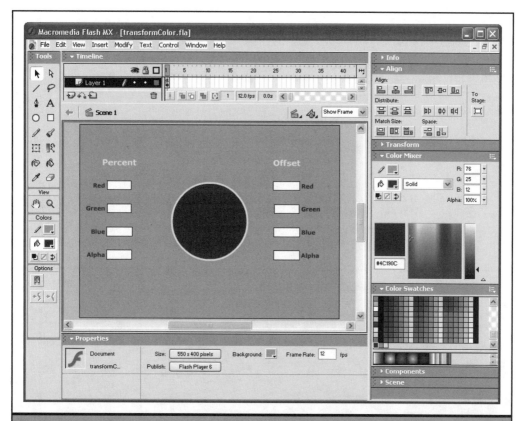

Figure 10-8. *The movie requires eight input text fields and a single larger round movie clip to set transform colors.*

4. Place four input text fields on the left and right sides of the movie clip in the center. From top to bottom on the left, provide them with the instance names raT, gaT, baT, and aaT. On the right, from top to bottom, use the instance names rbT, gbT, bbT, and abT.

5. Above the left column, use pale pale green to label the column Percent and the right column Offset. Using the deep brown, from top to bottom, label the input text fields Red, Green, Blue, and Alpha. Use Figure 10-8 as a guide.

6. Click the first frame and enter the following script:

```
_root.colorMC.onPress = function() {
    advPaint = new Color(colorMC);
```

```
advPaintTransform = new Object();
advPaintTransform.ra = parseInt(raT.text);
advPaintTransform.rb = parseInt(rbT.text);
advPaintTransform.ga = parseInt(gaT.text);
advPaintTransform.gb = parseInt(gbT.text);
advPaintTransform.ba = parseInt(baT.text);
advPaintTransform.bb = parseInt(bbT.text);
advPaintTransform.aa = parseInt(aaT.text);
advPaintTransform.ab = parseInt(abT.text);
advPaint.setTransform(advPaintTransform);
};
```

When you test the movie, enter the values in the left and right columns to see what you get. Figure 10-9 shows what you can expect to see when you test the movie. (Try the following values for an interesting color: Percent 255, 7, 8, 77; Offset 0, -55, 0, 77.)

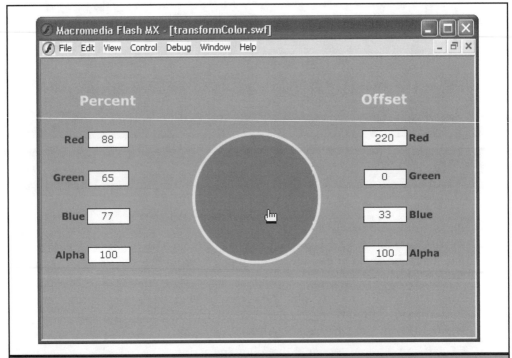

Figure 10-9. *The transform colors give you far more options to control as well as transparency.*

Key

The Key object can be used without using a constructor. To use the Key object most effectively, you will generally first create an Object object to be used as a listener to detect when a key has been pressed. You can place Key listeners like Key.isDown directly in a script which can be trapped by enterFrame clip events or simply the playhead running through the frame. However, a far more useful method is to create the Object object as a listener and use it with function literals. In the rest of this section, you will see examples using the Object object in this manner rather than the older methods of using an MC enterFrame event.

Methods

The methods associated with the Key object are generally connected with the two Key listeners. So in looking at the different methods, you will repeatedly see examples using the listeners as well as an Object object set up to trap events that will fire function literals. Of all of the objects examined so far, the Key object uses its listeners and methods interdependently.

addListener

Key.addListener(listenObj): Method

The addListener() method sets up an object to receive notification on an onKeyDown or onKeyUp event. Listening objects registered with addListener() have either their onKeyDown or onKeyUp method invoked, and you can register as many objects as you want. To show how all of these work together, the next movie uses several different Key object elements, including methods, listeners, events, and constants. The color palette is based on a Chinese design from Leslie Cabarga's book, *The Designer's Guide to Global Color Combinations* (Cincinnati, Ohio: How Design Books, 2001). To show how to use the keyboard controls in ActionScript, I designed a simple maze where a ball is moved by the arrow keys to its final destination—the Jade Treasure. Along the way, the script counts and displays the number of keystrokes as the ball moves through the maze to its goal. Table 10-6 shows the color values and Figure 10-10 shows the initial setup.

The following steps show how to set up the movie and the ActionScript that reads and responds to keyboard events:

1. Open a new movie, add two new layers, and rename all three layers from top to bottom, Move Ball, Maze, and Background.

2. Select the Background layer and select light blue for the background color. Select the Rectangle tool and draw a rectangle with a white fill and light brown 5-point stroke with the dimensions W = 485, H = 340. Lock the layer.

Name	R	G	B
Light brown	184	140	71
Light blue	99	189	192
Jade	127	200	107
Red	249	22	54
Black	0	0	0
White	255	255	255

Table 10-6. *Color Palette*

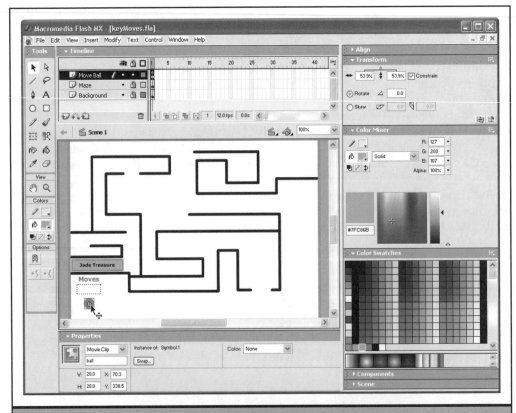

Figure 10-10. *In setting up the movie, both a movie clip and dynamic text field are connected to Key object events.*

3. Select the Maze layer and, using a 5-point black line, draw a maze similar to the one shown in Figure 10-10 or make up your own. Once the maze is complete, lock the layer.

4. Select the Move ball layer and draw a red circle with a 1-point light blue stroke with the dimensions W = 20, H = 20. Select it, convert it to a movie clip, and enter the instance name ball in the Properties panel. Once complete, position it in the lower-left corner of the stage.

5. Above the ball, use the Text tool to place a dynamic text field, giving it the instance name moves. Above the dynamic text field, type **Moves** using a static text field.

6. Using a light brown stroke and jade green fill, draw a rectangle with the dimensions W = 100, H = 20. Type **Jade Treasure** in black centered on top of the rectangle. Select the drawing and text and convert it to a movie clip, and give it the instance name finish.

7. Click the first frame of the Move ball layer and type in the following script:

```
ballListen = new Object();
ballListen.onKeyDown = function() {
    moveCounter++;
    _root.moves.text = moveCounter;
    if (Key.isDown(Key.RIGHT)) {
        _root.ball._x += 8;
    } else if (Key.isDown(Key.LEFT)) {
        _root.ball._x -= 8;
    } else if (Key.isDown(Key.UP)) {
        _root.ball._y -= 8;
    } else if (Key.isDown(Key.DOWN)) {
        _root.ball._y += 8;
    }
    if (_root.ball.hitTest(_root.finish)) {
        _root.ball._xscale = 120;
        _root.ball._yscale = 120;
    }
};

Key.addListener(ballListen);
```

When you test the movie, you should find that when you press an arrow key the ball moves 8 pixels in the direction indicated by the arrow. At the same time, the dynamic test field shows the number of moves (or key presses) you have taken. Each time you press a key, you initiate the isDown() method. Regardless of which key you press, including non-arrow keys, you will see the number under Moves increment by 1. If the isDown() method detects one of the four arrow keys, it triggers a condition that moves the ball object in one of four directions. When the ball and target come into contact, another condition signals the end by expanding the size of the ball 120%. Figure 10-11 shows the ball being moved through the maze.

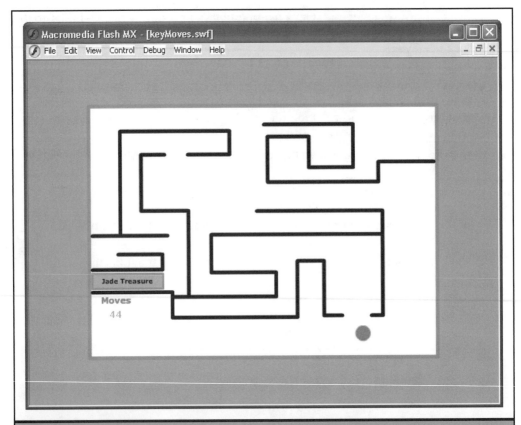

Figure 10-11.   *While only the arrow keys will move the ball object, any key press will increment the number of moves counted.*

getAscii

Key.getAscii(): Method

The getAscii() method returns the ASCII code of the last key pressed or released. If you press a combination (such as SHIFT-A), the ASCII values return the shifted value. For example, the ASCII value of lowercase *a* is 97 and uppercase *A* is 65. The SHIFT key itself returns a 0. (All returns are based on the English keyboard.) The following is a script that shows the ASCII value of the keys you press:

```
keyBee = new Object();
keyBee.onKeyDown = function() {
    var beta = Key.getAscii();
    trace(beta);
```

```
};
Key.addListener(keyBee);
```

getCode
Key.getCode(): Method

The getCode() method returns the key code value of the last key pressed. Sometimes key codes are the same as ASCII codes and sometimes not. Key codes do not distinguish between upper- and lowercase characters, but only recognize the key that has been pressed. The following script shows the difference between ASCII and key code values:

```
keyBee = new Object();
keyBee.onKeyDown = function() {
    var ascii=Key.getAscii();
    var code = Key.getCode();
    trace("ASCII= "+ascii);
    trace("Code= "+code);
};

Key.addListener(keyBee);
```

isDown
Key.isDown(keycode): Method

The isDown() method returns a Boolean true if the key specified in the keycode argument is pressed. The value of the argument can either be an actual key code value or the value of a Key object. For example, all of the Key constants can be trapped in this method, as was shown in the maze example. The following shows the two different ways this method works:

```
keyBee = new Object();
keyBee.onKeyDown = function() {
    if (Key.isDown(65)) {
        trace("You pressed the A key.");
    }
    if (Key.isDown(Key.SPACE)) {
        trace("You pressed the space bar.");
    }
};
Key.addListener(keyBee);
```

Notice that if you press upper- or lowercase A, the key code value 65 evaluates a Boolean true condition and sends the message in the output window.

isToggled

Key.isToggled(keycode): Method

The isToggled() method returns a Boolean true if either the CAPS LOCK or NUM LOCK is on, and the keycode value is either 20 (CAPS LOCK) or 144 (NUM LOCK). On the Macintosh, SHIFT-NUM LOCK achieves the key code of 144. The following script uses the isToggled() method for both keys:

```
keyBee = new Object();
keyBee.onKeyDown = function() {
    var lock = Key.isToggled(20);
    var numLock = Key.isToggled(144);
    if (lock) {
        trace("Caps lock is on.");
    } else if (numLock) {
        trace("Number lock is on.");
    }
};
Key.addListener(keyBee);
```

removeListener

Key.removeListener(listenObj): Method

The removeListener() method essentially turns off Key listening. If a Key object has been set to listen to a listener (onKeyDown or onKeyUp), the removeListener() method will stop all further listening. Thus, functions depending on the keyboard event will no longer respond. The following script will keep listening until the Q (for Quit) key is pressed. All subsequent key presses are no longer trapped for the object specified in the parameter.

```
keyBee = new Object();
keyBee.onKeyDown = function() {
    if (Key.isDown(81)) {
        Key.removeListener(keyBee);
    } else {
        trace("A key is pressed.");
    }
};
Key.addListener(keyBee);
```

Key Constants

Instead of using a key code value, some keys have special Key object status. These keys have constants associated with them, such as the arrow keys used in the maze example.

The format Key.CONSTANT recognizes the key being pressed. Table 10-7 shows all of the key constants in ActionScript.

Listeners

The Key listeners allow you to write scripts that will execute a function as soon as the event occurs. This allows function literals to be added to Key objects and then acted

Constant and Key Code	Key Action
BACKSPACE 8	BACKSPACE on Windows PC SHIFT-DELETE on Macintosh
CAPSLOCK 20	CAPS LOCK key
CONTROL 17	CTRL key on Windows PC Both CONTROL and COMMAND keys on Macintosh
DELETEKEY 46	DELETE key on Windows PC
DOWN 40	DOWN ARROW key
END 35	END key on Windows PC
ENTER 13	ENTER on Windows PC RETURN on Macintosh
ESCAPE 27	ESC key
HOME 36	HOME key
INSERT 45	INSERT key
LEFT 37	LEFT ARROW key
PGDN 34	PAGE DOWN key
PGUP 33	PAGE UP key
RIGHT 39	RIGHT ARROW key
SHIFT 16	SHIFT key
SPACE 32	SPACE BAR
TAB 9	TAB key
UP 38	UP ARROW key

Table 10-7.   *Key Constants*

upon by using the listeners instead of waiting for a clip event (for example, enterFrame) to coincide with the Key event. In most of the examples used earlier in discussing Key methods, listeners were employed so that the script could read a key's action.

onKeyDown

Key.onKeyDown: Listener

As a listener, onKeyDown requires a listener object. As seen in previous Key method examples, the listener object then sets up a function literal to execute as soon as the key is pressed. However, after defining the object and establishing the function literal, you must add the addListener() method targeting your listening object. The following shows the basic format required:

```
listenObj = new Object();
listenObj.onKeyDown = function() {
    trace("A key has been pressed.");
};
Key.addListener(listenObj);
```

Because you can add as many listeners to the same event as you want, you can coordinate several different objects and variables.

onKeyUp

Key.onKeyUp: Listener

As a listener, onKeyUp works just like onKeyDown and thus requires a listener object. As seen in previous Key method examples, the listener object then sets up a function literal to execute as soon as the key is pressed. Likewise, after defining the object and establishing the function literal, you must add the addListener() method targeting your listening object. You need the same basic format as with onKeyDown:

```
listenObj = new Object();
listenObj.onKeyUp = function() {
    trace("A key has been released.");
};
Key.addListener(listenObj);
```

You can add as many listeners with onKeyUp as you want, including multiple listeners for the same key event.

_level

_levelN: Property

The _level property is used when you have loaded SWF files using loadMovieNum(). The format of loadMovieNum() requires a level number to add a movie when an existing movie is in memory. For example, the following script loads a movie named spaceCreeps.swf to level 4:

```
loadMovieNum("spaceCreeps.swf",4);
```

A reference to objects from that movie must use _level4 to distinguish them from objects in the original level or _level0. For example, to extract data stored in a variable named fuel from a movie loaded in level 4, you would address it as follows:

```
var newFuel = _level4.fuel;
```

In referring to a path using the _level property, you would use it very much like you use _root. It is the highest level in a movie. In fact, in a typical movie, try substituting _level0 for _root. It works the same, and herein lies a problem. If you have a movie clip in the SWF on level 4 and you make a reference to the main timeline using _root, you will come to the main timeline of the movie clip on level 4 and not the original one. So instead of using _root, you would use _level0 if you wanted to address the main timeline of the original movie.

Note

Some programmers eschew the use of _root because it can be confusing when you have more than a single movie in memory. In fact, they assert that _root should never be used and you should only use _levelN when making references to the main timeline. Because _root is a relative reference and even vague in some contexts, the point is well taken. However, when only a single movie is used, _root is an easy way to remember the root level of the movie. Also, if you want a movie to be level-agnostic, then using _root makes the best sense.

Mouse

Like the Key object, the Mouse object is a top-level object that does not need a constructor. It also shares many of the same constructs as the Key object, and given the fact that they both involve input hardware, this should not be a surprise. In fact, the mouse is often considered an extension of the keyboard, and some laptops have even placed the mouse controller right on the keyboard.

ACTIONSCRIPT
OBJECTS

However, you will find important differences between the Mouse and Key objects. The Key object has both Key and ASCII codes, while the Mouse object has none. The Mouse object can hide and show the cursor, but the Key object cannot.

Methods

The Mouse object has four methods. Two involve listeners and two involve the mouse cursor's visibility. The listener methods are identical to those for the Key object, so if you are familiar with how the Key object uses listener methods, you will find the same with the Mouse object.

addListener
Mouse.addListener(listenObj): Method

The addListener() method works in conjunction with one of the Mouse listeners. It requires an Object object for a listener (a listener object.) The listener object is attached to one of the Mouse listeners. Finally, the listener object is placed in the argument of the Mouse.addListener() method. The following script shows how to construct a listener object for the mouse employing the addListener() method:

```
squeeky = new Object();
squeeky.onMouseDown = function() {
    trace("The mouse button is pressed.");
};
Mouse.addListener(squeeky);
```

hide
Mouse.hide(): Method

The hide() method simply hides the mouse cursor. Usually this method is employed when the developer wishes to replace the default arrow cursor with something related to his movie. The following script, however, simply shows how the script can be written to hide the mouse and then bring it back again:

```
squeeky = new Object();
squeeky.onMouseDown = function() {
    Mouse.hide();
    trace("Where's the mouse?");
};
squeeky.onMouseUp = function() {
    Mouse.show();
};
Mouse.addListener(squeeky);
```

removeListener

Mouse.removeListener(listenObj): Method

The removeListener() method essentially turns off the listening process that has been established using the Mouse.addListener() method. The following script shows how the position of the mouse cursor on the horizontal plane (_xmouse) can be used to remove the effect of the mouse listener:

```
squeeky = new Object();
squeeky.onMouseMove = function() {
    var showIt = _level0._xmouse;
    trace(showIt);
    if (showIt>300) {
        Mouse.removeListener(squeeky);
    }
};
Mouse.addListener(squeeky);
```

When you test the movie with the above script, keep the mouse on the left side of the stage for a while and then slowly move it to the right. Once you exceed the X = 300 position on the stage, moving the mouse back to the left side will not restore the listener.

show

Mouse.show(): Method

The show() method represents the default state of the mouse cursor—it shows it on the stage. The main use of Mouse.show() is to reshow the cursor after a Mouse.hide() method has been invoked. (See an example of using Mouse.show() and Mouse.hide() in the section on Mouse.hide().) The following script shows the Itchy and Scratchy of the Mouse object:

```
squeeky = new Object();
squeeky.onMouseMove = function() {
    var Itchy = (_level0._xmouse<200);
    var Scratchy = (_level0._xmouse>=200);
    if (Itchy) {
        Mouse.hide();
    } else if (Scratchy) {
        Mouse.show();
    }
};
Mouse.addListener(squeeky);
```

Listeners

The Mouse object has three listeners, one each for the mouse button up and down and one for moving the mouse. However, it does not have a listener for the several other mouse events such as drag and roll over. Nevertheless, the listeners are very important because they can be used with constructed objects and not objects on the stage such as movie clips or buttons. As a result, using purely mouse actions, you can capture mouse clicks and movement without a visible counterpart on the stage. The following three listeners all work the same except for the different events each is a listener for.

onMouseDown

Mouse.onMouseDown: Listener

The onMouseDown listener is notified when the mouse is down. It requires an object to be used as a listener. Used in conjunction with the addListener() method, the onMouseDown listener can be used to capture and employ events when the mouse key is pressed.

```
squeeky = new Object();
squeeky.onMouseDown = function() {
    trace("The mouse key is down.");
};
Mouse.addListener(squeeky);
```

onMouseMove

Mouse.onMouseMove: Listener

The onMouseMove listener is notified when the mouse is moved. Stated otherwise, the listener is notified when the _xmouse or _ymouse changes. It requires an object to be used as a listener. Used in conjunction with the addListener() method, the onMouseMove listener can be used to capture and employ events when the mouse changes positions.

```
squeeky = new Object();
squeeky.onMouseMove = function() {
    trace("The mouse key is moving.");
};
Mouse.addListener(squeeky);
```

onMouseUp

Mouse.onMouseUp: Listener

The onMouseUp listener is notified when the mouse key is in the non-pressed position. It requires an object to be used as a listener. Used in conjunction with the addListener() method, the onMouseUp listener can be used to capture and employ events when the mouse key is released or is simply not being pressed. The following example shows its employment:

```
squeeky = new Object();
squeeky.onMouseUp = function() {
    trace("The mouse button is released.");
};
Mouse.addListener(squeeky);
```

Conclusion

This chapter has examined a wide range of objects in Macromedia Flash MX ActionScript, ranging from accessibility to mouse events. However, the objects and their uses have changed considerably since Flash 5. Virtually all scripts can now be placed in one location, typically associated with a frame. This makes finding what you need much easier and the script of the movie objects less prone to bugs.

You have seen that many of the features that were once reserved for movie clips have now been made available to a wider range of objects, especially the Button object. However, movie clips have changed as well, and the next chapter examines them in detail. You will see similarities in many of the methods and properties found in this chapter. The material in this chapter will help you understand the next chapter, and at the same time, what you will learn in the next chapter will help clarify what you learned in this chapter.

The Complete Reference

ActionScript

Chapter 11

Movie Objects II

The MovieClip object in Macromedia Flash MX has been expanded more than in any other previous build of Flash. It is now a fully object-based element with a complete set of methods, properties, and events. Additionally, it has a whole new set of drawing methods

To understand any one of the movie clip's new characteristics, others will have to be used to illustrate points, and so while I've divided up the discussion into the different categories, you will find methods, properties, and events discussed in the others' respective sections.

> **Note** *In the Actions toolbox, you will find a folder reference to the MovieClip, an intercase contraction, but the term is very rarely used in ActionScript except to create an empty movie clip—MovieClip.createEmptyMovieClip(in,d). Movie clip instances are always referenced by the instance name or the "this" self-reference. Macromedia, Inc. uses MovieClip as a folder name and in its Reference panel to refer to the movie clip object as a generic substitute for an instance name. For example, the reference, MovieClip .attachMovie simply means that the method "attachMovie" belongs to the MovieClip objects. To help clarify the relationship between the movie clip instance and the method, property or event I've used the term "MCinstance" suggesting a movie clip instance name with the movie clip object implied.*

Movie Clip Methods

Macromedia Flash MX contains 26 movie clip methods. Table 11-1 provides a quick overview of the methods, and the rest of the section examines their use. After going

Method	Description
MCinstance.attachMovie()	Movie in the library is attached to movie on stage.
MCinstance.createEmptyMCinstance()	Script-based creation of empty movie clip.
MCinstance.createTextField()	An empty text field is created in MC.
MCinstance.duplicateMovieClip()	Movie clip is duplicated.
MCinstance.getBounds()	Minimum and maximum x and y positions are returned.
MCinstance.getBytesLoaded()	Returns current number of MC's bytes loaded.

Table 11-1. *Macromedia Flash MX Methods for the Movie Clip Object*

Method	Description
MCinstance.getBytesTotal()	Returns complete number of bytes in MC.
MCinstance.getDepth()	An MC's depth returned.
MCinstance.getURL()	Document from URL retrieved.
MCinstance.globalToLocal()	Changes object from Stage coordinates to coordinates of the specified movie clip.
MCinstance.gotoAndPlay()	Playhead moved to specified frame in MC and continues to play.
MCinstance.gotoAndStop()	Playhead moved to specified frame in MC and stops.
MCinstance.hitTest()	Boolean true returned if bounding box of the specified movie clip contacts (overlaps) the target movie clip.
MCinstance.loadMovie()	Movie loads into MC.
MCinstance.loadVariables()	Variables from external source loaded into MC.
MCinstance.localToGlobal()	Changes Point object from the local coordinates of MC to the global Stage coordinates.
MCinstance.nextFrame()	MC playhead moved to next frame.
MCinstance.play()	Forces MC to begin playing
MCinstance.prevFrame()	MC playhead moved to previous frame.
MCinstance.removeMovieClip()	MCs created with a duplicateMovieClip action or method or the attachMovie method are removed.
MCinstance.setMask()	The MC acts as a mask for specified movie clip.

Table 11-1. *Macromedia Flash MX Methods for the Movie Clip Object* (continued)

Method	Description
MCinstance.startDrag()	Sets MC to drag.
MCinstance.stop()	Forces MC to stop.
MCinstance.stopDrag()	Stops MC drag.
MCinstance.swapDepths	Two movies on stage have depths swapped.
MCinstance.unloadMovie()	MC loaded with the loadMovie() action is removed.

Table 11-1.   *Macromedia Flash MX Methods for the Movie Clip Object* (continued)

over the table list, you will find each method discussed and illustrated in greater detail in the subsections.

To best demonstrate how all of these movie clip methods work, a brief explanation will be accompanied with a brief script example. At the end of the section, an example movie illustrates several methods used together.

You will find the examples make extensive use of function literals used in conjunction with a movie clip event. The syntax and format better reflect the object-based nature of Macromedia Flash MX ActionScript, so instead of having to use a button to fire an event, or scripts associated with the example movie clips, the scripts are generally fired in a frame. In previous chapters, you have been introduced to using function literals in this manner, and as you continue in the book, you will see them used as a more efficient way to launch scripts. However, the button and MC event handlers discussed in previous chapters are not abandoned altogether, and some illustrations will use them.

For example, instead of creating an MC and using an event handler script like the following:

```
onClipEvent(mouseUp) {
    this.someMethod();
}
```

you will be more likely to see a script associated with a frame like this:

```
_root.MCname.onPress = function() {
    this.someMethod();
};
```

The advantage is that the scope of the event does not impact the entire movie. As discussed in Chapter 5, the onClipEvent() has a scope of the entire movie. If a clip event looks for any button press, for example, a click on a button or some other clip can launch a script even though you only want the event to scope a single movie clip's script. Using function literals, only when the event is on the movie clip will the method execute. In other words, you can set up movie clip events to work like button events that execute only when the cursor is over the movie itself. In the "Events" section later in this chapter, you will see how function literals can contain an event to a specific MC in other ways as well. However, don't forget that movie clip events such as onMouseUp still have a global scope, and if that is what you want, use them instead of the events associated with buttons. (Also, in Macromedia Flash MX and the Flash 6 player, the global scope of movie clip events can be used with button instances.)

attachMovie
MovieClip.attachMovie(ID, NIN, depth [optional obj props]): Method

Macromedia Flash MX provides methods whereby you can attach a movie to a current movie clip and later remove it. Basically, a movie clip in the library can be attached to a movie clip on the stage. The general format of the attach method is

```
MCinstance.attachMovie(identifier, newInstanceName, depth [optional obj props])
```

The movie in the library called by the method is then attached to the registration point of the movie on the stage at the depth specified in the depth parameter. The identifier is the name you give it in the Convert/Create Symbol dialog box, and the newInstanceName is the instance name for it as an object. The optional object properties are those that can be added to the dynamically created movie clip by an existing object.

To prepare a movie clip to be attached, you have to use the Advanced Convert To Symbol dialog box or apply the Linkage properties retroactively from the pop-up menu in the Library panel. The preparation steps are simple enough, but you need to understand that the name of a symbol, which has largely been ignored in favor of the instance name of the movie, becomes the linkage ID by default. Of course you can use any linkage ID name you want and ignore the symbol name. Use the following steps to set up a movie clip in the library to be attached to the movie clip on the stage:

1. Create the drawing you wish to be attached. Select it and press the F8 key to convert it to a symbol.

2. In the Convert To Symbol dialog box, click the Advanced button. (If the Basic button is showing on the Convert To Symbol dialog box, you are in the Advanced mode already.)

3. In the Name box, type a reference name with no spaces. In the example shown in Figure 11-1, the name "disc" is used. Then click the Export For ActionScript check box. The name you typed appears in the Identifier box. The Identifier

name is the reference name you will be using. Also, the Export In First Frame check box is automatically checked and should be left that way. Click OK, and your new symbol is all set to be attached. Remove the new symbol instance from the stage. (It will still be in the library.) Figure 11-1 shows the Convert To Symbol dialog box and the selected image (circle) to be converted to a symbol. The square on the stage is the movie clip that the circle will be loaded into.

4. Create a second drawing, and convert it to a movie clip. You don't have to use the Advanced mode. However, once created, give it an instance name. For this example, I have used the instance name block.

5. Finally, in the first frame of the movie, enter the following script:

```
_root.block.onPress=function() {
    _root.block.attachMovie("disc","newDisc",2);
}
```

When you test the movie, you will see the attached movie clip appear inside the MC on the stage. If the attached MC is larger than the one on the stage, it will

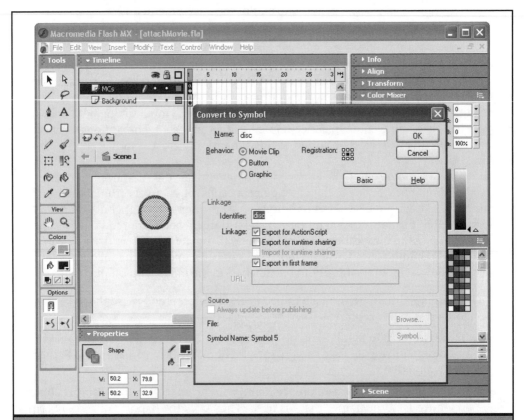

Figure 11-1.   *Converting a drawing to a symbol in the Advanced mode provides more options.*

completely cover it, otherwise, it sits right in the middle of the existing MC. A side-by-side comparison shows the relationship between the original MC on the stage and the attached MC.

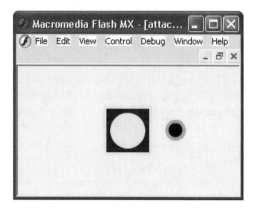

An interesting thing happens when a movie clip is attached to another movie clip. The attached movie clip becomes a child of the original movie clip. For example, if you want to reference the attached movie clip, the reference would be

```
_root.origClip.attachedClip
```

Using the sample script, to move the attached script elsewhere on the stage, you would write something like the following:

```
_root.block.newDisc._x=350;
```

The attached MC moves away from the original MC that was on the stage, but nevertheless, it is still referenced as a child of the original MC.

To remove the attached script requires a similar reference path, listing both parent and child objects. Thus, continuing with the sample movie, you could add a button to the movie and with the following script remove the movie added originally:

```
on(release) {
    _root.block.newDisc.removeMovieClip();
}
```

The ability to add and remove movie clips from a movie provides added flexibility to creating what will appear on the stage at any given time.

createEmptyMovieClip
MovieClip.createEmptyMovieClip("instanceName", nDepth): Method

This next movie clip method is something like attachMovie() except that the new movie is empty and needs no identifier. The empty movie clip becomes a child of the existing movie. The general format is

```
MCinstance.createEmptyMovieClip("instanceName", nDepth);
```

The instance name must be unique for the movie, and the depth must be an integer.

Because the main timeline is considered a movie clip, you can create an empty movie clip on the main timeline using the format in the following example:

```
_root.createEmptyMovieClip("myFigure", 1);
```

One of the primary reasons for creating an empty movie clip can be found when you take advantage of the new Macromedia Flash MX drawing methods discussed in the section "Drawing Methods," later in this chapter.

createTextField
MovieClip.createTextField("clip",d,x,y,width,height): Method

Creating a dynamic text field in Macromedia Flash MX is done using the createTextField() method. The text field is a child of the movie clip that creates it. The format is

```
MCinstance.createTextField("instanceName", depth,
x,y,width,height);
```

The movie clip can be any MC or the main timeline (_root). I found creating dynamic text fields on existing movie clips other than the main timeline more interesting because the position of the text field is relative to the position of the text movie clip and not the stage. In Chapter 12 where the text field object is discussed in detail, you can learn how to format any text in a dynamic text field, but here only the process of creating a text field is examined.

For a simple movie, create a 70 by 70 square on the stage and convert it to a movie clip. Give it the instance name block. Then, in the first frame, add the following script:

```
_root.block.onEnterFrame = function() {
    sayThis = new String();
    sayThis = "Blocko!";
    thisLong = sayThis.length * 12;
    _root.block.createTextField("message", this, -15, -10, thisLong, 15);
    _root.block.message.text = "Blocko!";
};
```

The string used to make up the message is transformed into an object to extract the length property to be used in the length of the text field. (The TextField object has an "auto-size" feature that will adjust to the size of the text, but that is covered in the next chapter, so a simpler and less accurate method was used to get the width of the text block.) The text field is given the instance name of message, and the current depth is established using the self-referral term, "this," to set the depth at that of the current movie clip. The other settings use numeric literals.

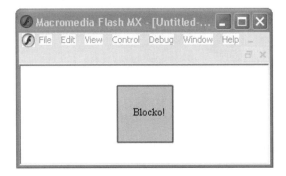

How the settings will actually be positioned on the screen depends on the many properties that make up a text field. Table 11-2 shows the default settings of the different text properties when you use the createTextField() method:

Property	Setting
type	dynamic
border	false
background	false
password	false
multiline	false
html	false
embedFonts	false
variable	null
maxChars	null
font	Times New Roman

Table 11-2.   *Default Text Field Settings*

Property	Setting
size	12
textColor	0x000000
bold	false
italic	false
underline	false
url	" " (none)
target	" " (none)
align	left
leftMargin	0
rightMargin	0
indent	0
leading	0
bullet	false
tabStops	an array of numbers provides stops

Table 11-2.   *Default Text Field Settings* (continued)

Chapter 12 shows how to change the many formatting elements of text fields, and once you have created a text field, you can change those properties.

duplicateMovieClip
MovieClip.duplicateMovieClip("name", depth): Method

The method for making a duplicate of an assigned movie clip comes in handy for filling up the screen with copies of a movie clip—such as one that scatters star movie clips randomly across the stage. The format for duplicating movie clips is

```
MCinstance.duplicateMovieClip("newInstanceName", depth);
```

When a movie clip is duplicated, it is positioned directly on top of the one it copied, and most scripts using a duplicate movie clip have some way of positioning them. Each newly duplicated MC needs to have not only a unique instance name, but also a unique depth. This is usually done using a loop with the index value generating the depth and a unique name for each new clip by concatenating a string with the index value.

One trick is to put a script into the original movie clip, and then when the movie clip is duplicated, so is the script. Then the new movie clips become self-positioning. For example, the following scripts placed in the first frame of the main timeline and in the first frame of the movie clip's timeline will generate three new instances of a movie clip named ball and then position the duplicated scripts on the stage. Follow these steps:

1. Create a round object using the Oval tool, convert it to a movie clip, and give it the instance name ball. Place the ball in the upper-left corner of the stage.

2. Double-click on the ball MC to enter the Symbol Editing mode. Click on the first frame of the MC's timeline, open the Actions panel, and enter the following script:

```
//In first frame of MC
this.onPress = function() {
    this._x = _root.stack.pop();
    this._y = _root.stack.pop();
};
```

The script uses an array created on the main timeline called stack. The Array object pop() method removes the last value in the array and assigns it first to the x position and then the y position of the movie clip each time the onPress event is detected. As the user clicks the MC, it moves one of the duplicated movie clips stacked up on the original to the next position provided by the array values.

3. Return to the main timeline, click on the first frame, and write the following script in the Actions panel:

```
//In first frame of main timeline
for (x=1; x < 4; x++) {
    _root.ball.duplicateMovieClip("ball" + x, x);
}
stack = new Array("100", "100", "200", "200", "300", "300");
```

Note   *Another trick would be to use the returned object reference to position the instances. duplicateMovieClip returns a reference to the new clip, so you could use this to avoid placing anything inside the MC symbol:*

```
//In first frame of main timeline
stack = new Array("100", "100", "200", "200", "300", "300");
for (x=1; x < 4; x++) {
    var temp = _root.ball.duplicateMovieClip("ball" + x, x);
    temp._x = stack.pop();
    temp._y = stack.pop();
}
```

Try it, it works! It can be used for attachMovieClip and createEmptyMovieClip as well.

The script first duplicates three copies of the object, and using the index value generates the instance names ball1, ball2, and ball3 with depths of 1 to 3. Then the script creates an array called stack. Each value in the stack is used in the MC's timeline script to position itself on the stage when clicked. (When running this script, be sure to click only the ball in the upper-left corner. You're actually clicking on four balls stacked on top of one another, and with each click, you move the next on the stack to another position.)

getBounds
MovieClip.getBounds(t): Method

Movie clips have boundaries that can be expressed in the properties xMin, xMax, yMin, and yMax. For example, a square movie clip's xMin and yMin are in the upper-left corner of the box, and the xMax and yMax are in the lower-right corner. You can find these values using the getBounds() method. The general format is

```
MCinstance.getBounds(target)
```

The target is the target path to the timeline you wish to find the boundaries. If you wanted the boundaries for an MC embedded in another MC, the target path would be through the main timeline (_root) to the instance name of the target. Of course, to get the boundaries for an MC on the main timeline, you would just have to use _root as the target. To get an idea of how this method works, create two MCs, a square and circle. Use the instance name block (square) for one, and pugs for the other. Then put the following script in the first frame of the main timeline:

```
beta = block.getBounds(_root);
_root.pugs._y=beta.yMin;
_root.pugs._x=beta.xMin;
```

The pugs object will immediately move to the upper-left corner of the box. The identifier beta is assigned the values of the properties xMin, xMax, yMin, and yMax. These values can them be placed into actual x and y positions of another object. Try changing the script so that you can place the ball at all four corners of the square.

getBytesLoaded and getBytesTotal
MovieClip.getBytesLoaded(): Method
MovieClip.getBytesTotal(): Method

Two methods determine how many bytes are loaded in a movie clip and the total number of bytes loaded. In Chapter 7, you saw how to make a preloader by determining the number of frames that had been loaded compared to the total number of frames in the movie. The methods for getting the current number of bytes loaded and total bytes work in a very similar manner. The methods can be used for both the main timeline and movie clips below the main timeline. They have the following formats:

```
MCinstance.getBytesLoaded();
MCinstance.getBytesTotal();
```

In the same way that frames can be compared to determine the percent of a movie loaded, bytes can be compared. Placed into variables, proportions can be generated and visual and textual clues offered to the user.

getDepth and swapDepths
MovieClip.getDepth(): Method
MovieClip.swapDepths(n *or* instance): Method

As seen in previous movie clip methods in this chapter, many require that a depth be specified. Macromedia Flash MX has two new methods for dealing with depth. One method gets and returns the depth of a movie clip using the format:

```
MCinstance.getDepth();
```

An integer is returned by getDepth() that can be placed in a variable or used in some other way in a script. For example, the following script finds the depth of the message movie clip embedded in the block MC on the main timeline:

```
var diver=_root.block.message.getDepth();
```

The second movie clip method dealing with depth has two formats:

```
MCinstance.swapDepths(integer);
MCinstance.swapDepths(MCinstance);
```

In the first usage, a movie clip swaps its current depth with another specified depth represented by an integer. For instance, if a movie clip named floater at a depth of 5 was to be moved to a depth of 17, the following script would do that:

```
floater.swapDepths(17);
```

To swap depths with another movie clip with the same parent, the script would be written as:

```
floater.swapDepths(sinker);
```

The following script shows an example using both getting and swapping depths beginning with a movie clip with the instance name block:

```
_root.block.duplicateMovieClip("punch", 5);
_root.block.duplicateMovieClip("judy", 17);
_root.punch.swapDepths(judy);
trace(_root.punch.getDepth()); // Returns 17
```

These methods can be handy when you want to use depths to maintain different statuses of movie clips and keep track of them.

getURL

getURL("URL", ["target", "method"]): Method

The getURL() method associated with a movie clip accesses a Web address from a specified movie clip instance. Using the following format, the method works similarly to the getURL function:

```
MCinstance.getURL("WebAddress" [," target window", "POST/GET"]);
```

The method is formatted in a similar manner to the anchor tag protocol in HTML. The URL (Web address) is placed in quotes, and the option target window can either be a specific name or one of the general references (_parent, _top, _blank, or _self). The difference lies in the placement of an optional method for getting the variables associated with the URL. Unlike loadVariables() and loadVariablesNum(), when the getURL() method sends variables from the current timeline, any information relating to those variables in the Web page called are displayed as regular Web content, and not as Flash. For example, the following statement would open the URL in a new browser window and send any variables using the POST method:

```
_root.block.getURL("http://www.sandlight.com","_blank","POST");
```

For working with server-side scripts such as PHP, ColdFusion, and ASP where you want the variables in the MC to be passed and used by the middleware and the middleware's variables passed back, you should use the LoadVars() object, described in Chapter 13.

globalToLocal and localToGlobal
globalToLocal(obj pt): Method
localToGlobal(obj pt): Method

The methods for changing local and global orientations refer to some point object with an x and y position property. The reversal in orientation means that the orientation changes from the stage 0,0 point (upper-left corner) to the MC's registration point or vice versa. The syntax for each is the following:

```
MCinstance.globalToLocal(obj point);
MCinstance.localToGlobal(obj point);
```

For example, with an MC on the stage with the instance name block, select the block instance, open the Actions panel, and type the following script:

```
onClipEvent(mouseMove) {
    phantom = new object();
    phantom.x = _root._xmouse;
    phantom.y = _root._ymouse;
    this.globalToLocal(phantom);
    trace("Unadjusted " + _root._xmouse + " " + _root._ymouse);
    trace("Global2Local " + phantom.x + " " + phantom.y);
    updateAfterEvent();
};
```

The object named phantom has been given x and y properties based on the position of the current mouse pointer position. By changing the phantom object's orientation from global to local, its center position is the registration point of the block object and not the stage. To reverse the orientation, use the localToGlobal() method.

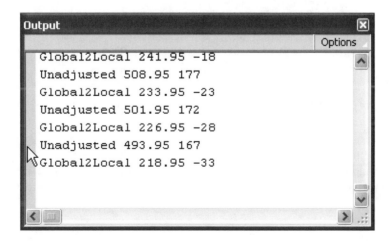

gotoAndPlay and gotoAndStop
MovieClip.gotoAndPlay(n): Method
MovieClip.gotoAndStop(): Method

When directing a movie clip to go to a specific frame in its timeline, the gotoAndPlay() and gotoAndStop() methods are invoked. The gotoAndPlay() method goes to the specified frame in the object's timeline and executes the script associated with the frame and then continues to the next frame. The gotoAndStop() method does the same thing except that it stops unless some kind of play action is in the script. The general format for the methods is the same as it is for the global actions, using either strings for named frames or integers for frame numbers:

```
MCinstance.gotoAndPlay(frame);
MCinstance.gotoAndStop(frame);
```

The following script in a frame will enable a movie clip with the instance name of block to move the playhead to the first frame, play the frame, and continue through the other frames until it encounters some kind of stop action. (The movie clip has a stop action in the first frame, and the method will override the stop action, causing the MC to play.)

```
_root.block.onPress =function() {
    this.gotoAndPlay(1);
};
```

Both of these methods provide ways to generate encapsulated movie control within movie clip timelines.

hitTest
MovieClip.hitTest(): Method

The hitTest() method in Flash is one of the primary methods for designing games and other movies where you want to determine when movie clips collide. If the conditions of the method occur, the method returns a Boolean true. Thus, the method is typically found in a conditional statement. The method has two formats:

```
MCinstance.hitTest(x, y, shape[true]/bounding box [false]);
Mcinstance.hitTest(targetInstance);
```

The second format is the simpler of the two. All you have to do is to name the target in the method of the targeting MC. For example, the following script set in a frame generates a function for an MC with the instance name missile. If the missile object hits the block object, the missile object has its transparency level (alpha) changed to 50 percent.

```
_root.missile.onEnterFrame= function() {
 if(this.hitTest(_root.block)) {
  this._alpha=50;
 }
};
```

The first method looks for a specific position, and as soon as that position is encountered, the method returns a Boolean true.

To see how the second method works, make a simple movie with a movie clip with the instance name of missile. Use the default 550 by 400 pixel size for the stage, and place vertical and horizontal lines in the middle of the stage. (They should intersect at x = 275, y = 200.) Click on the first frame and enter the following script:

```
_root.missile.onEnterFrame = function() {
    if (this.hitTest(275, 200, false)) {
        this._alpha = 50;
    }
    if (this.hitTest(300, 200, false)) {
        this._alpha = 100;
    }
};
_root.missile.onPress = function() {
    this.startDrag();
};
_root.missile.onRelease = function() {
    stopDrag();
};
```

Given the two formats in the method, any target or position on the stage can be used to launch a function, set a variable, or anything else the developer has in mind. Drag the missile object around the stage to see it change. Figure 11-2 shows the missile object dragged to the hit test point, and Figure 11-3 shows how the missile object is changed again when dragged away from the hit test point.

loadMovie and unloadMovie
MovieClip.loadMovie("url",[method]): Method
MovieClip.unloadMovie(): Method
The methods for loading and unloading movies apply to both Flash SWF files and JPEG files, so the methods are actually for loading and unloading movie and graphic

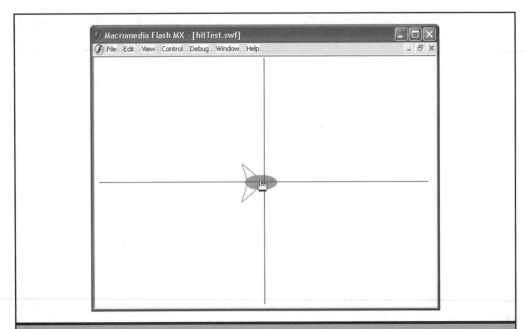

Figure 11-2.   *The object changes when it is positioned on the area designated for hitTest().*

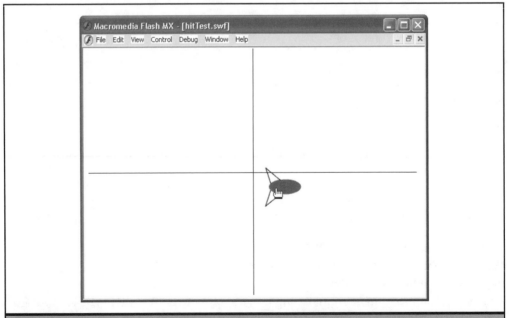

Figure 11-3.   *As the object is repositioned, a different hitTest() changes the transparency value a second time.*

images. The calling MC is replaced by the called movie or graphic. The format for the two methods is

```
MCinstance.loadMovie("URL", [POST/GET]);
MCinstance.unloadMovie();
```

The unload method has no parameters and unloads movies or JPEG files that were loaded with either loadMovie() or attachMovie() methods into a given MC. Unlike the attachMovie() method, the calling MC's content is removed when a new movie or JPEG file is loaded. For example, the following script replaces the block MC when it loads the JPEG file boop.jpg:

```
_root.block.onPress = function() {
    this.loadMovie("boop.jpg", 0);
};
```

To get rid of the JPEG file, the following script associated with a button does the trick:

```
on(release) {
    _root.block.unloadMovie();
}
```

Even through the object's image (block) disappeared when the file was loaded into the MC instance name, the reference to the same instance name is still valid.

When using these methods to load and unload movies related to a movie clip, the loaded SWF file (or JPEG file) loads relative to the calling MC's registration point and replaces the calling MC on the stage. The loaded file positions its upper-left corner as its own registration point. Hence, if the calling MC has its registration point in the middle of the object, the loaded file will appear to be aligned incorrectly because its registration point is in a different position relative to the object's center.

loadVariables
MovieClip.loadVariables("url", [method]): Method

Loading variables into a Flash movie clip can involve several different tasks. It can be as simple as loading a text file and passing variables and their values to a Flash movie. Or it can be as complex as calling a PHP script that receives variables and passes them to a database. The general format of the loadVariables() method is

```
MCinstance.loadVariables("URL", [POST/GET]);
```

The URL is any legitimate Web address (including a folder containing a text file formatted with Flash's special formatting for variables). The optional POST/GET methods are used when sending variables to an external file. (See Chapter 10 for a complete discussion of passing variables between Flash and external files. See Chapter 13 as well for a full discussion of the Macromedia Flash MX LoadVars object.)

To see how loading variables works, save the following script in a text file called connect.txt in the same folder you save the Flash file:

```
message=Hello Macromedia Flash MX
```

In the Flash variable format for external data, the variable is message and the following text is the variable's value.

Treating the main timeline as a movie clip, place a button with the instance name purple and a dynamic text field with the instance name sparky on the main timeline. The following script loads the variables into the main timeline MC and the text field variable message is passed to the text field sparky:

```
_root.purple.onPress = function() {
    _root.loadVariables("connect.txt");
    _root.sparky.text=message;
};
```

The variable named message can be data from any external file, including from server-side scripts. You might have to click the button a couple of times because of the latency between the load action and the variable actually being available. Using the LoadVars() object, you can use the onLoad() method to avoid this problem. See Chapter 13 for details of using LoadVars().

nextFrame and prevFrame
MovieClip.nextFrame(): Method
MovieClip.prevFrame(): Method

The methods for going to the next and previous frames are the same as going to and stopping at the next or previous frame. Because the methods only have a single option, neither contains any arguments. The formats are

```
MCinstance.nextFrame();
MCinstance.prevFrame();
```

The methods have no parameters and simply move the playhead to the next or previous frame and stop. For example, if the playhead is stopped in frame 10 in an MC named maze, the first of the two scripts would move the playhead to Frame 11 and the second to Frame 9.

```
_root.maze.nextFrame();
_root.maze.prevFrame();
```

Like the gotoAndPlay() and gotoAndStop() methods, the key to getting the scripts to work as planned is to have the right target path.

play and stop
play(): Method
stop(): Method

Two more simple methods stop or play movie clips. The formats are

```
MCinstance.play();
MCinstance.stop();
```

The methods have no parameters and work to direct movie clips to begin playing or stop. The following example illustrates using the methods with a movie clip named traffic that starts and stops the action with a button press and release:

```
_root.traffic.onRelease = function() {
    this.play();
};
_root.traffic.onPress = function() {
    this.stop();
};
```

To test this, just put a little animation in a movie clip (like a bouncing ball). When you press the MC button, the animation stops, but it resumes as soon as you release it. Like all other movie clip methods, they work with the main timeline as well.

setMask

MovieClip.setMask(m): Method

New in Macromedia Flash MX is the ability of one movie clip to mask another without having to use a mask layer. Once the mask method is applied, the entire movie clip that is masked disappears except for the portions of the masked object revealed by the masking MC. The format is

```
MCinstanceToBeMasked.setMask( maskingMCinstance);
```

For example if you have an MC named wand and you want wand to mask an MC named flower, you would use the following script:

```
flower.setMask(wand);
```

Both MCs can be on the same layer, and you can use multiple movie clips to act as masks, but you cannot mask more than one MC with a single MC. To turn off the masking effect, you substitute the null value for the masking MC. For example, to turn off the masking effect, you would write

```
flower.setMask(null);
```

Like other masking effects, you can animate both the masking and masked movie clip. Make two MCs, with one named daisy and the other named wand, and enter the following script in the first frame of the movie:

```
_root.wand.onPress = function() {
    daisy.setMask(wand);
    this.startDrag();
};
_root.wand.onRelease = function() {
    daisy.setMask(null);
    stopDrag();
};
```

Test the movie. Before you press the wand object, the daisy object appears beneath it.

As soon as you press the wand object, the daisy object disappears and all you see are those parts of the daisy object you drag the wand object over.

startDrag and stopDrag
MovieClip.startDrag(): Method
MovieClip.stopDrag(): Method

In Chapter 3, the different techniques and parameters used with both the movie clip control drag actions as well as the movie clip drag methods are discussed in detail, and should be consulted for using the drag methods with all of the available parameters. The following example shows a script associated with a frame that will drag an object with the MC name block when the mouse button is pressed and stop when the button is released:

```
_root.block.onPress = function() {
    this.startDrag();
};
_root.block.onRelease = function() {
    stopDrag();
};
```

Using drag methods instead of actions has the advantage of allowing multiple MCs to be dragged at once without multiple objects moving when a single object is dragged.

Drawing Methods

The drawing methods are all completely new to Macromedia Flash MX. The eight methods are used in conjunction with the createEmptyMovieClip() method to dynamically create images on the screen. Unlike the general movie clip methods that can be understood separately, these methods are best understood in the context of one another. Therefore, using a series of scripts, you'll see how to develop some different shapes using the drawing methods first, and then how the different methods were used to contribute to the drawing, examining parameters and techniques. Table 11-3 summarizes the different drawing methods.

Creating a Simple Figure

The best way to get started is to create a simple figure and then examine the methods used to do so. The following script associated with the first frame creates a simple square:

```
_root.createEmptyMovieClip("square",1);
with(_root.square)
{
    lineStyle(5,0xA65900,100);
    beginFill(0x664066, 60);
    moveTo(200,200);
    lineTo(200,100);
    lineTo(300,100);
    lineTo(300,200);
    lineTo(200,200);
    endFill();
}
```

The drawn object appears on the main timeline because the initial reference in creating the movie clip is _root. If you wanted the object to appear in another movie clip's timeline, the creating reference would be something like _root.myLittleClip .createEmptyMovieClip(). Using the with statement, all of the elements of the simple figure are laid out:

- **lineStyle([stroke[,color[, alpha]]]);**   The lineStyle() method expects a stroke (line thickness) between 0 and 255, with 0 being a hairline. If no stroke value is included, the figure is created without a stroke line. Optionally, you can include a color; if none is included, it uses a default of black. Finally, you can include an alpha value for the stroke, with a default of 100 if none is included.

- **beginFill([color [, alpha]]);** The fill color is expressed as a hexadecimal value using the 0x + hex value format (for example, 0xA7B4FF). If no color is included, the fill is omitted. An optional alpha value (0–100) can also be included, with the default being 100.

- **moveTo(x, y);** This drawing method "picks up the pencil" off the stage and moves it to another position without drawing. The parameters include the horizontal (x) and vertical (y) positions on the stage.

- **lineTo(x, y);** This drawing method draws a line from the current position to ending horizontal (x) and vertical (y) positions.

- **endFill();** This drawing method serves as a signal to fill to the lines and curves that began with the beginFill() method.

The simple figure that was generated used all but three of the drawing methods. Make some changes in the parameter values and try creating different shapes. You will find that a quick sketch on a piece of paper will help you plan where you want to begin with moveTo(), and where you want to draw your line to, using lineTo().

Drawing Method	Action
MCinstance.beginFill()	Starts the fill drawing on the stage.
MCinstance.beginGradientFill()	Starts the gradient fill drawing on the stage.
MCinstance.clear()	All of an MC instance's associated drawing commands are cleared.
MCinstance.curveTo()	With the latest line style, draws a curve.
MCinstance.endFill()	Terminates the fill initiated by beginFill() or beginGradientFill().
MCinstance.lineStyle()	Used with the lineTo() and curveTo() methods.
MCinstance.lineTo()	Draws a line using the current line style.
MCinstance.moveTo()	Moves the current drawing position to specified coordinates.

Table 11-3. *Movie Clip Drawing Methods*

Type 1 Gradient Fill

Macromedia Flash MX provides two methods for creating a gradient fill. The first
method uses a transformation matrix that describes a 3 by 3 table as a reference point.
To see how this first method works, create a new movie with two layers. In the bottom
layer, draw an 80 by 80 circle with a 3-point black stroke and white fill. Place the drawing
at x = 210 and y = 110. The gradient is set to an opaque level of 80 (alpha = 80) and so
has some transparency through which you can see the circle. Use #FFB3E6 for the
background color.

In the first (and only) frame of the top layer, type the following script:

```
_root.createEmptyMovieClip("blk2white",1);
with(_root.blk2white)
{
    lineStyle(.25,0xA65900,100);
    gradColors=[0x000000, 0xffffff];
    opaque=[ 80,80 ];
    ratios=[ 0, 0xaa ];
    matrix={a:250, b:0, c:0, d:0, e:250, f:0, g:250, h:250, i:1}
    beginGradientFill("linear",gradColors,opaque,ratios,matrix);
    moveTo(200,200);
    lineTo(200,100);
    lineTo(300,100);
    lineTo(300,200);
    lineTo(200,200);
    endFill();
}
```

When you test the movie, you will see the 80 percent opaque square directly
over the circle. To see what's going on, take a look at the following new terms and
parameters:

- **beginGradientFill("linear/radial", gradColors, opaque, ratios, matrix);**
  Beginning point of the gradient fill based on five parameters.

- **"linear/radial"**   The gradient can be either "linear" or "radial".

- **gradColors**   Two gradient colors expressed in the 0x hexadecimal format.
  The first will be the left color.

- **opaque**   Refers to the percent of opaqueness, an inverse value of the
  transparency level (higher = more opaque; lower = more transparent).

- **ratios**   Value between 0x0 and 0xff (0–255). Defines the percentage of
  the width where the color is sampled at 100 percent.

- **matrix**   Nine values identified as a, b, c, d, e, f, g, h, and i make up the transformation matrix, as seen in the first of the following two illustrations The second illstration shows the gradient generated.

3 X 3 Matrix

a	b	c
d	e	f
g	h	i

Change the values in the different attributes to see what changes occur. You might want to start by changing the opaque values to 100, and then experiment with different matrix values.

Type 2 Gradient Fill

The second type of gradient fill uses a different type of matrix—one that contains a matrixType property, called "box." It has the format:

```
matrix={matrixType:"box", x: upperLeftX, y: upperLeftY,
w:gradientWidth, h:gradientHeight, angleInRadians};
```

The registration point of the MC relative to the upper-left corner of the object is expressed in the x: and y: parameters, and the gradient width and height are expressed as values of w: and h:. To specify the angle of the gradient in the MC, use radians. To express radians as degrees, use the formula in ActionScript:

```
radians = degrees*Math.PI/180;
```

You can get a better idea of how degrees look in radians with the following values:

- 1 degree = PI/180 radians

- 180 degrees = PI radians

- 360 degrees = 2* PI radians

This next movie shows how to use the type 2 gradient fill dynamically. Create a new movie, give it a black background, and add a second frame. In the first frame, add the following script:

```
_root.createEmptyMovieClip("greenNblue", 1);
degrees ++;
if (degrees>360) {
    degrees = 1;
}
radians = degrees*Math.PI/180;
with (_root.greenNblue) {
    lineStyle(0, 0xffff00, 100);
    gradColors = [0x00ff00, 0x0000ff];
    opaque = [100, 100];
    ratios = [0, 0xff];
    matrix = {matrixType:"box", x:100, y:100, w:200, h:200, r:radians};
    beginGradientFill("linear", gradColors, opaque, ratios, matrix);
    moveTo(200, 200);
    lineTo(200, 100);
    lineTo(300, 100);
    lineTo(300, 200);
    lineTo(200, 200);
    endFill();
}
```

You will see a slow rotation of the gradient as the value of the radian changes with the changes in the degree variable.

Curves and Clear

In addition to drawing straight lines, the drawing methods include one for creating curved lines and a way to erase any drawn movie clip. The format is

```
curveTo(ptRegX, ptRegY, anchorX, anchorY);
```

The two sets of values specify a curve from the last point of the line or an original starting point. The first set of coordinates (ptPrgX, ptPrgY) curves from the last point to the new coordinates, and the second set of values (anchorX, anchorY) curves to the next coordinate. One way to think of a curve is this:

- Begin = lastX, lastY—result of moveTo() or last pair in curveTo()
- First pair = Curve to X, Y from lastX, lastY
- Second pair = Curve to point from last X, Y in first pair

To help you understand how the curveTo() method works, this next example carves initials in the screen with a black background and an eraser-shaped MC with the instance name eraser. The script can be placed in the first frame.

```
_root.createEmptyMovieClip("initials", 1);
with (_root.initials) {
    lineStyle(4, 0xffff00, 100);
    moveTo(200,200);
    curveTo(220, 300, 240, 240);
    curveTo(270,300,260,200);
    moveTo(330,200);
    curveTo(270,210,330,230)
    curveTo(355,250,300,260)
}
_root.eraser.onPress = function() {
    _root.initials.clear();
};
```

For some useful practice, try and script your own initials. You will see that it takes a surprising number of curves to create something as simple as initials. As with lines, you can enclose curved lines and fill them using the beginFill() and endFill() methods.

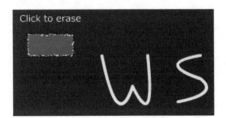

Movie Clip Properties

Many of the movie clip properties have been discussed and used in illustrations earlier in this chapter and in previous chapters. Many are familiar from previous versions of Flash as well; however, 12 of the 30 properties are new to Macromedia Flash MX. Table 11-4 shows the properties, a short description, whether they are new to Macromedia Flash MX, and whether they are read-only, can be read and set, or are references.

Movie clip properties can be assigned to any movie clip as well as other objects on the stage with instance names. Some of the new properties are best discussed in the context of either button or text field objects; you can read about them in Chapters 10 and 12. These include the button movie clip object properties in the three tab-related properties, the enabled properties, and the menu-related property. Most of the properties relate to appearance and position, and they are examined first. Then the other properties are discussed.

Property	Description	MX	Read/Set or Read-Only
MCinstance._alpha	MC transparency in percent (0 = fully transparent; 100 = fully opaque).		Read/Set
MCinstance._currentframe	The current position of the MC's playhead expressed as a frame number.		Read-only
MCinstance._droptarget	When an MC instance has a draggable MC dropped on it, its absolute path in slash syntax notation is stored in this property.		Read-only
MCinstance.enabled	Boolean value indicating if a button movie clip is enabled.	X	Read/Set
MCinstance.focusEnabled	Boolean value indicating if a button movie clip is enabled to receive focus.	X	Read/Set
MCinstance._focusrect	Boolean value indicating if a movie clip is enabled so that, when selected, a yellow rectangle appears around it.	X	Read-only
MCinstance._framesloaded	Returns the current number of frames loaded for specified MC.		Read-only
MCinstance._height	Height of MC in pixels.		Read/Set

Table 11-4.   *Movie Clip Properties and Read/Set Status*

Property	Description	MX	Read/Set or Read-Only
MCinstance.hitArea	Designates another movie clip to serve as the hit area for a button movie clip.	X	Read/Set
MCinstance._highquality	Global quality set as part of MC (overrides general quality property settings).	X	Read/Set
MCinstance._name	MC's instance name.		Read/Set
MCinstance._parent	MC's reference to MC that encloses it.	X	Reference
MCinstance._rotation	Rotation angle expressed in degrees (0–360).		Read/Set
MCinstance._soundbuftime	Sets or reads the number of seconds before a sound starts streaming.	X	Read/Set
MCinstance.tabChildren	Boolean (or undefined) value that sets the children of a movie clip to be included in automatic tab ordering. (Undefined default is the same as true.)	X	Read/Set
MCinstance.tabEnabled	Boolean (or undefined) value that sets a movie clip is automatically tab ordered. (Undefined default is the same as true.)	X	Read/Set

Table 11-4. *Movie Clip Properties and Read/Set Status* (continued)

Property	Description	MX	Read/Set or Read-Only
MCinstance.tabIndex	Returns and sets the order of MC in tab sequence	X	Read/Set
MCinstance._target	MC's instance target path.		Read-only
MCinstance._totalframes	The total number of frames in a movie clip instance.		Read-only
MCinstance.trackAsMenu	A Boolean value that must be set to true so that other buttons can receive mouse release events. (Default behavior is false.)	X	Read/Set
MCinstance._url	A downloaded SWF's URL containing MC		Read-only
MCinstance.useHandCursor	Boolean value indicating whether hand cursor (true) or arrow cursor (false) appears on screen.	X	Read/Set
MCinstance._visible	MC's visibility as a Boolean value.		Read/Set
MCinstance._width	MC's width in pixels.		Read/Set
MCinstance._x	MC's horizontal position on the screen.		Read/Set
MCinstance._xmouse	Current horizontal position of mouse cursor.		Read-only

Table 11-4. *Movie Clip Properties and Read/Set Status* (continued)

Property	Description	MX	Read/Set or Read-Only
MCinstance._xscale	Relative scale of MC's width.		Read/Set
MCinstance._y	MC's vertical position on the screen.		Read/Set
MCinstance._ymouse	Current vertical position of mouse cursor on the MC.		Read-only
MCinstance._yscale	Relative scale of MC's height.		Read/Set

Table 11-4. *Movie Clip Properties and Read/Set Status* (continued)

Appearance and Position

Most MC properties deal with a movie clip's appearance (transparency, visibility) or position. However, the difference between how a property is related to a movie clip and a general property is very different. For example, the _xmouse and _ymouse properties return the horizontal and vertical positions of the mouse cursor relative to the stage's upper-left corner, while the same properties of a movie clip return the mouse position relative to the registration point of the movie clip. To see this difference, open a new movie, add two dynamic text fields with the instance names myX and myY. Draw a circle, transform it into a movie clip, and give it the instance name disc. Add the following script to the first frame:

```
_root.disc.onMouseMove = function() {
    _root.myX.text = _root.disc._xmouse;
    _root.myY.text = _root.disc._ymouse;
    updateAfterEvent();
};
```

You will see that when you move the mouse to the center point of the MC, the text fields report 0,0, while all other movements of the mouse show positive and negative values relative to the movie clip's center point.

Using the other position and appearance properties is far more straightforward. To see how the different properties work, this next movie changes a simple square movie clip into a surprise using several properties. It's a simple movie as far as setting up the stage and movie clip is concerned. Figure 11-4 shows what the stage will look like when it's complete.

The movie has the following three layers:

- Script
- MC
- Background

As you will see, most of the moviemaking is done with the script that changes the MC's properties. Begin by setting up the color scheme shown in Table 11-5.

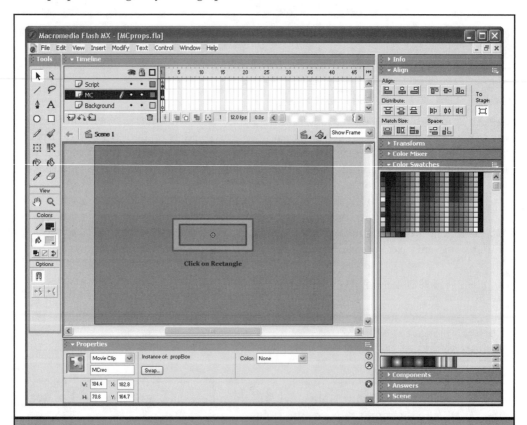

Figure 11-4. *A single rectangle movie clip is the sole object on the stage.*

Name	R	G	B
Tan	223	184	112
Orange	241	124	36
Slate green	89	157	127
Plum	128	0	83
Black	0	0	0

Table 11-5. *Color Values for Movie*

The following steps show how to make the movie:

1. Open a new movie and add the three layers noted above. Select the background layer. In the Background color well in the Properties panel, use slate green. Then with a 14-point Georgia black bold font, type the message Click on Rectangle. Lock the Background layer.

2. In the MC layer, using a 3-point plum-colored stroke and a tan fill, draw a rectangle with the dimensions w = 185, h = 71. Click on the stage and change the fill color to orange, and draw a second rectangle with dimensions of w = 185, h = 71. Place the second rectangle inside the first.

3. Select the two rectangles and press the F8 key to open the Convert To Symbol dialog box, selecting Movie Clip as the behavior. Click OK, select the new symbol instance on the stage, and give it the instance name MCrec in the Properties panel. You're all done with the layer. Lock the MC layer.

4. Click on the first (and only) frame on the Script layer. Open the Actions panel and enter the following script:

```
_root.MCrec.onPress = function() {
    fibonacci = .61080339;
    for (x=35; x>0; x--) {
        dup = "swirl"+x;
        //alternative rotation values;
        //newRot += int(x* (1+fibonacci));
```

ACTIONSCRIPT
OBJECTS

```
//newRot=int(x* (1+fibonacci));
newRot+=12;
offSet += int((fibonacci*x));
duplicateMovieClip(_root.MCrec, dup, x);
_root[dup]._rotation = newRot;
_root[dup]._xscale = offSet;
_root[dup]._yscale = offSet;
//Remove the comment slashes to see the effects
//and how much longer it takes using alpha
//_root[dup]._alpha = (90-x);
    }
  };
```

In the above script, the first time you test it, do it with the comment slashes in front of the ActionScript lines. You will find that calculating the alpha (transparency) level of a movie clip will be time-consuming, but the effect is interesting. When you uncomment (remove the slashes) in one or the other of the two lines beginning with newRot, be sure to place comment slashes in front of the line newRot+=12.

When creating the movie, I wanted to make each rectangle the "golden ratio" of the next one. However, after a few iterations, the rectangles would have been so large, they would have filled the screen. So, in honor of the Fibonacci series, each rectangle scale (generated by the index variable x) was multiplied by the variable named fibonacci with a value of the decimal golden ratio, .6180339. The fraction allowed more rectangles to be generated in a smaller space. For testing the golden ratio on rotation angles, substitute one of the rotation values with the comment slashes in front of them. You can experiment with any of the other properties as well with the script. Figure 11-5 shows what happens when the rectangle on the stage is clicked.

Other Movie Clip Properties

The movie clip properties that do not affect appearance or position are formatted in the same way as those that do affect appearance and position. For example, the property MCinstance.framesloaded is a read-only property used to determine the number of frames loaded in a particular MC. MCinstance.currentframe is another property, used to read the current frame of the movie clip. This allows you to check on movie clips that are being loaded dynamically in the same way that the frames and bytes can determine. However, the properties refer only to the movie clip itself being referenced, not the global movie. Therefore, when referencing movie clip properties, be careful to use them knowing that they can be expected to reference MCs.

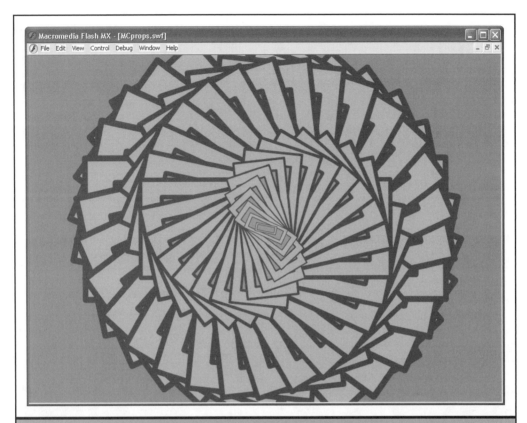

Figure 11-5.   *The script generates a spiral using the single rectangle as a base and changes several movie clip properties.*

Events

With Macromedia Flash MX, the emphasis has shifted from scripts that launch a set of actions associated with movie clips and buttons to scripts that define self-contained functions within objects. Part of these definitions always involves some kind of event handler that is defined as an event of the object, just as methods and properties are associated with an object. Table 11-6 provides an overview of the events that can be part of a movie clip.

Event	Description
MCinstance.onData	When all data is loaded into the MC, the script fires.
MCinstance.onDragOut	When the drag is off the MC after it has been on the MC.
MCinstance.onDragOver	Begin dragging inside the MC, drag it out and drag it in again.
MCinstance.onEnterFrame	Continuously invoked as the playhead enters new frame. These actions are processed prior to scripts associated directly with the frame.
MCinstance.onKeyDown	Responds to a key press using the Key.getCode and Key.getAscii methods to retrieve information about the last key pressed.
MCinstance.onKeyUp	Invoked when a key is released.
MCinstance.onKillFocus	Invoked when focus is removed from a button.
MCinstance.onLoad	Invoked when the movie clip is instantiated and appears in the timeline.
MCinstance.onMouseDown	Responds to left mouse button press.
MCinstance.onMouseMove	Responds to mouse movement.
MCinstance.onMouseUp	Responds when left mouse button is pressed and released.
MCinstance.onPress	Responds to left mouse button press on target MC.
MCinstance.onRelease	Responds when left mouse button press is released on target MC.
MCinstance.onReleaseOutside	Responds to left mouse button press over target MC and release off of target MC.
MCinstance.onRollOut	Responds when mouse pointer begins over target MC and rolls out.
MCinstance.onRollOver	Responds on mouse pointer moving over target MC.

Table 11-6.   *Movie Clip Events Include Both Movie Clip and Button Events*

Event	Description
MCinstance.onSetFocus	Responds when a button has input focus and a key is released.
MCinstance.onUnload	Responds as soon as the first frame after the movie clip is removed from the timeline.

Table 11-6. *Movie Clip Events Include Both Movie Clip and Button Events* (continued)

Movie Clip Event Characteristics

Chapter 3 covers all of the events for buttons and movie clips, along with quite a few others. The main difference between the events discussed in Chapter 3 and movie clip events is that MC events are typically written using a function literal to define them. The format:

```
mcInstance.event= function() {
    statements;
}
```

places the event as part of the MC's event definition and not as an external clip event. The scripts to create the events are associated with frames and not the clips. Throughout this chapter and previous chapters, you have seen examples using different events in this format. A single script associated with a frame can generate events for multiple objects, so you need not create separate event handlers in separate objects.

Movie Clip Events and Button Movie Clip Events

In Macromedia Flash MX, the line between buttons and movie clips is far more blurred. Buttons can now have instance names, and the button object can be changed dynamically by scripts. Likewise, movie clips can have events that require the mouse pointer to be over the MC and will only fire if the event is associated with the MC.

To see how the different events affect how movie clips respond in Macromedia Flash MX, this next movie uses three clip-type and three button-type events. Everything is done on a single layer in a single frame. Figure 11-6 shows the completed stage setup.

To get started, set up the color palette, using the colors from Table 11-7.

Name	R	G	B
Light green	166	243	192
Green	7	153	51
Olive	166	166	64
Maroon-brown	128	51	51
Yellow	255	255	128
Black	0	0	0

Table 11-7.   *Color Values for Movie*

Follow this next set of steps to create the movie:

1. Once you have your color palette established in the Swatches panel, use the yellow for the background color. Then draw a square with the rectangle tool with a light green border and green fill with a height and width of 43.

2. Select the square and press the F8 key to open the Convert To Symbol dialog box. Select Movie Clip as the behavior. Drag enough instances on the stage so that you have a total of six movie clips, and use the following instance names:

   - art
   - beans
   - charley
   - dog
   - effort
   - frog

3. Place art–charley in the first column and the others in the second column. Label them as shown in Figure 11-6.

4. Select the first frame, open the Actions panel, and enter the following script:

```
_root.art.onMouseDown=function() {
    this._alpha-=10;
}
_root.beans.onPress=function() {
    this._alpha-=10;
}
_root.charley.onMouseUp=function() {
    this._alpha -=10;
```

```
    }
_root.dog.onRelease=function() {
    this._alpha-=10;
}
_root.effort.onMouseMove=function() {
    this._alpha-=10;
}
_root.frog.onReleaseOutside=function() {
    this._alpha-=10;
}
```

Each of the function literals increases the transparency (or reduces the opacity) when each event occurs. When you test the movie (press CTRL-ENTER or CMD-RETURN), you will see that the MC whose event is the mouse movement disappears almost immediately, whereas the movie clips with button-like events only fade when the mouse pointer actually comes into contact with the movie clip and related event. Figure 11-7 shows what the screen looks like after a few clicks.

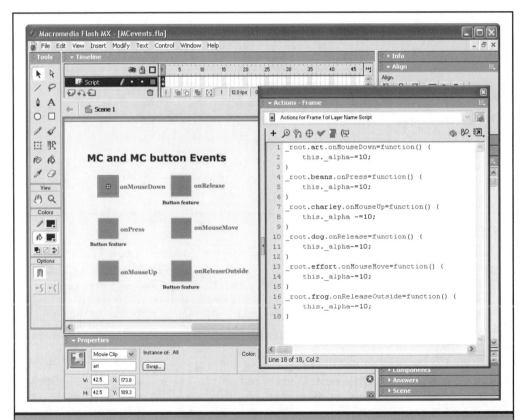

Figure 11-6. *Each instance on the stage contains a script using a different type of event.*

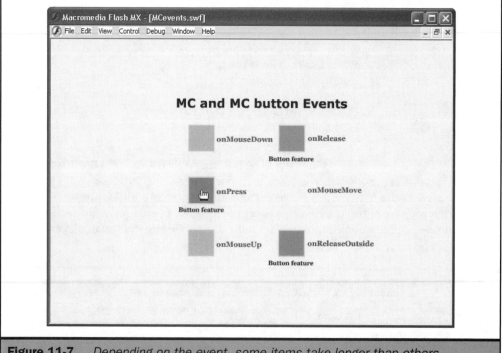

Figure 11-7. *Depending on the event, some items take longer than others to disappear.*

The important concept to learn from all of this is that MC-type events can occur anywhere on the stage, whereas button-type events must directly involve the MC itself.

Conclusion

The movie clip is the key element in a Flash movie, and in Macromedia Flash MX, several new features have been added to it. Perhaps the most important is the ability for movie clips to handle button-like events on the clip itself. Likewise, new methods for masking clips have made it far easier to create effects that were extremely difficult in earlier versions of Flash. As you saw in the previous chapter, the button object has changed dramatically since Flash 5 and in many ways can be treated in similar ways as movie clips.

The next chapter continues the examination of the objects in the Movie folder. Again you will see several different kinds of movie clip–like methods and properties added to objects that once could not be dynamically changed in a Flash movie. For example, while text fields have instance names, they do not have many properties you will recognize as being similar to movie clip properties. Likewise the selection, sound, stage, and text format objects all have methods and properties of their own, and yet they are applied in a similar fashion to those found in movie clips.

The
Complete
Reference

Chapter 12

Movie Objects III

I n the Movie folder in the ActionScript toolbox, the different subfolders have the full complement of the different types of object elements, including methods, properties, events, and listeners. In the Stage, TextField, and TextFormat subfolders, you will find a wide range of tools that will help format what the user sees on the stage, especially in text fields. To provide that control, the role of events and listeners is essential, and once you have mastered their use, you will find a whole new host of features in your Flash movies that you can control so that they will do what you want them to.

_parent

_parent: Property

When a movie clip references the timeline of the movie clip that contains it, it can do so by referencing _parent instead of the instance name of the movie clip. The reference is a relative one and can be used for more than one level. For example, the following are both legitimate relative references using _parent from a script within an embedded movie clip:

```
_parent._rotation=55;
```

```
_parent._parent.gotoAndPlay("addPoint");
```

To try out a script, create a movie clip embedded inside a movie clip that is embedded inside another movie clip. Give the innermost movie clip the instance name joe, and in the first frame of the joe clip type the following script:

```
this.onPress = function() {
        _parent._parent._alpha = 55;
};
```

When you run it, all of the alpha levels are affected in the three MCs. Change it to:

```
this.onPress = function() {
        this._alpha = 55;
};
```

and you will see that only the innermost MC is affected.

_root

_root: Property

The _root property references the root timeline within the context of a level. If referenced from _level0 (the default for movies), the root level is that of _level0. However, if you reference the root of a movie loaded into level 58, you will get the root of that level and not 0. As a general rule, when working with a movie with other SWF files loaded in different levels, avoid using _root and use _levelN to reference the main timeline of a movie. Otherwise, from any embedded or top-level position in a movie, the format is the same. For example, to reference the main timeline, the line:

```
_root.gotoAndPlay(6);
```

can be used from the main timeline or a movie clip embedded up to 15 levels within other movie clips. The result will be to go to the main timeline and play Frame 6.

Selection

The Selection object lets you set and control in which text field the cursor is located in a Flash movie. The text field that is said to have "focus" is the field in which the cursor is currently located. Selection-span indexes are zero-based (for example, the first position is 0, the second position is 1, and so on). There is no constructor method for the Selection object, as there can only be one currently focused field at a time.

Methods

To work through the examples in this section, add several Input text fields to a movie stage. You should be able to press the TAB key and go from one to the other.

addLearner

Selection.addListener(lisObj): Method

The addListener() method works in conjunction with the onSetFocus() method and an object you use for a listener. The method registers your "listening object" so that when a focus has been set on any selection, it receives notification that invokes any function waiting for the notification. The following example shows how:

```
formHear=new Object();
formHear.onSetFocus=function(){
     trace("You changed focus.")
}
Selection.addListener(formHear);
```

getBeginIndex

Selection.getBeginIndex(): Method

The getBeginIndex() method gets the index at the beginning of the selection span. A beginning index must be set with the setSelection() method or the method returns a -1.

For example, the following script places the beginning value of the selection span in the variable startSel:

```
var startSel = Selection.getBeginIndex();
```

Also see Selection.setSelection().

getCaretIndex
Selection.getCaretIndex(): Method

The caret position is the last selected character in a span. However, the caret position is relative to all of the text fields on the stage. The getCaretIndex() method returns the position of the caret position relative to all of the text fields. To see how this works, place two Input text fields on a page and a single button. Name the button clicker, the top text field Uname, and the bottom text field email. Select the first frame of the movie and type the following script:

```
formHear = new Object();
formHear.onSetFocus = function() {
      Selection.setSelection(0,1);
};
Selection.addListener(formHear);
_root.clicker.onPress = function() {
      Selection.setFocus("email");
      var wabbit = Selection.getCaretIndex();
      trace(wabbit);
};
```

Type 01234 in the top field and 56789 in the bottom field. The following shows what you should see:

The caret is placed over the first character of the second line. Beginning with 0, in the first text field, the setFocus() method forces the cursor to the email text field. The first character is selected in the text field because the setSelection() method is set at 0,1. Thus, the caret is in position 5 as both the Output window and text field revealed.

getEndIndex

Selection.getEndIndex(): Method

The getEndIndex() method gets the index at the end of selection span. An ending index must be set with the setSelection() method or the method returns a -1. For example, the following script places the ending value of the selection span in the variable endSel:

```
var endSel = Selection.getEndIndex();
```

Also see Selection.setSelection().

getFocus()

Selection.getFocus: Method

The getFocus() method returns the instance name of the object currently selected. For example, if your script set the focus on an object named flyer, the getFocus() method would return:

```
_level0.flyer
```

This method works in conjunction with the Selection.setFocus() method, and if no focus is set, it returns a null value:

```
Selection.setFocus("_root.email");
var where=Selection.getFocus()
//Returns _level0.email
```

removeListener

Selection.removeListener(listenObj): Method

The removeListener() method removes the listener from the object that was registered with addListener(). The only argument in the method is the listening object's name, and it is required. This next movie shows how the listener can be removed.

Place two Input text fields on the stage, giving one the instance name uno and the other dos. Add the following script to the first frame:

```
formHear = new Object();
formHear.onSetFocus = function() {
    Selection.setSelection(0, 1);
    var rightHere = Selection.getCaretIndex();
```

```
        trace(rightHere);
        counter++;
        _level0.dos.text=counter;
        if (counter>12) {
                Selection.removeListener(formHear);
        }
};
Selection.addListener(formHear);
```

Test the movie and click back and forth between the first and second text fields. As soon as the value is over 12, the script places one more value in the counter variable and quits. That's because the listener was removed after the counter exceeded 12.

setFocus

Selection.setFocus(instanceName): Method

The setFocus() method sets the focus to the object with the instance name in the argument. If using Flash 5, use the text field's variable name. The following example shows how a button with the instance name setter uses the method to set the focus on a text field with the instance name totalBill:

```
_level0.setter.onPress = function() {
        Selection.setFocus(_level0.totalBill);
};
```

setSelection

Selection.setSelection(b,e): Method

The setSelection() method requires two arguments. The first argument sets the first position of a selection span and the second sets the span's termination point. The first character is considered 0, so to set the first argument to the first character, you would use 0 and the termination point is the position after the last character you want in the movie. The following movie illustrates how to use the method:

```
formHear = new Object();
formHear.onSetFocus = function() {
        Selection.setSelection(2, 4);
        var startSel = Selection.getBeginIndex();
        var endSel = Selection.getEndIndex();
        trace(startSel+newline+endSel);
};
Selection.addListener(formHear);
```

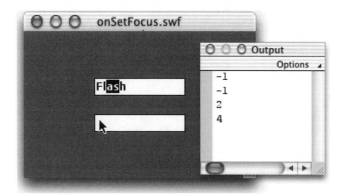

Listener

The single Selection listener looks for a changing focus. The focus change is accomplished by clicking on an Input text field or button object.

onSetFocus

Selection.onSetFocus: Listener

The onSetFocus listener must be used with the addListener() method and an object. It sets up the condition for notification when a focus has been changed from one object (text field or button) to another. The following script provides a demonstrative example:

```
formHear=new Object();
formHear.onSetFocus=function(){
      trace("You changed focus.")
}
Selection.addListener(formHear);
```

Sound

The sound object is built with the Sound constructor. Other than MP3 sound files loaded from external sources, all sounds used with the Sound object must first be imported to the library, then set to export for ActionScript. Using the Linkage selection in the Library panel context menu, sound files imported into the library are given names that can be linked to sound objects. Once linked, the Sound object provides several different methods, properties, and events that give you fuller control over sounds in Macromedia Flash MX.

new Sound

Establish a Sound object by assigning an identifier with a sound constructor. The format is similar to other objects in ActionScript MX. The following is the general construction format:

```
soundMind = new Sound();
```

All methods, properties, and events are attached to the identifier constructed as a Sound object.

Methods

The several methods in Macromedia Flash MX allow many different types of sound control in your movie. Using them either in conjunction with movies placed in different layers or on their own, the methods give you more precise control of volume and input through channels (speakers) as well as starting, stopping, and responding to Sound events.

attachSound

Sound.attachSound(soundObj): Method

The attachSound() method works in conjunction with a sound file in the Library panel, the start() method, and a sound object you have to create using the Sound constructor. To get sound working in this context, you also need to provide the sound with linkage that includes an identifier for the sound. The attachSound() method itself is pretty simple. It's all the other elements that must be in place that add some extra steps. So beginning with the following script in the first frame, each other step will be taken separately.

```
revive = new Sound();
revive.attachSound("revival"); //"revival" is the identifier
revive.start();
```

1. Create or download a sound file, and select File | Import To Library from the menu bar.

2. Once the sound file is in the Library panel, select it and then open the Library pop-up menu as shown in Figure 12-1 and select Linkage.

3. In the Linkage Properties dialog box, provide an identifier name and select the Export For ActionScript and Export In First Frame options.

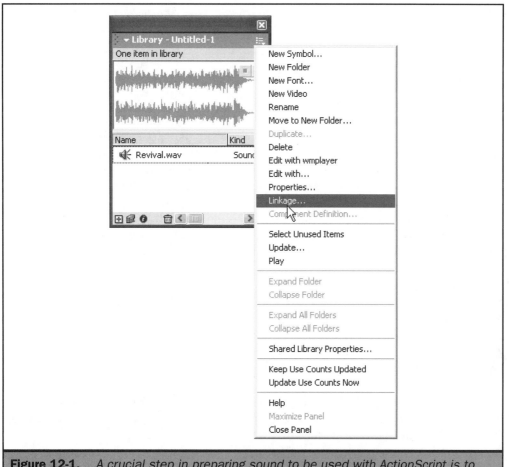

Figure 12-1.   *A crucial step in preparing sound to be used with ActionScript is to establish the linkage.*

Only after going through the previous three steps will the script work. When using any sound file in the Library panel, you must first set up the linkage as shown.

Lots of free music and sound can be found on the Web. At http://www.flashkit.com/ you can find some 6,000 sound effects and another 4,000 sound loops. These sounds have been contributed by Flash users and are royalty free.

getBytesLoaded()
Sound.getBytesLoaded(): Method

The getBytesLoaded() method returns an integer indicating the number of bytes currently streamed. First construct a Sound object and then attach the method to the object to get the current number of the movie streamed. The current number of bytes loaded for the specified Sound object are typically compared with getBytesTotal() to generate the proportion or percent of all of the bytes of a sound currently streamed. (For a complete example, see loadSound() later in this section.)

The following script uses dynamically loaded sounds rather than ones that have been imported and reside in the library. You will note that the sound type is MP3, which is indicated by the extension .mp3.

```
hotStuff = new Sound();
hotStuff.loadSound("http://www.sandlight.com/salsa.mp3", true);
hotStuff.start();
.....//More script
var loadie=hotStuff.getBytesLoaded();
....//More script
```

Before you can begin finding the number of bytes loaded, you must first begin the loading process using the Sound.loadSound() method. As the sound is streamed in, the getBytesLoaded() method is updated.

getBytesTotal()
Sound.getBytesTotal(): Method

The getBytesLoaded() method returns an integer indicating the number of bytes currently streamed. First construct a Sound object and then attach the method to the object to get the current number of the movie streamed. The total number of bytes in the sound file for the specified Sound object are typically compared with getBytesLoaded() to generate the proportion or percent of all of the bytes of a sound currently streamed. For a complete example, see loadSound() later in this section.

```
hotStuff = new Sound();
hotStuff.loadSound("http://www.sandlight.com/salsa.mp3", true);

.....//More script
var loadie=hotStuff.getBytesLoaded();
var allOfIt=hotStuff.getBytesTotal();
//Calculate percent of the total loaded.
percent=parseInt(loadie/allOfIt*100);
....//More script
```

Before you can begin finding the total number of bytes in a sound file, you must first begin the loading process using the Sound.loadSound() method. As the sound is streamed in, you immediately are able to find the total number of bytes.

getPan
Sound.getPan(): Method

The getPan() method returns the pan level that the last setPan() method established. The setPan() method is the most straightforward way of setting the volume level of the left and right speakers. If a 0 value is returned, it means that both the left and right speakers are equal. Negative values to -100 indicate more volume in the left speaker, and positive values up to 100 indicate more volume is set for the right speaker.

For example, the following script uses getPan() to make sure that if too much of the sound is going to the right speaker, it resets it to a balance with both speakers:

```
revive = new Sound();
revive.attachSound("revival");
revive.start();
upRight++;
revive.setPan(upRight);
var checkPan = revive.getPan();
if (checkPan>50) {
    revive.setPan(0);
}
```

getTransform
Sound.getTransform(): Method

Setting the speakers using setTransform() establishes how much of the left and right channels go to the left and right speakers using percentages of the channels' output based on four variables. The getTransform() method returns the value of these variables based on the previous setTransform call. (See the section on Sound .setTransform() for full details on what is returned in the getTransform() method.)

getVolume
Sound.getVolume(): Method

The getVolume() method returns the value of the last setVolume() method call. The method has no parameters. The following example shows how it works in the context of a script using a Sound object:

```
LCsound = new Sound();
LCsound.attachSound("revival");
LCsound.start();
LCsound.setVolume(67);
var viewVol=LCsound.getVolume();
trace(viewVol);
```

loadSound
Sound.loadSound("url", stream Boolean): Method

New to Macromedia Flash MX, the loadSound() method loads an MP3 file into an instance of the Sound object. The first parameter is the URL to the MP3 file, and the second argument is a Boolean for streaming. A Boolean true is for streaming sound, and false is for event sound. The streaming sounds play while loading and the event sounds completely load prior to playing. Both become part of the Sound object.

 Streamed sounds do not have the same controls as an event sound. For example, a streamed sound automatically plays, cannot be started at a particular timecode, or have its offset specified in a start() call even after being fully downloaded.

To see how to use the loadSound() method, in conjunction with preloading information using the getBytesLoaded() and getTotalBytes(), this next movie uses a movie clip to take care of all of the loading chores. As the movie loads, the MC gradually fades to serve as a loading icon. However, rather than seeing a loading bar, the viewer sees the movie clip fade. At the same time, the dynamic text is displayed without any loss of transparency level so that the user can see the loading values. When everything is loaded, the entire MC disappears from the stage. Table 12-1 shows the color palette used and Figure 12-2 shows the basic setup.

Use the following steps along with Figure 12-2 and Table 12-1 to create the movie. The movie is actually a single movie clip to be used for loading external sound files.

   1. Open a new movie and select Insert | New Symbol from the menu bar to open the Create New Symbol dialog box. Select Movie Clip for Behavior.

Name	R	G	B
Yellow	255	242	112
Red	225	0	25
Teal	79	166	176
Black-purple	64	36	83

Table 12-1. *Color Palette*

2. In the Symbol Editing Mode, add two layers to the existing layer and rename them from top to bottom Text Fields, Circle, and Background.

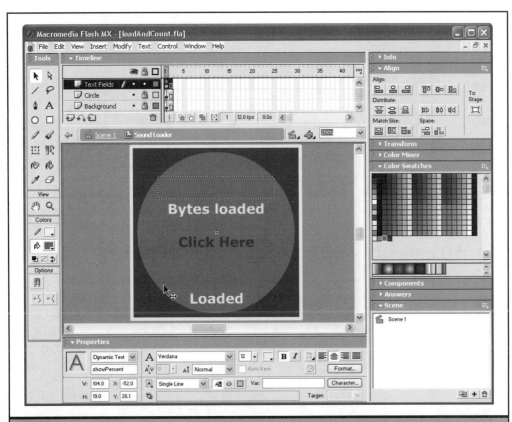

Figure 12-2. *By using a movie clip on the main timeline to load sound, the script first fades the clip and then makes it disappear altogether. (Shown at 200% magnification.)*

3. Select the Background layer and draw a square with each side 150 pixels, using a black-purple fill and yellow 3-point stroke. Lock the layer.

4. Select the Circle layer, and inside the square draw a red circle with a 140-pixel diameter. Lock the layer.

5. Select the Text Fields layer, and add two dynamic text fields, placing one near the top of the circle and the other near the bottom. Give the top one the instance name showBytes, and name the bottom one showPercent.

6. Add the labels as shown in Figure 12-2.

7. Select the first frame and enter the following script:

```
this.onPress = function() {
    _global.boogie = true;
};
if (boogie) {
    if (starter<1) {
        loJazz = new Sound();
        loJazz.loadSound("http://www.sandlight.com/hiphop.mp3", true);
        starter += 1;
    }
    nowUp = loJazz.getBytesLoaded();
    allUp = loJazz.getBytesTotal();
    showBytes.text = nowUP;
    percent = parseInt(nowUp/allUp*100);
    showPercent.text = percent+"%";
    this._alpha = 100-percent;
    if (percent == 100) {
        this._visible = false;
    }
}
```

The loadSound() method selected streaming by indicating "true" following the URL parameter. The external sound then became a property of the Sound object in a similar way as the sound in the Library panel became a property of the Sound object. (When testing this movie, you may find that the external MP3 sound loads so quickly that you cannot see the information process. If that happens, just comment out the script lines that reduce the alpha level and turn the visibility to false.) The following illustration shows the sound preloader indicating the amount of the sound that has been loaded into the Flash MX movie.

setPan

Sound.setPan(n): Method

The setPan() method sets the left/right balance of the sound.*pan*. Use an integer to set the left-right balance for a sound. The range of valid values is -100 to 100, where -100 uses only the left channel, 100 uses only the right channel, and 0 balances the sound evenly between the two channels. The following example shifts more sound to the left channel by using a negative value:

```
revive = new Sound();
revive.attachSound("revival");
revive.start();
revive.setPan(-34);
var nosey = revive.getPan();
trace(nosey);
```

A much more dynamic example of using setPan() can be found later in this section in the discussion of the start() method. Sliders are commonly used to shift sound from the left to the right and are used with the setPan() method in the start() method example.

setTransform

Sound.setTransform(soundTransformObject): Method

The Sound.setTransform() method uses the soundTransformObject. The soundTransformObject is created using the Object constructor. The format is relatively simple once you have your object established using the following format, where p is a percent value between 0–100:

```
trObj=new Object();
trObj.ll= p
```

```
trObj.lr= p
trObj.rr= p
trObj.rl= p
SoundObj.setTransform(trObj);
```

The soundSoundTransformObject represents the settings of the left and right channels as a percent of the input that will go to the speakers. The default settings are that 100 percent of the right input goes to the left channel and 100 percent of the right input goes to the right channel. However, to allow experimentation and develop interesting sounds, the soundSoundTransformObject allows the user to add a percent of the left input to go to the right speaker and vice versa. The following property/ variable names are used with their associated meanings:

- **ll**   Left input to left channel/speaker
- **lr**   Left input to right channel/speaker
- **rr**   Right input to right channel/speaker
- **rl**   Right input to left channel/speaker

The following example places 30 percent of the input to the opposite speaker. The soundSoundTransformObject is setChannel and the Sound object is salsaMi.

```
salsaMi = new Sound();
salsaMi.attachSound("salsa");
salsaMi.start();
setChannel = new Object();
setChannel.ll = 70;
setChannel.lr = 30;
setChannel.rr = 70;
setChannel.rl = 30;
salsaMi.setTransform(setChannel);
```

Use the setTransform() method to experiment with different mixes of sound. While not much can be done with mono sounds, the method does offer a wide (and wild) set of possibilities for mixing sound.

setVolume

Sound.setVolume(v): Method

The setVolume() method sets the volume level with values ranging from 0 (mute) to 100 (highest volume.) The v parameter can be any value from 0 to 100. The following shows a simple setting of the volume in the context of a Sound object movie:

```
revive = new Sound();
revive.attachSound("revival");
revive.start();
revive.setVolume(67);
```

You can use sliders, knobs, and keys to dynamically change the volume of the sound in a movie. See the extended example in the next section to see how setVolume() is controlled by pressing the UP ARROW and DOWN ARROW keys.

start

Sound.start(o,l): Method

The start() method initiates a sound with two optional parameters. The first optional parameter is an offset that specifies the number of seconds into the sound to begin playing. If you have a 60-second sound and you want the sound to begin at the 12-second point, you would specify the offset to be 12. For example:

```
coolSound.start(12);
```

would only play the last 48 seconds of the 60-second sound

The loop parameter is the second optional argument to be included in the start() method. If you are using a music loop, you will find this option perfect for running the loop the length of the movie or a specified number of iterations. The following example begins at the beginning of the sound and loops it five times:

```
coolLoop.start(0,5);
```

To show you how to use the start() method and several other methods in the context of different sound controls, parameters, and methods, the following example project offers several different ways to control a sound. Table 12-2 shows the color palette for the movie, and Figure 12-3 shows the basic layout.

Name	R	G	B
Yellow	235	204	2
Red	179	0	13
Light brown	200	173	129

Table 12-2. *Color Palette*

Name	R	G	B
Light tan	242	237	160
Light peach	254	217	153
Black	0	0	0

Table 12-2.   *Color Palette* (continued)

The following steps show how to build the movie. Feel free to add your own flourishes and modifications.

1. Open a new movie and add three layers for a total of four. From top to bottom, name them Actions, Speakers, Controls, and Background.

2. Select the Background layer, click on the stage, and set the background color to light brown. Use the Rectangle tool to draw a 10-point yellow rectangle just inside the stage area as shown in Figure 12-3. Place all of the labels for the

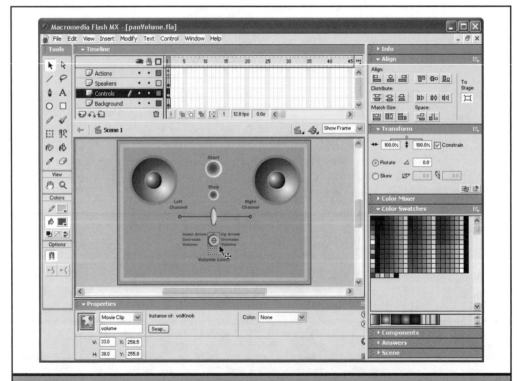

Figure 12-3.   *All of the script associated with a single frame enables the several different controls that affect the sound in the movie.*

different controls, including Start, Stop, Left Channel, Right Channel, Down Arrow Decrease Volume, Up Arrow Increase Volume, and Volume Layer. Use 12-point bold Verdana red font for the labels.

3. Use the line tool to draw a 2-point 200-pixel wide line to server as a slider guide. At the opposite ends of the line draw terminal circles. Group the line and the terminal circles and then position the group in the horizontal center of the stage at Y = 185. Lock the layer.

4. Select the Controls layer and create a 48-pixel diameter button with a red radial fill and yellow gradient fill stroke. Place the button at the top center of the stage directly beneath the Start label. Give it the instance name startPlay.

> **Tip**
>
> *To convert a stroke line to a fill, select Modify | Shape | Convert Lines To Fills from the menu bar. While you can no longer use the Ink Well tool on the stroke lines, you can use gradient and radial fills.*

1. Drag a second instance of the Start button beneath the Stop label. Reduce the button size to 60%. Give it the instance name stopPlay.

2. Use the Oval tool to draw a slider handle. Give it a yellow gradient fill and a red gradient stroke. Convert the drawing into a movie clip. Position it in the center of the slider guide line and give it the instance name slide.

3. Use the Oval tool to draw a circle with a yellow center and black gradient stroke line. Add a little pointer stick to the top of the circle and convert it into a movie clip. Give it the instance name volume. The object is the volume knob controlled by the UP ARROW and DOWN ARROW keys.

4. Beneath the volume knob, directly above the Volume Level label, place a dynamic text field including a 12-point Verdana font. Provide the instance name volT for the text field. Lock the layer.

5. Select the Speakers layer. Create a movie clip of a pulsing speaker. The easiest way to do this is to draw a speaker, and then over about 20–30 frames oscillate between full size and 60% size. Place blank keyframes between the changing sizes to give it a punch effect. Place two instances of the speakers on the stage, providing the instance names speak1 and speak2. Lock the layer.

6. Click on the first frame of the Actions layers and enter the following script in the Actions panel:

```
speak1.stop();
speak2.stop();
startPlay.onPress = function() {
    leRue = new Sound();
    leRue.attachSound("sideWalk");
    leRue.start(0, 4);
    leRue.setVolume(50);
```

```
        speak1.play();
        speak2.play();
        leRue.onSoundComplete = function() {
            speak1.stop();
            speak2.stop();
        };
    };
    stopPlay.onPress = function() {
        leRue.stop();
        speak1.stop();
        speak2.stop();
    };
    slide.onPress = function() {
        this.startDrag(false, 182, 211.5, 382, 211.5);
        lePan = slide._x-282;
    };
    slide.onRelease = function() {
        stopDrag();
        leRue.setPan(lePan);
    };
    //Volume Control
    volListen = new Object();
    volListen.onKeyDown = function() {
        if (Key.isDown(Key.UP)) {
            loud += 1;
            volume._rotation = parseInt(loud*3.6);
        } else if (Key.isDown(Key.DOWN)) {
            loud -= 1;
            volume._rotation = parseInt(loud*3.6);
        }
        volT.text = loud;
        leRue.setVolume(loud);
    };
    Key.addListener(volListen);
```

When you play the movie, you will begin with the volume set at 50. Because the volume is tied into the rotating knob, the first time you press the UP ARROW key, the volume will fall because it begins at the 0 rotation position. (You could easily change that so that the volume knob begins at 50 as well—which would be 180 degrees because the volume is 3.6 times the value of the rotation position.) Figure 12-4 shows the movie being played.

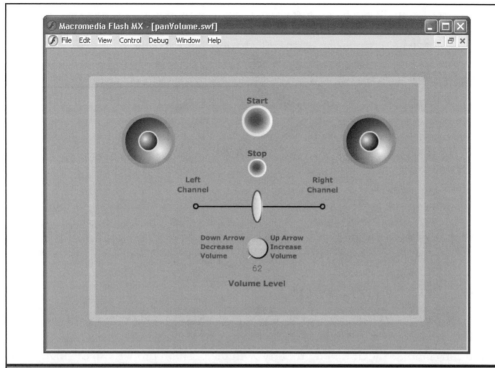

Figure 12-4. *Multiple controls affect the volume, channel, start, and stop of the sound, and sound events can affect the rest of the movie.*

ACTIONSCRIPT
OBJECTS

stop

Sound.stop(idName): Method

The stop() method stops all sounds if no argument is used. Otherwise, it only stops the sound in the idName parameter. The following shows how to incorporate the method into a button using the optional idName:

```
NightSounds = new Sound();
NightSounds.attachSound("dog_bark");
NightSounds.start();
_root.haltSound.onPress = function() {
    NightSounds.stop("dog_bark");
};
```

The above script would have stopped only the sound dog_bark, and if other sounds were also playing, only the dog_bark sound would have quit. This is useful when you have several sounds working together—for example, if you have a series of sounds typically heard at night, such as crickets, frogs, sounds of light traffic, and the occasional barking dog. By having the ability to turn off any one sound belonging to a set, you have better control over the effect you want to create.

Properties

The Sound object only has two properties. One property contains the length of the sound in milliseconds and the other the position of the playhead in the movie. Used in conjunction with Sound methods, you can calculate how long a sound has to play.

duration
Sound.duration: Property

This property may be a good one to show viewers because it tells them how long the sound is in milliseconds, or adjusted to seconds or minutes. For example, the following script translates the duration into seconds:

```
LCsound = new Sound();
LCsound.attachSound("revival");
LCsound.start();
howLong.text=(LCsound.duration)/1000 + " seconds"
```

You can combine the duration property with the position property to calculate what percent of a sound has played.

position
Sound.position: Property

The position property seems somewhat misnamed because it shows how long the sound has been playing. If looped, it resets to 0 for each loop. This next script needs to have at least two frames and as the frames are entered, the display shows how long the sound has been playing.

```
if (starter<1) {
    LCsound = new Sound();
    LCsound.attachSound("revival");
    LCsound.start();
    starter += 1;
}
howLong.text = (LCsound.position)/1000 + " seconds";
```

To create a sound testing utility, you can use the position and duration properties to create a script that shows the percent of the sound that has been played.

Events

The Sound events recognize when a sound loads and when it has completed playing. Both of these events are useful for coordinating any number of other objects, including other sounds, in a movie.

onLoad

Sound.onLoad: Event

The onLoad event is invoked as soon as a sound loads. When you use this event, you need to write a function literal or regular function for the set of actions to be launched when the event occurs. The following example shows the format for using this Sound event:

```
sweetMaryJane = new Sound();
sweetMaryJane.loadSound("http://www.sandlight.com/sweetStuff.mp3", true);

sweetMaryJane.onLoad = function() {
    trace("Sound is now loaded");
};
```

onSoundComplete

Sound.onSoundComplete: Event

As soon as a sound stops playing, the event fires. You can use it to control other objects in the movie that may be related to the sound. As soon as the sound stops, movement, visibility, or any other property could be stopped as well. Typically, the event would be used with a function literal. The general format is:

```
coolSound.onSoundComplete = function() {
 //Some actions
}
```

For example, this next movie is a fairly simple one. Follow these steps and use Figure 12-5 as a guide to create it:

1. Open a new movie and add a layer to it. Name the top layer Actions and the bottom layer Rotate.

2. Select the Rotate layer, set a black background and in a yellow 52-point Verdana font, type **Le Club Jazz**. Convert the text block to a movie clip and center it in the middle of the stage.

ACTIONSCRIPT OBJECTS

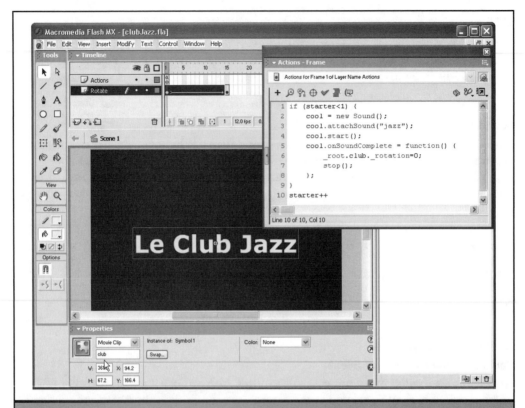

Figure 12-5.   *The script in the first frame uses the end of the sound to stop the movie.*

3. Select the Le Club Jazz MC and type **club** for an instance name.

4. Add a frame and then a keyframe in Frame 15. Rotate the movie 30 degrees.

5. Select the first frame and in the Properties panel, select Motion from the Tween pop-up menu. Lock the layer.

6. Select File | Import To Library from the menu bar and select the file jazz.wav from the downloaded files. Set the file's compression to MP3 in the Sound Properties dialog box.

7. Click on Frame 1 of the Actions layer and enter the following script in the Actions panel:

```
if (starter<1) {
    cool = new Sound();
    cool.attachSound("jazz");
```

```
        cool.start();
        cool.onSoundComplete = function() {
            _root.club._rotation=0;
            stop();
        };
    }
    starter += 1;
```

When you test the movie, the Le Club Jazz movie clip rocks back and forth until the sound ends. The end of the sound is trapped using the onSoundComplete event, which invokes a function to restore the MC's rotation to 0 and the stop the movie.

Stage

As a top-level object, the Stage object has no constructor. With a single event and two methods, the value in the Stage object is to use changes in the movie environment to launch functions that respond to changes in the stage.

Methods

The two listeners associated with the Stage object require an Object object constructed for the purpose of being a listener. One method adds the listener, and the other removes it.

addListener

Stage.addListener(listenerObj): Method

The addListener() method works in conjunction with the onResize event to notify when the stage has been resized. As with other listeners, you need to create a listener from an Object object. The listener object is then placed in the parameter for method. Because the Stage object only has a single event, onResize, where you find the Stage.addListener() method, you will find the onResize event in the script. The following script is a fairly simple one. Create a movie clip with a dark-colored fill and a light-colored static text message, "Resized." Give it the instance name announce and set the alpha level to 0, making it invisible on the stage. Select the first frame and then put the following script in the Actions panel:

```
stageHand = new Object();
stageHand.onResize = function() {
    _root.announce._alpha = 100;
};
Stage.addListener(stageHand);
```

When you test the movie, you should see a blank stage. As soon as you resize the stage, the movie clip appears.

removeListener

Stage.removeListener(listenObj): Method

At some point in a movie, you may want the listener used to launch a set of actions to be removed. The removeListener() method does that. The only argument is the name of the object used as a listener. The parameter must be identical to the one used in the related addListener() method. In the example below, the listener object is named stageHand. The following script uses a dark-colored box MC with the message "Resize" with the alpha value set to 0, the instance name announce, and a button with the instance name RSoff.

```
stageHand = new Object();
stageHand.onResize = function() {
    _root.announce._alpha = 100;
};
Stage.addListener(stageHand);
_root.RSoff.onPress = function() {
    Stage.removeListener(stageHand);
};
```

When you first test the movie, resize the stage to see that it triggers the function to add visibility to the movie clip. Then test it a second time, but this time click the button first. When you resize the stage, the onResize event does not fire and shows the movie clip at 100 percent alpha.

Properties

The several Stage object properties are used to specify settings so that the stage objects and those objects on the stage have the right proportion and position. Most of the properties deal with some dimension that can be dynamically set for the stage.

align

Stage.align: Property

The align property establishes the position of the stage in the browser. The position codes are set up as a default center if the value has one character, while a two-character value provides left and right positions and top and bottom positions. For example, B is the bottom center, and BL is the bottom-left position. Table 12-3 shows all of the values used with Stage.align. If the property is assigned a value not in the table, the alignment will be the horizontal and vertical center of the stage.

To get an idea of what happens using Stage.align, create a movie with a 50-by-50-pixel square, centered aligned to all sides of the stage. In the first frame, type:

```
Stage.align="BR";
```

Test your movie and you should see the position of the square in the lower-right side of the stage.

Value	Vertical	Horizontal
T	Top	Center
B	Bottom	Center
L	Center	Left
R	Center	Right
TL	Top	Left
TR	Top	Right
BL	Bottom	Left
BR	Bottom	Right

Table 12-3. *Align Values and Their Positions*

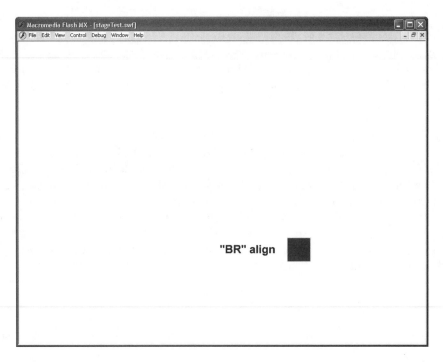

Using the same movie, change the align property value to TL. As you will see, the alignment is toward the opposite corner.

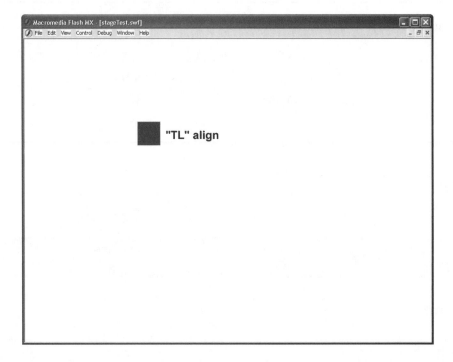

You can also change the Stage.align property dynamically. For example, add a button with the instance name punch to the stage, along with the centered square, and put the following script into the first frame:

```
Stage.align = "TL";
punch.onPress = function() {
    Stage.align = "BR";
};
```

When you click the button, not only will the position of the box shift from the top left to the bottom of the stage, so too will the button.

height

Stage.height: Property (read only)

The height property contains either the height of the Flash player or the height of the stage. If the Stage.noScale property is a Boolean true, then it's the height of the Flash player, but if Stage.noScale is a Boolean false, it is the height of the stage. To see the difference, type in the following script:

```
Stage.noScale = true;
trace(Stage.height);
punch.onPress = function() {
  Stage.noScale = false;
  trace(Stage.height);
};
```

When you test the movie, you should first see the height of the Flash player, and then when you click the button, you will see the height of the stage. (If they happen to be identical, you will see the same value twice.) Otherwise, you will see a difference as shown below:

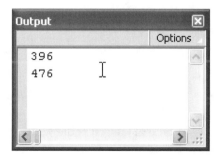

ACTIONSCRIPT OBJECTS

scaleMode

Stage.scaleMode: Property

The scaleMode property has the following four values:

- "exactFit"
- "showAll"
- "noBorder"
- "noScale"

The property sets the movie's scaling mode. These values correspond to those set in the HTML parameters set in the Publish Settings dialog box. (Select File | Publish Settings | HTML from the menu bar and TAB selections.) If you put in a value other than the four values, the scale is set to the default "showAll." The following script sets the scaling mode to no borders:

```
Stage.scaleMode = "noBorder";
```

showMenu

Stage.showMenu: Property

The showMenu() property turns on or turns off the display options in the Flash player context menu. The following options are available:

- Zoom In
- Zoom Out
- 100%
- Show All

Setting a Boolean value of false hides the options, while a Boolean true shows them. For example, the following script hides the menu options in the Flash player:

```
Stage.showMenu=false;
```

width

Stage.width: Property (read only)

The width property contains either the width of the Flash player or the width of the stage. If the Stage.noScale property is a Boolean true, then it's the width of the Flash player, but if Stage.noScale is a Boolean false, it is the width of the stage. To see the difference, type in the following script:

```
Stage.noScale = true;
trace(Stage.width);
punch.onPress = function() {
 Stage.noScale = false;
 trace(Stage.width);
};
```

When you test the movie, you should first see the width of the Flash player, and then when you press the button, you will see the width of the stage. If they happen to be identical, you will see the same value twice. When that happens, resize the view window and click the button again.

Event

By dragging the corner pull tab, users can resize a movie, and in doing so can fire any functions the developer wants. The Stage event recognizes when the dragging occurs.

onResize

Stage.onResize: Event

The onResize event requires a listener to notify it that the Flash player window has been resized. Adjusting windows in the player is a common enough activity, and when that happens, you can trap the event and launch a function. The onResize event is the only Stage event and has important implications for designs. If a window is resized, the resizing can throw off a design. To see how the onResize can be used to stabilize a design, the following movie uses the onResize event to adjust the height and width of two movie clip bars.

Using Figure 12-6 as a setup guide and Table 12-4 for the color palette, the following steps show how to set up the onResize event example.

Name	R	G	B
Dusty blue	79	112	162
Old gold	226	153	57
Red	171	17	0
Muted dusty green	217	233	208

Table 12-4. *Color Palette*

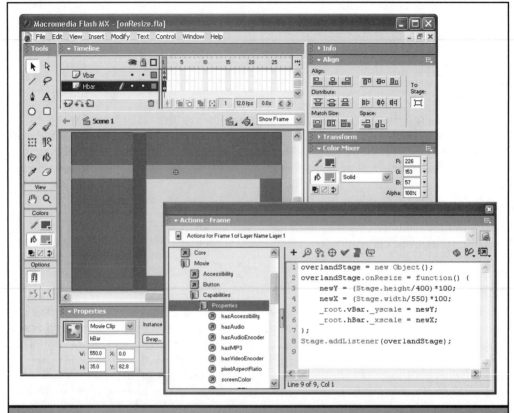

Figure 12-6. *The horizontal and vertical movie clips in this movie show how the onResize event can capture and affect the appearance of a page.*

1. Open a new movie, add a layer, and name the top one Vbar and the bottom one Hbar. Set the background color to dusty blue.

2. Draw a 300-by-250-pixel muted green rectangle in the middle of stage.

3. Select the Hbar layer and draw a rectangle the horizontal length of the stage, with no stroke and the old gold color. Its dimensions should be H = 550, W = 35. Center it horizontally using the Align panel tools. Select the rectangle, convert it to a movie clip, and give it the instance name hBar. Lock the layer.

4. Select the Vbar and draw a red rectangle the vertical height of the stage with no stroke. Its dimensions should be H = 400, W = 35. Center it vertically using the Align panel tools. Select the rectangle, convert it to a movie clip, and give it the instance name vBar. Lock the layer.

5. Select the first frame of the Vbar layer and enter the following script:

```
overlandStage = new Object();
overlandStage.onResize = function() {
    newY = (Stage.height/400)*100;
    newX = (Stage.width/550)*100;
    _root.vBar._yscale = newY;
    _root.hBar._xscale = newX;
};
Stage.addListener(overlandStage);
```

When you test the movie, you should be able to resize the stage all you want. You will notice that the horizontal and vertical bars maintain their size. Figure 12-7 shows two different screens with different sizing, but with the horizontal lines maintaining their full horizontal and vertical positions on the stage. (Unfortunately, this script only works with the player because the browser does not change the stage size.)

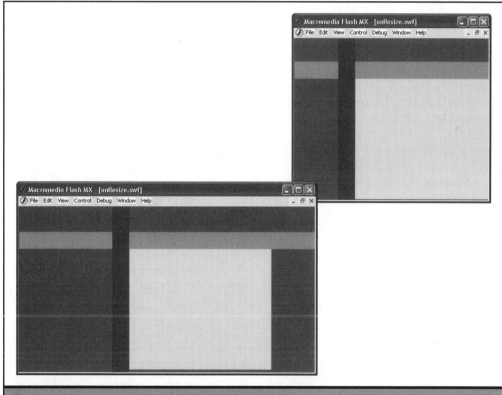

Figure 12-7.   *No matter what resizing is done, the horizontal and vertical bars keep their full span size.*

System

System.capabilities: Object

All of the Capabilities object's properties are System.capabilities properties. In a somewhat awkward arrangement of objects, the Actions toolbox has a single object with no properties, System.capabilities, in the System folder. The properties used with the System.capabilities are in the Capabilities | Properties folders. All properties of the Capabilities object require the System.capabilities object. So to use this object, see the section "Capabilities" in Chapter 10 for explanations and examples.

TextField

The TextField object in Macromedia Flash MX has expanded considerably. It can now be constructed dynamically using a movie clip method as described in Chapter 11, and text fields can be established on the stage using the Text tool and Properties panel. To begin this section, it would be useful to take a look at creating a text field using the MovieClip.createTextField method. By selecting the _root level, the text field will be created on the main timeline without the necessity of having to create a separate movie clip.

By first creating this next example project, you will be able to see how a number of text field properties are employed in ActionScript instead of using the Properties panel. The movie uses several text fields for data entry, and like all good data-entry movies, it checks for blank fields. If a blank field is found, it will not send in the form, and it lets the user know which fields are blank. By using MovieClip.createTextField, it not only shows how to use the dynamically created text field, it also shows how to use several of the properties that are part of the TextField object. Table 12-5 shows the color palette and Figure 12-8 shows the initial setup.

A set of text fields on the stage are constructed using the Text tool and Properties panel. The following steps will walk you through the process.

Name	R	G	B
Mustard	226	209	85
Muddy red	152	56	3
Old brass	227	145	2
Black	0	0	0

Table 12-5. *Color Palette*

1. Open a new movie and insert four new layers. From top to bottom, name the layers, Forms, Labels, Backdrop, Backdrop2, and Background.

2. Select the Background layer, set the background color to mustard, and use the Oval tool to draw a large oval with a muddy red fill and old brass stroke. Use a 10-point stroke and have the oval's sides touch the sides of the stage. Lock the layer.

3. Select the Backdrop2 layer, and use the rectangle tool to draw a rectangle inside the oval that covers most of the horizontal width of the oval. Use a mustard fill and old brass 4-point stroke. The dimensions are W = 486, H = 90. Lock the layer.

4. Select the Backdrop layer and draw two black rectangles with old brass 2.5-point wide strokes. Each should have the dimensions W = 153, H = 287. Lock the layer.

5. Select the Labels layer, and near the center inside top of the background oval, type **Information Form**. At the bottom of the background oval, type **Submit**. Over the two black boxes, add the labels for two columns, as shown in Table 12-6, and then lock the layer.

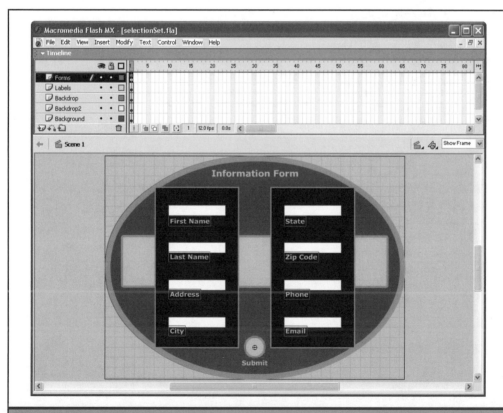

Figure 12-8. *Eight text fields and a button are on the stage, and a ninth text field is generated in ActionScript.*

Left Column	Right Column
First Name	State
Last Name	Zip Code
Address	Phone
City	Email

Table 12-6. *Text Field Labels*

6. Select the Forms layer and place eight dynamic text fields directly above the eight labels. Beginning in the left column, provide the instance names f1 through f4 and in the right column, f5 through f8. The instance names are numbered sequentially so a loop can sequence through them when checking to make sure that they have been filled.

7. Create a button with a mustard fill and old brass stroke and place it above the Submit label. Give it the instance name checkNsend.

8. Click the first frame of the Forms layer and enter the following script:

```
//Establish tab order
place = new Array();
for (var order = 1; order<9; order++) {
    place[order] = eval("f"+order);
    place[order].tabIndex = order;
}
//Limit the number of characters for state and zip code
_level0.f5.maxChars = 2;
_level0.f6.maxChars = 5;
//Create name array for forms
_root.checkNsend.onPress = function() {
    formNames = new Array("First Name", "Last Name");
    formNames.push("Address", "City", "State", "Zip Code");
    formNames.push("Phone", "Email");
    cr = newline;
    blankProblem = "";
    //Check for blanks
    blank = new Array();
    for (x=1; x<9; x++) {
        blank[x] = eval("f"+x);
        if (blank[x].text == "") {
```

```
                    blankProblem += formNames[x-1]+" is blank."+cr;
            }
        }
        //Create popup text field
        _root.createTextField("feedback", 0, 200, 150, 150, 100);
        with (feedback) {
            border = true;
            borderColor = 0xab1100;
            background = true;
            type = "dynamic";
            backgroundColor = 0xE2D155;
            if (blankProblem == "") {
                blankProblem = "Form has been sent.";
                //Script for sending data would go here
                //See LoadVars() object in Chapter 13
            }
            text = blankProblem;
        }
    };
    //Remove text field when button released.
    _root.checkNsend.onRelease = function() {
        feedback.removeTextField();
    };
```

The script uses several properties of the TextField object. The first array establishes tab order (tabIndex) for each of the eight fields. The default tab order would be from left–right and then top–bottom. The script rearranges the order to go down the first column and then the second.

Second, the script sets the maximum number of characters for the State and Zip Code fields. The script performs the same function as would typing them in the Properties panel. Third, the script creates an output array and then an array to check if any of the fields are left empty. It stores the information about the empty fields in a compound-assigned variable named blankProblem.

Next, the script uses the MovieClip.createTextField to generate a dynamic text field that displays information about any blank fields or informs the user that the form has been sent (see Figure 12-9). Note the several different TextField properties that are assigned values in this portion of the script and how they are defined using the with action (statement) to assign different properties values. Thus where the script shows:

```
text=blankProblem
```

it's another way of stating:

```
feedback.text=blankProblem
```

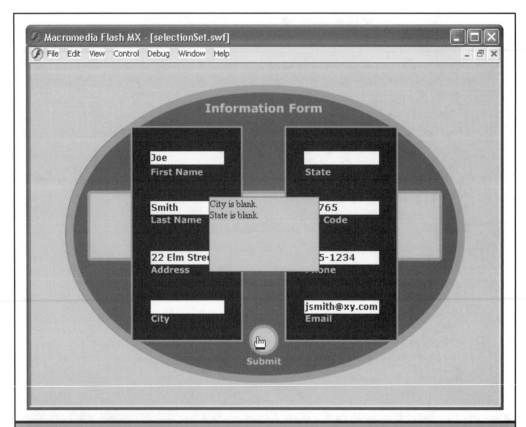

Figure 12-9.   *When the form is submitted, an additional text field appears when the Submit button is clicked to inform the user whether the form was completed correctly.*

Using the with action makes it a lot simpler because you can specify several different TextField properties with a single reference to the object.

The final segment of the script is a function literal hooked up to the checkNsend button object. Its purpose is to get rid of the text field when the button is released. If you've ever filled out a form and had to backtrack pages to find out what you left out, you might find this method a little quicker and less tiresome to the user. What is interesting about the removeTextField() method is that it is associated with the TextField object. Since the createTextField() method belongs to the MovieClip object, you would expect the removal method to belong to the same object. However, in this case, the creation method belongs to one object and the removal method to another.

Through the rest of this section, you will find references to this movie and example excerpts taken from it. The movie is a good one to use as a test bench to try out different script elements associated with the TextField object.

Methods

The TextField object methods are of the get/set and add/remove variety. You can get various text field–related characteristics such as formats and font list. You can also set formats. These methods allow for extremely dynamic text fields that not only change content but form as well.

addListener

TextField.addListener(listenObj): Method

The addListener() method works with only two of the TextField events, onChanged or onScroller. You can use listenObj to listen with more than a single object. For example, the following script adds a listener using the Object object hearIt. It uses two Input text fields named tf1 and tf2. A third Dynamic text field, tf3, is used to further show the listener at work.

```
hearIt = new Object();
hearIt.onChanged = function() {
    trace(tf1.text);
    tf3.text = tf1.text;
};
tf1.addListener(hearIt);
```

Because both onChanged and onScroller are TextField events, you do not need to add a listener object to launch an action, but using a listener, you can add several different sets of actions to a single event using the format in the above script. The outcome shows that the event fires at every stage of the change.

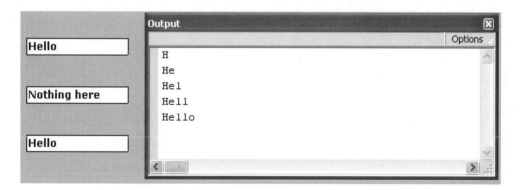

getDepth
TextField.getDepth(): Method

The getDepth() method returns the depth of a text field. The values returned are negative values beginning with -16383. As each field is added, the depth decreases upward toward 0. Try out the following script with two Input text fields and one Dynamic text field using the instance names tf1 through tf3:

```
var howDeep = tf1.getDepth();
var howDeep2 = tf2.getDepth();
_root.tf3.text = howDeep+" "+howDeep2;
//Shows -16383 -16382
```

getFontList
TextField.getFontList: Method

The getFontList() method retrieves all of the fonts on the host's system. The font list is returned as an array. For example, to see all the fonts on a system, the following script brings them all up:

```
var gimmeFonts = new Array();
gimmeFonts = TextField.getFontList();
for (x=1; x<gimmeFonts.length; x++) {
    trace(gimmeFonts[x]);
}
```

A common use of this method is to check a system to see if it contains a crucial font that is part of your movie. For example, when not using the embedded font information that accompanies Macromedia Flash MX SWF files, the following script checks to see if you have a particular font in your collection:

```
var gimmeFonts = new Array();
gimmeFonts = TextField.getFontList();
for (x=1; x<gimmeFonts.length; x++) {
    if (gimmeFonts[x] == "Putz bold") {
        var flag = 1;
    }
}
if (flag != 1) {
    trace("You do not have one of the key fonts in this movie");
} else {
    trace("You have the necessary font.");
}
```

This particular type of script is handy when using device fonts. Because Macromedia Flash MX embeds font information when using a specialized font, you don't have to worry about what the font will look like on the viewer's computer. However, to reduce file size some developers opt to use device fonts. The getFontList() method can be used to check the users' fonts and inform them whether the font is available on their system or not.

getNewTextFormat
TextField.getNewTextFormat(): Method

The getNewTextFormat() method returns a TextFormat object with a copy of the text field's text format object. When you type in new text, if you use the method, you can find what text format is used. (For details on this method, please see the "TextFormat" section in this chapter.)

getTextFormat
TextField.getTextFormat(): Method

The getTextFormat() method has three uses:

- Using getTextFormat() returns a TextFormat object containing formatting information for all text in a text field. Properties that are common to all text in the text field are set in the resulting TextFormat object. Properties with different values at different points in the text are set to null. You can store the text format in an Object object as shown in the following script:

```
var storeTextFormat = new Object();
storeTextFormat = coolTextField.getTextFormat();
//The object storeTextFormat contains the text format
//information from coolTextField
```

- Using TextFormat(*index*) returns an object containing a copy of the text field's text format at *index*.

- Using getTextFormat(beginIndex,endIndex) returns the TextFormat object containing formatting information for the span between the arguments.

(For details on this method, please see the "TextFormat" section later in this chapter, and the setTextFormat() method later in this section.)

removeListener
TextField.removeListener(listenObj): Method

The removeListener() method simply takes away the functionality of a listener object previously set up using the TextField.addListener() method. For example, create the next movie using a single Input text field with the instance name tf1 and a button with the instance name killer. As soon as you add anything to the text field, a function fires that places a message in the output box. As soon as you click the button, the effect stops.

```
hearIt = new Object();
hearIt.onChanged = function() {
    trace("You will see this until the button is pressed.");
};
tf1.addListener(hearIt);
killer.onPress = function() {
    tf1.removeListener(hearIt);
};
```

removeTextField
TextField.removeTextField(): Method

The removeTextField() method removes a text field dynamically using the MovieClip .createTextField() method. In the introduction to the section on the TextField object, the movie first creates a text field with the instance name feedback and then uses a function literal associated with a button to remove it. This is the script segment employing the removeTextField() method:

```
//Remove text field when button released.
_root.checkNsend.onRelease = function() {
    feedback.removeTextField();
};
```

replaceSel
TextField.replaceSel(text): Method

Using the replaceSel() method requires that text be selected dynamically and then replaced. Selecting text and then firing a function that will do something with the text requires more than just selecting the text by dragging. One way to ensure you have selected text is to use the Selection object and setSelection() method. Then by clicking on an Input or selectable Dynamic text field, you can invoke a function that selects the text you want to replace.

The following example requires one Input text field with the instance name tf1 and a button with the instance name swapper. Click on the first frame to select it and enter the following script:

```
switcheroo = new Object();
switcheroo.onSetFocus = function() {
```

```
    Selection.setSelection(8, 14);
};
Selection.addListener(switcheroo);
swapper.onPress = function() {
    tf1.replaceSel("break!");
};
```

Before you first launch the movie, type **Gimme a cake!** in the Input text field.

Once the movie is launched, click the text field and see how "cake" gets replaced.

setNewTextFormat
TextField.setNewTextFormat(): Method

When text is inserted, either manually or using coded actions (for example, replaceSel), you can set a new text format using this method. The setNewTextFormat() method includes information for character formatting such as font name, point size, color, and associated URL. The method also includes the paragraph formatting information describing such paragraph settings as the margins, indentation, and alignment. (See also setTextFormat() next and the "TextFormat" section later in this chapter.)

setTextFormat

TextField.setTextFormat (textFormat): Method
TextField.setTextFormat (index, textFormat): Method
TextField.setTextFormat (beginIndex, endIndex, textFormat): Method

One of the most important features of the TextField.setTextFormat is that you can give individual characters their own text format. Thus, you can have dynamic text fields with bold and italicized characters or even a highlighted background. The setTextFormat method has three uses.

The simplest is to use the properties of textFormat() to format all text in the text field. This next example requires only two Input text fields with the instance names tf1 and tf2, and a button with the instance name clicker. Set different fonts, sizes, and colors for the two text fields. For example, set one text field to black 12-point Verdana font, and the other to green 24-point Times font. Then click on the first frame and enter the following script:

```
clicker.onPress = function() {
    var beta = new Object();
    beta = tf1.getTextFormat();
    tf2.setTextFormat(beta);
};
```

When you test the movie, type anything you want in the two text fields. The object named beta gets its text format information from the tf1 text field object using the getTextFormat() method. Then it takes that very same information and resets the format for the tf2 text field object. Thus when you click the button, the formats of the two different text fields become identical.

The second use of the setTextFormat() method uses two arguments, index and textFormat. The index parameter specifies where the text formatting is applied. For example, the script line:

```
coolText.setTextFormat(7, someFormat);
```

would set the eighth character with the format someFormat. (The first character is 0, so position 7 is occupied by the eighth character.)

The third usage is like the second except that rather than a single character, it applies to a range of characters between the first and second parameters, using the text format object in the third argument. For example, the following script applies the text format to the word "wonderful" in the sentence, "It was wonderful." In a new movie, add a button named clicker and a Dynamic text field named tf1. Type the phrase **It was wonderful.** in the Dynamic text field. Select the first frame and enter the following script:

```
clicker.onPress = function() {
    doormat = new TextFormat();
    doormat.italic = true;
    tf1.setTextFormat(6, 16, doormat);
};
```

When you test the movie and click the button, the phrase in the text field will change to "It was *wonderful.*"

Properties

The TextField object properties contain a wide range of characteristics that you can use to dynamically format and change text fields. You will find a whole new set of scroll properties that effectively replace former scrolling terms in Flash 5 and add horizontal scrolling. Other properties are familiar ones you can set in the Properties panel, but using script, you can change text field properties while the movie is playing.

autosize

TextField.autosize: Property

The autosize property has the following values that control automatic sizing of text fields. The values marked with an asterisk (*) are not yet implemented, but are planned for future updates.

- **true**   The text field automatically resizes to the text entered in the field. Expands to the right and bottom to contain the text. The left and top positions remain constant.
- **left***   Same as true.
- **right***   The text field automatically resizes to the text entered in the field. Expands to the left and bottom to contain the text. The right and top positions remain constant.
- **center***   The text field automatically resizes to the text entered in the field. Expands to the bottom to contain the text. The left, right, and top positions remain constant.
- **false**   Turns off autosizing.
- **none***   Same as false.

For example, the following script forces the text field to expand to accept the different size text values:

```
stretcher.onPress = function() {
    tf1.autosize = true;
    tf1.text = "Short";
};
stretcher.onRelease = function() {
    tf1.text = "Very, very, very, very Loooong";
};
```

background
TextField.background: Property

The background property is a Boolean that provides a backdrop for background color. The default background color is white (0xffffff), and if a field's background property is defined as true, it appears as a white rectangle on the stage. The following codes set the background:

```
tf1.background=true;
```

backgroundColor
TextField.backgroundColor: Property

The backgroundColor property of a text field is visible only if the background property is set as true. (The TextField.border property does not have to be set.) The colors are established using hexadecimal values in the format:

```
0xRRGGBB;
```

where RR is the red value (0–FF), BB is the blue value (0–FF), and GG is the green value (0–FF).

```
tf1.background = true;
changer.onRollOver = function() {
    tf1.backgroundColor = 0xff0000;
};
changer.onPress = function() {
    tf1.backgroundColor = 0xffff00;
};
changer.onRelease = function() {
    tf1.backgroundColor = 0xff00ff;
};
```

border

TextField.border: Property

The border property is set with a Boolean value and sets a border around the text field. The default color is white, but can be changed with the borderColor property, and it must be set to use the borderColor property.

```
infoField.border=true;
```

borderColor

TextField.borderColor: Property

The borderColor property sets the color of the border property if the border property is assigned a true value. The colors are established using hexadecimal values in the format:

```
0xRRGGBB;
```

where RR is the red value (0–FF), BB is the blue value (0–FF), and GG is the green value (0–FF).

```
infoField.border = true;
infoField.borderColor = 0xaabbcc;
```

bottomScroll

TextField.bottomScroll: Property (read only)

The bottomScroll property is a read-only property that stores the line number of the last visible value in a text field. In cases where you have multiline text fields, text may scroll off the bottom or the top. Suppose you had 100 lines of text, 10 lines could fit into the text window, and the visible portion of your screen displayed lines 40–49. The bottomScroll value would be 49. To see one application, create a movie with a multiline Dynamic text field with the instance name infoField, a single-line Dynamic text field named scrollHere, and a button with the instance name viewer. Click on the first frame and add the following script:

```
infoField.border = true;
infoField.background = true;
viewer.onPress = function() {
    var cr = newline;
    for (x=1; x<20; x++) {
        infoField.text += x+newline;
    }
```

```
    scrollHere.border = true;
    scrollHere.autosize = true;
    scrollHere.text = infoField.bottomScroll;
};
```

You can see the bottom number is also the value of the bottomScroll property, but keep in mind that this is only true when no other line numbers scroll above the text field.

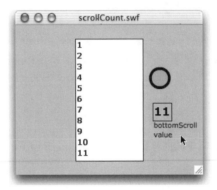

embedFonts

TextField.embedFonts: Property

The embedFonts property is a Boolean value that is used to turn device fonts off and on. The default of this property is true so that the text field uses embedded font outlines. To use device fonts, set the value to false.

```
//Use device fonts
infoField.embedFonts = false;
```

hscroll

TextField.hscroll: Property

The hscroll property is a read-and-write property, either returning or setting the horizontal scroll position of a TextField object. By increasing or decreasing the hscroll value of a text field, text can be moved to the left or right. For example, the following script generates text and then scrolls it left and right across the screen. To set it up, place a Dynamic text field on the stage and select multiline no wrap in the Properties panel for the text field, with the instance name infoField. Add two buttons with the instance names sRight and sLeft. (You can get left and right arrow buttons from the Buttons Library Panel.) Place another Dynamic text field with the instance name scrollHere on the stage.

```
infoField.border = true;
infoField.background = true;
```

```
scrollHere.autoSize = true;
for (x=1; x<20; x++) {
    infoField.text += x + "-";
}
sRight.onPress = function() {
    infoField.hscroll += 1;
    scrollHere.text = infoField.hscroll;
};
sLeft.onPress = function() {
    infoField.hscroll -= 1;
    scrollHere.text = infoField.hscroll;
};
```

When you test the movie and click the right button, the movie scrolls to the left, revealing hidden text on the right. The opposite occurs when you click the left button. While clicking the button, you can see the hscroll value.

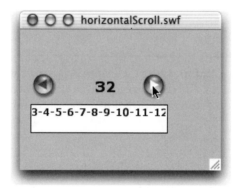

html
TextField.html: Property

In order to use HTML markup tags in a text field, you first have to set a Boolean flag in the TextField.html property to true. If you attempt to use the htmlText property without setting the html property flag first, any text assigned to the text field that contains HTML tags simply displays the entire text, including the markup tags.

```
hyperField.html=true;
//Sets the field to an HTML text field
```

htmlText
TextField.htmlText: Property

The htmlText property is something like the TextField.text property, but it is used to display HTML formatting in a text field. To use the htmlText property, you must first set the TextField.html property to a Boolean true. The following example uses HTML formatting to make the first letter of "Welcome" boldface:

```
webField.html=true;
webField.htmlText="<B>W</B>elcome";
//Bold 'W' in 'Welcome'
```

length
TextField.length: Property (read only)

The length property stores the number of characters in a text field at any given time. It is a read-only property. The following example uses two Dynamic text fields, one with the instance name infoField and the other with the instance name showMe:

```
infoField.text="Welcome to Macromedia Flash MX";
showMe.text=infoField.length;
//Displays 30
```

maxChars
TextField.maxChars: Property

The maxChars property limits the number of characters that a user can enter in a text field. Usually associated with Input text fields, the property can help in prescreening forms. For example, a text field set up to accept a state's two-character abbreviation or a five-character zip code could be scripted like the following:

```
stateField.maxChars=2;
zipField.maxChars=5;
```

If you use a script to dynamically enter new text in a field beyond the maximum characters, they will be accepted. Thus, for all intents and purposes, the property only applies to Input text fields.

maxhscroll
TextField.maxhscroll: Property (read only)

The maxhscroll property is a read-only property containing the maximum horizontal scroll possible in a text field. It is the maximum hscroll value in a text field. For example, the following script shifts to the maximum horizontal scroll:

```
maxShift.onPress = function() {
    var allTheWay = infoField.maxhscroll;
```

```
    infoField.hscroll = infoField.maxhscroll;
};
```

maxscroll

TextField.maxscroll: Property (read only)

The maxscroll property represents the top line when the scroll reaches the bottom of a scroll. To understand this, consider 50 names in a list and only five names that can be seen in the text field at one time. When the text field scrolls all the way to the bottom, the last five names begin with the name on line 46 and you can see the names from 46 to 50—five names in all. Thus, the maxscroll value will be 46 because it is at the top of the text field once the scroll is at the vertical bottom.

The following movie has two Dynamic text fields. One is long and wide enough to contain six 24-point values (the instance name is infoField) and the other is an auto-sized field with the instance name scrollHere. A button with the instance name viewer must also be on the stage.

```
infoField.border = true;
infoField.background = true;
//Fill the text field with 20 numbers
viewer.onPress = function() {
    var cr = newline;
    for (x=1; x<21; x++) {
        infoField.text += x+newline;
    }
    //Display the value of maxscroll
    infoField.scroll = infoField.maxscroll;
    scrollHere.border = true;
    scrollHere.autosize = true;
    //Scroll to the maximum
    scrollHere.text = infoField.maxscroll;
};
```

When you test the movie, you can see that the text field called infoField has scrolled all the way to the bottom, and the number in the scrollHere text field shows the same value that is at the top of the viewable area.

multiline

TextField.multiline: Property

The multiline property establishes the text field as having multiple lines. A Boolean value sets the field to multiline or not.

```
infoField.multiline=true;
```

password

TextField.password: Property

The password property with a Boolean value sets a text field to show encoded materials or not. If the password property is true, a series of asterisks appear when the user enters information in an Input text field. However, the information is preserved as text entered in the Input text field. The following example shows how text entered in the password text field becomes visible in a Dynamic output field:

```
bluto.password = true;
bluto.background = true;
clicker.onPress = function() {
    popeye.text = bluto.text;
};
```

As you will see when you test the movie, whatever you type in the password field emerges as clear text when shown in a text field that is not password enabled.

restrict

TextField.restrict: Property

The restrict property helps "idiot-proof" input forms. The property lists the characters that the Input text field is restricted to. A hyphen (-) ranges the characters. For example:

```
TxtInstanceName.restrict = "a-n 0-4";
```

restricts the input to lowercase alphabetic from the letter *a* to the letter *n*. The letter *m* would not be accepted. It also allows the numeric characters 0 through 4, but no other characters.

The caret character (^) is used to include everything but the characters following the caret. For example, the following only excludes uppercase X, Y, and Z:

```
TxtInstanceName.restrict = "^X-Z";
```

In a more practical vein, the following shows how to use the restrict and maxChars properties to help in the idiot-proofing of a zip code. The restrict property only allows numbers, and maxChars keeps the user from putting in more than five numbers.

```
zipCode.background = true;
zipCode.border = true;
zipCode.maxChars = 5;
zipCode.restrict = "0-9";
```

ACTIONSCRIPT
OBJECTS

scroll
TextField.scroll: Property

The scroll property establishes the vertical position of text in a text field. It can be used with different events to either smoothly scroll through a long vertical body of text or jump to different paragraphs, not unlike anchors in HTML. The following shows an example of scrolling using two buttons and a single text field. Take two left-pointing arrows from the Buttons library, and using the Free Transform tool, rotate one up and the other down. Give one the instance name sUp and the other sDown. Place a Dynamic text field with the dimensions W = 125, H = 155. (The example uses a 24-point font to give you plenty to scroll.) Select the first frame and enter the following script:

```
tigers = new Array("Bobby", "Sue", "Peg", "Bill");
tigers.push("Jane", "Jack", "Ralph", "Grace");
tigers.push("Nancy", "Ruth", "Betsy", "George");
tigers.sort();
for (x=0; x<tigers.length; x++) {
    team.text += tigers[x]+newline;
}
team.border = true;
team.borderColor = 0x009900;
sUp.onPress = function() {
    team.scroll -= 1;
};
sDown.onPress = function() {
    team.scroll += 1;
};
```

As an added bonus, the script sorts the data in the array. When you push the upward-pointing button, the script should scroll upward and vice versa with the downward-pointing button.

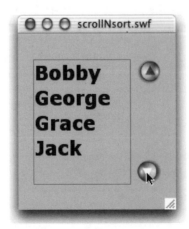

selectable

TextField.selectable: Property

The selectable property takes a Boolean value of true or false. When a true flag is set, the text in the text field can be selected (and copied) by the user. In many applications the designer wants to make information easily available to the user, and making it selectable helps.

```
coolTextField.selectable = true;
```

tabEnabled

TextField.tabEnabled: Property

The default setting of the tabEnabled property is undefined or true. When the property is in the default state, the object is included in tailored TAB ordering in combination with the tabIndex. Generally when creating a user form to be completed online, the tabEnabled and tabIndex properties are used to let the user move from one field to the next by pressing the TAB key.

```
infoForm.tabEnabled = true;
```

tabIndex

TextField.tabIndex: Property

Used in conjunction with the tabEnabled property, the tabIndex property allows you to place text fields in the order to be completed when the user presses the TAB key to move from one field to the next. If you are creating a text field dynamically, as was done in the example at the beginning of the section on the TextField object, you can assign tabIndex properties dynamically as well:

```
position = new Array();
for (var x = 1; x<21; x++) {
    position[x] = eval("myField"+x);
    position[x].tabIndex = x;
}
```

If the text fields have been defined in the Properties panel, you assign each one a value in ascending order of the TAB position. For example, the following might be used to order fields accepting first and last names and city and state:

```
fName.tabIndex = 1;
lName.tabIndex = 2;
city.tabIndex = 3;
state.tabIndex = 4;
```

ACTIONSCRIPT OBJECTS

text
TextField.text: Property

The text property is one of the most-used TextField properties because it stores the information placed into a text field or retrieved from it. Any valid data type can be assigned to a text property, but it will revert to text. For example, the following script places a Boolean value into a text field with the instance name easy. However, when the information in the text field is passed to a variable, the Boolean true that was generated by the expression 7 > 2 is now "true," a string value.

```
easy.text = 7>2;
var calc = easy.text;
if (calc) {
    trace("It's true.");
} else {
    trace("It's text!");
}
```

When you test the movie, the output correctly evaluates the calc variable and decides that it is "true" but not a Boolean true.

textColor
TextField.textColor: Property

Not surprisingly, the textColor property defines the color of the text in the text field. The colors are established using hexadecimal values in the format:

```
0xRRGGBB;
```

where RR is the red value (0–FF), BB is the blue value (0–FF), and GG is the green value (0–FF). For example, the following would establish a pure red text color:

```
hotField.textColor = 0xff0000;
```

No background or border is required to set or change the textColor property. (Just be sure your text color contrasts with your text field's background color.)

textHeight
TextField.textHeight: Property

The textHeight property is an indicator of the height of text.

```
someTextField.textHeight
```

textWidth

TextField.textWidth: Property

The textWidth property is an indicator of the width of text.

```
someTextField.textWidth
```

type

TextField.type: Property

The type property has two values, dynamic and input. (The third type of text field, static, is not an option, nor do static text fields have instance names.) You can set a text field to either type and would generally use the MovieClip.createTextField method. However, you will find occasions to change the type of text field from one type to another. For example, if you have several parts to a form, and you want part of the form "frozen" as Dynamic text fields until the user has completed another part, you can keep one or more text fields unusable until the user has triggered an event to change their type. The following example shows how a Dynamic text field only becomes dynamic when a button is pressed:

```
nextQuestion.onPress = function() {
    frozen.text = "";
    frozen.background=true;
    frozen.type = "input";
};
```

One possible use of the TextField type property is to use screen real estate more effectively. The initial text fields could be a set of instructions in the Dynamic configuration, and when an event is triggered, the information in the Dynamic text fields is cleared, backgrounds are activated (and therefore visible targets for entering text) and the fields are changed to input.

variable

TextField.variable: Property

Each text field can have a variable associated with it. It is not the same type of relationship that was found in Flash 5. In Flash 5, a variable associated with a text field could be used to display the value of the variable in the text field. Flash 5 text fields did not have instance names, and so dynamic change to what appeared in text fields was handled by changing the associated variable's value. However, to change what appears in a text field in Macromedia Flash MX, the text property must be changed. Changing the text property value does not change the variable's value. To see the separation between the text and variable properties, the following script illustrates associating a text field (tf1) with a variable and then assigning the TextField.variable property to a TextField.text property:

```
changer.onPress = function() {
    var feature=50;
    tf1.variable = feature;
    tf1.text = tf1.variable;
};
```

If you deal with external data from a SQL database (including MySQL), the data are loaded into Macromedia Flash MX variables. To display data values, you must assign the variable to the TextField.text property. In Flash 5, you would have simply associated the text field to the variable used to store the data. (See loadVars() in Chapter 13.)

wordWrap
TextField.wordWrap: Property

The wordWrap property sets the ability of a text field to continue a line of text in a field once it has reached the horizontal margin of the field. When wordWrap is set to a Boolean true, the text at the end of the text field window shifts down to the next line, while a Boolean false setting sends the text off to a non-viewable portion of the text field. The following example uses two identical Dynamic text fields with the instance names tf1 and tf2, and a button with the instance name filler:

```
filler.onPress = function() {
    var numUp = new Array();
    tf1.wordWrap = false;
    tf2.wordWrap = true;
    for (x=0; x<30; x++) {
        tf1.text += x+"-";
        tf2.text += x+"-";
    }
};
```

As you can see, the text on the right wraps around so that all of the text is visible. In some applications you may want the wordWrap option to be false to save space and use a horizontal scroll to view it.

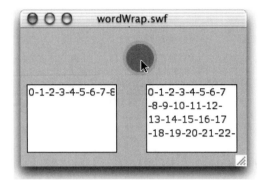

Events

The different TextField object events work independent of listeners. All that is required of an event is that it is attached to a TextField object, and a function literal specifies the actions to be taken once the event occurs in the movie. You may want to note that the onChanged and onSetFocus events are subtly different. Using the former, you must at least press the SPACE BAR or some other key before the event is recognized, while simply clicking on the text field is sufficient to launch the onSetFocus event.

onChanged

TextField.onChanged: Event

The onChanged event handler fires whenever script-driven or user-invoked changes occur in a text field. The act of simply filling out a form triggers the onChanged event. For example, the following script has two text fields with the instance names tf1 and tf2:

```
tf1.onChanged = function() {
    tf2.wordWrap=true;
    tf2.text = "You changed the page.";
};
```

As soon as text is entered into the tf1 field, the message appears in the page of tf2.

onKillFocus

TextField.onKillFocus: Event

The onKillFocus event is triggered after a user has focused on a text field and then leaves the text field. The event is linked to the text field that will be "de-focused." For example, create a movie with two text fields. Give one the instance name tf1 and the other tf2. Select the first frame and enter the following script in the Actions panel:

```
tf1.onKillFocus = function() {
    tf1.wordWrap = true;
```

```
        tf1.text = "Come back here!";
};
```

Click on the first text field (tf1) and press the TAB key. As soon as you press the TAB key to leave the frame, the event triggers the function and places a message in the first field.

onScroller

TextField.onScroller: Event

The onScroller event handler is alerted by any changes in the values of the scroll properties, including scroll, hscroll, maxscroll, and maxhscroll. A typical way to invoke it would be to set up a scrolling text field and then have it fired with each change. The following script illustrates this principle using instance names tf1 and tf2 for two text fields, and sUp and sDown for two buttons on the stage:

```
//Create an array to fill text field
var cars = new Array("Ford", "VW");
cars.push("Dodge", "Audi", "Toyota", "Buick");
cars.push("Infiniti", "Mercedes Benz", "Hyundai");
cars.sort();
//Fill up text Field with car makes and models
for (x=0; x<cars.length; x++) {
    tf1.text += cars[x]+newline;
}
//Trigger function when text scrolls
tf1.onScroller = function() {
    tf2.wordWrap = true;
    tf2.text += "They're scrolling."+newline;
};
//Up and down scroll changes using buttons
sUp.onPress = function() {
    tf1.scroll -= 1;
};
sDown.onPress = function() {
    tf1.scroll += 1;
};
```

Notice that each time either button is pressed, the second text field indicates that the event is triggered. Only when you reach the limits of the text field does the event stop firing.

Besides pressing the scroll buttons, you can also get the scroll effect (and set off an onScroller event) by clicking in the text field and using the arrow keys to move up and down through the text.

onSetFocus

TextField.onSetFocus: Event

The onSetFocus event handler triggers when the text field is clicked into focus. The event is focusing on a text field by clicking on it but not yet having to change it. The following script uses two text fields with the instance names tf1 and tf2, and you trigger the event by clicking tf1.

```
tf1.onSetFocus = function() {
    tf2.wordWrap = true;
    tf2.text += "Focus is set on tf1.";
};
```

Once the first text field receives focus, it sets off the message in the second text field. If you repeatedly click the first text field, you will notice that the event did not send another message to the second text field. However, if you click (set focus) on the second text field and then go back to the first text field, you will find that the event is triggered again.

Listeners

Listeners are just a little different from events. The listeners look for one of two listener events and are attached to an Object object. The listener events must be connected to a text field using the addListener() method.

onChanged

Object.onChanged: Listener

The onChanged listener is first attached to an Object object and assigned an unnamed function to launch. The Object object then becomes the parameter for as many TextField objects as you want to use as listeners for the onChanged listener. For example, the following script creates a listener that is then used by three different text fields. Rather than having to rewrite the same event handler separately for each text field, just add a listener to each text field you want to respond to a changed event.

```
hearIt = new Object();
hearIt.onChanged = function() {
    tf1.text += "I heard that!" + newline;
};
tf2.addListener(hearIt);
```

```
tf3.addListener(hearIt);
tf4.addListener(hearIt);
```

onScroller

Object.onScroller: Listener

The onScroller listener can be applied to any text field using the addListener() method. An Object object with the onScroller listener attached generates an unnamed function with associated actions. When the text field with the attached listener detects scrolling within itself, it fires the function connected to the Object object with the onScroller listener. The following example shows how this is set up using the horizontal scroll method (hscroll). All the movie needs is two text fields, one with the instance name tf1 and the other named tf2.

```
scrollEar = new Object();
scrollEar.onScroller = function() {
    tf2.text += "Someone is scrolling."+newline;
};
for (x=0; x<21; x++) {
    tf1.text += x;
}
bLeft.onPress = function() {
    tf1.hscroll -= 1;
};
bRight.onPress = function() {
    tf1.hscroll += 1;
};
tf1.addListener(scrollEar);
```

You can listen to as many text field scroll-related events as you want with the single listener. Simply use the addListener() method and attach it to text fields with scrolling possibilities.

TextFormat

The TextField object has a number of properties that can be changed individually to effect a format. Using the TextFormat object, however, you can create a single format and apply it to several different text fields. Not only will the TextFormat object save time in formatting text fields, you can create a consistent style for your text fields no matter how many you use. If a format needs to be changed dynamically, the TextFormat object can be used to do it efficiently and consistently throughout the movie.

new TextFormat

Setting up a text format for application to a text field requires constructing a TextFormat object and then defining the different properties that make up the bulk of the TextFormat object. The basic format is:

```
TFObject = new TextFormat();
with (TFObject) {
    formatProp1 = value;
    formatProp2 = value;
}
textField.setTextFormat(TFObject);
```

> **Note** *You can set up the TextFormat() object by establishing all of the values as arguments, but doing so is both unclear and awkward. For example:*
> `TFObject = new TextFormat("Arial",12,0xffff00,true,true);`
> *leaves one wondering what the 12 and hex values are for and what the two Boolean true values are for. However, if you prefer the format, the arguments are in the following order:*

```
TextFormat(font, size, color, bold, italic, underline, url, target, align,
leftMargin, rightMargin, indent, leading)
```

The following example uses 15 of the text format properties. Begin with a Dynamic text field with the instance name tWind and place some text in the text field using Figure 12-10 as a guide. Then click on the first frame and enter the following script:

```
tWind.wordWrap = true;
billz = new TextFormat();
billzTabs = new Array(12, 16, 24, 32, 48);
with (billz) {
    bold = true;
    blockIndent = 15;
    bullet = false;
    color = 0x336633;
    font = "Georgia";
    indent = 12;
    italic = false;
    leading = 13;
    leftMargin = 50;
    rightMargin = 30;
    size = 11;
    tabStops = billzTabs;
```

```
    target = n
    underline = false;
    url = null;
}
tWind.setTextFormat(billz);
```

> **Note**   *If you place text into your text field dynamically using the TextField text property, you must have the code in place (on a lower line number) before you apply the TextFormat object.*

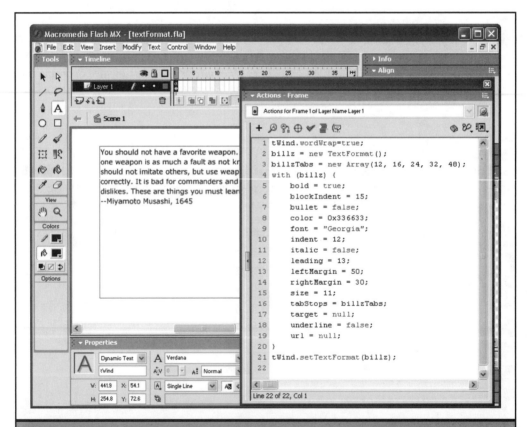

Figure 12-10.   *You must place text in a text field before you apply a format for it to affect the text.*

When you test the movie, you should see the text appear with the margins established in the formatting definitions. Figure 12-11 shows how the movie should appear when tested.

Properties

The TextFormat properties available in Macromedia Flash MX allow you to format dynamically all of the text field attributes in the Properties panel. However, you can fine-tune and adjust the text format while the movie plays and changes—an adjustment not possible using the Properties panel.

Note   *When creating dynamic formatting for text fields, you might want to have a "shadow" format on the stage so that you can see what the text will look like on the stage when you run the movie. You can use the Properties panel to set up and display samples of the format you will see when the movie is tested. This preview on the stage can be removed once you are finished developing your movie. Otherwise, you might be looking at a blank stage as you develop your movie.*

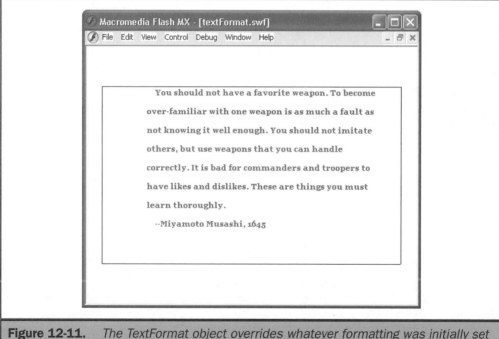

Figure 12-11.   *The TextFormat object overrides whatever formatting was initially set in the Properties panel.*

align
TextFormat.align: Property

The align property has three values expressed as strings: "left," "right", and "center". No assignment of a value or null uses left as default alignment. The property sets the alignment of the text in the text field. The following example will center all the text:

```
pageDesign = new TextFormat();
pageDesign.align = "center";
designText.setTextFormat(pageDesign);
```

blockIndent
TextFormat.blockIndent: Property

The blockIndent property indents all of the text in a text field and not just the first line of a paragraph as is the case with the TextFormat.indent property. The following example indents the text block five points:

```
pageDesign = new TextFormat();
pageDesign.blockIndent = 5;
designText.setTextFormat(pageDesign);
```

bold
TextFormat.bold: Property

The bold property is a Boolean value used to set the bold typeface. By default the property is not set, and a Boolean true sets it. The following sample script sets the bold property:

```
pageDesign = new TextFormat();
pageDesign.bold = true;
designText.setTextFormat(pageDesign);
```

bullet
TextFormat.bullet: Property

The bullet property is a Boolean value used to set the text to a bullet list. By default the property is not set, and a Boolean true sets it. The following sample script sets the bullet property:

```
for (x=0; x<9; x++) {
    shootMe.text += "Line of text"+newline;
}
```

```
bang = new TextFormat();
bang.bullet = true;
shootMe.setTextFormat(bang);
```

The format indents the text and places a bullet next to each line.

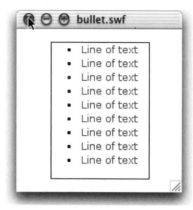

color
TextFormat.color: Property

The color property establishes the color of text in the format. The colors are established using hexadecimal values in the format:

```
0xRRGGBB;
```

where RR is the red value (0–FF), BB is the blue value (0–FF), and GG is the green value (0–FF). For example, the following format produces a maroon colored text:

```
pageDesign = new TextFormat();
pageDesign.color = 0x6C2831;
designText.setTextFormat(pageDesign);
```

font
TextFormat.font: Property

The font property has a string value indicating the name of a font. A null value produces the font selected in the Properties panel when the text field was initially set up. The following script sets the font type as Georgia, a serif font developed specifically for the 72dpi environment of the Web.

```
pageDesign = new TextFormat();
pageDesign.font = "Georgia";
designText.setTextFormat(pageDesign);
```

indent

TextFormat.indent: Property

The indent property indents just the first line of paragraph. (The TextFormat.block Indent property indents all text.) The following example indents the text block 15 points on the left:

```
pageDesign = new TextFormat();
pageDesign.indent = 15;
designText.setTextFormat(pageDesign);
```

italic

TextFormat.italic: Property

The italic property is a Boolean value used to set the italic typeface. By default the property is not set, and a Boolean true sets it. The following sample script sets the italic property:

```
pageDesign = new TextFormat();
pageDesign.italic = true;
designText.setTextFormat(pageDesign);
```

leading

TextFormat.leading: Property

The leading property derives its name from the old hot metal method of setting type. To add or subtract the vertical space between lines, the typesetter would add thin strips of lead, each strip representing 1 point of vertical space. The leading is automatically set depending on the font and size of the text, but you can add or subtract leading points using the leading property. One of my favorite combinations of text size and leading is 11/13 (typesetter talk for an 11-point font using a 13-point leading.)

```
sunTzu.wordWrap = true;
sunTzu.autoSize = true;
nobleSpirit = new TextFormat();
nobleSpirit.size = 11;
```

```
nobleSpirit.leading = 13;
nobleSpirit.color = 0x666666;
sunTzu.setTextFormat(nobleSpirit);
```

When experimenting with leading you will want to use the TextField.autosize property set to Boolean true. Otherwise, it might not appear where you expect.

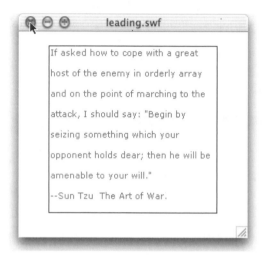

leftMargin
TextFormat.leftMargin: Property

The leftMargin property sets the left margin in points from the left side of the text field's border. The following example includes both the left and right margin settings:

```
sunTzu.wordWrap = true;
sunTzu.autoSize = true;
nobleSpirit = new TextFormat();
nobleSpirit.leftMargin =17;
nobleSpirit.rightMargin=8;
nobleSpirit.color = 0x333333;
sunTzu.setTextFormat(nobleSpirit);
```

When you test the movie, note the amount of space on the left and right side.

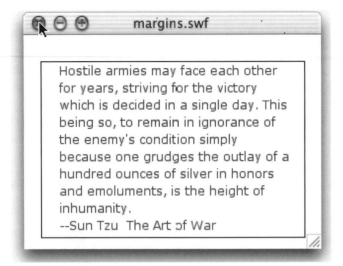

rightMargin

TextFormat.rightMargin: Property

The rightMargin property sets the right margin in points from the right side of the text field's border. (See leftMargin for an example of both left and right margins.)

size

TextFormat:size: Property

The size property sets the point size of the text. The default null value is actually set by the value placed in the Properties panel. Common sizes are between 10–12 points for body text. With Web pages, anything below 10 points can be difficult to read.

```
pageDesign = new TextFormat();
pageDesign.size = 12;
designText.setTextFormat(pageDesign);
```

tabStops

TextFormat.tabStops: Property

The tabStops property has a default value of 4. You can reset it with an array with a set of positive integers. Then you can assign the array as the value assigned to the tabStops property.

```
var myTabSet = new Array(12, 16, 20, 24);
pageDesign = new TextFormat();
pageDesign.tabStops = myTabSet;
designText.setTextFormat(pageDesign);
```

target

TextFormat.target: Property

The target property specifies the window in a frameset where the hyperlink is displayed. The default is _self, but others, either named or general such as _blank, can be assigned as well.

```
pageDesign = new TextFormat();
pageDesign.target = "_blank";
designText.setTextFormat(pageDesign);
```

underline

TextFormat.underline: Property

The underline property is a style last popular with secretaries in the 1970s just before the advent of word processors. It is a style to be avoided at all costs, and used in combination with all caps and bold typefaces, can render a body of text almost unreadable. The following example shows how to make sure it's kept from your Macromedia Flash MX pages:

```
pageDesign = new TextFormat();
//How to keep this noxious style from corrupting your text.
pageDesign.underline = false;
designText.setTextFormat(pageDesign);
```

If you must use it (such as putting your return address on a ransom note), simply assign it a Boolean value of true.

url

TextFormat.url: Property

The url property specifies the URL target link. If this property is unassigned, it will specify null or no URL.

```
linko.text="Link Me";
pageDesign = new TextFormat();
pageDesign.url="http://www.sandlight.com";
pageDesign.target = "_blank";
linko.setTextFormat(pageDesign);
```

ACTIONSCRIPT
OBJECTS

Conclusion

This chapter has covered a wide range of material, but the new methods, properties, events, and listeners in Macromedia Flash MX ActionScript in the Stage, TextField, and TextFormat objects require a good deal of explanation and examples. With the information from this chapter, you will be able to control how text and other objects appear on the stage more than with any previous version of Flash.

The next chapter is the last one that covers the many new objects in Flash. In using the new loadVars() object, you will need the skills from this chapter to format materials that you bring in from remote sources. Likewise, when loading data from XML files, you will need to format the gathered information. So all the time you have spent learning how to work with the Stage, TextField, and TextFormat objects will pay off in the next chapter and just about every time you use Macromedia Flash MX.

The
Complete
Reference

ActionScript

Chapter 13

Client/Server
and Authoring

The main objects in this chapter deal with data that enters the Flash Player after the movie has begun playing. In Flash 5, the main actions handling data were loadVariables() and loadVariablesNum(). The LoadVars object and its associated methods, properties, and events offer a far more powerful alternative to these older actions. Using LoadVars you will see how to bring external data into a Macromedia Flash MX movie whether it's a text file in the same folder as the SWF file or from a server-side script.

The second object you will become familiar with in this chapter is the XML object. While the LoadVars object is new to Flash MX, you will find just a few changes in it or associated elements. However, XML files load much quicker in the Flash 6 Player than in previous versions. Also, you will learn about using the XMLSocket object. A complete, simple example using a free socket server shows you how to add open socket technology to your Macromedia Flash MX movies.

Finally you will learn about using the new Authoring objects, CustomActions, and Live Preview. While these are relatively minor objects, you will find them quite useful.

LoadVars

The LoadVars object is used to manage sending data to and loading data from external sources. At the simplest level, its methods can be used to load text files for display in a text field window. However, the LoadVars object is also used in loading data from a database via middleware such as PHP, ASP, CGI, and ColdFusion MX. As such it is the key object to use in managing non-XML files with Flash.

Whether you plan to use LoadVars as an interface to a back end sending and receiving data between Flash MX and databases, such as MySQL or Microsoft Access, or use it for shuffling different text files into text fields, it is the key object to learn for working with external files. It has replaced much of what was done with loadVariables() and loadVariablesNum() in previous versions of Flash.

When using the LoadVars object with the onLoad event, you need to use the Flash-readable format for all files, whether text files or files passed on from middleware. The format assigns variables with values in the following arrangement:

```
fVariable1=anyData you want&fVariable2=moreData you want
```

The variable identifiers (fVariable1 and fVariable2) are assigned everything from the right side of the equal sign (=) to the end of the line or until the line encounters an ampersand (&). The ampersand serves as a delimiter between variables. No spaces should be placed between the variable name and the beginning of the data or between the ampersand and the next variable name. However, the values assigned to variables can have all the spaces you want. Therefore, in the examples, you will see this format employed both in examples using simple text fields and middleware.

new LoadVars

The constructor for the LoadVars object follows standard ActionScript format for object construction. Simply assign new LoadVars() to an identifier such as:

```
hopLoader = new LoadVars();
```

Once constructed, the object can be employed with the LoadVars methods, properties, and event.

Methods

The LoadVars methods are used to direct data coming into and leaving through the Flash player, to keep track of how much data has been loaded, and to do similar data-handling chores. You will find that the methods add a far more robust and malleable set of functions to deal with variables and data from external sources.

getBytesLoaded
LoadVars.getBytesLoaded(): Method

The getBytesLoaded() method returns an integer indicating the number of bytes that have been downloaded after a load() or sendAndLoad() method has been issued. For example, the following routine is placed on a little movie clip with two frames that traces the bytes of an external object as it is being loaded. When the load is complete, it politely disappears. (On the main timeline, the LoadVars() object, dataLoad, has been assigned a load() method.)

```
var nowLoaded = _root.dataLoad.getBytesLoaded();
trace(nowLoaded);
if (_root.dataLoad.loaded) {
     this._visible = false;
     this.stop();
}
```

getBytesTotal
LoadVars.getBytesTotal(): Method

The getBytesTotal() method returns an integer indicating the total number of bytes in the file being loaded. Until the load operation is in progress, the method returns a value of undefined. The following example uses a movie clip to generate a percent value of a LoadVars object on the main timeline with the name dataLoad. It compares the total number of bytes loaded with the amount currently loaded in exactly the same way you would do in a preloader that compares the total number of bytes in a movie that have been loaded with the total number of bytes currently loaded.

```
var nowLoaded = _root.dataLoad.getBytesLoaded();
var allLoaded = _root.dataLoad.getBytesTotal();
if (allLoaded != undefined) {
        var percent = parseInt(nowLoaded/allLoaded*100);
        trace(percent+"%");
}
if (_root.dataLoad.loaded) {
        this._visible = false;
        this.stop();
}
```

load

LoadVars.load(url): Method

The load() method loads a variable from an external file and places it into the LoadVars object. For text files as well as data formatted by middleware such as ASP, PHP, or Cold Fusion, any variables passed to Flash must be formatted with the variable name, the equal sign, and the data. The load method is used only in asynchronous downloading.

To see how this all works, begin with a text file. Because the example uses the onLoad event, the text must be configured as a variable with the text you want to load assigned to it. Since the text is from William Shakespeare's Love's Labour's Lost, the variable name "willie" is used. The following steps show how to create the movie:

1. Use NotePad or some other text editor and save the file as "loveLost.txt" in the same folder where you will be putting your SWF file. Figure 13-1 shows the text you will be using in the correct format. Be sure not to have any spaces between the variable name, the equal (=) sign, and the beginning of the assigned data.

2. With an external text file formatted for the onLoad event, all that's needed is a single dynamic text field with the instance name showAll. By using the autoSize property set as true, you can take the guesswork out of trying to set the correct multiple-line text field. Figure 13-2 shows the rest of the setup.

3. Select the first frame and add the following script:

```
showAll.autoSize = true;
showAll.background = true;
dataLoad = new LoadVars();
dataLoad.onLoad = function() {
        showAll.text = this.willie;
};
dataLoad.load("loveLost.txt");
```

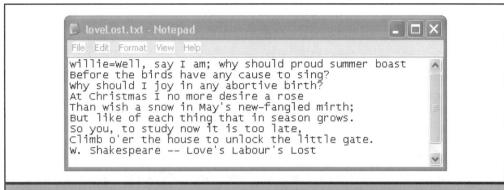

Figure 13-1.   *All of the data should be assigned to a variable.*

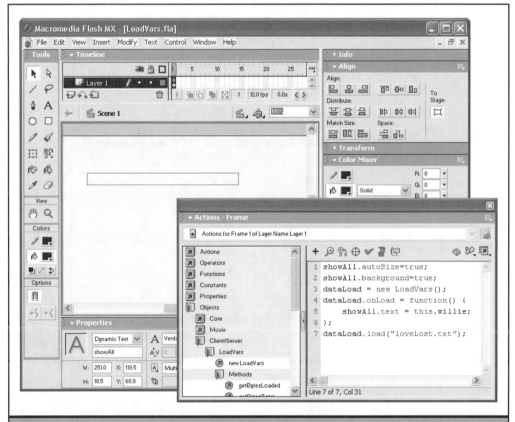

Figure 13-2.   *The stage only has the empty dynamic text field, and the script will load the file to fill the text field.*

ACTIONSCRIPT
OBJECTS

4. Save the file in the same directory (folder) as the loveLost.txt text file. Figure 13-3 shows what you should see when you test the movie.

send

LoadVars.send(url[,target, method]): Method

The send() method sends variables to a specified URL, typically a middleware file (such as PHP, ASP, CFM). The variables in the LoadVars object are combined into a string that is sent to the target URL, for example, if you had two variables you wanted to put into a database, nameM and team. The current value of those variables in the current level where you are sending them from in Flash is included in the LoadVars object when you use the send() method. The following shows a very simple example:

```
var nameM = Uname.text;
var team = Uteam.text;
sendIt.onPress = function() {
      teamStore = new LoadVars();
      teamStore.teamL = team;
      teamStore.nameML = nameM;
      teamStore.send("myURL/team.ASP", "showSer", "GET");
};
```

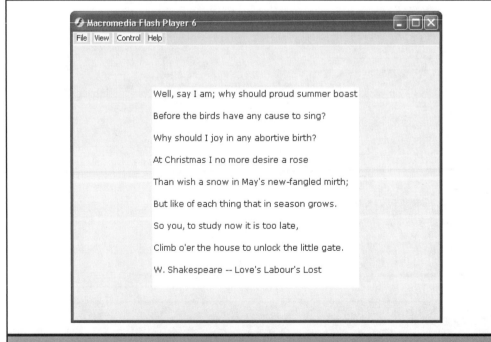

Figure 13-3. *The text assigned to the variable "willie" is loaded into the text field.*

Because the send() method returns a Boolean string but not data, the most likely use for the method is to store data in a database.

By specifying a target parameter, the server's response appears in the named frame ("showSer") in the browser. By leaving the method argument blank, POST acts as the default method.

sendAndLoad
LoadVars.sendAndLoad(url, targetObject[,method]): Method

The sendAndLoad() method is the most likely method you will be using when dealing with databases. The "send" portion of the method sends variables in the LoadVars object, while the "load" portion downloads the server response. The downloaded data is placed in the targetObject. The target object can be the same or a different LoadVars object than is used for the send portion of the sendAndLoad() method. The following movie illustrates how this works using a single LoadVars object:

```
sendIt.onPress = function() {
    var team = Uteam.text;
    teamStore = new LoadVars();
    teamStore.teamL = team;
    teamStore.onLoad = function() {
        //Once loaded place the data into the output
        //window. "this"= teamStore object.
        _root.output.text = this.comeback;
    };
    teamStore.sendAndLoad("http://myURL.com/billz.php", teamStore);
};
```

The script connects up with a PHP script, but it could just as easily have been one written in Perl, ASP, or ColdFusion. In the following PHP script, you can see that the sent variable, teamL, is found in PHP now, except the name has a dollar sign ($) in front of it as PHP is wont to do. The dot (.) in PHP is used to concatenate strings, so .= is the same as += in ActionScript. The following PHP script shows how the variables from Flash are turned around and sent back to Flash:

```
<?php
$teamL .= " from the backend";
//Format variable for Flash.
$output="comeback=$teamL";
echo $output;
?>
```

ACTIONSCRIPT OBJECTS

The variable name "comeback" is added to the string "$teamL" and then sent back in the variable $output. However, in the Flash script, to trap the variable, the variable name "comeback" is used because it is formatted for Flash.

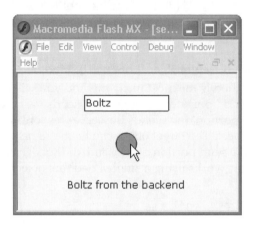

toString

LoadVars.toString(): Method

The toString() method is very helpful to see what the LoadVars object looks like when it contains data. All enumerable variables are contained in the string that is returned when using this method. Understanding this helps to better control and use the LoadVars object. It is formatted in the urlform-encoded syntax. To see the data without the coded spaces and other coded elements, use the unescape() function. The following shows an example of using the LoadVars.toString() method:

```
var penFill = new LoadVars();
penFill.color = "black and green";
penFill.ink = "blue";
penFill.model = "ballpoint";
trace(unescape(penFill.toString()));
```

Notice how the output uses the same familiar format that all Flash external documents do, and how the variable names and data are connected using the equal (=) sign.

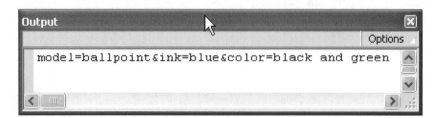

Properties

The two properties associated with the LoadVars object provide information about the type of materials loaded and, more importantly, whether they were loaded successfully. Both can be important in operations where data of all sorts is being brought into the Flash movie.

contentType

LoadVars.contentType: Property

The contentType property can be assessed when either the LoadVars.send() or LoadVars.sendAndLoad() method is employed. It returns the MIME type sent to the server when either the send() or sendAndLoad() method is used. If the contentType property is placed in a position where it will be triggered by an LoadVars.onLoad() event, you can trap the contentType property and read it. The default type is application/x-www-form-urlencoded. (See the LoadVars.toString() method above.) The following script segment shows how to find the contentType property:

```
pcData.onLoad = function() {
      trace(pcData.contentType);
};
```

As you can see, the MIME type shown in the Output window is what was expected.

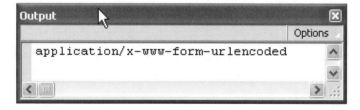

With scripts where you need to change the MIME type, this property is the most useful. When changed to another MIME type, it maintains that type until it receives a different value from the script. In this way the MIME type can be kept consistent throughout the movie.

loaded

LoadVars.loaded: Property

The loaded property returns a Boolean true after a load() or sendAndLoad() method is called. Until the target is fully loaded, the loaded property maintains a Boolean false value. For example, the following shows another way to track how many bytes have been loaded using the loaded property:

```
if (flag<1) {
      sweetMaryJane = new LoadVars();
      sweetMaryJane.load("loveLost.txt");
}
flag++;
if (!sweetMaryJane.loaded) {
      trace(sweetMaryJane.getBytesLoaded());
}
sweetMaryJane.onLoad = function() {
      showWords.text = this.willie;
};
```

Event

The only LoadVars event is onLoad, and as you may have seen, it permeates the examples in this section. The amount of time between when a load call of some sort has been made and when data from a file (whether from a text file or a big database) has been loaded can vary considerably. Therefore, having the onLoad event handler available makes it possible to better position statements that need to wait for all of the data to be loaded before being put into action.

onLoad

LoadVars.onLoad: Event

The onLoad event is triggered when called data has been successfully loaded. Generally used with an unnamed function, the onLoad event handler is crucial because if you attempt to make assignments using the loading data prior to its full and successful loading, the action fails. For example, if you simply assign data being loaded to a text field to be viewed prior to all of the data being in memory, nothing will appear. Therefore, an essential step in building most applications that requires waiting for data to be loaded also needs the onLoad event handler. The following example shows a typical use of the event:

```
snowBall = new LoadVars();
snowBall.onLoad = function() {
      pictureWindowA.text = this.flake;
      pictureWindowB.text = this.avalanche;
      pictureWindowC.text = this.plow;
};
snowBall.load("blizzard.txt");
```

Several different variables can inhabit a single external file, and if this is the case, you can pull out each one separately using the LoadVars object and onLoad event handler.

Note   *One other event can be used with the LoadVars object: onData. While this event is not documented as a LoadVars event, it can be employed as such. As soon as the data loads, the onData event is invoked. Unlike onLoad, the text does not have to be broken into variables to be displayed. The syntax of onData employs an argument that is passed to a function and then placed as the contents of the loaded file. The following shows an example of using onData with LoadVars:*

```
myStuff = new LoadVars();
myStuff.onData = function(stuff) {
    stuffUp.text = stuff;
};
myStuff.load("anImportantMessage.txt")'
```

See Branden Hall's "Macromedia Flash Extreme" at http://www.macromedia.com/desdev/mx/flash/extreme/extreme001.html for more information on this topic. Also, see Chapter 19's main example for use of onData with the LoadVars object and an external text field.

XML

Flash 5 introduced the XML object to Flash, and Flash MX uses a very similar set of objects, methods, and events as Flash 5. New XML methods in Flash MX include getBytesLoaded() and getBytesTotal(). Flash MX also includes a new XML property, contentType. Otherwise, if you are familiar with Flash 5 and XML, you will be in comfortable surroundings.

If you are new to XML, you can find several good tutorials online as well as a number of excellent books on using XML. I generally recommend Simon St. Laurent's *XML: A Primer 2nd Edition* (New York: M&T Books, 1999) because it is a clear and thorough introduction to XML. Online, you can't find a much better place to begin than Mike Chambers' soup-to-nuts coverage of Flash and XML at http://www.macromedia.com/desdev/articles/learning_xml.html.

You will also find good ActionScript tips with XML at Helen Triolo's site, http://actionscript-toolbox.com/.

Well-Formed XML

In writing XML, one of the important features is creating what are called "well-formed" XML documents. To do this, you need to add document type definitions (DTD) at the

ACTIONSCRIPT OBJECTS

beginning of your XML document. Once your XML document has been created with a DTD header, you can validate it using XML tools like Microsoft's XML Notepad or at online sources such as Brown University's XML Validation Form page at http://www. stg.brown.edu/service/xmlvalid/. At the Brown University site, you just browse your drive to find the file you want to validate and then click a Validate button.

Validating your XML may seem like a pain in the neck, but you will be assured that your code is well formed. However, the good news is that Flash MX does not require that you have DTD at the beginning of your XML page, and believe me, without the DTD header, working with Flash and XML is a lot easier. So to have well-formed XML and work effectively with Flash, put your DTD head on your XML, validate it, and then once you know it's well formed, remove the DTD head and work with it in Flash.

To keep the focus on what you can do with Flash MX and XML, the same XML file will be used throughout this section. In that way you can better see what each XML method, property, and event in Flash MX does with the XML file. Also, you should spend some time looking at XML tutorials if you are not familiar with it. Otherwise, very little of this section will make much sense.

For purposes of understanding ActionScript, the following script will be used and should be saved in text file format as books.xml:

```xml
<books cat="Recent">
  <computer>
   <title rating="good">Flash in 30 Seconds</title>
   <title rating="bad">ActionScript in 1 Minute</title>
   <title rating="ugly">XML in a Lifetime</title>
  </computer>
  <fiction>
   <title rating="ugly">The Honest Accountant</title>
   <title rating="bad">Adventure in Iowa City</title>
   <title rating="good">Romance in the Computer Lab</title>
  </fiction>
  <nonFiction>
   <title rating="ugly">Build Your Own House With a Saw</title>
   <title rating="good">Cat Herding for Fun and Profit</title>
   <title rating="bad">Post-Modern Money Laundering</title>
  </nonFiction>
</books>
```

When you're finished typing in the file, or any XML file, save it to disk and then have it validated. You can do it either using the DTD and one of the validation sites, or use software that validates XML without DTD. For example, on Windows platforms, the XML Notepad will do it for you. You can get it free at http://www.microsoft.com/. Just go to their home page and put in XML Notepad as the search word, and it'll find it for you.

View Current XML Source

```
<books cat="Recent">
  <computer>
    <title rating="good">Flash in 30 Seconds</title>
    <title rating="bad">ActionScript in 1 Minute</title>
    <title rating="ugly">XML in a Lifetime</title>
  </computer>
  <fiction>
    <title rating="ugly">The Honest Accountant</title>
    <title rating="bad">Adventure in Iowa City</title>
    <title rating="good">Romance in the Computer Lab</title>
  </fiction>
  <nonFiction>
    <title rating="ugly">Build Your Own House With a Saw</title>
    <title rating="good">Cat Herding for Fun and Profit</title>
    <title rating="bad">Post-Modern Money Laundering</title>
  </nonFiction>
</books>
```

The current XML definition is well formed.

| OK | Help |

Children and Siblings

When working with XML files you need to understand the very simple and intuitive arrangement of parent nodes, child nodes, and sibling nodes. The sample XML file, books.xml, contains three levels of child nodes:

- **Level 1** Books (parent of Level 2 child nodes)
- **Level 2** Computer, fiction, and nonfiction (parent of Level 3 child nodes, sibling of nodes on the same level; for example, computer and fiction are siblings of one another, as is nonfiction)
- **Level 3** Title (child of Level 2 nodes and sibling to other title nodes)

```
<books cat="Recent">        Level 1 Child Node
  <computer>                Level 2 Child Node
    <title rating="good">Flash in 30 Seconds</title> Level 3
    <title rating="bad">ActionScript in 1 Minute</title> Level 3
```

Some of the child nodes also have attributes. The books have a cat attribute, and title has a rating attribute. This information is also available through ActionScript.

new XML

To create a new XML object, use the constructor method very much in the same way as when constructing any other object. Likewise, you have to construct the XML object prior to using any of the XML object methods. Use the general format:

```
someXML = new XML();
```

In the example movie below, you will see the script that will be referenced throughout this section on the XML objects, methods, properties, and events. It uses several different methods and contains the XML constructor near the end of the script. As with other objects that involve loading external data, you can generally place the constructors and loaders near the end of the script. The functions they call must be ready when the data is loaded into Flash, so you will see the key functions built first and then the load methods later. Figure 13-4 shows the script and the portion of the stage where the scroll bar UI component is set to the text field. Table 13-1 shows the color palette used for the movie.

As you are introduced to the different methods, properties, and events in this section, you will be referred back to this Constructor script and you should have a fuller understanding of how ActionScript works with XML files. Use the following steps to create the movie:

1. Open a new movie and add two layers to the existing layer. From top to bottom, name them Text Field, Background, and Backdrop. Use green-blue for the background color.

2. In the Background layer, draw a rectangle with a 4.5-point maroon stroke and orange fill with the dimensions H = 350, W = 215. Center the rectangle vertically and horizontally on the stage. Lock the layer.

Name	R	G	B
Green-blue	78	181	135
Orange	255	161	0
Maroon	155	0	53
White	255	255	255
Black	0	0	0

Table 13-1.   *Color Palette*

3. In the Backdrop layer, draw two black rectangles with no stroke and the dimensions W = 67, H = 400. Place them in the vertical center of the stage, but to the left and right of the center, leaving room for a white vertical rectangle about the same size.

4. Draw a vertical white rectangle with the dimensions W = 82, H = 400. Center the rectangle in the vertical and horizontal center of the stage and then nudge the two black rectangles so they are adjacent and just touching the white rectangle. Lock the layer.

5. In the Text Field layer, place a Dynamic text field with the dimensions W = 240, H = 117 with the border showing. In Properties panel, give the text field the instance name showXML.

6. Drag a ScrollBar from the Components panel and attach it to the left side of the text field. Click the Parameters tab in the Properties panel with the scroll bar selected. Type **showXML** next to the Target TextField and leave Horizontal at the default "false." Take a look at Figures 13-4 and 13-5 to get an idea of how the stage should look when you're finished.

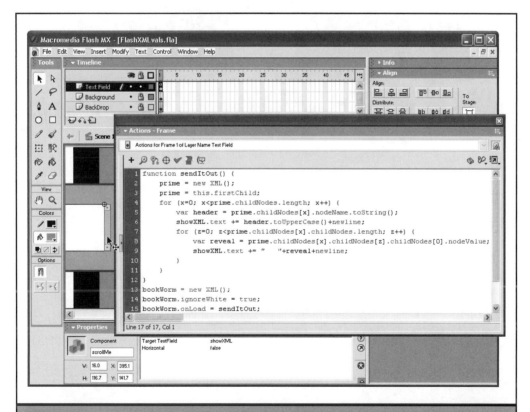

Figure 13-4. *Most of the movie revolves around the tiered ActionScript that loads the XML file and formats its output.*

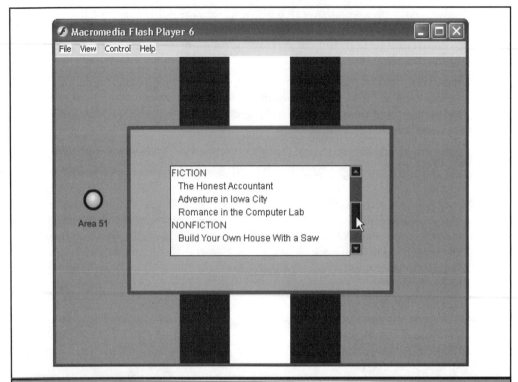

Figure 13-5. *XML-coded files can be brought into Flash MX and displayed clearly; they lend themselves to easy updating and display.*

7. Click the first frame of the Text Field layer and enter the following script. (Line 8 is flush left so that you could see it in one line. It will automatically place itself in the line tiers when you type it in the Actions panel.)

```
function sendItOut() {
        prime = new XML();
        prime = this.firstChild;
        for (x=0; x<prime.childNodes.length; x++) {
                var header = prime.childNodes[x].nodeName.toString();
                showXML.text += header.toUpperCase()+newline;
                for (z=0; z<prime.childNodes[x].childNodes.length; z++) {
var reveal = prime.childNodes[x].childNodes[z].childNodes[0].nodeValue;
```

```
                    showXML.text += "  "+reveal+newline;
            }
        }
    }
    bookWorm = new XML();
    bookWorm.ignoreWhite = true;
    bookWorm.onLoad = sendItOut;
    bookWorm.load("books.xml");
```

Two different XML objects were created in the script, both using the XML() constructor. One of the objects is used to load and direct the script to the main function that parses the information from the XML file, and the other XML object is used to define the top level node.

You can parse an XML file using a second method that does not involve loading an external XML file. You create the XML code within the constructor object and then the defined XML object is used to parse it. For example, the following construction creates a simple XML fragment on the fly:

```
XemailML = new XML("<name>Sue M. All<email>lawyer@court</email></name>");
```

The same XML markup would look like the following were it in an external file:

```
<name>Sue M. All
<email>lawyer@court</email>
</name>
```

It may not look it, but it is well-formed XML. Generally, this second format is used for testing different modules that you may be parsing with Flash MX ActionScript rather than a replacement for a big database file in XML on a disk file. In the XML sections discussing XML methods and properties, some of the examples are of this nature.

Methods

The methods associated with XML help to pull out the various properties of the XML file. By working with the different methods, you should be able to manipulate files that have been loaded from an external source and create XML objects dynamically. You can also add nodes and data to XML files using the XML object methods.

In looking at the examples, you will find many of them relating to the general XML file shown above. However, within the file, you will find a comment section, "Area 51", where you can insert the sample code for various methods that use the same XML file that is loaded from the disk (or server). In this way, the examples of the different methods should be a bit more coherent and show how to use them with a familiar XML file.

appendChild
XML.appendChild(childNode): Method

The appendChild() method is used to add a node in an existing XML file. The parameter is the node to be appended to the existing XML in memory. It does not affect the XML file loaded from the disk, just what will be seen. The appended child node is added to the XML's child list.

The following example clones the fourth element of the third element in the node tree, and then adds it to the newly created primeAdd XML object:

```
prime = new XML();
primeAdd = new XML();
newNode = prime.childNodes[2].childNodes[3].cloneNode(true);
primeAdd.appendChild(newNode);
```

cloneNode
XML.cloneNode(deep): Method

The cloneNode() method creates a new XML node that is identical in every way to the cloning target. It has all the same values and attributes as well as being the same type and having the same name as the XML node it was cloned from. Its single parameter, deep, is a Boolean value. If set to true, all child nodes are recursively cloned. This preserves the original object's document tree. However, the returned clone node is not associated with the cloned target's tree.

```
//Area 51 X-[ml] tests in progress
viewIt.onPress = function() {
    X51 = prime.firstChild.firstChild.nodeName;
    X51c = prime.firstChild.firstChild.cloneNode(true);
    trace(X51);
    trace(X51c);
    trace(X51c.firstChild.nodeValue);
};
```

As can be seen in the following Output window, the node was indeed cloned:

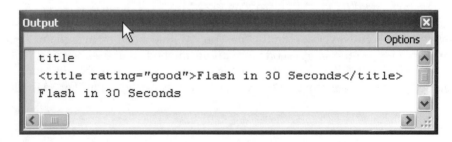

createElement
XML.createElement(name): Method

The createElement() method has a single argument, which is the name of the new element tag. Used together with the createTextNode() method, they constitute the constructor methods for making new nodes for an XML object. When the new element is first defined, there are no related elements in the XML trees (no parent, children, or siblings).

```
//Area 51 X-[ml] tests in progress
viewIt.onPress = function() {
    X51 = new XML();
    testBench = X51.createElement("Author");
    X51.appendChild(testBench);
    trace(X51.firstChild);
};
```

The new element can now be seen looking like an XML tag:

```
<Author />
```

Note   *Once you have created the new element, you can begin to add attributes to it in the same way you would in XML, except you use the ActionScript XML object rather than the tag language of XML.*

createTextNode
XML.createTextNode(text): Method

A text node is essentially a "data node" where the data is in the form of text. The createTextNode() method creates a node made up of a text string. The actual text string appears as the sole parameter in the method. You need to create an element for it and append it to the element for it to be part of the XML object.

The following creates a new element, <Author>, and then appends the text within the opening and closing tags of the element. The script shows both the source code and the text in two separate operations:

```
//Area 51 X-[ml] tests in progress
viewIt.onPress = function() {
    X51 = new XML();
    testBench = X51.createElement("Author");
    X51.appendChild(testBench);
    anotherAuthor = X51.createTextNode("Mark Syntax");
    X51.firstChild.appendChild(anotherAuthor);
  //Source Code
```

```
    trace(X51.firstChild);
    //Data
       trace(X51.firstChild.childNodes[0]);
};
```

The following Output window shows that the text node was added and can be accessed as such:

getBytesLoaded
XML.getBytesLoaded(): Method

The getBytesLoaded() method returns an integer with the number of bytes of the XML file currently loading. A simple way to make a preloader for large XML files is with a movie clip that outputs the current number of bytes being loaded.

```
    trace(_root.bookWorm.getBytesLoaded());
```

Using the XML.getBytesTotal method with XML.GetBytesLoaded you can easily create a proportional preloader giving the user information about the percent of the XML file that has been loaded.

getBytesTotal
XML.getBytesTotal(): Method

The getBytesTotal() method returns an integer with the total number of bytes in the entire file. This method can be used to create a preloader in combination with the XML.getBytesLoaded() method, or it can be used to determine the size of the loaded XML file. The following script change can be made to the script used for this section (FlashXMLvals.fla).

```
function sendItOut() {
    trace(bookWork.getBytesTotal());
....
```

hasChildNodes
XML.hasChildNodes(): Method

The hasChildNodes() method returns a Boolean value. During a scan for values in an XML file, you can find which nodes have child nodes. Those elements with nodes can be further examined for data to be brought to the screen. The following script simply finds if any child nodes are associated with the prime XML object and if so, how many:

```
//Area 51 X-[ml] tests in progress
viewIt.onPress = function() {
 if (prime.hasChildNodes()) {
  trace("prime has "+prime.childNodes.length+" child nodes!");
 } else {
  trace("prime has no child nodes.");
 }
};
```

The Output window clearly shows the number of nodes:

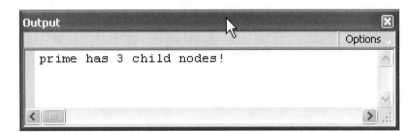

```
Output                                    [x]
                                   Options
  prime has 3 child nodes!
```

insertBefore
XML.insertBefore(childNode, beforeNode): Method

The insertBefore() method is used to insert nodes in an existing XML object. The two parameters identify the node to be inserted (childNode) and the node before which it is to be inserted (beforeNode).

Using a new element, this next example shows an XML object with initial nodes. The goal is to insert a node right between the existing nodes. Not only does the script create a new element, it can place it where you want it to go. The createElement() method creates another <review> tag, and then createTextNode() creates new text. The new text is appended to the new <review> tag. Thus, the node <review>Pass it up</review> is now available for placement in the XML object with the identifier newReview. To place the new node between the existing nodes, the line:

```
bookLook.insertBefore(newReview, bookLook.firstChild.nextSibling);
```

places newReview in front of the next sibling of the first child. Thus, the new node is positioned in the middle. The following script shows the entire process:

```
viewIt.onPress = function() {
    bookLook = new XML("<review>Hot</review><review>Great</review>");
    newReview = bookLook.createElement("review");
    newWords = bookLook.createTextNode("Pass it up");
    newReview.appendChild(newWords);
    bookLook.insertBefore(newReview, bookLook.firstChild.nextSibling);
    trace(bookLook);
};
```

As you can see in the Output window, the new node is right where it's supposed to be.

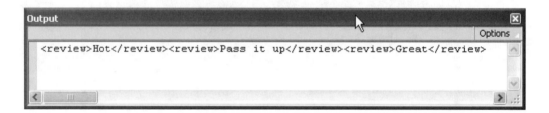

load

XML.load(url): Method

The load() method is used to load an external XML file into a Flash MX XML object. The single argument, url, is the absolute or relative address to the actual XML file stored on disk space. In the XML movie for this section, the method was used to load the file books.xml.

In the sample XML movie, the XML object bookWorm was created and then later used to load the XML file on the disk:

```
bookWorm = new XML();
....
bookWorm.load("books.xml");
```

parseXML
XML.parseXML(source): Method

The parseXML() method parses the XML object specified in the source parameter. The plain source text is parsed into a live XML tree and then placed in the target object. The following example shows how the method is applied and the resulting outcome using the XML sample movie:

```
//Area 51 X-[ml] tests in progress
viewIt.onPress = function() {
    parser = new XML();
    parser.parseXML(bookWorm);
    trace(parser);
};
```

removeNode
XML.childNodes[1].removeNode(): Method

The removeNode() method removes the XML object's specified childNode. When the child node is removed, all of its descendents are removed as well. The analogy of sawing off the limb of an oak tree comes to mind. The trunk (parent node) and all the other limbs (sibling nodes) are unaffected, but all of the branches, leaves, acorns, and bird nests on the limb are eliminated along with the limb.

```
//Area 51 X-[ml] tests in progress
viewIt.onPress = function() {
    lastOne = new XML();
    goneOne = new XML();
    lastOne = prime.firstChild.childNodes[2].childNodes[0].nodeValue;
  //Next line removes the node
    prime.firstChild.childNodes[2].childNodes[0].removeNode();
    goneOne = prime.firstChild.childNodes[2].childNodes[0].nodeValue;
    if (goneOne == null) {
```

```
            goneOne = "Nobody home!";
      }
      trace(lastOne+newline+goneOne);
};
```

The Output window shows the following:

```
XML in a Lifetime
Nobody home!
```

send

XML.send(url, [window]): Method

The XML send() method is something like the loadVars.send() method. The two arguments are a string for the Web address, and an optional window for showing data the server returns. The following window references may be used along with any named window the HTML site has defined:

- **_self**   Current frame (default if no window specified)
- **_blank**   New window
- **_parent**   Parent of current frame
- **_top**   Top-level frame of current window

The following example specifies the output to be sent to a new window:

```
prime.send("http://www.sandlight.com/xml.php", "_blank");
```

sendAndLoad

XML.sendAndLoad(url,targetXMLobject): Method

The sendAndLoad() method is something like the LoadVars.sendAndLoad() method, but XML data is transferred rather than strictly text. The first argument is the URL for the file in the target server. The XML data associated with the sending XML object is sent and any returns are placed into an object specified in the second parameter to receive data returned from the server. The sending and receiving XML object can be the same, but usually they are separate to preserve the data in the sending object. For example, the following PHP script is used to return a message in XML source format when called:

```
<?php
$message= "<serverSaid>Something!</serverSaid>";
echo $message;
?>
```

The following script sends one XML object, and then receives a return from the server captured in a receiving XML object. The sending XML object is sender and the one to receive the returns of the server is catcher:

```
viewIt.onPress = function() {
      catcher = new XML();
      sender = new XML("<serverSaid>Say something</serverSaid>");
      catcher.onLoad = function() {
            trace(this.toString());
      };
      sender.sendAndLoad("http://www.sandlight.com/xml.php", catcher);
};
```

toString
XML.toString(): Method

The toString() method formulates the XML into a string. Generally, the use of converting XML into a string would be for output to a text field or for reformatting for comparisons. The following example extracts a node from the XML file and then outputs it as a string:

```
//Area 51 X-[ml] tests in progress
viewIt.onPress = function() {
      looker = new XML();
      looker = prime.firstChild.childNodes[2].childNodes[0].nodeValue;
      trace(looker.toString());
};
```

The results are the string:

```
XML in a Lifetime
```

Properties

In looking at the properties associated with the XML object, you will find elements of standard XML. For example, the attributes property is used in exactly the same way and reference as it is with XML—a term that refers to characteristics within a tag definition. So in addition to examining the text nodes for information, you can also examine other information stored within an XML file.

attributes

XML.attributes: Property

One of the node or element characteristics of XML files is attributes. The attributes are embedded in the tags that make up the nodes. For example, the following XML segment contains tags with two different attributes:

```
<books cat="Recent">
  <computer>
   <title rating="good">Flash in 30 Seconds</title>
   <title rating="bad">ActionScript in 1 Minute</title>
   <title rating="ugly">XML in a Lifetime</title>
  </computer>
....
```

One attribute, cat, is part of the <books> node, and the other, rating, is part of the <title> nodes. The attributes property in ActionScript returns the value of the attribute following the XML branch to which it is attached. The following script shows how to extract and display XML attributes:

```
//Area 51 X-[ml] tests in progress
viewIt.onPress = function() {
  book = new XML();
  book.bookTitle = prime.childNodes[0].childNodes[1].childNodes[0].nodeValue;
  book.bookRating = prime.childNodes[0].childNodes[1].attributes.rating;
  trace(book.BookTitle+" is rated "+book.bookRating);
};
```

The Output window formats the value of the attribute in a way that clarifies the relationship between the parent node (title) and its child node (text node with the name of the book) as shown in the following:

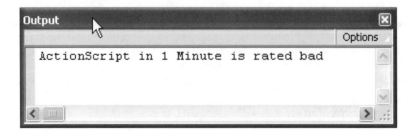

childNodes
XML.childNodes: Property

In the sample script for XML, the childNodes property was used to sort out the different information so that it could be clearly displayed in the Output window. The property returns an array made up of the XML object's children arranged along the lines of the XML tree structure. Learning how to work with the childNodes property as an array is key to using the information in an XML file. Like all arrays, the first element is always [0], and so the first node has a value of childNodes[0]. To find the number of child nodes in an XML object, use childNodes.length, in exactly the same way you would for any array.

The following shows the different uses of childNodes as an array and as array elements:

```
for (x=0; x<prime.childNodes.length; x++) {
    var header = prime.childNodes[x].nodeName.toString();
    showXML.text += header.toUpperCase()+newline;
    for (z=0; z<prime.childNodes[x].childNodes.length; z++) {
var reveal = prime.childNodes[x].childNodes[z].childNodes[0].nodeValue;
        showXML.text += "  "+reveal+newline;
    }
```

contentType
XML.contentType: Property

The "type" in the contentType property refers to the MIME sent to the server. The following example shows that using the default assignment results in application/x-www-form-urlencoded.

```
//Area 51 X-[ml] tests in progress
viewIt.onPress = function() {
    book = new XML();
    book.contentType = "application/x-www-form-urlencoded";
    trace(book.contentType);
};
```

docTypeDecl
XML.XMLdocTypeDecl: Property

The DOCTYPE declaration is important to well-formed XML because it contains key information for the parser. However, as noted at the beginning of the section on XML,

Flash MX can parse XML without the DTD (document type definitions) generally required in HTML parsers. Because ActionScript's XML parser does not validate an XML file, it does not require the DTD-related tags. As suggested, prior to using Flash to parse an XML file, validate it and then strip the declaration tags and code to simplify use with ActionScript.

However, if you do have occasion to include a DTD tag in your file, the docTypeDecl property uses the standard tags and escape codes. For example, the following calls up an external file to fill in the longer !DOCTYPE tag information typically associated with DTD:

```
viewIt.onPress = function() {
    onlyText = new XML();
    onlyText.docTypeDecl = "<!DOCTYPE DOCUMENT SYSTEM \" min.dtd\">";
    trace(onlyText);
};
```

firstChild
XML.firstChild: Property

The firstChild property is the first child of a given XML node. When the first child (or only child) is a text node, the return is undefined, while a null value is returned to nodes with no children. In the XML sample movie, the XML object prime is defined as the first child of the newly loaded XML file using the following script:

```
prime = new XML();
prime = this.firstChild;
```

The this object is the bookWorm XML object that called the function using the onLoad event. The first child of an XML object loaded with an XML file is the entire script. If you make the following adjustment to the script, you will be able to see the entire script outlined as a long line of tags:

```
prime = new XML();
prime = this.firstChild;
trace(prime)
```

ignoreWhite
XML.ignoreWhite: Property
XML.prototype.ignorewhite: Property

When an XML file is parsed, any spaces, tabs, or carriage returns are read as new nodes or other information you do not want to be part of the parsed material. The ignoreWhite property ignores the spaces, carriage returns, and tab spaces. In the XML sample, the following line made sure that the white spaces between nodes were ignored:

```
bookWorm.ignoreWhite = true;
```

To set all XML objects to ignore the extraneous spaces and symbols, use the following script:

```
XML.prototype.ignoreWhite=true;
```

This latter format will save time and make sure all of the XML objects in the script ignore the white spaces.

To see the effect of not setting the ignoreWhite property to true, comment out the following line:

```
// bookWorm.ignoreWhite = true;
```

Test the script, and you will see spaces between the lines in the output. Those spaces represent an attempt by the parser to add carriage returns as new nodes that are placed between the real nodes. Because the ignoreWhite property is set to false by default, by commenting out the script that set ignoreWhite to true, it became false.

lastChild

XML.lastChild: Property

The lastChild property identifies the last child node of the selected parent. In the XML example, the last child of the primary node, prime, is <nonFiction>. The last node of <nonFiction> was a <title> node with a text node, and the node's value is "Post Modern Money Laundering". This next script uses the lastChild property to find the last book in the list:

```
//Area 51 X-[ml] tests in progress
viewIt.onPress = function() {
     book = new XML();
     book = prime.lastChild.lastChild.lastChild.nodeValue;
     trace(book);
};
```

The node value of the last node is shown in the Output window:

```
Post Modern Money Laundering
```

ACTIONSCRIPT
OBJECTS

loaded
XML.loaded: Property

The loaded property returns a Boolean true if the XML file is loaded and false if it is still loading. The following script returns true because the script has already loaded the movie by the time the script below is launched by the Area 51 button:

```
//Area 51 X-[ml] tests in progress
viewIt.onPress = function() {
        if (bookWorm.loaded) {
                trace("all loaded");
        } else {
                trace("still loading");
        }
};
```

nextSibling
XML.nextSibling: Property

Each node that shares the same parent node is a sibling. In the sequence of the XML file the "next" sibling is the one in the next node. For example, in the following XML file segment, all of the title nodes are siblings:

```
<computer>
   <title rating="good">Flash in 30 Seconds</title>
   <title rating="bad">ActionScript in 1 Minute</title>
   <title rating="ugly">XML in a Lifetime</title>
</computer>
```

The top title node's next sibling is the one below it, and the third title node is the next sibling of the second title node. The third title node has no next sibling and so would return null if referenced. The following example shows how the property can be used in a script:

```
//Area 51 X-[ml] tests in progress
viewIt.onPress = function() {
        rival = new XML();
        rival = prime.childNodes[0].childNodes[0].nextSibling;
        trace(rival.childNodes[0].nodeValue);
};
```

The outcome shows the next sibling to be the title value of the second node, which is exactly what can be seen in the XML file list:

```
ActionScript in 1 Minute
```

nodeName
XML.nodeName: Property

The nodeName property only works with XML bracket nodes and returns a null value for text nodes. For example, the <title> nodes would return "title", but their titles will return null because each is a text node. The following script gets the node name for the great-grandchild of the main XML object:

```
//Area 51 X-[ml] tests in progress
viewIt.onPress = function() {
      rival = new XML();
      rival = prime.childNodes[0].childNodes[0].nextSibling;
      trace(rival.nodeName);
};
```

nodeType
XML.nodeType: Property

The nodeType property returns two values for valid nodes. If the node is an XML element, it returns 1, and text nodes return 3. The following script identifies one of each:

```
//Area 51 X-[ml] tests in progress
viewIt.onPress = function() {
      whatElement = new XML();
      whatText = new XML();
      whatElement = prime.childNodes[0].childNodes[0].nodeType;
      whatText = prime.childNodes[0].childNodes[0].childNodes[0].nodeType;
      isElement = (whatElement == 1);
      isText = (whatText == 3);
      if (isElement && isText) {
            trace("whatElement is indeed an element");
            trace("whatText is certainly text");
      }
};
```

nodeValue
XML.nodeValue: Property

The nodeValue property is used to return the actual text of a text node. In the XML sample movie, all of the titles were generated using the following line:

```
var reveal = prime.childNodes[x].childNodes[z].childNodes[0].nodeValue;
```

ACTIONSCRIPT
OBJECTS

If you attempt to get an XML node's value, the return is null. The following script gives some more practice in generating node values:

```
//Area 51 X-[ml] tests in progress
viewIt.onPress = function() {
     rival = new XML();
     rival = prime.childNodes[0].childNodes[0].nextSibling;
     trace(rival.childNodes[0].nodeValue);
};
```

parentNode
XML.parentNode: Property

The parentNode property indicates the parent of the specified XML node. One way to think about the parentNode is that it goes in the opposite direction of the childNodes, but unlike childNodes, the parentNode (notice it is singular compared to the plural name in childNodes) is not an array nor does it contain array elements. The following example goes to the end of the XML tree and then backs up using the parentNode property:

```
//Area 51 X-[ml] tests in progress
viewIt.onPress = function() {
   caboose = new XML();
     caboose = prime.lastChild.lastChild.lastChild;
     trace(caboose.parentNode.parentNode.nodeName);
};
```

previousSibling
XML.previousSibling: Property

The previousSibling property refers to the sibling in the previous position in the same node group as the selected node. The property has the same branching map as the nextSibling property (discussed earlier), but it is the sibling prior to the one selected. The following script shows how it can be used to target a node:

```
//Area 51 X-[ml] tests in progress
viewIt.onPress = function() {
     prior = new XML();
     prior = prime.childNodes[2].previousSibling;
     trace(prior.childNodes[0].childNodes[0].nodeValue);
};
```

status
XML.status: Property

The status property acts somewhat like XML validation in that it returns different problems in your XML file. Depending on the problem (or lack thereof), the property generates the following codes with the adjacent meanings:

- **0**   Success
- **2**   A CDATA not terminated correctly
- **3**   Improper XML declaration termination
- **4**   Improper DOCTYPE declaration termination
- **5**   A comment was not properly terminated
- **6**   Malformed XML element
- **7**   Out of memory
- **8**   Improper attribute value termination
- **9**   No matching end tag for existing start tag
- **10**   No matching start tag for existing end tag

If your code is well formed, you should receive a 0 value. Otherwise, you will get one of the other nine values. (There is no 1 value; after 0 follows 2 through 9.)

```
//Area 51 X-[ml] tests in progress
viewIt.onPress = function() {
        trace(bookWorm.status);
};
//Output shows 0
```

xmlDecl
XML.xmlDecl: Property

If the XML document your ActionScript program is parsing contains a declaration, you can check its contents with the information in the xmlDecl property. Flash MX can parse a valid XML file without the declaration line, but if you include one, you can parse it with the xmlDecl property.

```
viewIt.onPress = function() {
        wellFormed = new XML("<?xml version=\"1.0\" ?>");
        trace(wellFormed.xmlDecl);
};
```

Events

The events used with the XML object both involve the status of the XML file loaded. The two events look at the loading materials before and after the data is parsed.

onData
myXML.onData: Event

The onData event handler launches when XML text has been downloaded fully from the server but before it has been parsed. It can also be invoked by an error. If this event and an onLoad event handler are set simultaneously, the onLoad event is blocked. Also, the XML data is not parsed when the onData event handler is invoked.

To see how the onData event handler works, add the following script to the XML movie:

```
//Area 51 X-[ml] tests in progress
bookWorm.onData = function(src) {
    showXML.text = src;
};
```

When you test the movie, you will see that the XML source code appears in the Output window where you had seen the parsed XML in prior tests. The function that parses and organizes the XML is blocked because the onData event handler occurs first. (In fact, if you just comment out the line to load the source code into the Dynamic text field, you will see that the parsed and formatted output does not appear in the text field.) The src parameter is the source of the loaded data.

onLoad
myXML.onLoad(success): Event

The onLoad event handler can be used with or without a parameter area. Typically, the onLoad event handler is expressed without a parameter, but it will accept a Boolean value. The event is invoked by the arrival of an XML document in the Flash player. The parameter, success, (using any name you want) contains the XML just loaded and is passed to a function. Then the function uses that parameter to pass the XML on to another XML object.

In the XML sample movie, the onLoad() method was used to launch the main function that parsed the XML and displayed it in the text window using the following script:

```
bookWorm.onLoad = sendItOut;
```

XML Socket

If you are unfamiliar with open socket technology, you will find that the basics are straightforward, but using open socket connections with Flash MX and XML is a bit different than regular XML and Web usage. Whenever a Web page or Flash SWF file loads from a server to a client's computer, the connection between the server and client is broken. With an open socket server, the connection stays open between the client and server so that data can be constantly streamed to the client.

The advantage of open socket XML and of open socket technology in general is the constant connectivity. This type of connectivity allows for synchronous operations such as online chats. Because the socket remains open, the stream of information keeps flowing as it becomes available and not in a "package" as an entire Web page or XML file.

In order to work with XMLSocket objects, you will need an open socket server. One you can download at no charge (at the time of this writing) is available from Figleaf Software at http://www.figleaf.com/development/flash5/. Written by Branden Hall, the server runs in the Java 2 Runtime Environment, version 1.3.1 or higher. If your computer does not have JRE installed, you can download it from Sun Microsystems at http://www.sun.com/. From that Web page, select Downloads | Technologies | Java Technology Java 2 Platform, Standard Edition v1.4. The example movie for XML socket servers was tested using JRE v1.4.1.

Use your command prompt in Windows (it resides in the Accessories folder in Windows, and older versions of Windows reference it as MS-DOS) or the Terminal application in Macintosh OS X platforms to start the AquaServer. Navigate to the folder (directory) with the AquaServer components and type:

```
java AquaServer 6744
```

That sets up the server to listen to port 6744. Actually, you can use any unused port greater than 1023, but some ports, such as 1935 (default port for Flash Communication Server), may conflict with other servers you have running. I picked 6744 because I know of nothing else that uses that port. If you change that port number, be sure to change the reference to that port in the script in the sample XML socket movie and any scripts you develop on your own.

Once you start the AquaServer, you can shut the server down using the quit command. This command can be useful to test the onClose() XMLSocket event handler.

new XMLSocket

new XMLSocket(): Constructor

Creating a new XMLSocket object is just like any other object that requires a constructor. For instance, in the movie that follows, the XMLSocket object is defined as:

```
hotSocket = new XMLSocket();
```

To better understand how the different methods and events associated with the XMLSocket object work, this section contains a movie using most of these methods and events. As you will see, you can use the same XML structures as the Flash MX XML object uses, and by adding a few methods and events, you can use Flash with open socket technology. Figure 13-6 shows the general layout of the page and Table 13-2 shows the color palette used.

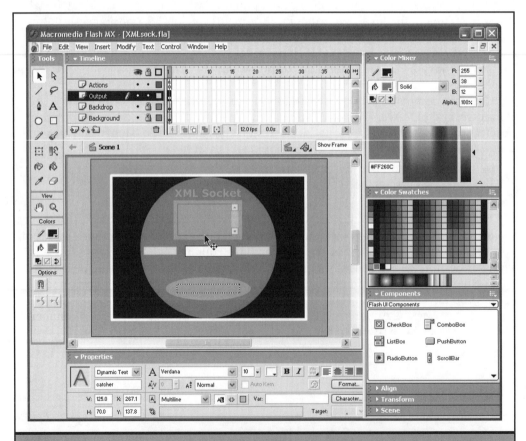

Figure 13-6. *The stage contains two text fields for sending materials out to the server and then receiving it back through the server.*

Name	R	G	B
Gray	179	179	153
Red	255	38	12
White	255	255	255
Black	0	0	0

Table 13-2. *Color Palette*

The sample movie demonstrates how the open socket technology can be used to create a text communication application. It's quite primitive, but it is meant to show you the basics of the XMLSocket methods and events. The movie connects and disconnects to an open socket server, then sends a message in XML format to the server which is bounced back and parsed into a clear message in a Dynamic text field. The message is originally created in an Input text field, and going from one text field to another may not be too impressive except for one fact. The same message also appears if another instance of the SWF file is also hooked into the same server. In other words, while you're entering text on one instance you can see it appear on another instance sharing the same connections (see Figure 13-7). To recreate the movie, use the following steps:

1. Open a new movie, add three layers to the existing one, and name them from top to bottom Actions, Output, Backdrop, and Background. Set the background color to gray.

2. Select the Background layer and use the Rectangle tool to draw a rectangle with a black fill and 7-point white stroke with the dimensions W = 450, H = 325. On top of the rectangle, draw a red circle with no stroke with the dimensions W = 318, H = 318. Center the circle and rectangle vertically and horizontally with the stage. Lock the layer.

3. Select the Backdrop layer and draw a gray rectangle near the top of the red circle with the dimensions W = 162, H = 90 with no stroke. Center the rectangle and set the vertical position to Y = 138.

4. Near the bottom of the red circle draw a gray oval with the dimensions W = 200, H = 55 with the vertical position at Y = 293. Lock the layer.

5. Select the Output layer and place a Dynamic text field with a 12-point Verdana bold black font centered over the gray oval. Give it the instance name serverBack.

6. Place an Input text field in the horizontal and vertical center of the stage selecting a 10-point Verdana font. Select the text field and press the SHIFT key

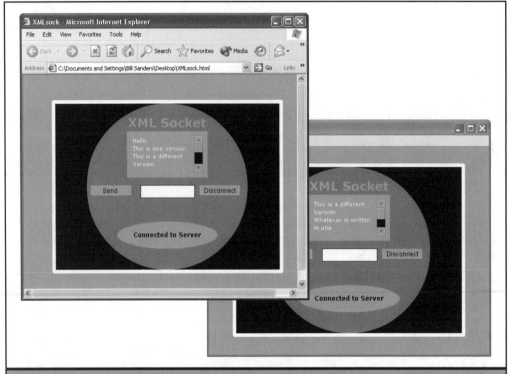

Figure 13-7. *When more than one instance of the movie run simultaneously connected to the same server, whatever is sent to the server on one appears on both.*

and DOWN ARROW to move it down 8 pixels. Give it the instance name sender. On either side of the Input text field, place a PushButton UI component. Give the push button on the left the instance name doSend and the one on the right hookUp. The script will provide each with appropriate labels and related functions.

7. Directly over the gray rectangle, place a multiline Dynamic text field with the dimensions W = 125, H = 70, and a white 10-point Verdana font. Give the text field the instance name catcher. Drag a ScrollBar UI component next to the text field on its right side. Set the dimensions of the scroll bar component to W = 16, H = 70 so that it will fit exactly with the text field. Give the scroll bar the instance name sBar. Finally, type **XML Socket** in a 24-point Verdana gray font at the top of the circle. Use Figure 13-6 as a guide. Lock the layer.

8. Click the first frame of the Actions layer and add the following script:

```
//Connect and Disconnect Buttons
function linkUp() {
```

```
        if (hookUp.getLabel() == "Connect") {
            hookUp.setLabel("Disconnect");
            hotSocket.connect("localhost", 6744);
        } else {
            hotSocket.close();
            hookUp.setLabel("Connect");
            serverBack.text = "Disconnected";
        }
}
//Inform user that the server has quit
function shutIt() {
        serverBack.text = "Server Shutoff.";
}
//Display Information from Server
function showIt(hotXML) {
        var holdIt = hotXML.firstChild.childNodes[0].nodeValue;
        catcher.text += holdIt+newline;
}
//Send Information to Server
function messageOut() {
        hotSocket.send("<socketM>"+sender.text+"</socketM>");
        sender.text = "";
}
//Confirm Connection
function socketConnect(success) {
        if (success) {
            serverBack.text = "Connected to Server";
        } else {
            serverBack.text = "Failed to Connect";
        }
}
//Initialize XML Socket
XML.prototype.ignoreWhite = true;
hotSocket = new XMLSocket();
hotSocket.onConnect = socketConnect;
hotSocket.onXML = showIt;
hotSocket.onClose = shutIt;
//
//Set up UI Components
doSend.setLabel("Send");
doSend.setClickHandler("messageOut");
hookUp.setLabel("Connect");
hookUp.setClickHandler("linkUp");
sBar.setScrollTarget(catcher);
//UI Components Style
```

```
btnStyle = new FStyleFormat();
btnStyle.face = 0xB3B399;
btnStyle.arrow = 0xFF260C;
btnStyle.scrollTrack = 0x000000;
btnStyle.addListener(doSend, hookUp, sBar);
```

The script handles the details for styling the UI components and putting them together with the right click handler or scrolling target. Because the UI components can change dynamically, they can be used to save space on the stage when needed. Figure 13-7 shows two instances of the movie sharing the same server and messages. (Look closely and you can see that one of the movies started sending and receiving text before the other because the text is slightly different.)

Methods

The XMLSocket object has only three methods, and all three are used for communication with the open socket servers. Two are used for opening and closing connections with the movie and the server, and the third is for sending it messages.

close

XMLSocketInstance.close(): Method

The close() method terminates the connection with the server. It is sometimes used in conjunction with the XMLSocket event onClose to launch a function. However, by itself, the method does nothing more than sever the connection. In the socket server example, the following segment of the linkUp function shows how it was used:

```
} else {
    hotSocket.close();
    hookUp.setLabel("Connect");
    serverBack.text = "Disconnected";
}
```

connect

XMLSocketInstance.connect(host, port): Method

The connect() method uses two parameters. The first parameter can be a DNS domain name, an IP address, or the local host name assigned to your system (usually it's "localhost"). The port parameter refers to an available TCP port on your computer, and largely depends on your configuration. The TCP port number must be higher than 1023, but otherwise, just use any available port number. The XML socket example uses 6744, which is both unused on the system tested (and most others as well) and totally arbitrary.

This method opens a connection between the Flash movie and the Internet host through the named TCP port. If the connection is established, the method returns a Boolean true. A false return means that the connection failed. If you are using a remote hosting system with an open socket server, you will have to get a port number from the hosting service. In some circumstances you need to have the same subdomain for the host named in the parameter and from where you download the movie. Generally, you will find it easier to place your open socket server and movie in the same folder in the root directory with your Web server. If you're using your own Windows computer as a server, you are likely to find the root in C:\Inetpub\wwwroot. However, that may not be the case with your system, and on Macintoshes it varies as well, depending not only on your configuration, but also on whether the configuration is based on an OS X or OS 9.x or earlier. In the sample movie, the following script segment shows where the open() method is used as part of the linkUp function:

```
//Connect and Disconnect Buttons
function linkUp() {
        if (hookUp.getLabel() == "Connect") {
                hookUp.setLabel("Disconnect");
                hotSocket.connect("localhost", 6744);
        }
```

The connection specifies the host as "localhost", but if you want to use the movie as a limited chat system, use your IP address in place of "localhost". For example, change it to:

```
hotSocket.connect("12.345.67.890", 6744);
```

substituting your actual IP address for the fictitious one supplied.

Tip *You can quickly find out what your IP address is by checking the following URL: http://checkip.dyndns.org/. If you have a dynamic (DHCP) IP address, as is the case with many cable modems and DSL lines, it might change regularly. Some ISPs provide their clients with DHCP but rarely change the IP address, so it has the virtual functionality of a stable IP address.*

If you want to use your XML socket movie to chat with someone on another computer, you can give them the full URL. If you place your movie in a folder with your open socket server in the Internet root folder for your system, they can easily access it like a regular Web server. For example, if you place your movie in a folder called XMLos and name your movie XMLsock, it could be accessed with the following URL:

```
http://12.345.67.890/XMLos/XMLsock.swf
```

On my computer, the file address is C:\Inetpub\wwwroot\XMLos\XMLsock.swf, but because the Internet root is where the IP address begins, it and the Inetpub folder need not be part of the URL.

ACTIONSCRIPT OBJECTS

Tip   *If your system is running Windows XP Pro, you will find a link to your own system at http://localhost/iishelp/iis/misc/default.asp. There you will find IIS documentation.*

send
XMLSocketInstance.send(object): Method

What you send using the send() method can be a simple XML and text node, as was done in the sample movie, or it can be a full-blown XML file in an XML object or some other type of data. The send() method converts whatever is in the object into a string and sends it to the server, but it does not indicate whether the transmission is successful.

In a minimalist application of the send() method, the object in the sample movie is an XML and text node. The tag <socketM> provides the only XML node, and the text currently in the text field named sender makes up the text node.

```
//Send Information to Server
function messageOut() {
     hotSocket.send("<socketM>"+sender.text+"</socketM>");
     sender.text = "";
}
```

The send() method is executed by invoking the messageOut() function, which is launched by a button press. The last line in the function simply clears the text window, which gives the illusion of the message being sent when the button is pressed.

Events

The events associated with the XMLSocket object include events that involve opening and closing the open socket. Obviously, when one of the key features of open socket technology and Flash MX objects that use that technology is a continuous connection, the status of that connection is an event that needs to be trapped. Besides connection events, the XMLSocket events include whether data, XML or unparsed data, has been loaded.

onClose
XMLSocketInstance.onClose: Event

The onClose event is fired when the server sends a message indicating it is closing. It is not invoked by the XMLSocket.close() method, and you may have noticed in the sample movie that no attempt was made to link onClose with the close() method. Generally, the utility of this event is found where the server quits, and you find that your movie is not working as it should be. When the server quits on its own or is terminated intentionally, the onClose event fires and can be used to inform the user that something is amiss (or that the server is shutting off as planned).

In the sample movie, the event is used in the following script:

```
hotSocket.onClose = shutIt;
```

The script fires the following function:

```
//Inform user that the server has quit
function shutIt() {
      serverBack.text = "Server Shutoff";
}
```

The event is not controlled at all by the user unless he has control of the server. As soon as the server disconnects for some other reason than a close() method being invoked, the onClose event is triggered and lets the user know that the server has precipitated the loss of connection.

onConnect

XMLSocketInstance.onConnect(success): Event

When a connection is attempted using the connect() method, the onConnect event generates a Boolean value for the success parameter. This parameter can then be used in a called function to send feedback to the user to indicate whether the attempt was successful or not.

In the sample XMLSocket movie, the event handler is used to launch a function that used the success parameter as shown in the following:

```
hotSocket.onConnect = socketConnect;
```

The success parameter is passed to the function to determine whether the connection was a success or not:

```
//Confirm Connection
function socketConnect(success) {
      if (success) {
            serverBack.text = "Connected to Server";
      } else {
            serverBack.text = "Failed to Connect";
      }
}
```

onData
XMLSocket.onData(): Event

The onData event is triggered by XML data arriving from the server. The default for this event is to fire the onXML event method. However, if you want to work with data using a different set of behaviors than the default, you will have to change the onData prototype (for example, XMLSocket.prototype.onData = function (src)...). The onData event method can be employed where you need to do something else with the data other than parse the XML, which is handled by onXML. Add the following to the current XMLSocket sample script to see the difference between using onData and onXML events:

```
function hereComes(osData) {
        catchrer.text = "Data Coming!"+osData;
}
hotSocket.onData = hereComes;
```

The data is not parsed, so what you get is the raw material that was sent to the server. For example, if you typed in "Hello" your output would be:

```
Data
Coming!<socketM>Hello
</socketM>
```

onXML
XMLSocketInstance.onXML(object): Event

By assigning the onXML event method to a function, the object argument, which contains whatever was received from the server, is passed on to the function. Therefore, whatever term is used in the argument in the function contains the object passed from the onXML event method. This method is the key one to take whatever the server sends and pass it on to the current movie. It works similarly to the onLoad() method for the Flash MX XML object. In the sample XMLSocket movie the event method was used to call a function that interpreted the data as an XML object to locate the text node.

The event was used as the following script segment shows:

```
hotSocket.onXML = showIt;
```

The XML object coming from the server is in the object parameter in the function the XML object was passed to. In the function, the object parameter is named hotXML.

It becomes the XML object in the same way as an XML object constructed with the XML constructor is an XML object. So when locating the node you want to display, treat the object parameter as an XML object as shown in the following function:

```
//Display Information from Server
function showIt(hotXML) {
      var holdIt = hotXML.firstChild.childNodes[0].nodeValue;
      catcher.text += holdIt+newline;
}
```

Authoring

The authoring actions are more advanced and are used to add materials to both the Actions toolbox and the References panel. You can use plain text to add to the References panel, but you will need XML to add to the Actions toolbox.

CustomActions

To create and use CustomActions, you need to access the Configuration\ActionsPanel\ CustomActions folder in your Macromedia Flash MX folder. Depending on your operating system, the file can be found in different locations. The following cover most of the popular operating systems:

- **OS:** Windows 2000 or XP Professional/Home
  Path: C:\Documents and Settings\user\Application Data\Macromedia\ Flash MX\

- **OS:** Windows 98 or ME
  Path: C:\Windows\Application Data\Macromedia\Flash MX\

- **OS:** Windows NT
  Path: Windows directory\profiles\user\Application Data\Macromedia\ Flash MX\

- **OS:** Macintosh OS X
  Path: Hard Drive/Users/Library/Application Support/Macromedia/FlashMX/

- **OS:** Macintosh System 9.x, single user
  Path: Hard Drive/System folder/Application Support/Macromedia/ Flash MX/

- **OS:** Macintosh System 9.x, multiple users
  Path: Hard Drive/Users/user/Documents/Macromedia/FlashMX/

The Configuration\ActionsPanel\CustomActions folder is where you will be placing any custom action files that you create in either in plain text or XML. If you cannot find your CustomActions folder, use your Search feature (Sherlock on the Macintosh) to locate it. Sometimes they end up in unexpected places.

In order to have a reference point, I will use the following CustomActions saved in a file, sysSec.xml:

```
<customactions>
    <actionspanel>
<string name="allow" tipText="XDo" text="System.security.allowDomain()"/>
    </actionspanel>
</customactions>
```

The file is strictly for the Actions panel and not the Reference panel. It sets up an undocumented Flash MX method for allowing cross-domain data transfer. By adding the custom action, it will be available in the Actions toolbox under the name "allow." By double-clicking "allow", the line System.security.allowDomain() appears in the main ActionScript pane.

Methods

The methods consist of four functions to get, install, list, and uninstall CustomActions objects.

get
CustomActions.get(customActionsName): Method
The get() method returns the contents of the CustomActions file. A single parameter is the name of the file without the .xml file extension or any directory separators. For example, the sysSec.xml file would be addressed as sysSec, and the get() method would return the file's source code. The following script uses the get() method in this manner:

```
var CA = CustomActions.get("sysSec")
```

install
CustomActions.install(customActionsName, customXMLDefinition): Method
To install custom actions, the install() method works like an automated version of installing the custom action in a folder by dragging it there. The method expects two arguments, the name of the custom action and the XML definition. The name is whatever you want to appear in the Actions panel. The XML definition requires an entire XML

file in a string. By concatenating a string with itself, you can add the same kind of XML file that you would by keying it into a text file and saving it, but you have to pay attention to the escape characters. (The Auto Format tool in the Actions panel will do most of it for you.) The following code adds a custom action using this method:

```
var caXML = "<customactions><actionspanel>";
caXML += '<string name=\"decode\" tipText=\"decode UNIcode\"';
caXML += 'text=\"LoadVars.decode()\"/>';
caXML += "</actionspanel></customactions>";
CustomActions.install(decode, caXML);
```

list
CustomActions.list(): Method
The list() method lists all of the custom actions in the CustomActions folder. It does not list the one created using the CustomActions.install() method, however. The following script shows the format:

```
trace(CustomActions.list());
```

The output is an array of the custom actions in your system.

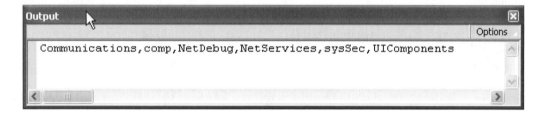

```
Output
Communications,comp,NetDebug,NetServices,sysSec,UIComponents
```

uninstall
CustomActions.uninstall(customActionsName): Method
The uninstall() method simply removes the unwanted custom actions. Its only parameter is the name of the file without the extension name or the path elements. When this method is used, the effect is only temporary, and after quitting and restarting Flash MX, all of the custom actions in the CustomActions folder reappear in the Actions toolbox. To see the effect of this method, combine it with the list() method as shown in the following:

```
CustomActions.uninstall("sysSec");
trace(CustomActions.list());
```

If you have placed the sysSec.xml script in the CustomActions folder, you will see it missing from the Output window. However, when you quit Flash and restart it, the list() method shows that it is still extant.

Live Preview

Live Preview is a partially documented feature of Flash MX. When creating your own components, one of the options is to make a Live Preview file that allows you to see what your component is going to look like before you use Test Movie to see it. To see how to build your own components and Live Preview file, see Macromedia's support note/tutorial at the following address:

http://www.macromedia.com/support/flash/applications/creating_comps/index.html

In the Live Preview folder in the Actions toolbox, you will find a single function, onUpdate(). To understand what this function actually is doing, take a look at the process for creating a Live Preview with a tailor-made component first.

onUpdate

onUpdate(): Callback Function

When building your own components in Flash MX, you will need to know when your component variables change. Keeping in mind the onUpdate() function is only for the Live Update while authoring components, it is set up on the main timeline of your movie where the component is under construction. To use onUpdate(), you need an empty movie clip with the name "xch" in the Live Preview movie. Then you can write a script that will update the Live Preview of your component. For example, suppose you're working on a list box and you want the scroll track color to update in your Live Preview. The following script provides the update information to be passed to the Live Preview:

```
myScroller.scrollTrack = colorScroll;
 function onUpdate() {
    myScroller.scrollTrack = xch.colorScroll;
 }
```

Conclusion

This chapter has shown how to use Flash MX as a robust front end for working with external files. The new LoadVars object provides a powerful tool to interface with back-end scripts and databases. As such, it makes Flash MX the front-end choice because of its ease of use and power in working with different middleware and databases.

XML has a hidden feature in Flash MX not seen in Flash 5. While most of the methods are the same, the speed with which Flash MX loads XML files is significantly faster than Flash 5. Otherwise, those familiar with Flash 5 XML will feel very comfortable with the new Flash XML methods and events.

The open socket XML features of Flash MX make Flash a powerful communication tool by providing a continuous open channel to port data. Even with a simple open socket server like Branden Hall's AquaServer, Flash was shown to perform as a simple yet effective chat room.

Finally, the CustomActions methods can be used to create additional actions to be stored in your Actions toolbox. When you need a special term, combination of actions, or undocumented action to appear in the Actions panel, creating your own can ease a serious workload.

Following this chapter is a series of chapters that show how to configure and use the UI components. Designers who shudder at the idea of using "prefab" buttons, scroll bars, and other ready-built parts for a Flash movie are in for a pleasant surprise. You can work with the design features of components in just about any way you want. As a little preview of Part IV, the components used in the sample movies were configured using ActionScript rather than the Properties panel. As always with ActionScript, you have maximum control over the materials you use in Flash.

ACTIONSCRIPT
OBJECTS

The Complete Reference

ActionScript

Part IV

ActionScript User Interface Components

The Complete Reference

ActionScript

Chapter 14

FCheckBox

The FCheckBox object has its counterpart in HTML and methods in JavaScript in the form of the check box. The check box is typically used when multiple choices are available that are not mutually exclusive. The check box's implementation in Flash MX is similar to HTML's, and while it typically has a similar use as HTML's check box, it works differently and can be molded by the developer in many different ways.

Scripting Components

In this chapter and the others on the UI components, a single large script and movie that encompasses all or most of the component's methods will be used to illustrate the component's features. As each method is discussed, pertinent script examples are taken from the larger script so you can see how they are used specifically and in the context of the movie.

Methods

To see how the methods work, this movie uses all but one of the FCheckBox object's methods. Table 14-1 shows the color palette used. Figure 14-1 shows the general layout and some component information in the Properties panel, and Figure 14-2 shows the movie clip timeline.

Use the following steps to recreate the movie:

1. Open a new movie and add three layers, naming them from top to bottom, Check Boxes, Movie Clips, Backdrop, and Background.

2. In the Background layer, use the beige color for the background color, and then draw a red circle with a 7-point orange stroke with a diameter of 371 pixels. Lock the layer.

Name	R	G	B
Green	33	109	72
Orange	252	116	74
Red	223	37	86
Yellow	255	230	49
Beige	246	239	223
Black	0	0	0

Table 14-1. *Color Palette*

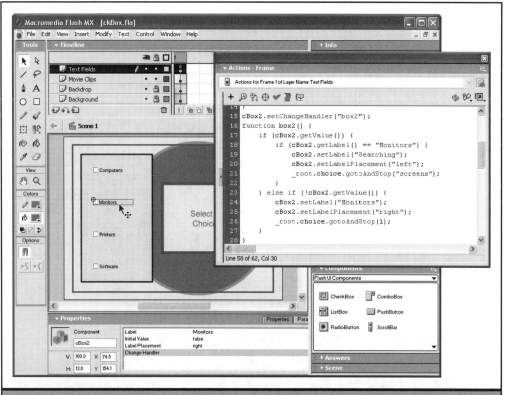

Figure 14-1.   *The check box components control themselves, other components, and the movie clip on the stage.*

3. In the Backdrop layer, draw a yellow rectangle with a 3.25-point black stroke. Use the dimensions W = 179, H = 313. Then around the outside margins, using only a 4-point green stroke line with no fill, draw a rectangle with the dimensions W = 505, H = 361. Lock the layer.

4. In the Movie Clips layer, create a rectangle with the dimensions W = 209, H = 169, using a beige fill and green 7-point stroke. Select the rectangle and press the F8 key to convert it to a movie clip. Give the clip the instance name choice in the Properties panel.

5. Double-click the new movie clip to enter the Symbol Editing mode. Add a second layer and name the top layer Stops and the bottom layer Background. Create five frames on both layers, and five keyframes on the top layer. The rectangle drawing makes up the contents of the Background layer. Lock the layer. (See Figure 14-2 for visual details.)

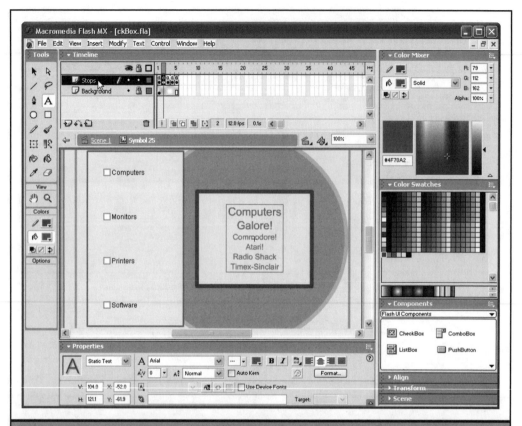

Figure 14-2. The movie clip has different messages linked to four different keyframes that will be linked by the component scripts.

6. In each of the five keyframes on the top layer, add a stop() action. Beginning with the second frame on the top layer, provide the following keyframe names: compute, screens, print, and soft.

7. Select the second keyframe in the first layer and add red static text with the message, "Computers Galore! Commodore! Atari! Radio Shack, Timex-Sinclair." Select the third keyframe and add the message "Flatscreen Monitors, Pancake, RoadKill, Super Model, Rail." Select the fourth keyframe and add the message "No Printers!" and place a red circle outline with a diagonal red line through it right on top of the message. Select the last keyframe and type the text, "Software, 300 baud com, pong, pacman 1, Windows 3.1." Lock the layer and return to the main timeline.

8. Select the Check Boxes layer and drag four Check Box components to the stage, distributed on the yellow vertical rectangle.

9. Select the top check box and then click on Parameters in the Properties panel. In the label column, use the label Computers. Do the same with the other three components, naming them from top to bottom, Monitors, Printers, and Software. Figure 14-1 shows what they should look like once you have them labeled and arranged.

10. Click on the first frame and enter the following script in the Actions panel:

```
//The first check box -- Computers
//Sets the Change Handler to box1
//The box1 function checks to see if check box is enabled first
//Then it changes the label, placement and sends an
//action to the MC named "choice."
cBox1.setChangeHandler("box1");
function box1() {
    if (cBox1.getEnabled()) {
        if (cBox1.getLabel() == "Computers") {
            cBox1.setLabel("Searching");
            cBox1.setLabelPlacement("left");
            _root.choice.gotoAndStop("compute");
        } else {
            cBox1.setLabel("Computers");
            cBox1.setLabelPlacement("right");
            _root.choice.gotoAndStop(1);
        }
    }
}
//The second check box -- Monitors
//Sets the Change Handler to box2
//The box1 function checks to see if check box is checked
//Then it changes the label, placement and sends an
//action to the MC named "choice."
cBox2.setChangeHandler("box2");
function box2() {
    if (cBox2.getValue()) {
        if (cBox2.getLabel() == "Monitors") {
            cBox2.setLabel("Searching");
            cBox2.setLabelPlacement("left");
            _root.choice.gotoAndStop("screens");
        }
    } else if (!cBox2.getValue()) {
        cBox2.setLabel("Monitors");
        cBox2.setLabelPlacement("right");
        _root.choice.gotoAndStop(1);
```

```
        }
    }
//The third check box -- Printers is sabotaged!
//Sets the Change Handler to box3
//The box3 function checks to see if check box is enabled first
//Then it changes the label, placement and sends an
//action to the MC named "choice." Then it changes the field size
// and sets the Enabled status to "false"
cBox3.setChangeHandler("box3");
function box3() {
    if (cBox3.getValue()) {
        if (cBox3.getLabel() == "Printers") {
            cBox3.setLabel("Paper Jam! Disabled");
            cBox3.setLabelPlacement("left");
            _root.choice.gotoAndStop("print");
            cBox3.setSize(150);
            cBox3.setEnabled(false);
        }
    }
}
//The fourth check box -- Software
//Sets the Change Handler to box4
//The box4 function checks to see if check box is enabled first
//Then it changes the label, placement, style and sends an
//action to the MC named "choice."
//After that it takes care of the disabled cBox3 instance of the
//check box object by enabling it and resetting it to the original
cBox4.setChangeHandler("box4");
function box4() {
    if (cBox4.getEnabled()) {
        if (cBox4.getLabel() == "Software") {
            cBox4.setLabel("Searching");
            cBox4.setStyleProperty("background", 0xdf2556);
            cBox4.setLabelPlacement("left");
            _root.choice.gotoAndStop("soft");
            if (!cBox3.getEnabled()) {
                cBox3.setEnabled(true);
                cBox3.setValue(false);
                cBox3.setLabel("Printers");
                cBox3.setLabelPlacement("right");
            }
        } else {
            cBox4.setLabel("Software");
```

```
                cBox4.setLabelPlacement("right");
                _root.choice.gotoAndStop(1);
            }
        }
    }
```

When you test the movie, you will see the check boxes go through their paces for you. Figure 14-3 shows the Printer check box in the disabled stage and the other text boxes in different stages.

In examining the different methods for the FCheckBox object, keep this listing and movie handy to see how the different methods have been used. When you test the movie, note how each method affects the different check boxes.

getEnabled
FCheckBox.getEnabled(): Method

The default condition of a check box instance dragged on the stage is a Boolean true enabled. When you use the getEnabled() method, you receive the Boolean value of true or false indicating that the check box is enabled or not. If you want to disable it,

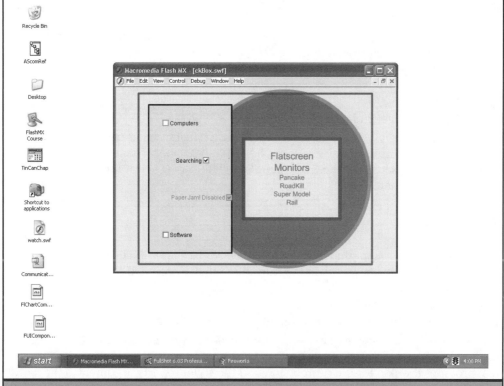

Figure 14-3. *By using the different FCheckBox methods, your interface can give the user more information about what is going on.*

you would use the setEnabled() method. The following example is one instance of the method's use from the sample movie:

```
function box1() {
    if (cBox1.getEnabled()) {
        if (cBox1.getLabel() == "Computers") {
```

Because the method returns a Boolean value, you can use it as such without a comparative operator in a conditional statement. Unless set to false, the enabled state of a component is true.

getLabel
FCheckBox.getLabel(): Method

One of the more useful enhancements of the check box object is the ability to retrieve and change its label. Using the getLabel() method, you can search through several check box instances to find a particular one, or as was done repeatedly in the sample movie, use it to determine the state of the check box instance.

```
if (cBox4.getLabel() == "Software") {
```

Usually the next step after a conditional statement is to change the label to something else using the setLabel() method. By changing labels depending on the check box's current status, the user has far more information, increasing the page's usability.

getValue
FCheckBox.getValue(): Method

The getValue() method checks to see if the check box instance has been checked or not. A Boolean true indicates that it has and a false that it has not. The default state of the check box is unchecked or false. For example, the following script forces the check box to the unchecked state:

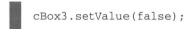

```
cBox3.setValue(false);
```

In some cases, you might want to uncheck the boxes after the user has checked them but has not unchecked them to return them to their original state.

registerSkinElement
FCheckBox.registerSkinElement(element, styleProperty): Method

The only method applying to the check box object is the registerSkinElement() method. The method has two arguments. The element parameter refers to the movie clip instance that provides the skin for the component, and the styleProperty argument is the name of the FStyleFormat property. The method registers the skin element to a style property specified. The following example shows a movie clip with the instance name billzSkin_mc that replaces the default highlight3D styleProperty:

```
cBox2.registerSkinElement(billzSkin_mc, "highlight3D");
```

setChangeHandler
FCheckBox.setChangeHandler(functionName, [location]): Method

The change handler can be placed in the Properties panel with the Parameters tab selected. The setChangeHandler() method does essentially the same thing. The method has two parameters. The functionName must be named as a string indicating a unique name for a function. Optionally, you can specify the path (location) to the function in a movie clip or timeline. If no location parameter is indicated, the change handler function must be on the same timeline as the check box instance. The following example illustrates this point:

```
cBox4.setChangeHandler("box4");
function box4() {
```

The function for the change handler begins in the line after it has been set. In this way, you can set the handler and define its function in the same code segment.

setEnabled
FCheckBox.setEnabled(enable): Method

The setEnabled() method has a single Boolean parameter that can be set to true or false. The Boolean true enables the check box instance, and the Boolean false disables it. Disabled check boxes cannot accept keyboard or mouse input from the user, and the labels turn gray as well. When you test the sample movie, as soon as the Printers check box is checked, it disables the check box *after* it has attended to several chores first.

The following example shows how the Printer check box is re-enabled:

```
if (!cBox3.getEnabled()) {
    cBox3.setEnabled(true);
```

setLabel
FCheckBox.setLabel(label): Method

The setLabel() method accepts a string as its parameter and then changes the check box's label to the string specified in the argument. The label it sets can also be used as a value with the getLabel() method. Used together, the getLabel() and setLabel() methods are used to toggle UI component labels, including the check box object.

In the sample movie, all of the labels are reset to "Searching" when their value is set to true (they are checked):

```
cBox4.setLabel("Searching");
```

setLabelPlacement
FCheckBox.setLabelPlacement(labelPosition): Method

The setLabelPlacement() method sets the check box label to the left or right of the box itself. A "left" or "right" string argument is used to position the label relative to the check box. In the sample movie, whenever a check box is checked, its label position changes.
   The following code places the label for checkBox1 to the right of the check box:

```
cBox3.setLabelPlacement("right");
```

setSize
FCheckBox.setSize(width): Method

The setSize() method sets or resets the width of the check box "window"—the combined check box and its label. In the sample movie, the one place where the size of the check box had to be changed was where the label was too long to be contained by the label window.
   The following script shows why the size had to be changed:

```
cBox3.setLabel("Paper Jam! Disabled");
cBox3.setLabelPlacement("left");
_root.choice.gotoAndStop("print");
cBox3.setSize(150);
```

The new label set, "Paper Jam! Disabled", was too long a string to fit into the conventional width, and so the check box instance was reset to 150 pixels, giving it ample room to fit the new string.

setStyleProperty
FCheckBox.setStyleProperty(styleProperty, value): Method

The setStyleProperty() method has two parameters. The styleProperty is an FStyleFormat property that can be used with components in general, with a subset that can be used for only certain components. For example, the arrow style property is used with scroll bars but not with check boxes. (See the table in the section "FStyleFormat Properties" for all of the FStyleFormats.)
   The second parameter is the color of the styleProperty. Use the format 0xRRGGBB where RR (0–FF) is red, GG (0–FF) is green, and BB (0–FF) is blue. For example, 0x00ff00

is pure green. The color only applies to the specified styleProperty and not other properties that may make up the component.

In the bottom check box in the sample movie, you may have noticed that when the script is run, as soon as you click the Software component, the little box's background turns red. That is due to the following script:

```
cBox4.setStyleProperty("background", 0xdf2556);
```

setValue
FCheckBox.setValue(select): Method

You have to be careful using the setValue() method because it fires off the change handler associated with the check box instance. Basically, the value is set to a Boolean true or false, with true being checked or selected. It does not matter whether you set it to true or false because either setting will invoke the event handler. In the script, the disabled cBox3 had its value reset from true to false (uncheck). However, the change handler filtered for a true, and because the script set the value to false, the event handler, while launched, did nothing because of the trap to filter out unchecked or unselected boxes, as shown in the following script segment:

```
function box3() {
    if (cBox3.getValue()) {
        if (cBox3.getLabel() == "Printers")
cBox3.setValue(false);
```

However, because the first condition of the function is that cBox3.getValue() must be true, and cBox3 has just been deselected, nothing more will happen in the function after the first line.

FStyleFormat Properties

The following table contains the different FStyleFormat properties and their descriptions. Use these properties with the setStyleProperty() and registerSkinElement() methods.

Property	Description
arrow	Color of arrow (scroll bars and drop-down lists only)
background	Background color of a component
backgroundDisabled	Background color of a disabled component
check	Check mark color in check box

Property	Description
darkshadow	Inner border or darker shadow portion color of a component
face	Main color of the component
foregroundDisabled	Foreground color of a disabled component
highlight	Inner border or darker shadow portion color of a selected component
highlight3D	Outer border or light shadow portion color of a selected component
radioDot	Dot color in a selected radio button
scrollTrack	Track color in a scroll bar
selection	Selection bar color highlighting a list item in a component
selectionDisabled	Selection bar color that highlights a list item in a disabled component
selectionUnfocused	Selection bar color of a component without keyboard focus
shadow	Outer border or light shadow portion color of a component
textAlign	Left, right, or center alignment for text displayed in or on a component
textBold	Boolean true value assigns bold style to text
textColor	All components assigned this default text color to the style format
textDisabled	Text color in a disabled component
textFont	Font name
textIndent	First indentation
textItalic	Boolean true value assigns italic style to text
textLeftMargin	Left paragraph margin in pixels for text
textRightMargin	Right paragraph margin in pixels for text
textSelected	Selected list color item in a component
textSize	Size of text in points
textUnderline	Boolean true value assigns underline style to text

Conclusion

One way to achieve better Web page usability is with a set of common and clear interface elements. The FCheckBox component objects not only provide a clear and intuitive set of interface elements, they can be customized using their different methods to bring them alive and add another layer of interactive usability in a Web page.

In the next chapter, you will be introduced to the FComboBox component, which has some elements in common with the FCheckBox component, but is a very different type of component with different methods. With it you can create scrollable drop-down lists with selectable items. You will use the same FStyleFormat table for changing different style properties.

The Complete Reference

ActionScript

Chapter 15

FComboBox

T
he FComboBox (or just combo box) is best understood as a versatile drop-down menu. By adding items along with their properties of labels and data, you can script a wide variety of effects with the combo box. You will also find it adaptable enough to fit into just about any design. Because the component takes up so little room on the stage, its power and versatility may be overlooked. However, if you want a powerful menu object for your Macromedia Flash MX movies, be sure to see what the combo box can do.

The Sample Program

The sample program for this chapter is a bit long so that I could put in as many methods for the FComboBox object as possible. One of the features I like about the combo box object is that you can pack a lot of information in a little space, and when that's what you want to do, the combo box is the component to do the job.

Methods

Each of the methods is discussed in turn, and you can find most of the methods used in the movie. The movie itself only uses a single frame and gives you most of the FComboBox methods so you can see them in context. Use Table 15-1 for the color palette used in this movie. The colors in the color palette are extended to the combo box object, so after you punch in the decimal values for the colors, look at the hexadecimal values for the colors as well. (You can see the hexadecimal colors in the Swatches panel and the other pop-up swatches, but the best place is the Color Mixer panel right beneath the main selected color.) Figure 15-1 shows how the stage is set up to begin the project. The large movie clip with three additional buttons and text fields will only become visible when the Add/Remove button on the stage is clicked, so you can put it anywhere you want on the stage. It has its own layer, so instead of trying to work around it, just click the Eye column to make it disappear. Then, before you test the movie, place it in the middle of the stage where it will pop up when the user wants it.

Name	R	G	B
Blue-gray	226	223	238
Brown	131	101	86
Dark maroon	121	37	46
Black	0	0	0

Table 15-1.   *Color Palette*

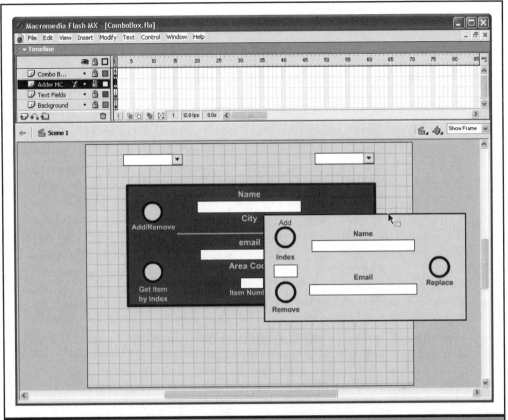

Figure 15-1.   *When creating the movie, very little space on the stage is occupied by the combo boxes even though each contains six items.*

Also feel free to substitute actual names and e-mail addresses for the ones provided. It's very handy for looking up e-mails. Also, you can add to the Area Code list or incorporate it in some other way into your own movies.

1. Open a new movie and add three layers to the existing one. Name them from top to bottom, Combo Boxes, Add MC, Text Fields, and Background. Set the background color to blue-gray.

2. Select the background layer and draw a rectangle with a dark maroon fill and 4-point black stroke with the dimensions W = 416, H = 198. Lock the layer.

3. Select the text field layer. Create a button with a 31.5-pixel diameter, a blue-gray fill and 4-point black stroke. Place two instances of the button on the stage positioned near the upper- and lower-left corners of the background rectangle. Give the top one the instance name addIt and the bottom one the instance name peekItem.

4. Add three Dynamic text fields over the middle of the background rectangle. The top two should have a width of 175 and the bottom one a width of 37.5. Each should use 12-point Arial font and brown for the font color.

5. Use the following labels: Beneath the top button, Add/Remove; beneath the bottom button, Get Item by Index; above the top text field, Name, and City beneath it; above the middle text field, email, and Area Code beneath it; beneath the bottom text field, Item Number.

6. Give the following instance names to the text fields in the order from top to bottom: fName, fMail, and menuIndex. Lock the layer.

7. Create a rectangle with a blue-gray fill and 2-point black stroke line with the dimensions W = 340, H = 175. Convert it into a movie clip, give it the instance name addStuff, and then double-click it to enter the Symbol Editing Mode.

8. In the Symbol Editing Mode, add a layer and name it Text Field. Place three instances of the same button symbol used on the main timeline. Place two on the left side near the corners and the third one on the right side in the center. Use the following instance names: upper-left button, addBtn; lower-left button, killBtn; and right-side button, rplBtn. Place the label Add above the one in the upper left, Remove below the one in the lower left, and Replace beneath the button on the right side. Use a bold dark maroon 12-point font for the labels.

9. Add three Dynamic text fields, a small one between the two buttons on the left, and two larger ones in the center of the movie clip. Use the following instance names: left, addIndex; top, addName; and bottom, addEmail. Place the label Index above the one on the left, Name above the top-middle text field, and Email above the bottom text field. Lock both layers and return to the main timeline. Lock the Add MC layer

10. Select the Combo Boxes layer. Above the dark maroon backdrop, place two instances of the ComboBox UI Component from the Components panel. Place one above the left-top corner of the rectangle background and give it the instance name friendsEmail. Place the other above the top-right corner, giving it the instance name areaCodes. Lock the layer.

11. Click in the first frame of the Combo Boxes layer, open the Actions panel, and enter the following script:

```
var x, long, longest, combosize, fEmailSize;
addStuff._visible = false;
//Create array for label and value
//The first element in each pair is the label
//The second element in each pair is the value
var fEmail = new Array("Sue Zee", "suZ@fufu.com");
fEmail.push("Darrel Duce", "ddDo@duceme.com");
fEmail.push("Wally Woo", "whowoo@freeMe.com");
```

```
fEmail.push("JoJo Peters", "jjp@hereNow.net");
fEmail.push("Darla Wawa", "dwow@ohmeohmy.com");
fEmail.push("Betty Jo Flapjack", "preacher@tv.com");
//Find the longest name and use it to factor in the number
//of pixels used for the width of the combo box.
for (long=2; long<fEmail.length; long += 2) {
    if (fEmail[long].length>fEmail[long-2].length) {
        longest = fEmail[long];
    } else {
        longest = fEmail[long-2];
    }
}
//Set the width of the Combo Box
//Multiply the longest string by 7 --adding pixels not
//characters
comboSize = longest.length*7;
friendsEmail.setSize(comboSize);
//Put the values into the Combo Box
//The pop() method takes information from the top of the
//Array and works downwards.
//The pop() method also makes the length of the array
//shorter with each iteration so be sure to put the
//length of the original array in a variable before you start
//popping off elements!
fEmailSize = fEmail.length;
for (var x = 0; x<fEmailSize; x += 2) {
    eData = fEmail.pop();
    eLabel = fEmail.pop();
    friendsEmail.addItem(eLabel, eData);
}
//Now Sort them by the label
friendsEmail.sortItemsBy("label", "ASC");
//Set Change Handler
eGrabber = new Object();
eGrabber.eHandler = function(component) {
    fName.text = friendsEmail.getSelectedItem().label;
    fMail.text = friendsEmail.getSelectedItem().data;
};
friendsEmail.setChangeHandler("eHandler", eGrabber);
//Make the MC with the Add/Remove/Replace buttons
//visible on the screen.
addIt.onPress = function() {
    addStuff._visible = true;
```

```
};
addStuff.addBtn.onPress = function() {
    aIndex = parseInt(_root.addStuff.addIndex.text);
    aName = _root.addStuff.addName.text;
    aEmail = _root.addStuff.addEmail.text;
    _root.friendsEmail.addItemAt(aIndex, aName, aEmail);
    _root.addStuff._visible = false;
};
//Remove an item using an index value
addStuff.killBtn.onPress = function() {
    aIndex = parseInt(_root.addStuff.addIndex.text);
    _root.friendsEmail.removeItemAt(aIndex);
    _root.addStuff._visible = false;
};
//Replace one item with another
addStuff.rplBtn.onPress = function() {
    aIndex = parseInt(_root.addStuff.addIndex.text);
    aName = _root.addStuff.addName.text;
    aEmail = _root.addStuff.addEmail.text;
    _root.friendsEmail.replaceItemAt(aIndex, aName, aEmail);
    _root.addStuff._visible = false;
};
//Examine item using index value
peekItem.onPress = function() {
    nowIndex = parseInt(menuIndex.text);
    fID = friendsEmail.getItemAt(nowIndex).label;
    eID = friendsEmail.getItemAt(nowIndex).data;
    fName.text = fID;
    fMail.text = eID;
};
/////////////////////////////////////////////
// Make another Menu with Editable Feature //
/////////////////////////////////////////////
var fAreaCode = new Array("San Diego", "619");
fAreaCode.push("Portland ME", "207");
fAreaCode.push("Miami", "305");
fAreaCode.push("Bloomfield", "860");
fAreaCode.push("Seattle", "206");
fAreaCode.push("Denver", "303");
//Set size manually
areaCodes.setSize(100);
//Put the values into the Combo Box
fACsize = fAreaCode.length;
```

```
for (var x = 0; x<fACsize; x += 2) {
    eData = fAreaCode.pop();
    eLabel = fAreaCode.pop();
    areaCodes.addItem(eLabel, eData);
}
//Now Sort them by the label
areaCodes.sortItemsBy("label", "ASC");
//Set Editable to true
areaCodes.setEditable(true);
//Set Change Handler
//Use a simple function as a change handler
function areaHandler() {
    fName.text = areaCodes.getSelectedItem().label;
    fMail.text = areaCodes.getSelectedItem().data;
}
areaCodes.setChangeHandler("areaHandler");
//Give the new menu a title
areaCodes.setValue("Area Codes");
//Add some style to both components
friendsEmail.setStyleProperty("arrow", 0x79252e);
areaCodes.setStyleProperty("arrow", 0x79252e);
friendsEmail.setStyleProperty("face", 0x7E2DFEE);
areaCodes.setStyleProperty("face", 0xE2DFEE);
friendsEmail.setStyleProperty("background", 0x7E2DFEE);
areaCodes.setStyleProperty("background", 0xE2DFEE);
friendsEmail.setStyleProperty("selection", 0x836556);
areaCodes.setStyleProperty("selection", 0x836556);
//Get the number of rows and scroll position
friendsRows = friendsEmail.getRowCount();
areaRows = areaCodes.getScrollPosition();
fName.text = "Friends Emails has "+friendsRows+" rows";
fMail.text = "Area Codes scrolled to: "+areaRows;
```

When you test the movie, be sure to use the "pop out" movie clip that lets you add, remove, and replace items in the friendsEmail instance of the combo box. Make some changes and then look at the choices in the menus. Also, you may find that the look of the combo boxes has changed even though you did nothing to it. The changes you see when you test the movie are due to the changes invoked by the script as can be seen in Figure 15-2.

addItem()
FComboBox.addItem(label [,data]): Method

The addItem() method adds new items to the combo box instance. The method has two arguments, label and data. Essentially, the data parameter is the value of the

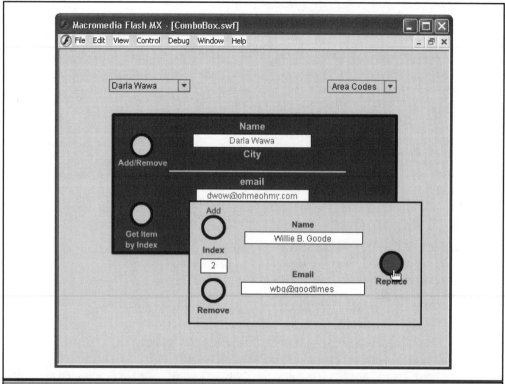

Figure 15-2.   *When you test the movie you can make changes to the combo boxes dynamically by using the movie clip that allows adding and removing items from the friendEmails instance of the combo box.*

label parameter. Generally, an array is used to add items to a combo box instance. It uses the format:

```
comBxInstance.addItem("myStuff", "myStuffValue");
```

Macromedia recommends that you limit your list of labels to 400. I'm not sure why anyone would place 400 items in a combo box (I can't handle the ones with 50 states), but if you really need more than 400 items, just break them up into more combo boxes. The following script segment from the chapter sample movie shows how data from an array is put into a combo box using the Array.pop() method:

```
for (var x = 0; x<fEmailSize; x += 2) {
    eData = fEmail.pop();
    eLabel = fEmail.pop();
    friendsEmail.addItem(eLabel, eData);
}
```

The array fEmail.pop() method begins removing elements from the end of the array and placing the data and label values into the FComboBox object using the addItem() method. When using the pop() method, you have to do things backwards, and so the first item popped is data, and the second is the label. However, it's a quick way to fill up the combo box instance with labels and data.

addItemAt
FComboBox.addItemAt(index, label [,data]): Method

The addItemAt() method is just like the addItem() methods except it has an additional parameter, index. The 0-based system of item assignment used with combo boxes sets up an index with 0 being the top of the menu and the length of the combo box being the bottom. By specifying the index value, you can specify where you want to insert an item, while using the addItem() method places the newest items at the bottom of the menu. The label is a string and the data can be any acceptable Macromedia Flash MX data type, including a Flash object or movie clip.

In the sample movie, a button on the movie clip scripted with an unnamed function uses information from a text field to insert a new name and e-mail address. The following script shows how information entered into the combo box from text fields with the instance names addName and addEmail is used to add items to the friendsEmail combo box object:

```
addStuff.addBtn.onPress = function() {
    aIndex = parseInt(_root.addStuff.addIndex.text);
    aName = _root.addStuff.addName.text;
    aEmail = _root.addStuff.addEmail.text;
    _root.friendsEmail.addItemAt(aIndex, aName, aEmail);
    _root.addStuff._visible = false;
};
```

getEnabled
FComboBox.getEnabled(): Method

The getEnabled() method contains a Boolean true if the combo box is enabled and a false if it is not. Try putting the following code at the beginning of the sample movie:

```
trace(areaCodes.getEnabled());
```

Right away you will see that the combo box is enabled. It is on the stage with an instance name; since its default enabled status is true, that is what you will see in the output window. A combo box does not have to contain items to be enabled.

getItemAt
FComboBox.getItemAt(index): Method

When you use getItemAt(), it returns an object with the label and data information. The single argument in the method is any integer that is within the range of items on the combo box. For example, the following code segment uses a value from an input text field instance (menuIndex) as an index to view the label and data in the item at the specified index:

```
//Examine item using index value
peekItem.onPress = function() {
    nowIndex = parseInt(menuIndex.text);
    fID = friendsEmail.getItemAt(nowIndex).label;
    eID = friendsEmail.getItemAt(nowIndex).data;
    fName.text = fID;
    fMail.text = eID;
};
```

The button instance, peekItem, simply fires the function that takes the index from the text field and uses it to place the label and data property values in two dynamic text fields.

getLength
FComboBox.getLength(): Method

The getLength() method returns the number of items currently in the combo box list. For an interesting experiment, place the following script at the beginning of the sample movie:

```
trace(friendsEmail.getLength())
```

You will get 0. That is because at the beginning of the movie, no items have been entered into the combo box. However, if you place the same script at the end of the movie, the Output box shows 6.

getRowCount
FComboBox.getRowCount(): Method

The getRowCount() method returns the number of rows that have been set as being visible without scrolling. The default is 8 rows, and you may have noticed when you ran the movie that the initial value in the Name text field indicates that "Friends Emails has 8 rows." If that confused you because the array only contained six items, it is referring to the number of possible visible items at one time and not the number of items. The following script shows how the row count is placed into a variable and then displayed in the fName text field:

```
//Get the number of rows and scroll position
friendsRows = friendsEmail.getRowCount();
areaRows = areaCodes.getScrollPosition();
fName.text = "Friends Emails has "+friendsRows+" rows";
fMail.text = "Area Codes scrolled to: "+areaRows;
```

getScrollPosition
FComboBox.getScrollPosition(): Method

The getScrollPosition() method returns an integer with the position of the item at the top of the combo box. At the outset, the scroll position will be 0 because the 0-based index is the starting point for all items in the combo box. At the beginning of the movie (and the end of the script) you will see the message:

```
Area Codes scrolled to: 0
```

because the following script first retrieves the scroll position of the areaCodes combo box instance and then places it in a text field for viewing:

```
areaRows = areaCodes.getScrollPosition();
....
fMail.text = "Area Codes scrolled to: "+areaRows;
```

getSelectedIndex
FComboBox.getSelectedIndex(): Method

The getSelectedIndex() method retrieves the index value of the currently selected item. For example, if the item on the fourth row were selected, its index value would be 3 because the index is 0-based. If the getSelectedIndex() method were invoked at that time, it would return 3.

The following script would place the index value of the areaCodes combo box instance into a variable named showIndexS:

```
var showIndexS=areaCodes.getSelectedIndex();
```

getSelectedItem
FComboBox.getSelectedItem(): Method

The getSelectedItem() method returns an object currently selected in the combo box or undefined. (The selected item is the one highlighted.) However, to use the method effectively, you need to specify what properties of the object to get. Generally, you will want to get the label and data value of the selected item rather than the object without any reference to either the label or data. In the sample movie, the change handlers retrieved the values of both the label and data properties as shown in the following script segment:

```
fName.text = friendsEmail.getSelectedItem().label;
fMail.text = friendsEmail.getSelectedItem().data;
```

Both label and data values are passed to Dynamic text fields for viewing. However, both must be specified when the getSelectedItem() method is being used.

getValue
FComboBox.getValue(): Method

In an editable combo box, such as the areaCodes instance, the getValue() method returns the text in the field at the top of the combo box. The same method used with the static combo box, like the friendsEmail instance, the value returned is the data of the label in the top field of the combo box. For example, enter the following code at the end of the sample movie:

```
trace(friendsEmail.getValue());
trace(areaCodes.getValue());
```

The top value in the Output window will be an e-mail address, and the bottom value will be "Area Codes," the value set with the FComboBox.setValue() method. (Unlike some components, setting a value in an editable combo box instance will not trigger the change handler.)

registerSkinElement
FComboBox.registerSkinElement(element, styleProperty): Method

The registerSkinElement() method is used to customize the look of the combo box instances. The method has two arguments. The element parameter refers to the movie clip instance that provides the skin for the component, and the styleProperty argument is the name of the FStyleFormat property. The method registers the skin element to a style property specified. The following example shows a movie clip with the instance name silky_mc that replaces the default selection styleProperty in the "selection" element:

```
areaCodes.registerSkinElement(silky_mc, "selection");
```

removeAll
FComboBox.removeAll(): Method

The removeAll() method removes all of the items and their label and data properties from the combo box instance. For example, to remove all of the names and e-mail addresses in the sample movie, use the following code:

```
friendsEmail.removeAll();
```

Ironically, if the combo box is disabled, this method cannot be applied. However, an enabled combo box can, and the removeAll() method can be used to clean out a combo box whose items are no longer required.

removeItemAt

FComboBox.removeItemAt(index): Method

The removeItemAt() method requires a 0-based index value (integer). The item at the index is removed. A combo box that has been sorted will not automatically resort itself if the insertion point is not in alphabetical order. When the item is removed, the list is updated so you won't see gaps where the item has been removed. The following was used in the sample movie to remove an item based on user-supplied value in an input text field:

```
//Remove an item using an index value
addStuff.killBtn.onPress = function() {
    aIndex = parseInt(_root.addStuff.addIndex.text);
    _root.friendsEmail.removeItemAt(aIndex);
    _root.addStuff._visible = false;
};
```

The page viewer types in an integer in the addIndex.text field that is contained on the addStuff instance of the movie clip. When you test the sample movie, you will see any item you have removed using this method disappear from the menu list.

replaceItemAt

FComboBox.replaceItemAt(index, label [,data]): Method

The replaceItemAt() method uses an index value to replace a combo box item at the index position. Unlike the removeItemAt() method, this method requires a substitute label and optional data. The following script references a button (rplBtn) that invokes an unnamed function that includes viewer-supplied label and data information:

```
//Replace one item with another
addStuff.rplBtn.onPress = function() {
    aIndex = parseInt(_root.addStuff.addIndex.text);
    aName = _root.addStuff.addName.text;
    aEmail = _root.addStuff.addEmail.text;
    _root.friendsEmail.replaceItemAt(aIndex, aName, aEmail);
    _root.addStuff._visible = false;
};
```

As soon as the method is invoked, the menu list changes with the new label and data. Use the sample movie to see how it affects a menu.

setChangeHandler
FComboBox.setChangeHandler(functionName, [location]): Method

The setChangeHandler() method essentially names the function that fires when a combo box change occurs. The change with the combo box is typically a change in the selected item. A simple function is sufficient to work with the combo box. In the sample movie, the function for the areaCodes instance of the combo box uses a function named areaHandler. The function sets up the actions that occur when a selection change occurs.

```
//Use a simple function as a change handler
function areaHandler() {
    fName.text = areaCodes.getSelectedItem().label;
    fMail.text = areaCodes.getSelectedItem().data;
}
areaCodes.setChangeHandler("areaHandler");
```

The handler function simply transfers the label and data value of the selected item to the viewable output text fields. You want to be sure to place the setChangeHandler() method after the function that it calls.

setDataProvider
FComboBox.setDataProvider(dataProvider): Method

The setDataProvider() method is an advanced technique involving creating an array with string elements specifying the items to add to the combo box. The dataProvider is an outside data source and can be an Array object that specifies the label and data. For example, the following code specifies cityAC as the dataProvider object:

```
areaCodes.setDataProvider(cityAC);
```

One way of creating an object with both label and data properties would be the following:

```
var fAreaCode = new Array("San Diego", "619");
fAreaCode.push("Portland ME", "207");
fAreaCode.push("Miami", "305");
fAreaCode.push("Bloomfield", "860");
fAreaCode.push("Seattle", "206");
fAreaCode.push("Denver", "303");
var cityAC= new Object();
for(x=0;x<6;x+=2) {
 cityAC.label=fAreaCode[x];
```

```
    cityAC.data=fAreaCode[x+1];
}
```

setEditable
FComboBox.setEditable(editable): Method

The setEditable() method defines a combo box as being static (false) or editable (true) using the method's single argument. In the sample movie, the friendsEmail instance is static and the areaCodes instance of the combo box is editable. If a combo box is editable, you can use the setValue() method to change the text field element of the combo box dynamically. The following is a code segment from the sample movie that shows how the areaCodes instance of the combo box became editable:

```
//Set Editable to true
areaCodes.setEditable(true);
```

setEnabled
FComboBox.setEnabled(enable): Method

By default, the combo boxes set on the stage with an instance name are enabled. A Boolean value determines whether the combo box is enabled (true) or disabled (false). In some applications, you will want to "freeze" a combo box until some other element of the movie has been attended to. By setting setEnabled() to false, the combo box no longer responds to mouse or keyboard controls. However, as soon as the combo box instance is assigned setEnabled(), either with no Boolean true or with a Boolean true in the argument, it becomes fully functional again. The following would disable the areaCodes instance of the combo box:

```
areaCodes.setEnabled(false);
```

setItemSymbol
FComboBox.setItemSymbol(symbolID): Method

The setItemSymbol() method registers the symbol linkage ID of a graphic symbol to show the contents of a combo box. FComboBoxItem in the library is the default value. As an advanced programming concept, you need to understand the linkage between the library objects and the graphic symbols to represent the combo box elements. To set a symbolID to the areaCodes instance of the combo box in the sample movie, the format would be

```
areaCodes.setItemSymbol(myOwnGr)
```

The "graphic symbol" would have to be a Movie Clip symbol and not a Symbol with Graphic behavior.

setRowCount
FComboBox.setRowCount(rows): Method

The setRowCount() method is deceptively useful. The number of rows that can be displayed in a combo box may not seem to be a matter to ponder, but because the number of visible rows that can be seen without scrolling can affect both design and usability, it can be very useful. You may even need to consider having a different number of visible rows for different combo boxes in the same movie. The following sets a longer row count than the default of 8 rows:

```
friendsEmail.setRowCount(10);
```

setSelectedIndex
FComboBox.setSelectedIndex(index): Method

The setSelectedIndex() method can be used to select an item in the combo box. It has the same effect as selecting an item from the menu using the mouse. The parameter is an integer from 0 to the number of items in the menu minus 1. The change handler is involved by this method as well. The following example would select the third item in a combo box list:

```
areaCodes.setSelectedIndex(2);
```

setSize
FComboBox.setSize(width): Method

Use the setSize() method to dynamically set the size of your combo box relative to the size of the longest item label. The width parameter is the size in pixels, and depending on the type and size of the font you are using, the width can vary. In the sample movie, I used 7 as a multiplier based on the string length of an item label. Thus a label with 12 characters would be multiplied by 7, resulting in a width parameter of 84. The following is a segment of the script that used a variable to set the width of the friendsEmail combo box instance:

```
//Set the width of the Combo Box
//Multiply the longest string by 7 --adding pixels not
//characters
comboSize = longest.length*7;
friendsEmail.setSize(comboSize);
```

setStyleProperty
FComboBox.setStyleProperty(styleProperty, value): Method

The setStyleProperty() method has two parameters. The styleProperty is an FStyleFormat property that can be used with components in general, with a subset that can be used for only certain components. For example, the arrow style property is used with combo boxes, but not with check boxes. (See the table in the section "FStyleFormat Properties" for all of the FStyleFormats.)

The second parameter is the color of the styleProperty. Use the format 0xRRGGBB where RR (0–FF) is red, GG (0–FF) is green, and BB (0–FF) is blue. For example, 0x00ff00 is pure green. The color only applies to the specified styleProperty and not other properties that may make up the component.

The sample movie uses information from both the section "FStyleFormat Properties" and the color palette to better integrate the combo boxes into the color scheme. The following script shows the different properties changed along with the color values:

```
//Add some style to both components
friendsEmail.setStyleProperty("arrow", 0x79252e);
areaCodes.setStyleProperty("arrow", 0x79252e);
friendsEmail.setStyleProperty("face", 0x7E2DFEE);
areaCodes.setStyleProperty("face", 0xE2DFEE);
friendsEmail.setStyleProperty("background", 0x7E2DFEE);
areaCodes.setStyleProperty("background", 0xE2DFEE);
friendsEmail.setStyleProperty("selection", 0x836556);
areaCodes.setStyleProperty("selection", 0x836556);
```

setValue
FComboBox.setValue(editableText): Method

If a combo box instance has FComboBox.setEditable set to true, you can add text to the top (editable) text box in the combo box. The single parameter in the method expects a string that will be placed in the input field at the top of the combo box.

In the sample movie, the following sets the areaCodes instance text box with the heading "Area Codes":

```
//Give it the new menu a title
areaCodes.setValue("Area Codes");
```

sortItemsBy
FComboBox.sortItemsBy(fieldName, order): Method

The sortItemsBy() method has two parameters. The first, fieldName, is either label or data. If your items contain first and last names, the sorting will be on the first names unless the surname is placed first in the item. The second parameter specifies ascending (ASC) or descending (DESC) order. In the sample movie, the following script places the items in the friendsEmail instance in alphabetical order by first name:

```
//Now Sort them by the label
friendsEmail.sortItemsBy("label", "ASC");
```

FStyleFormat Properties

The following table contains the different FStyleFormat Properties and their descriptions. Use these properties with the setStyleProperty() and registerSkinElement() methods.

Property	Description
arrow	Color of arrow (scroll bars and drop-down lists only)
background	Background color of a component
backgroundDisabled	Background color disabled component
check	Check mark color in check box
darkshadow	Inner border or darker shadow portion color of a component
face	Main color of the component
foregroundDisabled	Foreground color of a disabled component
highlight	Inner border or darker shadow portion color of selected component
highlight3D	Outer border or light shadow portion color of a selected component
radioDot	Dot color in a selected radio button
scrollTrack	Track color in a scroll bar
selection	Selection bar color highlighting a list item in a component
selectionDisabled	Selection bar color that highlights a list item in a disabled component
selectionUnfocused	Selection bar color when the component does not have keyboard focus
shadow	Outer border or light shadow portion color of component

Property	Description
textAlign	Left, right, or center alignment for text displayed in or on a component
textBold	Boolean true value assigns bold style to text
textColor	All components assigned this default text color to the style format
textDisabled	Text color in a disabled component
textFont	Font name
textIndent	First indentation
textItalic	Boolean true value assigns italic style to text
textLeftMargin	Left paragraph margin in pixels for text
textRightMargin	Right paragraph margin in pixels for text
textSelected	Selected list color item in a component
textSize	Size of text in points
textUnderline	Boolean true value assigns underline style to text

Conclusion

In looking at all the code and considering the possibilities that can be placed in the combo boxes, the idea that "great things come in small packages" resonates. The little pop-up menu that characterizes the combo box component hides a great many possibilities for an efficient user interface that takes up precious little screen real estate. The fact that the component has so many methods speaks to the fact of the combo box's many different uses and adaptability to different tasks.

In the next chapter, you will find a similar component, the FListBox. The great majority of the methods are the same, but enough are unique and different that you will find working with the list box component another clear choice of components to use in developing and designing your movie.

The
Complete
Reference

ActionScript

Chapter 16

FListBox

T he FListBox (or just list box) is another type of menu component. By adding items along with their properties of labels and data, you can script a wide variety of effects with the list box. You will also find it adaptable enough to fit into just about any design. The amount of space list box components take up on the stage depends on how much you want the user to see initially. They are designed to immediately show the viewer more options than the FComboBox object, but because they have scroll ability, they can take up as much or little room on the stage as you want.

Using the List Box Component

The purpose of the list box component is to show or list choices without making the viewer open the menu. So if you want to have a pop-up menu object you might want to consider the combo box. Otherwise, you will find the list box easy to use and versatile for showing off a set of selections. As you will see in both the example and methods available for the component, you can match it to just about any design.

Methods

The sample movie for this chapter contains as many methods for the FListBox object as possible. With the list box, the user can make multiple selections, and you can script in selections to highlight the choices in the list box.

Use Table 16-1 for the color palette used in this movie. The colors in the color palette are extended to the list box object as well, so after you punch in the decimal values for the colors, look at the hexadecimal values for the colors as well. (You can see the hexadecimal colors in the Swatches panel and the other pop-up swatches, but the best place is the Color Mixer panel right beneath the main selected color. You can even copy and paste the hexadecimal values from the Color Mixer panel to the Actions panel.) Figure 16-1 shows how the stage is set up to begin the project. The two list boxes are on top of two different colored squares. The tops of the list boxes can be

Name	R	G	B
Orange-tan	214	134	20
Yellow	240	221	56
Dark maroon	106	0	18
Pale, pale blue	229	241	245
Gray	131	143	142

Table 16-1. *Color Palette*

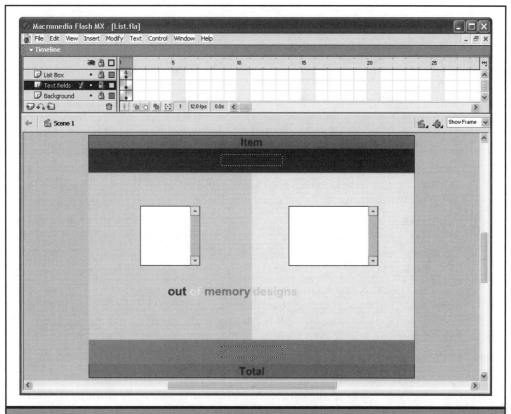

Figure 16-1.   *The two list boxes' tops are aligned vertically, but their horizontal position on the stage is controlled by the ActionScript.*

top-aligned using the Align panel. However, because the ActionScript changes both list boxes' horizontal dimensions, it is difficult to place them in the correct horizontal position on the stage before testing the movie. Therefore, the ActionScript places both list boxes in the horizontal center of the respective background square each resides on.

The sample movie shows a hypothetical online Web design company, Out of Memory Designs. The list box on the left shows the company's services, and the one on the right shows its products for sale. As each item is selected, its cost is displayed in a text field at the top of the stage area, and a running total is displayed at the bottom.

1. Open a new movie and add two layers to the existing one in the movie. Name them from top to bottom, List Box, Text Fields, and Background. Set the background color to gray. Use the default stage size of 550-by-400 pixels.

2. Select the Background layer and draw a square with a yellow fill and no stroke with the dimensions W = 275, H = 275. Align it to the left of the stage and center it vertically. Draw an identical square on the right side of the stage using pale, pale blue and no stroke.

3. Draw a dark maroon rectangle with the dimensions W = 550, H = 39. Center it horizontally and position it directly on top of the two squares. Draw an identical orange-tan rectangle and place it directly beneath the two squares. Lock the layer.

4. Select the Text fields layer. Place two Dynamic text fields on the stage set for yellow 12-point Arial font and dimensions of W = 104, H = 18. Position one vertically and horizontally in the middle of the dark maroon rectangle. Give it the instance name item. Position the other one centered vertically and horizontally on the orange-tan rectangle and give it the instance name total.

5. Using a 20-point Arial bold font in a Static text field place the title, "out of memory designs", using dark maroon for "out", pale, pale blue for "of", gray for "memory", and yellow for "designs". Place the text as shown in Figure 16-1.

6. Centered above the dark maroon rectangle using a bold dark maroon 18-point Arial font, place the label "Item" in a Static text field. Centered below the bottom orange-tan rectangle, place the label "Total" using the same font dimensions. Lock the layer.

7. Select the List Box layer. Drag two ListBox components to the stage. Place one over the yellow square and give it the instance name WebSer. Place the other ListBox component over the pale, pale blue square and give it the instance name WebProd.

8. Position each in the middle of their respective squares and then use the Align panel to top-align them. Lock the layer.

9. Click the first frame of the top layer and enter the following script:

```
//Array for Services
var Wservices = new Array("Page Design", "200");
Wservices.push("Site Design", "500");
Wservices.push("Site Development", "1000");
Wservices.push("Template Design", "400");
Wservices.push("Site Re-design", "1500");
Wservices.push("Site Development & Design", "2000");
Wservices.push("Backend & Database", "3200");
//Loop to place them into the ListBox
for (x=0; x<Wservices.length; x += 2) {
    WebSer.addItem(Wservices[x], Wservices[x+1]);
}
//Set Size, visible rows, multiple selection
//Auto hide the scroll bar and sort
WebSer.setSize(175);
//Set position on stage
WebSer._x = (275/2)-(175/2);
WebSer.setRowCount(4);
```

```
WebSer.setSelectMultiple(false);
WebSer.setAutoHideScrollBar(true);
WebSer.sortItemsBy("label", "ASC");
//Array for Products
var Wproducts = new Array("Clip Art: Travel", "345");
Wproducts.push("Clip Art: Business", "490");
Wproducts.push("Clip Art: Play", "188");
Wproducts.push("Fonts Pack 1 : All Display", "288");
Wproducts.push("Fonts Pack 2 : Headers", "188");
Wproducts.push("Fonts Pack 3 : Cursive", "175");
Wproducts.push("Fonts Pack 4 : Classic", "258");
for (k=0; k<Wproducts.length; k += 2) {
    WebProd.addItem(Wproducts[k], Wproducts[k+1]);
}
//Set Size, visible rows, multiple selection
//Auto hide the scroll bar and sort
WebProd.setSize(27*7);
//Position in the middle of the right column
WebProd._x = (275+275/2)-(189/2);
WebProd.setRowCount(6);
WebProd.setSelectMultiple(true);
WebProd.setAutoHideScrollBar(true);
//Create array to set selected indices
var selEm = new Array(0, 2, 4, 6);
WebProd.setSelectedIndices(selEm);
//Add some style
WebSer.setStyleProperty("arrow", 0x6A0012);
WebSer.setStyleProperty("selection", 0xD68614);
WebSer.setStyleProperty("scrollTrack", 0x6A0012);
WebSer.setStyleProperty("face", 0xF0DD38);
WebSer.setStyleProperty("selectionUnfocused", 0x838F8E);
WebProd.setStyleProperty("arrow", 0x6A0012);
WebProd.setStyleProperty("selection", 0xD68614);
WebProd.setStyleProperty("arrow", 0x6A0012);
WebProd.setStyleProperty("scrollTrack", 0x6A0012);
WebProd.setStyleProperty("face", 0xE5F1F5);
WebProd.setStyleProperty("selectionUnfocused", 0x838F8E);
//Change Handlers
//Service Change Handler
webHand = new Object();
webHand.serHand = function(component) {
    item.text = "$"+WebSer.getSelectedItem().data;
    var single = parseFloat(WebSer.getSelectedItem().data);
    _global.totalBill += single;
```

```
         total.text = "$"+totalBill;
      };
      WebSer.setChangeHandler("serHand", webHand);
      //Product Change Handler
      webHand.prodHand = function(component) {
       item.text = "$"+WebProd.getValue();
       var single = parseFloat(WebProd.getValue());
       _global.totalBill += single;
       total.text = "$"+totalBill;
      };
      WebProd.setChangeHandler("prodHand", webHand);
      //Area 51 -- Hazardous Tests in Progress
      //Use this area to add suggested test scripts.
```

When you test the movie, select items from both sides. You will notice that the Total keeps accumulating no matter what item or which list box you select from. That's because the variable totalBill is a global one used in both change handler scripts. At the same time, the single variable is a local one to each function and so the values of one and the other do not get mixed up. Figure 16-2 shows the movie presenting each item's value individually and the accumulated total.

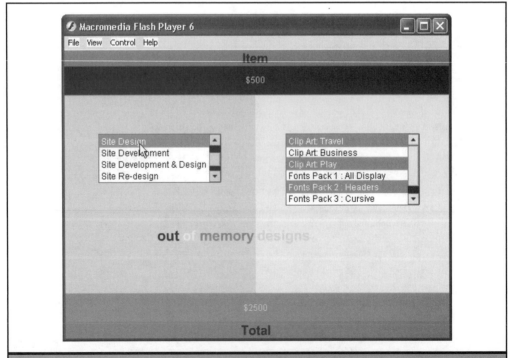

Figure 16-2. *When you test the movie you will see the values in the top and bottom text fields change.*

addItem

FListBox.addItem(label [,data]): Method

The addItem() method adds new items to the list box instance. The method has two arguments, label and data. Essentially, the data parameter is the value of the label parameter. Generally, an array is used to add items to a list box instance. It uses the following format:

```
listBoxInstance.addItem("myStuff", "myStuffValue");
```

The following script segment from the chapter sample movie shows how data stored in an array is put into a list box using a loop:

```
//Loop to place them into the ListBox
for (x=0; x<Wservices.length; x += 2) {
    WebSer.addItem(Wservices[x], Wservices[x+1]);
}
```

Because the label and data properties were arranged in pairs in the array, removing them from the array and placing them into the list boxes is simply a sequential loop using a step of two rather than one.

addItemAt

FListBox.addItemAt(index, label [,data]): Method

The addItemAt() method is just like the addItem() methods except it has an additional parameter, index. The 0-based system of item assignment used with list boxes sets up an index with 0 being the top of the menu and the length of the list box being the bottom. By specifying the index value, you can specify where you want to insert an item, while using the addItem() method places the newest items at the bottom of the menu. The label is a string and the data can be any acceptable Macromedia Flash MX data type, including a Flash object or movie clip.

The method had no natural place in the sample movie, but you could add script to insert additional items. For example, the following would add an item in index position 2 (which would be item number 3):

```
WebSer.addItemAt(2,"Font Design", "3000");
```

The most useful application of the method is when you want to insert an item in an existing list. Because of the index value, you can position it anywhere you want.

getEnabled
FListBox.getEnabled(): Method
The getEnabled() method contains a Boolean true if the list box is enabled and a false if it is not. Try putting the following code at the beginning of the sample movie:

```
trace(WebSer.getEnabled());
```

Right away you will see that the list box is enabled. List boxes on the stage have a default state of being enabled. A list box does not have to contain items to be enabled.

getItemAt
FListBox.getItemAt(index): Method
When you use getItemAt(), it returns an object with the label and data information. The single argument in the method is any integer within the range of items on the list box. For example, the following code uses a value from an assigned variable to extract label and data information:

```
//Examine item using index value
nowIndex = 3;
WSlab = WebSer.getItemAt(nowIndex).label;
WSdata = WebSer.getItemAt(nowIndex).data;
```

The values of both the label and associated data from the fourth list box item are stored in the variables WSlab and WSdata. (Using a 0-index, the value 3 returns the fourth item.)

getLength
FListBox.getLength(): Method
The getLength() method returns the number of items currently in the list box list. For an interesting experiment, place the following script at the beginning of the sample movie:

```
trace(WebSer.getLength()
```

You will get 0 because, at the beginning of the movie, no items have been entered into the list box. However, if you place the same script at the end of the movie, the Output box shows 7.

getRowCount
FListBox.getRowCount(): Method

The getRowCount() method returns the number of rows that have been set as being visible without scrolling. The default is 8 rows. The following script shows how the row count is retrieved from a list box:

```
//Get the number of rows
serRows = WebSer.getRowCount();
trace(serRows);
```

If you place that script at the end of the sample movie script, you will see 4 in the Output window when you test the movie.

getScrollPosition
FListBox.getScrollPosition(): Method

The getScrollPosition() returns an integer with the position of the item at the top of the list box. At the outset, the scroll position will be 0 because the 0-based index is the starting point for all items in the list box. This will occur even if you have scripted items to be selected as was done with the WebProd list box object. Using the setSelectedIndices() method, the sample movie selected four items. However, you still get an output of 0 using the following script at the end of the movie:

```
trace(WebProd.getScrollPosition());
```

At first you may suspect that the 0 is returned because one of the array elements used to set the selected indices was 0. However, even if you remove the 0 from the array, you will still find that the return is 0. Furthermore, if you select an item beyond the visible number of rows which would require a scroll to see it using setSelectedIndices() or setSelectedIndex(), the initial scroll position is still going to be 0. This is because a scroll is not required when an ActionScript method is used to select the item.

getSelectedIndex
FListBox.getSelectedIndex(): Method

The getSelectedIndex() method retrieves the index value of the currently selected item. For example, if the item on the fourth row were selected, its index value would be 3 because the index is 0-based. If the getSelectedIndex() method were invoked at that time, it would return 3.

However, because you can select indices using the setSelectedIndices() method, the selection can be made with ActionScript code rather than a mouse-click. For example, add the following line at the end of the sample movie:

```
trace(WebProd.getSelectedIndex());
```

At first you may suspect that the 0 is returned because the first of the array elements used to set the select indices is 0. However, you will see 6 because it gets the most recently selected index. (The value 6 was the last value in the array and so is the most "recent.")

getSelectedIndices
FListBox.getSelectedIndices(): Method

The getSelectedIndices() method returns the index values of all of the items currently selected in a multiple-selection list box. The values are returned as an array, but the array is in the reverse order in which the items were selected. In the sample movie, add the following script to the end of the existing script:

```
gimmeIndices = new Array();
gimmeIndices = WebProd.getSelectedIndices();
for (v=0; v<gimmeIndices.length; v++) {
    trace(gimmeIndices[v]);
}
```

You will see the values stacked up in the Output window:

```
6
4
2
0
```

getSelectedItem
FListBox.getSelectedItem(): Method

The getSelectedItem() method returns an object currently selected in the list box or undefined. (The selected item is the one highlighted.) However, to use the method effectively, you need to specify what properties of the object to get. Generally, you will want to get the label and data value of the selected item rather than the object without any reference to either the label or data. For example, the first of the two change handler scripts in the sample movie used the getSelectedItem() method to retrieve the data associated with the selected item:

```
webHand.serHand = function(component) {
```

```
    item.text = "$"+WebSer.getSelectedItem().data;
    var single = parseFloat(WebSer.getSelectedItem().data);
    _global.totalBill += single;
    total.text = "$"+totalBill;
};
```

The label did not need to be selected because it is visible on the stage during the selection process, but the data needs to be added to the text file at the top of the stage.

getSelectedItems
FListBox.getSelectedItems(): Method

Because list boxes (unlike combo boxes) allow the selection of multiple items, more than a single item can be selected simultaneously. The getSelectedItems() method returns an array with all of the currently selected items as label and data property values. Since the sample script has multiple sections in the WebProd component instance at the outset, the following ActionScript added at the end of the sample script will display all of the item labels and associated data properties:

```
thisThat = new Array();
thisThat = WebProd.getSelectedItems();
for (v=0; v<thisThat.length; v++) {
    trace(thisThat[v].label);
    trace(thisThat[v].data);
}
```

When you test the movie, you will see all the labels and data in the Output window.

getSelectedMultiple
FListBox.getSelectedMultiple(): Method

The getSelectedMultiple() method returns a Boolean value indicating whether the list box can have multiple selections. The WebProd component instance had its value set to true and the WebSer component instance had its value set to false. The following script shows these settings:

```
trace(WebProd.getSelectedMultiple());
trace(WebSer.getSelectedMultiple());
```

The Output window indicates

```
true
false
```

getValue
FListBox.getValue(): Method

The data value from the currently selected item (or most recently selected if multiple items are selected) is returned by the getValue() method. In the sample movie, the change handler function for the WebProd component instance used the getValue() method to get the data from the selected item in the list box:

```
webHand.prodHand = function(component) {
  item.text = "$"+WebProd.getValue();
  var single = parseFloat(WebProd.getValue());
  _global.totalBill += single;
  total.text = "$"+totalBill;
};
```

It might help to think of the getValue() method as a "getData()" method because it is the data property that the method returns.

registerSkinElement
FListBox.registerSkinElement(element, styleProperty): Method

The registerSkinElement() method is used to customize the look of the list box instances. The method has two arguments. The element parameter refers to the movie clip instance that provides the skin for the component, and the styleProperty argument is the name of the FStyleFormat property. The method registers the skin element to a style property specified. The following example shows a movie clip with the instance name business_ mc that replaces the default selection styleProperty in the "selection" element:

```
WebProd.registerSkinElement(business_mc, "selection");
```

removeAll
FListBox.removeAll(): Method

The removeAll() method removes all of the items and their label and data properties from the list box instance. For example, to remove all of the items in the WebSer component instance in the sample movie, use the following code:

```
WebSer.removeAll();
```

If the list box is disabled, this method cannot be applied. However, an enabled list box can, and the removeAll() method can be used to clean out a list box whose items are no longer required.

removeItemAt
FListBox.removeItemAt(index): Method

The removeItemAt() method requires a 0-based index value (integer). The item at the index is removed. A list box that has been sorted will not automatically resort itself if the insertion point is not in alphabetical order. When the item is removed, the list is updated so you will not see gaps where the item has been removed. Add the following line to the end of the sample movie script:

```
//Remove an item using an index value
 WebSer.removeItemAt(1);
```

When you test the movie, you will see that the item "Page Design" has disappeared from the list box on the left. That item was the second one (0 was the first) in the menu list, and its index value was selected for removal.

replaceItemAt
FListBox.replaceItemAt(index, label [,data]): Method

The replaceItemAt() method uses an index value to replace a list box item at the index position. Unlike the removeItemAt() method, this method requires a substitute label and optional data. Add the following lines at the end of the sample script:

```
//Replace one item with another
WebSer.replaceItemAt(1,"New Stuff",123);
```

You will see in the list box on the left that "Page Design" has been replaced by "New Stuff" with a value of 123.

setAutoHideScrollBar
FListBox.setAutoHideScrollBar(true/false): Method

The setAutoHideScrollBar() method accepts a Boolean value to turn it on or off (true for on). When the number of items is at or below the maximum number of viewable rows, the scroll bar disappears, but as soon as the number of items exceeds the maximum viewable rows, the scroll bar appears. In the sample movie, the following line uses the method:

```
WebSer.setAutoHideScrollBar(true);
```

To see how it works, comment out the last array values for the WebProd component instance in the sample movie script:

```
// Wproducts.push("Fonts Pack 4 : Classic", "258");
```

Now when you test the movie, you will no longer see the scroll bar in the list box on the right. When you remove the comment slashes (//), the scroll bar reappears when you test the movie.

setChangeHandler
FListBox.setChangeHandler(functionName, [location]): Method

The setChangeHandler() method essentially names the function that fires when a list box change occurs. The change with the list box is typically a change in the selected item. To create two change handlers for the sample movie, a webHand object was constructed and then used for both list boxes. The webHand object is the location of both the serHand and prodHand functions (or methods of the webHand object).

```
//Change Handlers
//Service Change Handler
webHand = new Object();
webHand.serHand = function(component) {
    item.text = "$"+WebSer.getSelectedItem().data;
    var single = parseFloat(WebSer.getSelectedItem().data);
    _global.totalBill += single;
    total.text = "$"+totalBill;
};
WebSer.setChangeHandler("serHand", webHand);
//Product Change Handler
webHand.prodHand = function(component) {
  item.text = "$"+WebProd.getValue();
  var single = parseFloat(WebProd.getValue());
  _global.totalBill += single;
  total.text = "$"+totalBill;
};
WebProd.setChangeHandler("prodHand", webHand);
```

The handler function simply transfers the label and data value of the selected item to the viewable output text fields. You want to be sure to place the setChangeHandler() method after the function that it calls.

setDataProvider
FListBox.setDataProvider(dataProvider): Method

The setDataProvider() method is an advanced technique involving creating an array with string elements specifying the items to add to the list box. The dataProvider is an outside data source and can be an Array object that specifies the label and data. For example, the following code specifies artProds as the dataProvider object:

```
WebProd.setDataProvider(cityAC);
```

One way of creating an object with both label and data properties would be the following:

```
var fWebProduct = new Array("Mouse", "10.15");
fWebProduct.push("Fonts", "40");
fWebProduct.push("Stylus", "10");
fWebProduct.push("Drawing pad", "98");
fWebProduct.push("Clip Art", "76.95");
var artProds= new Object();
for(x=0;x<5;x+=2) {
 artProds.label=fWebProduct[x];
 artProds.data=fWebProduct[x+1];
}
```

setEnabled

FListBox.setEnabled(enable): Method

By default, the list boxes set on the stage with an instance name are enabled. A Boolean value determines whether the list box is enabled (true) or disabled (false). In some applications, you will want to "freeze" a list box until some other element of the movie has been attended to. By setting setEnabled() to false, the list box no longer responds to mouse or keyboard controls. However, as soon as the list box instance is assigned setEnabled(), either with no Boolean true or with a Boolean true in the argument, it becomes fully functional again. The following would disable the WebProd instance of the list box:

```
WebProd.setEnabled(false);
```

setItemSymbol

FListBox.setItemSymbol(symbolID): Method

The setItemSymbol() method registers the symbol linkage ID of a graphic symbol to show the contents of a list box. FListBoxItem in the library is the default value. You need to understand the linkage between the library objects and the graphic symbols used to represent the list box elements. To set a symbolID to the WebProd instance of the list box in the sample movie, the format would be

```
WebProd.setItemSymbol(businessGR)
```

 The graphic symbol would be Movie Clip and not a symbol with Graphic behavior.

setRowCount
FListBox.setRowCount(rows): Method

The setRowCount() method is important for design considerations. The number of rows that can be displayed in a list box can affect both design and usability. You may even need to consider having a different number of visible rows for different list boxes in the same movie as was done in the sample movie. The following sets a shorter row count than the default of 6 rows:

```
WebSer.setRowCount(3);
```

setScrollPosition
FListBox.setScrollPosition(index): Method

The setScrollPosition() method forces the list box to scroll so that the item at the index value specified in the parameter moves to the top of the list. The position set is not the scroll position's value, but rather the index value of the item. For example, when item 7 (eighth item) in the WebProd component instance is forced to the top of the menu, the scroll position is 1. That's because scroll position 0 is forced up out of sight. Add the following script to the end of the sample movie script and see both the item's position and its index value:

```
WebProd.setScrollPosition(7);
trace(WebProd.getScrollPosition());
```

You will see the value 1 in the Output window.

setSelectedIndex
FListBox.setSelectedIndex(index): Method

The setSelectedIndex() method can be used to select an item in the list box. It has the same effect as selecting an item from the menu using the mouse. The parameter is an integer from 0 to the number of items in the menu minus 1. The change handler is involved by this method as well. The following example would select the third item in a list box list:

```
WebProd.setSelectedIndex(2);
```

setSelectedIndices
FListBox.setSelectedIndices(index): Method

Use the setSelectedIndices() method to select multiple items in the list box. The parameter uses an array to identify the items you want selected. In the sample movie, the following script sets up an array named selEm that becomes the argument for the setSelectedIndices() method:

```
//Create array to set selected indices
var selEm = new Array(0, 2, 4, 6);
WebProd.setSelectedIndices(selEm);
```

When you test the movie, you will see the first, third, fifth, and seventh items in the list box on the right highlighted. Those are the indices specified in the 0-based array.

setSelectMultiple
FListBox.setSelectMultiple(t/f): Method

The setSelectMultiple() method expects a Boolean argument to set the list box to multiple selections. The default selection is a single selection. That is, setSelectMultiple() is set to false. In the sample movie for this chapter, one list box was set to true and the other to false.

```
WebSer.setSelectMultiple(false);
WebProd.setSelectMultiple(true);
```

When you test the movie, you can select multiple items in the list box on the right by clicking on the item and holding down the CTRL key (CMD on Macintosh). However, when you try it with the list box on the left, you will find that only a single item can be selected at a time.

setSize
FListBox.setSize(width,height): Method

With list boxes, use the setSize() method when you are not using the setRowCount() method. The width and height parameters are the number of pixels you want to use to make your list box. For example, add the following script to the end of the sample movie script:

```
WebProd.setSize(200,300);
```

When you run the movie, you will see that the list box on the right is now much larger than the previous setting based on the number of rows to show and width based on the longest string of the label properties.

setStyleProperty
FListBox.setStyleProperty(styleProperty, value): Method

The setStyleProperty() method has two parameters. The styleProperty is an FStyleFormat property that can be used with components in general, with a subset that can be used for only certain components. For example, the arrow style property is used with list boxes but not with check boxes. (See the section "FStyleFormat Properties" for all of the FStyleFormats.)

ACTIONSCRIPT USER
INTERFACE COMPONENTS

The second parameter is the color of the styleProperty. Use the format 0xRRGGBB where RR (0–FF) is red, GG (0–FF) is green, and BB (0–FF) is blue. For example, 0x00ff00 is pure green. The color only applies to the specified styleProperty and not other properties that may make up the component.

The sample movie uses information from both the table in the "FStyleFormat Properties" section and the color palette to better integrate the list boxes into the color scheme. The following script shows the different properties changed along with the color values:

```
//Add some style
WebSer.setStyleProperty("arrow", 0x6A0012);
WebSer.setStyleProperty("selection", 0xD68614);
WebSer.setStyleProperty("scrollTrack", 0x6A0012);
WebSer.setStyleProperty("face", 0xF0DD38);
WebSer.setStyleProperty("selectionUnfocused", 0x838F8E);
WebProd.setStyleProperty("arrow", 0x6A0012);
WebProd.setStyleProperty("selection", 0xD68614);
WebProd.setStyleProperty("arrow", 0x6A0012);
WebProd.setStyleProperty("scrollTrack", 0x6A0012);
WebProd.setStyleProperty("face", 0xE5F1F5);
WebProd.setStyleProperty("selectionUnfocused", 0x838F8E);
```

setWidth

FListBox.setWidth(n): Method

Use the setWidth() method to dynamically set the size of your list box relative to the size of the longest item label. The width parameter is the size in pixels, and depending on the type and size of the font you are using, the width can vary. In the sample movie, I used 7 as a multiplier based on the string length of an item label. For example, the WebProd component instance was set at 27 * 7 (189) because the longest label was 27 characters long, including spaces. The following script shows how the size was set:

```
WebProd.setWidth(27*7);
//Position in the middle of the right column
WebProd._x = (275+275/2)-(189/2);
```

Then the size of the boxes was used to calculate the center position of the square on the right where the list box is positioned. Both squares are 275 pixels wide. So center _x value for the square on the right should be the value of the width of the square on the left plus one half of the square on the right. Then by subtracting one half of the width of the list box, it can be placed squarely in the middle of the square on the right.

sortItemsBy
FListBox.sortItemsBy(fieldName, order): Method

The sortItemsBy() method has two parameters. The first, fieldName, is either "label" or "data." If your items contain first and last names, the sorting will be on the first names unless the surname is placed first in the item. The second parameter specifies ascending ("ASC") or descending ("DESC") order. In the sample movie, the following script places the items in the WebSer instance in alphabetical order:

```
//Now Sort them by the label
WebSer.sortItemsBy("label", "ASC");
```

FStyleFormat Properties

The following table contains the different FStyleFormat properties and their descriptions. Use these properties with the setStyleProperty() and registerSkinElement() methods.

Property	Description
arrow	Color of arrow (scroll bars and drop-down lists only)
background	Background color of a component
backgroundDisabled	Background color of a disabled component
check	Check mark color in check box
darkshadow	Inner border or darker shadow portion color of a component
face	Main color of the component
foregroundDisabled	Foreground color of a disabled component
highlight	Inner border or darker shadow portion color of a selected component
highlight3D	Outer border or light shadow portion color of a selected component
radioDot	Dot color in a selected radio button
scrollTrack	Track color in a scroll bar
selection	Selection bar color highlighting a list item in a component
selectionDisabled	Selection bar color that highlights a list item in a disabled component

Property	Description
selectionUnfocused	Selection bar color when of component without keyboard focus
shadow	Outer border or light shadow portion color of a component
textAlign	Left, right, or center alignment for text displayed in or on a component
textBold	Boolean true value assigns bold style to text
textColor	All components assigned this default text color to the style format
textDisabled	Text color in a disabled component
textFont	Font name
textIndent	First indentation
textItalic	Boolean true value assigns italic style to text
textLeftMargin	Left paragraph margin in pixels for text
textRightMargin	Right paragraph margin in pixels for text
textSelected	Selected list color item in a component
textSize	Size of text in points
textUnderline	Boolean true value assigns underline style to text

Conclusion

If you've looked at the preceding chapter, you undoubtedly noticed the similarities between the combo box and the list box components. However, they are also very different. The list boxes are used to show more than a single item when first viewed. The combo boxes are great for saving space, but that is not the primary purpose of the list boxes. They are designed to show a certain number of choices that suggest to the user scrolling for more choices. Alternatively, you can place all selections in view at one time so that the entire set of selections is viewed without scrolling

In the next chapter, you will find a much simpler component, the push button. The push button is used to launch one event instead of many, as with the list box. Several push buttons are used to provide user-initiated actions in several different locations on the stage or organized as part of a navigation system. So while you will find similarities in the use of a connection to a change handler, otherwise you will find the push button to be a simple component by comparison to the list box.

The Complete Reference

ActionScript

Chapter 17

FPushButton

O ne of the most familiar symbols in Macromedia Flash MX has always been the Button object. The push button, though, is not just another Button object. As a component, it has many methods in common with other UI components. Push buttons do not have a special timeline with Up, Over, Down, and Hit frames, but you will find changing button states to be very simple using the button click handlers and the different methods with which you can apply the FStyleFormat properties and their values. (A table in the section "FStyleFormat Properties" at the end of the chapter provides a full list of the FStyleFormat properties.)

Using the Push Button Component

Push buttons have a number of different uses. Besides their use for navigation, they can be employed on different movie clips to invoke scripts. Their common look helps the user immediately identify them as buttons and not something else. So they score high on usability, and they are also flexible enough to be used in most designs.

Methods

Of all of the components, the PushButton component has the fewest methods. Further, you will find that most of the other UI components have all of the methods found in push buttons. However, you will find a good deal of flexibility using the FPushButton methods, and the methods can be used to provide the user with a good deal of information.

The sample movie for this chapter is relatively simple, but it employs most of the push button's methods. It is designed to show how to "batch-process" several buttons at once and to change their appearance when clicked. Figure 17-1 shows the basic stage setup and Table 17-1 has the values for the color palette used in the movie.

The following steps provide a guide to putting the movie together:

1. Open a new movie and add three layers to the existing layer and name them, from top to bottom, Push Button, MC, Backdrop, and Background. Use blue for the background color.

Name	R	G	B
Blue	79	112	162
Dark tan	226	153	57
Deep red	171	17	0
Pale blue-green	217	233	208

Table 17-1.   *Color Palette*

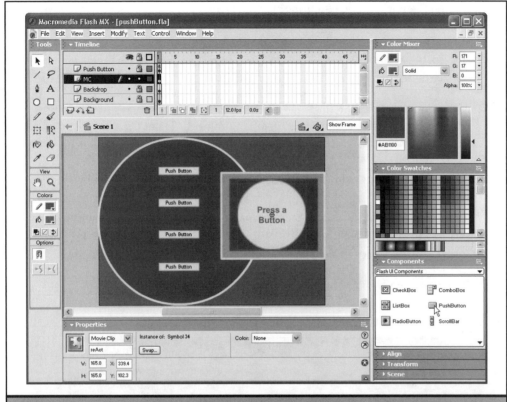

Figure 17-1.   *Four instances of the push button object begin on the stage with the generic label "Push Button" that is dynamically changed by the script.*

ACTIONSCRIPT USER
INTERFACE COMPONENTS

2. Select the Background layer and draw a circle using the deep red fill and 5-point pale blue-green stroke with the dimensions W = 395, H = 395. Center-align the circle vertically and left-align it horizontally with the stage. Lock the layer.

3. Select the Backdrop layer and draw a rectangle with a 5-point pale blue-green stroke and dark tan fill with the dimensions W = 250, H = 204. Inside the first rectangle, draw another rectangle with a 3-point blue stroke and deep red fill with the dimensions W = 212, H = 169. Center it inside the first rectangle. Select both rectangles. Right align and vertically center them on the stage. (See Figure 17-1 to get a visual idea of where to position the rectangle.) Lock the layer.

4. Select the MC layer and draw a circle with a 3-point dark tan stroke and a pale blue-green fill. The circle dimensions are W = 164, H = 164.

5. Select the circle and press the F8 key to convert it to a movie clip. Double-click the MC to enter the Symbol Editing Mode and add a layer to the existing layer.

Name the bottom layer Actions and the top layer Frames. The drawing of the circle should be on the Actions layer. Add five frames to both layers, and to the Frames layer, add four keyframes beginning with the second frame. Lock the Actions layer.

6. Click the first keyframe (Frame 1) on the Frames layer. Add a 20-point bold blue Arial static text message, "Press a Button", in the middle of the circle. Using the same font, style, color, and size, add the following messages in keyframes 2 through 5: "Alpha" in Frame 2; "Beta" in Frame 3; "Delta Disabled!" surrounded by a red circle with a 6-point stroke and no fill with a slash through it in Frame 4 (see Figure 17-2); and "Gamma" in Frame 5. Lock the layer.

7. Select the first frame of the Actions layer and add a stop(); action in the Actions panel.

8. On the main timeline, select the movie clip and type the instance name reAct in the Properties panel. Lock the MC layer and select the Push Button layer.

9. Drag four instances of the PushButton component and position them in the center of the circle. Distribute them evenly as shown in Figure 17-1. From top to bottom, provide them with the instance names pb1, pb2, pb3, and pb4.

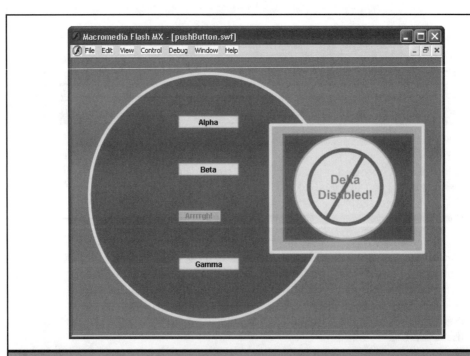

Figure 17-2.   *When you test the movie, you will see that all of the buttons have changed color, the labels are in bold, and each button sets a different frame in the movie clip.*

10. Select the first frame in the Push Button layer and enter the following script:

```
//Label all of the buttons
var loadBtn = new Array("Alpha", "Beta");
loadBtn.push("Delta", "Gamma");
for (x=0; x<loadBtn.length; x++) {
    var myName = eval("pb"+(x+1));
    var myHandle = "doBtn"+x;
    myName.setLabel(loadBtn[x]);
    myName.setStyleProperty("face", 0xD9E9D0);
    myName.setStyleProperty("textBold", true);
    myName.setClickHandler(myHandle);
}
//Change handlers
//Alpha
function doBtn0() {
    if (pb1.getLabel() == "Alpha") {
        pb1.setLabel("Punched Out");
        pb1.setStyleProperty("face", 0xE29939);
        _root.reAct.gotoAndStop(2);
    } else {
        pb1.setLabel("Alpha");
        pb1.setStyleProperty("face", 0xD9E9D0);
        _root.reAct.gotoAndStop(1);
    }
}
//Beta
function doBtn1() {
    if (pb2.getLabel() == "Beta") {
        pb2.setLabel("Punched Out");
        pb2.setStyleProperty("face", 0xE29939);
        _root.reAct.gotoAndStop(3);
    } else {
        pb2.setLabel("Beta");
        pb2.setStyleProperty("face", 0xD9E9D0);
        _root.reAct.gotoAndStop(1);
    }
}
//Delta
function doBtn2() {
    if (pb3.getLabel() == "Delta") {
        pb3.setLabel("Arrrrgh!");
        pb3.setStyleProperty("face", 0xE29939);
        pb3.setEnabled(false);
        pb3.setSize(70);
```

```
        _root.reAct.gotoAndStop(4);
    } else {
        pb3.setLabel("Delta");
        pb3.setStyleProperty("face", 0xD9E9D0);
        _root.reAct.gotoAndStop(1);
    }
}
//Gamma
function doBtn3() {
    if (pb4.getLabel() == "Gamma") {
        pb4.setLabel("Punched Out");
        pb4.setStyleProperty("face", 0xE29939);
        _root.reAct.gotoAndStop(5);
        if (!pb3.getEnabled()) {
            pb3.setEnabled(true);
        }
        pb3.setLabel("Delta");
        pb3.setSize(100);
        pb3.setStyleProperty("face", 0xD9E9D0);
    } else {
        pb4.setLabel("Gamma");
        pb4.setStyleProperty("face", 0xD9E9D0);
        _root.reAct.gotoAndStop(1);
    }
}
```

When you test the movie, the first two buttons perform almost identical tasks, illustrating the kind of tasks usually assigned to buttons. However, the third button is self-disabling and is only enabled by the fourth button. The point, of course, is to demonstrate the disable/enable sequence. Also, in looking at the methods in this chapter, you will find that most of them are used in the script.

getEnabled
FPushButton.getEnabled(): Method

The getEnabled() method returns a Boolean true if the button is enabled and a Boolean false if it is disabled. In their default state, buttons with an assigned click handler are functionally enabled. Until they are disabled by a new setting, they will stay enabled. However, in the sample script, one of the buttons is disabled, and part of the script uses the Boolean value returned to re-enable it. The following script segment shows how the getEnabled() method is used in a conditional statement:

```
if (!pb3.getEnabled()) {
    pb3.setEnabled(true);
}
```

getLabel
FPushButton.getLabel(): Method

The getLabel() method returns a string with the name of the button's label. This method is used extensively with buttons where more than a single label is used to provide feedback about the button's current state. In the sample movie, the getLabel() method is used several times to retrieve the button's label. The following shows how the pb2 (Beta) push button instance is examined by its click handler function to determine the button's state:

```
if (pb2.getLabel() == "Beta") {
    pb2.setLabel("Punched Out");
```

The getLabel() method is often used in conjunction with the setLabel() method. As each label is examined in turn, the setLabel() responds based on what the getLabel() method returns.

registerSkinElement
FPushButton.registerSkinElement(element, styleProperty): Method

The registerSkinElement() method is used to customize the look of the push button instances. The method has two arguments. The element parameter refers to the movie clip instance that provides the skin for the component, and the styleProperty argument is the name of the FStyleFormat property. The method registers the skin element to a style property specified. The following example shows a movie clip with the instance name panic_mc that replaces the default selection styleProperty in the "face" element:

```
pb2.registerSkinElement(panic_mc, "face");
```

setClickHandler
FPushButton.setClickHandler(functionName, [location]): Method

You may have noticed that most of the other UI components use a change handler. The push button object uses a click handler. The setClickHandler() method is very specific—it's waiting for a click to handle rather than a nonspecific change as the other components are. However, the click handler is pretty much like a change handler because it just looks for clicks and nothing else.

The click handler itself is a function of some kind that is invoked by clicking the button. In the sample script, all four buttons were assigned sequential click handler functions using a batch process in the form of a loop, as the following shows:

```
for (x=0; x<loadBtn.length; x++) {
    var myName = eval("pb"+(x+1));
    var myHandle = "doBtn"+x;
```

```
. . . . .
. . . . .
myName.setClickHandler(myHandle);
}
```

In the script segment, the functions were all named "doBtnN" where "N" is a number between 0 and 3. The index value of the loop is concatenated with a string and placed into a variable which is then used as the argument in the setClickHandler() method.

setEnabled
FPushButton.setEnabled(enable): Method

The setEnabled() method accepts a Boolean argument for enabling and disabling a button. Unless set to false using the setEnabled() method, the buttons are enabled by default. In the sample script, one script segment turned off a button (disabled) and another turned it back on (enabled). The following script was used:

```
pb3.setEnabled(false);
. . . .
pb3.setEnabled(true);
```

When you want certain portions of your movie disabled (because of some condition in the movie), you can dynamically disable it, and then (under different conditions) re-enable it.

setLabel
FPushButton.setLabel(label): Method

Using the setLabel() method, you can name push buttons anything you want. If you have an especially long or short label, you may want to change the size of the button (see setSize()), but otherwise, all you need to do is specify the push button's instance name and place a string in the method's parameter. In the sample movie, the names change after the button has been clicked, and as a result, the setLabel() method is used often. The following example shows how the name is made to change with each click:

```
function doBtn0() {
    if (pb1.getLabel() == "Alpha") {
        pb1.setLabel("Punched Out");
        pb1.setStyleProperty("face", 0xE29939);
        _root.reAct.gotoAndStop(2);
    } else {
        pb1.setLabel("Alpha");
```

```
        pb1.setStyleProperty("face", 0xD9E9D0);
        _root.reAct.gotoAndStop(1);
    }
}
```

setSize

FPushButton.setSize(width, height): Method

The setSize() method sets the push button instance width pixels wide and height pixels high. The default size of push buttons dragged to the stage is W = 100, H = 20. If only the first parameter is given a value, the height reverts to 20. For example, if your script uses the following code:

```
pb3.setSize(70,50);
```

and then posts the following:

```
pb3.setSize(100);
```

the second parameter defaults to 20.

In the sample script, only one parameter was used. Try adding some different parameter values to the line:

```
pb3.setSize(70);
```

For example, try the following, and when you test the movie, notice that the text in the button is not distorted by the change in the button size:

```
pb3.setSize(150,150);
pb3.setSize(pb3.setSize(50,200);
pb3.setSize(35,10);
```

setStyleProperty()

FPushButton.setStyleProperty(styleProperty, value): Method

The setStyleProperty() method has two parameters. The styleProperty is an FStyleFormat property that can be used with components in general, with a subset that can be used for only certain components. For example, the arrow style property is used with list boxes but not with check boxes. (See the section "FStyleFormat Properties" for all of the FStyleFormats.)

The second parameter is the color of the styleProperty. Use the format 0xRRGGBB where RR (0–FF) is red, GG (0–FF) is green, and BB (0–FF) is blue. For example, 0x00ff00 is pure green. The color only applies to the specified styleProperty and not other properties that may make up the component. The second parameter can be any other value that the styleProperty accepts, such as a Boolean value. (The table in the section "FStyleFormat Properties" shows other values accepted as values for the second parameter.)

The sample movie uses information from both the following table and the color palette to better integrate the list boxes into the color scheme. In the sample movie, all of the buttons were given the same changes in style properties. The following script shows the different properties changed along with the color values:

```
myName.setStyleProperty("face", 0xD9E9D0);
myName.setStyleProperty("textBold", true);
```

FStyleFormat Properties

The following table contains the different FStyleFormat properties and their descriptions. Use these properties with the setStyleProperty() and registerSkinElement() methods.

Property	Description
arrow	Color of arrow (scroll bars and drop-down lists only)
background	Background color of a component
backgroundDisabled	Background color of a disabled component
check	Check mark color in check box
darkshadow	Inner border or darker shadow portion color of a component
face	Main color of the component
foregroundDisabled	Foreground color of a disabled component
highlight	Inner border or darker shadow portion color of a selected component
highlight3D	Outer border or light shadow portion color of a selected component
radioDot	Dot color in a selected radio button
scrollTrack	Track color in a scroll bar
selection	Selection bar color highlighting a list item in a component

Property	Description
selectionDisabled	Selection bar color that highlights a list item in a disabled component
selectionUnfocused	Selection bar color of component without keyboard focus
shadow	Outer border or light shadow portion color of a component
textAlign	Left, right, or center alignment for text displayed in or on a component
textBold	Boolean true value assigns bold style to text
textColor	All components assigned this default text color to the style format
textDisabled	Text color in a disabled component
textFont	Font name
textIndent	First indentation
textItalic	Boolean true value assigns italic style to text
textLeftMargin	Left paragraph margin in pixels for text
textRightMargin	Right paragraph margin in pixels for text
textSelected	Selected list color item in a component
textSize	Size of text in points
textUnderline	Boolean true value assigns underline style to text

Conclusion

While the push button is a relatively simple component, it can be a very powerful one. Its unique click handler (as opposed to change handler) provides a focused event. By changing the label and style parameters, the push button can be very versatile. By using ActionScript to "batch" define buttons, using arrays and loops, it can be very simple to generate multiple buttons on your Flash stage.

While buttons have only a few methods, the next chapter deals with radio button components that have a double set of methods. Radio buttons have a set of methods for both FRadioButtonGroup and FRadioButton. Selections of buttons in a group are mutually exclusive, while radio buttons themselves are much like check boxes but with major important differences.

The Complete Reference

ActionScript

Chapter 18

FRadioButton

T he Macromedia Flash MX radio button has two overlapping configurations. In the FRadioButton folder in the ActionScript toolbox, the first subfolder is FRadioButtonGroup. This folder contains several items that look suspiciously like methods. In fact, they are methods to be used with radio button groups. If you look at the reference materials, though, you see that the methods can be used with individual radio buttons as well as radio button groups. Further, when you look in the Methods subfolder of the FRadioButton folder, you will see several identical methods and the reference is identical to the method in the FRadioButtonGroup subfolder.

Rather than dwelling on the confusing nature of this particular UI component, a better approach lies in looking at what happens with radio buttons that are part of a group and ones that are not. If you are familiar with radio buttons in HTML, you're aware of the possible grouping of radio buttons into mutually exclusive selections. If one button in the group is selected, the others are automatically deselected. Thus, when the designer wants the user to select a single choice, he employs the radio button group. For example, you can inquire into the viewer's current marital status with the following selections:

- Single
- Married
- Separated
- Divorced

Only a single category can apply at any one time. To prevent a helpful user who was divorced and is now remarried from clicking both Married and Divorced, the radio button group forces a single choice.

When a radio button is not part of a group, it can be selected, given an instance name, and then used wholly independently of a group. If it is clicked "on," it can invoke a change handler and is unaffected by any other radio button unless a script has been written so that another radio button affects it. As soon as a radio button is part of a group, the simple inclusion in the group makes it subject to the state of other buttons in the same group.

Introduction to FRadioButton

The best way to understand exactly how buttons work as part of a group and independently can best be understood by developing a movie that uses both. In the sample movie you will see that two questions are posed. Each question has a single answer, and in selecting a radio button, the user is notified that he has the correct or incorrect answer. Because only a single answer is correct, the radio buttons associated with the two questions are placed into groups. The process is very simple. All that needs to be done is that each button in the group be assigned to the group using the setGroupName() method. The group name becomes something like an object,

Name	R	G	B
Green	54	161	43
Red	255	0	0
Blue	14	50	147
White	255	255	255

Table 18-1. *Color Palette*

and all of the buttons assigned to the group as properties inherit all of the group characteristics. However, each button in the group has its own label and data.

Using Figure 18-1 and the color palette in Table 18-1 as guides, create this next movie to see how individual and group radio buttons work together.

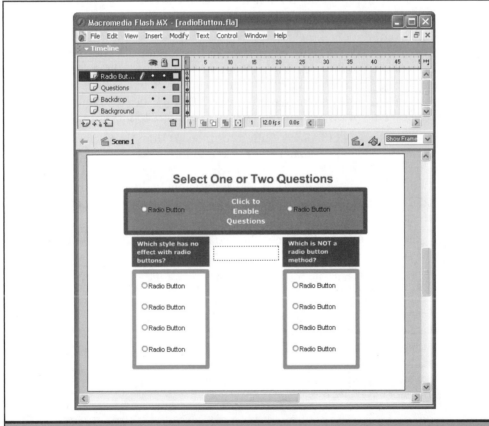

Figure 18-1.   *When the radio buttons are initially placed on the stage, they all look the same, but when the script runs, they all change.*

1. Open a new movie and add three layers to the existing one with the following names from top to bottom: Radio Buttons, Questions, Backdrop, and Background.

2. In the Background layer, create a rectangle with a red fill and 7-point blue stroke with the dimensions W = 414, H = 72 positioned centered horizontally near the top of the stage. (See Figure 18-1 for positioning.)

3. Create a rectangle with a green 7-point stroke and no fill with the dimensions W = 126, H = 162. Make a copy of the rectangle and position each beneath the red and blue rectangle. Leave about 60 pixels between the bottom of the red and blue rectangle and the tops of the green rectangles. (See Figure 18-1 for positioning.) Lock the layer.

4. In the Backdrop layer, draw two blue rectangles with no stroke directly above the green outline rectangles. Use the dimensions W = 133, H = 50. Lock the layer.

5. Select the Questions layer and using a 10-point white Verdana font type in the questions directly on top of the blue rectangles created in Step 4. On the one on the left type, "Which style has no effect with radio buttons?" and on the right, "Which is NOT a radio button method?" Lock the layer.

6. Select the Radio Buttons layer. Drag two instances of the RadioButton component from the Components panel and place them on the red and blue rectangle. Position them vertically centered on the rectangle on the left and right. Give the instance name q1 to the one on the left and q2 to the one on the right. Using a 12-point white Verdana bold font, type the message "Click to Enable Questions" between the two radio buttons. (See Figure 18-1.) Above the red and blue rectangle type, "Select One or Two Questions" using 20-point bold blue Verdana.

7. Drag four instances of the RadioButton component from the Components panel for each of the two green rectangles. Place four in the green outline of the rectangle on the left and four on the right. Select each radio button on the left in turn and give them the instance names a1 to a4. Do the same to the radio buttons on the right, giving them the instance names b1 to b4. Refer to Figure 18-1 for positioning. Lock the layer.

8. Place a Dynamic text field between the two questions using a red bold 16-point Verdana font. Give the text field the instance name ans.

9. Click the first button in the top layer and enter the following script:

```
//Define buttons and groups
//Independent Enable button for Question 1
q1.setLabel("Question 1");
q1.setData("doOne");
q1.setChangeHandler("allow");
q1.setLabelPlacement("left");
//Independent Enable button for Question 2
```

```
q2.setLabel("Question 2");
q2.setData("doTwo");
q2.setChangeHandler("allow");
//Define First Group and Radio Buttons
var quesA = new Array("textBold", "incorrect");
quesA.push("radioDot", "incorrect");
quesA.push("background", "incorrect");
quesA.push("arrow", "correct");
howLongA = quesA.length;
for (x=0; x<howLongA; x++) {
    var question = eval("a"+(x+1));
    yourData = quesA.pop();
    yourName = quesA.pop();
    question.setLabel(yourName);
    question.setData(yourData);
    question.setGroupName("ahOne");
}
//Set group methods()
ahOne.setStyleProperty("textColor", 0x0E3293);
ahOne.setStyleProperty("radioDot", 0xff0000);
ahOne.setSize(150);
ahOne.setChangeHandler("goFigure");
ahOne.setEnabled(false);
//Define Second Group and Radio Buttons
var quesB = new Array("getData()", "incorrect");
quesB.push("getRowCount()", "correct");
quesB.push("setState()", "incorrect");
quesB.push("getValue()", "incorrect");
howLongB = quesB.length;
for (x=0; x<howLongB; x++) {
    var question = eval("b"+(x+1));
    yourData = quesB.pop();
    yourName = quesB.pop();
    question.setLabel(yourName);
    question.setData(yourData);
    question.setGroupName("ahTwo");
}
//Set group methods()
ahTwo.setStyleProperty("textColor", 0x0E3293);
ahTwo.setStyleProperty("radioDot", 0xff0000);
ahTwo.setSize(150);
ahTwo.setEnabled(false);
ahTwo.setChangeHandler("goFigure");
```

```
//Change Handler for Enable
function allow(component) {
    if (component.getValue() == "doOne") {
        ahOne.setEnabled(true);
    } else if (component.getValue() == "doTwo") {
        ahTwo.setEnabled(true);
    }
}
//Change Handler for Groups
function goFigure(component) {
    if (component.getValue() == "correct") {
        ans.text = "You got it.";
    } else {
        ans.text = "D'oh!";
        //Phrase "d'oh" is in the
        //online version of the Oxford
        //English Dictionary
    }
}
```

When you test the movie, all of the answers to the questions are disabled. To enable the questions, you must first click the Question 1 and Question 2 buttons. Then click the radio buttons beneath the two questions to see the correct answers. Figure 18-2 shows what you can expect to see when you test the movie.

FRadioButtonGroup Methods

The methods associated with the FRadioButtonGroup UI component reference the entire group, not just a single button. While the FRadioButton and FRadioButtonGroup methods are quite similar, keep in mind that a method reference to a group object is a collective one and not the instance name of a single radio button.

getEnabled
FRadioButtonGroup.getEnabled(): Method

The default condition of a radio button group is a Boolean true enabled. When you use the getEnabled() method, you receive the Boolean value of true or false indicating that the radio button group is enabled or not. If you want to disable it, you would use the setEnabled() method. For example, add the following lines at the end of the movie:

```
trace(ahOne.getEnabled());
trace(q1.getEnabled());
```

Because the radio button group ahOne is disabled at the outset, the Output window shows "false," while the output for the q1 instance is "true" because it begins the movie as enabled. (Both groups and individual buttons use this method.)

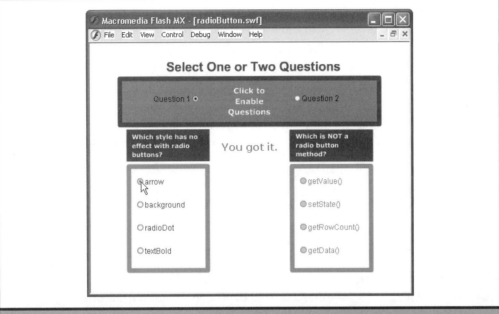

Figure 18-2. *To enable the radio buttons beneath the questions, the Question 1 and Question 2 radio buttons must be clicked.*

getGroupName
FRadioButtonGroup.getGroupName(): Method

The getGroupName() method can be used with either groups or individual radio buttons. The method returns the name of the group attached to the beginning of the method. So the name of the group that gets the name is the same name that is returned as a string. For example, add the following line at the end of the movie to test this:

```
trace(ahOne.getGroupName());
```

The output is, "ahOne." (Both groups and individual buttons use this method.)

getValue
FRadioButtonGroup.getValue(): Method

The getValue() method returns the data associated with the selected radio button in the radio button group. The value of the label is returned if no data has been given.

In the sample movie, a function uses the getValue() method when determining the correct answer:

```
function goFigure(component) {
    if (component.getValue() == "correct") {
```

```
        ans.text = "You got it.";
    }
}
```

registerSkinElement
FRadioButtonGroup.registerSkinElement(element, styleProperty): Method

The registerSkinElement() method can be applied to button groups and instances of the radio button. The method has two arguments. The element parameter refers to the movie clip instance that provides the skin for the component, and the styleProperty argument is the name of the FStyleFormat property. The method registers the skin element to a style property specified. The following example shows a movie clip with the instance name newRadio_mc that replaces the default radioDot styleProperty:

```
ahTwo.registerSkinElement(newRadio_mc, "radioDot");
```

setChangeHandler
FRadioButtonGroup.setChangeHandler(functionName, [location]): Method

The change handler can be placed in the Properties panel with the Parameters tab selected. The setChangeHandler() method does essentially the same thing with or without a group. The method has two parameters. The functionName must be named as a string indicating a unique name for a function. Optionally, you can specify the path (location) to the function in a movie clip or timeline. If no location parameter is indicated, the change handler function must be on the same timeline as the radio button instance. The following example illustrates this point:

```
ahOne.setChangeHandler("goFigure");
```

The function for the change handler begins in the line after it has been set. In this way, you can set the handler and define its function in the same code segment.

setEnabled
FRadioButtonGroup.setEnabled(enable): Method

The setEnabled() method has a single Boolean parameter that can be set to true or false. The Boolean true enables the radio button instance and the Boolean false disables it. Disabled radio buttons cannot accept keyboard or mouse input from the user, and the labels turn gray as well. When you test the example movie, you will see that both groups of buttons to answer the questions have their enabled status set to false— they're disabled at the outset. The following script is used to enable them:

```
//Change Handler for Enable
```

```
function allow(component) {
    if (component.getValue() == "doOne") {
        ahOne.setEnabled(true);
    } else if (component.getValue() == "doTwo") {
        ahTwo.setEnabled(true);
    }
}
```

setGroupName
FRadioButtonGroup.setGroupName(groupName): Method

The setGroupName() method assigns a new group name for all of the radio buttons in FRadioButtonGroup. For example, if you wanted to change the group name for a set of buttons in a group, you could use this method to make that change. Using the group names from the sample movie you might want to make the following change:

```
ahOne.setGroupName("setOne");
```

After that code is encountered, all buttons in the group ahOne would be in the group setOne.

setLabelPlacement
FRadioButtonGroup.setLabelPlacement(labelPosition): Method

The setLabelPlacement() method sets the radio button label to the left or right of the box itself. Use a "left" or "right" string argument to position the label relative to the radio button. In the example movie, whenever a checkbox is checked, its label position changes.

The following code places the label for group ahOne to the left of the radio button:

```
ahOne.setLabelPlacement("left");
```

Place the code at the end of the current sample movie script and see what happens to the radio buttons on the left.

setSize
FRadioButtonGroup.setSize(width): Method

The setSize() method sets or resets the width of the radio button "window"—the combined radio button and its label. In the sample movie, both groups set the size of the radio buttons in their group at 150 using the following script:

```
ahTwo.setSize(150);
```

If you change the width parameter to 20, all of the buttons on the right will have truncated answer selections. When using setSize() with a group, it affects all the buttons in the group.

setStyleProperty
FRadioButtonGroup.setStyleProperty(styleProperty, value): Method

The setStyleProperty() method has two parameters. The styleProperty is an FStyleFormat property that can be used with components in general, with a subset that can be used for only certain components. For example, the arrow style property is used with scroll bars but not with radio buttons. (See the section "FStyleFormat Properties" for a list of all of the FStyleFormats.)

The second parameter is the color or some other parameter of the styleProperty. Use the format 0xRRGGBB where RR (0–FF) is red, GG (0–FF) is green, and BB (0–FF) is blue. For example, 0x00ff00 is pure green. The color only applies to the specified styleProperty and not other properties that may make up the component.

In the sample movie, the changes were all made using the group name because it involves so much less code. It would have taken eight lines of code to do the same thing were it necessary to define each button individually.

```
ahOne.setStyleProperty("textColor", 0x0E3293);
ahOne.setStyleProperty("radioDot", 0xff0000);
```

setValue()
FRadioButtonGroup.setValue(select): Method

The setValue() method used with radio button groups sets the value of the data parameter of the selected radio button within the group. For example, in the sample movie using radio buttons, if you wanted to change the data in the "correct" answer so that there was an indication that it was answered already, you could use the following script to do so:

```
function goFigure(component) {
    if (component.getValue() == "correct") {
        component.setValue("answered");
    }
}
```

The next time the function was invoked, it would evaluate the data to be "answered" instead of "correct."

FRadioButton Methods

You will find that the methods used for radio buttons and radio button groups to be almost identical. The only main difference is that the object is a single component instance rather than a whole group of them.

getData
FRadioButton.getData(): Method

The getData() method works like the getValue() method for radio button groups. The method returns a string with the value of the "data" element in the radio button instance. Add the following to the end of the sample movie to see what it returns:

```
trace(b2.getData());
```

getEnabled
FRadioButton.getEnabled(): Method

The default condition of a radio button instance dragged on the stage is a Boolean true enabled. When you use the getEnabled() method, you receive the Boolean value of true or false indicating that the radio button is enabled or not. If you want to disable it, you would use the setEnabled() method. Add the following line to the end of the movie's script:

```
trace(b2.getEnabled())
```

Because the movie sets the radio button instance as disabled in the script, the Output window shows "false." However, if you put the same line at the very beginning of the movie, the output is "true" because the default state of radio button instances is enabled.

getLabel
FRadioButton.getLabel(): Method

One of the more useful enhancements of the radio button object is the ability to retrieve and change its label. Using the getLabel() method, you can search through several radio button instances to find a particular one. In the sample movie, the search retrieved data using the getValue() method. To see how the getLabel() method works, add the following script to the end of the movie:

```
trace(b2.getLabel());
```

The Output window shows, "setState()," one of the answer choices in the second question.

getState
FRadioButton.getState(): Method

The getState() method returns a Boolean true if a radio button is selected and a false if it is not. Instead of selecting the data from an answer choice to indicate a correct or incorrect answer in the sample movie, it would have been possible to do the same thing using the getState() method. For example, if you put in the conditional statement:

```
if(a1.getState()) {
    ans.test = "You got it.";
    ....
```

the movie would work the same for the first question, but not the second question. Because the correct choice in Question 1 is the a1 instance of the radio button, if that radio button is selected, the condition evaluates to "true" and invokes the correct answer response. However, had the getState() method been used instead of getValue() for the data indicating "correct," a new else if statement would have to be written for the second question. That's not much more work for a second question, but imagine how much more it would be with 100 questions.

registerSkinElement
FRadioButtonGroup.registerSkinElement(element, styleProperty): Method

The registerSkinElement() method can be applied to button groups and instances of the radio button. The method has two arguments. The element parameter refers to the movie clip instance that provides the skin for the component, and the styleProperty argument is the name of the FStyleFormat property. The method registers the skin element to a style property specified. The following example shows a movie clip with the instance name newRadio_mc that replaces the default radioDot styleProperty:

```
b1.registerSkinElement(newRadio_mc, "radioDot");
```

setChangeHandler
FRadioButton.setChangeHandler(functionName, [location]): Method

The change handler can be placed in the Properties panel with the Parameters tab selected. The setChangeHandler() method does essentially the same thing with or without a group. The method has two parameters. The functionName must be named as a string indicating a unique name for a function. Optionally, you can specify the path (location) to the function in a movie clip or timeline. If no location parameter is indicated, the change handler function must be on the same timeline as the radio button instance. The following example illustrates this point:

```
q1.setChangeHandler("allow");
```

The function for the change handler begins in the line after it has been set. In this way, you can set the handler and define its function in the same code segment.

setEnabled
FRadioButton.setEnabled(enable): Method

The setEnabled() method has a single Boolean parameter that can be set to true or false. The Boolean true enables the radio button instance and the Boolean false disables it. Disabled radio buttons cannot accept keyboard or mouse input from the user, and the labels turn gray as well. When you test the example movie, you will see that both groups of buttons used to answer the questions have their enabled status set to false—they're disabled at the outset. The sample movie script used group settings instead of individual buttons to enable the disabled groups. To see how the method works with individual radio buttons, add the following to the end of the sample movie script:

```
q1.setEnabled(false);
```

With the q1 instance disabled, you will find you have no way of enabling the disabled radio buttons in Question 1, so be sure to remove it after testing it.

setGroupName
FRadioButton.setGroupName(groupName): Method

The setGroupName() method assigns a new group name for the radio button instance calling the method. In the sample movie, a variable (question) containing the evaluated value of the different instances invokes the method as follows:

```
question.setGroupName("ahOne");
```

Once the method is invoked, all calls made with the group name affect the individual radio buttons in the group.

setLabel
FRadioButton.setLabel(label): Method

The setLabel() method accepts a string as its parameter and then changes the radio button's label to the string specified in the argument. The setLabel() method can be employed to change the radio buttons when they are selected or deselected. However, in the sample movie, the labels were set in a loop using data from an array as shown in the following:

```
question.setLabel(yourName);
```

The value of the parameter yourName resulted from a label being popped off an array.

setSize
FRadioButton.setSize(width): Method

The setSize() method sets or resets the width of the radio button "window"—the combined radio button and its label in pixels. The default size is 100. In the sample movie, both of the radio button instances that were not part of a group used that default size by not calling the setSize() method at all. However, if you want to change an individual radio button size, simply use the instance name and the method with the specified number of pixels you want the radio button window to be. For example, the following sets the size of instance q2 to 120 pixels:

```
q2.setSize(120);
```

setState
FRadioButton.setState("select"): Method

The setState() method accepts a Boolean value to set the selected state of a radio button to true or false. A true setting displays the radio button as selected. However, the method does not invoke the change handler associated with the radio button instance. For example, add the following script to the end of the sample movie script:

```
q1.setState(true);
```

When you test the movie, you will see that the Question 1 radio button has been selected, but you will also see that the first set of questions is still disabled. In some respects you can think of setting the state to true as disabling the button from mouse clicks and negating any change handler the instance invokes. By passing false as an argument to the setState() method, it becomes "clickable" and able to invoke its associated functions.

setStyleProperty
FRadioButton.setStyleProperty(styleProperty, value): Method

The setStyleProperty() method has two parameters. The styleProperty is an FStyleFormat property that can be used with components in general, with a subset that can be used for only certain components. For example, the arrow style property is used with scroll bars but not with radio buttons. (See the section "FStyleFormat Properties" for all of the FStyleFormats.)

The second parameter is the color or some other parameter of the styleProperty. Use the format 0xRRGGBB where RR (0–FF) is red, GG (0–FF) is green, and BB (0–FF) is blue. For example, 0x00ff00 is pure green. The color only applies to the specified styleProperty and not other properties that may make up the component.

In the sample movie, the changes were all made using the group name, but by using the instance names of the radio button, you can get the same results as shown in the following example:

```
b3.setStyleProperty("textColor", 0x0E3293);
b3.setStyleProperty("radioDot", 0xff0000);
```

FStyleFormat Properties

The following table contains the different FStyleFormat properties and their descriptions. Use these properties with the setStyleProperty() and registerSkinElement() methods.

Property	Description
arrow	Color of arrow (scroll bars and drop-down lists only)
background	Background color of a component
backgroundDisabled	Background color of a disabled component
check	Check mark color in check box
darkshadow	Inner border or darker shadow portion color of a component
face	Main color of the component
foregroundDisabled	Foreground color of a disabled component
highlight	Inner border or darker shadow portion color of a selected component
highlight3D	Outer border or light shadow portion color of a selected component
radioDot	Dot color in a selected radio button
scrollTrack	Track color in a scroll bar
selection	Selection bar color highlighting a list item in a component
selectionDisabled	Selection bar color that highlights a list item in a disabled component
selectionUnfocused	Selection bar color when of a component without keyboard focus
shadow	Outer border or light shadow portion color of a component

Property	Description
textAlign	Left, right, or center alignment for text displayed in or on a component
textBold	Boolean true value assigns bold style to text
textColor	All components assigned this default text color to the style format
textDisabled	Text color in a disabled component
textFont	Font name
textIndent	First indentation
textItalic	Boolean true value assigns italic style to text
textLeftMargin	Left paragraph margin in pixels for text
textRightMargin	Right paragraph margin in pixels for text
textSelected	Selected list color item in a component
textSize	Size of text in points
textUnderline	Boolean true value assigns underline style to text

Conclusion

This chapter has been "A Tale of Two Radio Buttons"—the group and individual buttons. While you found a good deal of duplication of methods in the two configurations, each had its own unique methods as well. So whether used in sets to distinguish mutually exclusive choices or used in individual units, the radio button UI component has many uses.

The next chapter examines the FScrollBar UI component, a decidedly unitary component. Its function is to scroll text in Dynamic text fields. Beside making scrolling very easy, the scroll bar has a surprising number of methods that can be used to configure it and affect other aspects of the movie.

Chapter 19

FScrollBar

L ike the other UI components in Macromedia Flash MX, the FScrollBar UI component comes with a set of methods that are used to control different aspects of the component. The general use of the scroll bar is to provide an easy scrolling capability to a text Dynamic text field. This is especially important with externally loaded text that flows beyond the boundaries of the text field or even the stage. Only by scrolling the text can the viewer see it. As you will see in this chapter, you can use the scroll bar for more than scrolling text.

Introduction to Scroll Bar

The scroll bar is relatively simple in most respects. If you plan to use the scroll bar primarily for scrolling text, you will find several different methods to customize the scroll bar for your needs. However, some of the methods cannot be used with text fields and are designed to work with non-text objects. So while the chapter sample movie centers on text fields, a little extra movie had to be added to this chapter to show how non-text fields operate in conjunction with the scroll bar.

Methods

The scroll bar has 12 methods, some of which are found with other UI components, and other methods that are unique to the FScrollBar component object. Like other components, scroll bars are referenced by an instance name allowing control of multiple scroll bars on the stage simultaneously. The main sample movie for this chapter uses only a single scroll bar, but it uses several of the methods associated with the scroll bar component. Also, the setScrollProperties() method requires a movie because it cannot be used with a text field which dominates the first movie. Figure 19-1 provides a visual overview of the stage being set. A red filter made up of a solid red movie clip with adjusting alpha level covers up the underlying text field, but both are identical in size, and the filter places a red hue over the text as the scroll bar (called a "thumb") is moved up and down the scrolling groove. Table 19-1 shows the color palette for the movie. It contains

Name	R	G	B
Green	54	161	43
Red	255	0	0
Orange	255	125	0
Black	0	0	0
White	255	255	255

Table 19-1. *Color Palette*

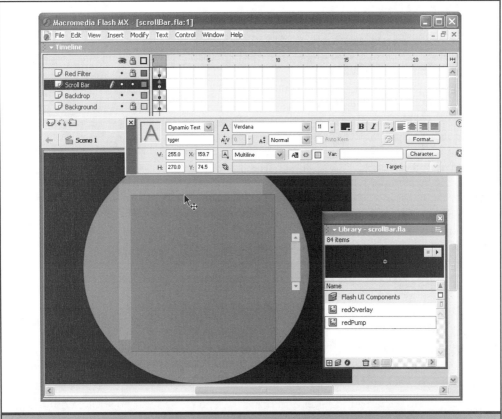

Figure 19-1. *The scroll bar component can be placed anywhere on the stage because the script positions and sizes it to fit the text field hidden beneath the red movie clip*

the colors of a tiger—orange, black, and white. The red is added as an element of drama to William Blake's poem, "The Tyger." When the text scrolls, the alpha (transparency) level of a red filter made up of a solid red movie clip casts a red mist over the poem.

The following steps show how to reproduce the movie. I used William Blake's famous poem, "The Tyger," but you can put in any text you want.

1. First create a text file and put it in the same folder where you will save your Flash movie. You can use application programs like Notepad (Windows) or SimpleText (Macintosh) to save the file as a text file. Save the file as tyger.txt.

```
Tyger Tyger, burning bright,
In the forests of the night:
What immortal hand or eye,
Could frame thy fearful symmetry?
```

```
In what distant deeps or skies
Burnt the fire of thine eyes?
On what wings dare he aspire?
What the hand dare seize the fire?
And what shoulder and what art
Could twist the sinews of thy heart?
And when thy heart began to beat,
What dread hand and what dread feet?
What the hammer and what the chain?
In what furnace was thy brain?
What the anvil? What dread grasp
Dare its deadly terrors clasp?
When the stars threw down their spears
And water'd heaven with their tears:
Did he smile his work to see?
Did he who made the Lamb make thee?
Tyger Tyger, burning bright,
In the forests of the night:
What immortal hand or eye
Dare frame thy fearful symmetry?
—William Blake, 1794
```

2. Open a new movie and add 3 layers to the existing layer. Name them from top to bottom: Red Filter, Scroll Bar, Backdrop, and Background. Set the background color to black.

3. Select the Background layer and draw a green circle with no stroke with the dimensions W = 400, H = 400. Center it horizontally and vertically on the stage. Lock the layer.

4. Select the Backdrop level and draw an orange rectangle with the dimensions W = 255, H = 270 positioned at x = 138, y = 55 so that the upper-left corner touches the edge of the circle. Lock the layer.

5. Select the Scroll Bar layer and add a Dynamic text field with the dimensions W = 255, X = 270, positioning it to overlap the underlying orange rectangle. Its lower-right corner should just touch the lower-right side of the green circle. Give it the instance name tyger.

6. Drag an FScrollBar UI component from the Components panel. Place it to the right side of the stage on the circle. The ActionScript will resize and reposition it for you. Lock the layer.

7. Select the Red Filter layer and draw a red rectangle directly over the Dynamic text field using exactly the same position and dimensions. (See Step 5.) Select the red rectangle, press the F8 key to convert it into a movie clip, giving it the symbol name redOverlay and the instance name redFilter.

8. Select Insert | New Symbol from the menu bar. Select Movie Clip for Behavior, and provide the symbol name redPump, then click OK to enter the Symbol Editing Mode. Add a frame to the existing layer in the Symbol Editing mode for a total of two frames. Select the first frame and in the Actions panel add the following script:

```
pump = _root.tygerBar.getScrollPosition()*4;
_root.redFilter._alpha = pump;
```

9. Click the Scene icon to return to the main timeline, click the first frame of the Scroll Bar layer, and enter the following script:

```
//Load some text into the text field.
redFilter._alpha = 0;
tygerUp = new LoadVars();
tygerUp.onData = function(contents) {
    tyger.text = contents;
};
tygerUp.load("tyger.txt");
//Establish Settings
tygerBar.setScrollTarget(tyger);
tygerBar.setEnabled(true);
tygerBar.setHorizontal(false);
tygerBar.setSize(270);
tygerBar.setLargeScroll(10);
tygerBar.setSmallScroll(4);
tygerBar.setStyleProperty("arrow", 0x36A12B);
tygerBar.setStyleProperty("scrollTrack", 0xFF7D00);
tygerBar.setStyleProperty("face", 0x000000);
//Position Scroll Bar
tygerBar._y = tyger._y;
tygerBar._x = tyger._x+255;
```

The scroll bar was updated by the movie clip's second frame. It kept refreshing the scroll position of the scroll bar by rerunning the same script, while at the same time the scroll bar was moving the text in the Dynamic text field. Figure 19-2 shows that the red filter disappears and the scroll bar has changed shape and position.

getEnabled

FScrollBar.getEnabled(): Method

The default condition of a scroll bar is a Boolean true enabled. When you use the getEnabled() method, you receive the Boolean value of true or false indicating that the scroll bar is enabled or not. If you want to disable it, you would use the setEnabled() method. For example, the following line gets the enabled status of a scroll bar with the

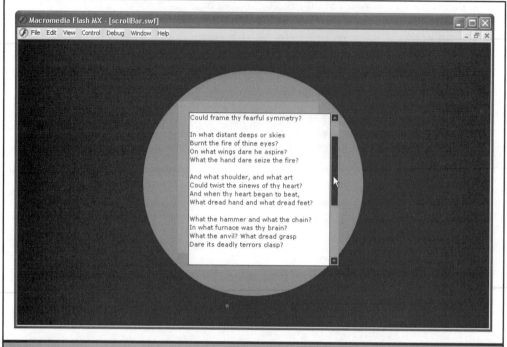

Figure 19-2.   *When you scroll the text, the red filter's alpha level increases to put a red mist over the text.*

instance name "tygerBar" and places it in the Output window. You should see a "true" in the Output window if you attach the script to the end of your movie.

```
trace(tygerBar.getEnabled());
```

getScrollPosition
FScrollBar.getScrollPosition(): Method

The getScrollPosition() method returns an integer with the current scroll position based on the minPos and maxPos settings or the size of the text field the scroll bar is attached to. The initial position value at the top of the scroll bar is 0. Each time the scroll goes one line below the visible text, the scroll position increases by 1. For example, if you can see 7 lines of text in the text window, to see line 8 you have to scroll down 1. The scroll position becomes 1 when line 8 is first visible, 2 when line 9 becomes visible, and so forth to the bottom of the scroll.

In the sample movie, the movie clip redPump uses the scroll position to increase the amount of alpha that the red filter receives based on the current scroll position using the following script:

```
pump = _root.tygerBar.getScrollPosition()*4;
_root.redFilter._alpha = pump;
```

registerSkinElement

FScrollBar.registerSkinElement(element, styleProperty): Method

The registerSkinElement() method has two arguments. The element parameter refers to the movie clip instance that provides the skin for the component, and the styleProperty argument is the name of the FStyleFormat property. The method registers the skin element to a style property specified. The following example shows a movie clip with the instance name scrollMe_mc that replaces the default scrollTrack styleProperty:

```
tygerBar.registerSkinElement(scrollMe_mc, "scrollTrack");
```

setChangeHandler

FScrollBar.setChangeHandler(functionName, [location]): Method

The setChangeHandler() method has two parameters. The functionName must be named as a string indicating a unique name for a function. Optionally, you can specify the path (location) to the function in a movie clip or timeline. If no location parameter is indicated, the change handler function must be on the same timeline as the scroll bar instance.

The sample movie did not have a change handler because the scroll bar attaches to the movie and changes the text position without any need for specifying a change handler and a function to carry out related actions. However, if dealing with a non-text object such as a movie clip, the scroll bar needs a change handler to make something happen. To make a simple movie to see how this works, place a single scroll bar and a movie clip in the shape of a filled circle. Give the circle the instance name ball and place an instance of the MC in the middle of the stage. Position the scroll bar component on the far left at the edge of the stage, and give the scroll bar the instance name hor. Click on the first frame and enter the following script:

```
hor.setHorizontal(true);
hor.setSize(500);
hor.setChangeHandler("moveX");
hor.setScrollProperties(1, 0, 550);
function moveX() {
    _root.ball._x = hor.getScrollPosition();
}
```

The change handler identifies moveX as the change function. The moveX() function links the ball's horizontal (_x) position with the scroll bar's position moving it left and right. The following illustration gives you an idea of what you can expect to see:

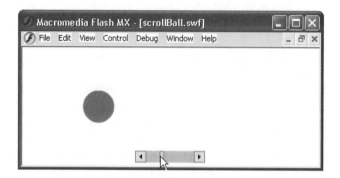

setEnabled

FScrollBar.setEnabled(enable): Method

The setEnabled() method has a single Boolean parameter that can be set to true or false. The Boolean true enables the scroll bar instance, and the Boolean false disables it. Disabled scroll bars cannot accept keyboard or mouse input from the user, and the bar turns gray as well. When you test the sample movie, the scroll bar is enabled by default. The following was included even though it is redundant to the default condition of the scroll bar:

```
tygerBar.setEnabled(true);
```

setHorizontal

FScrollBar.setHorizontal(horizontalScroll): Method

The setHorizontal() method uses a Boolean true as a parameter value to change the default orientation of a scroll bar from vertical to horizontal. For horizontal scrolling in a text field or some other object (see the setChangeHandler() section), set the parameter to true. To make sure it stays vertical, you can use what was done in the sample movie script as the following shows:

```
tygerBar.setHorizontal(false);
```

Note *If you place a scroll bar on the stage and then use the Free Transform tool to place it in a horizontal position, the setHorizontal() method will not change the position to vertical. However, if the scroll bar is set to setHorizontal(false), moving the scroll bar left and right will scroll the text up and down. As a general rule of thumb, only change the horizontal position of the scroll bar using the Parameters tab in the Properties panel or in your ActionScript code. However, if you want your design to move text vertically with the scroll bar in a horizontal position, you know the secret of doing it.*

setLargeScroll
FScrollBar.setLargeScroll(largeScroll): Method

The setLargeScroll() method is used to set the number of positions the scroll moves when the track receives one click. If no setting is made, the large scroll defaults to the size of the viewable page.

In the sample movie, the value 10 is used because it jumped a single stanza of the poem. The following script made that setting:

```
tygerBar.setLargeScroll(10);
```

setScrollPosition
FScrollBar.setScrollPosition(position): Method

The setScrollPosition() method sets the position of the scroller or thumb on the scroll bar. Like some other components that invoke the change handler when the setValue() method is invoked, the scroll bar fires the change handler when the thumb is set to a new position on the scroll bar:

```
tygerBar.setScrollPosition(15);
```

If you insert the above line of code at the end of the sample movie, you will find a very interesting phenomenon. The movie will briefly scroll to the new position, but it immediately bounces back to the default position of 0. However, if you add the line:

```
hor.setScrollPosition(400);
```

at the end of the ball movie script, when you test the movie, the ball will move and stay at the uncentered position. (See the setChangeHandler section.) The ball movie contains settings for the scroll bar that the main sample movie does not and so does not snap to defaults as is the case when connected to text fields.

setScrollProperties
FScrollBar.setScrollProperties(pageSize, minPos, maxPos): Method

While considered a more advanced method, the setScrollProperties() method is not that difficult to set. The problem with the method is that it does not work with scroll bars attached to text fields. Text fields with attached scroll bars automatically set the scroll properties. That was why the method was used in the example moving the ball from side to side on the stage. The pageSize parameter refers to the number of rows in a page view. The ball movie used a single row, and so this parameter was set to 1. The minPos parameter is the minimum position for scrolling. The ball movie was moving a ball MC from left to right across the stage. To move it all the way to the left, it needed a value of 0, and so the minPos was set to 0. Finally, the maxPos represents the maximum index value for a scrolled position. Since the stage is 550, it was set to that value. Also because the size of the scroll bar was set to 550, the ball stayed directly above the thumb on the scroll bar as it slid to the left and right. The following code was used to make that setting:

```
hor.setScrollProperties(1, 0, 550);
```

setScrollTarget
FScrollBar.setScrollTarget(target): Method

The setScrollTarget() method accepts an argument that is the instance name of the target. *Do not place quotation marks around the instance name.* This method links the scroll bar to the text field or other target. Moreover, the scroll bar does not have to physically connect with the target on the stage. In the sample movie, the scroll bar was moved next to the text field, but in the ball example, no such connection on the stage is made. So while text fields generally have scroll bars "attached" (touching), all that is actually required in the script is the setScrollTarget() method with the target name:

```
tygerBar.setScrollTarget(tyger);
```

setSize
FScrollBar.setSize(length): Method

The setSize() method sets or resets the length of the scroll bar—the combined scroll bar and its scroll arrows. In the sample movie, the scroll bar is set to 270, the height of the text field it is associated with using the following script:

```
tygerBar.setSize(270);
```

setSmallScroll()
FScrollBar.setSmallScroll(smallScroll): Method

When you click the little arrows on either end of the scroll bar, it invokes the smallScroll parameter. The purpose of the small scroll movement is to move small increments for detailed postioning. (This contrasts with the large scroll movement established with the setLargeScroll() method.) The default small scroll movement is 1, but you can set it for any number you want. In the sample movie, the small scroll was set to 4 with the following script:

```
tygerBar.setSmallScroll(4);
```

setStyleProperty

FScrollBar.setStyleProperty(styleProperty, value): Method

The setStyleProperty() method has two parameters. The styleProperty is an FStyleFormat property that can be used with components in general, with a subset that can be used for only certain components. For example, the arrow style property is used with scroll bars, but not with check boxes. (See the table in the next section for all of the FStyleFormats.)

The second parameter is the color or some other parameter of the styleProperty. Use the format 0xRRGGBB where RR (0–FF) is red, GG (0–FF) is green, and BB (0–FF) is blue. For example, 0x00ff00 is pure green. The color only applies to the specified styleProperty and not other properties that may make up the component.

In the sample movie, the changes to the arrow, scroll track, and face are made so that the colors fit the color palette selections. The following script made the settings:

```
tygerBar.setStyleProperty("arrow", 0x36A12B);
tygerBar.setStyleProperty("scrollTrack", 0xFF7D00);
tygerBar.setStyleProperty("face", 0x000000);
```

FStyleFormat Properties

The following table contains the different FStyleFormat properties and their descriptions. Use these properties with the setStyleProperty() and registerSkinElement() methods.

Property	Description
arrow	Color of arrow (scroll bars and drop-down lists only)
background	Background color of a component
backgroundDisabled	Background color of a disabled component
check	Check mark color in a check box
darkshadow	Inner border or darker shadow portion color of a component
face	Main color of the component
foregroundDisabled	Foreground color of a disabled component
highlight	Inner border or darker shadow portion color of a selected component

Property	Description
highlight3D	Outer border or light shadow portion color of a selected component
radioDot	Dot color in a selected scroll bar
scrollTrack	Track color in a scroll bar
selection	Selection bar color highlighting a list item in a component
selectionDisabled	Selection bar color that highlights a list item in a disabled component
selectionUnfocused	Selection bar color when of a component without keyboard focus
shadow	Outer border or light shadow portion color of a component
textAlign	Left, right, or center alignment for text displayed in or on a component
textBold	Boolean true value assigns bold style to text
textColor	All components assigned this default text color to the style format
textDisabled	Text color in a disabled component
textFont	Font name
textIndent	First indentation
textItalic	Boolean true value assigns italic style to text
textLeftMargin	Left paragraph margin in pixels for text
textRightMargin	Right paragraph margin in pixels for text
textSelected	Selected list color item in a component
textSize	Size of text in points
textUnderline	Boolean true value assigns underline style to text

Conclusion

While the great majority of uses of the FScrollBar UI component will no doubt continue to be an easy scrolling tool for text fields, other uses should be considered as well. They can be used to control movie clips as was seen in both the little ball movie and in the movie clip that assigned the scroll position to changing the alpha level in the filter over the text fields. For such a seemingly specialized UI component, the scroll bar has a surprising number of applications and a good deal of flexibility in the way material is scrolled.

The next chapter examines not only the last UI component, but also another way that materials are scrolled. The FScrollPane UI component is not used to display text, but rather to display movie clips. The component allows any number of movie clips to be scrolled in a confined space, allowing the viewer to see different items without having to search the Internet.

The Complete Reference

ActionScript

Chapter 20

FScrollPane

The FScrollPane UI component is used to contain and display movie clips, SWF, and JPEG files. In some respects the scroll pane is a graphic scroll box, but instead of text, you scroll MCs and external SWF and JPEG files. It is unique to Macromedia Flash MX, and I can think of no counterpart in HTML except perhaps layers, but layers can contain both text and graphics. So if you have a project where you need large MCs or graphics files available in scrollable format, look into the scroll pane.

Introduction to FScrollPane

When you first start using FScrollPane component instances, you may have a little trouble wrapping your head around the idea of movie clips and external files in a scrolling context. The basic idea is to fit far more objects on the stage than you would be able to do without scrolling them. Of course, the idea of thumbnails lets you do the same thing without scrolling, but some graphics might be well placed within a scroll pane. For example, if you had a number of different graphic font sets you wanted to show on a page, you could arrange them to be horizontally or vertically scrolled. In that way, each set would be available for viewing but not take up much room on the screen.

Methods

The FScrollPane UI component has several unique methods not found in other components. When looking at the different methods and the sample movie, keep in mind the two-dimensional scrolling. Usually when dealing with text scrolling, it is only scrolled vertically or horizontally but not both. With graphics and movie clips, though, it makes perfect sense to scroll in both directions. You can also resize the element inside the scroll pane. While the pane maintains a stable size, the movie clip, SWF file, or JPEG file can be changed to different horizontal and vertical configurations.

The sample movie shows examples of different characteristics and uses for the scroll pane to illustrate most of the methods. Two SWF files need to be created prior to running the main movie. They load into the scroll panes as external files. A movie clip is created and resides in the Library panel, but not on the stage. Figure 20-1 shows how the materials on the stage are arranged, and Table 20-1 provides the color codes used.

The following steps provide a guide to constructing the sample movie:

1. Create two small movies to be loaded into the main Macromedia Flash MX movie. One movie should be created on a 200 by 200 stage, and in 42-point red font type, "B is for baby bottles" on the top layer. The bottom layer should be a dark purple 200 by 200 square with no strokes. Save the movie as bFont.fla and publish the bFont.swf file. The second movie should be created on a 160 by 120 stage with two layers. On the top layer, in a 42-point teal font, type "Call 555-1234" in the middle of the stage. On the bottom layer, create a 160 by 120 yellow rectangle with no stroke. Save the movie as cFont.fla and publish the cFont.swf file. When you begin the main movie, be sure to place the SWF files in the same folder as the main movie.

Name	R	G	B
Yellow	255	242	112
Teal	79	166	176
Red	255	0	25
Dark purple	64	36	83

Table 20-1.   *Color Palette*

2. Open a new movie with a 550 by 400 stage and add a yellow background color. Add two layers to the existing layer and name them, from top to bottom, Pane, Buttons, and Background.

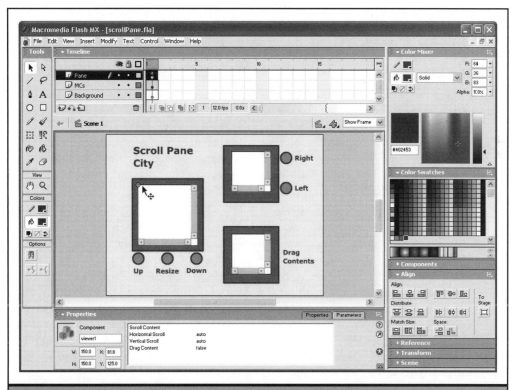

Figure 20-1.   *Three scroll panes on the stage accept content from external files and a movie clip in the Library panel, and the ActionScript further configures all of the panels.*

3. In the background layer, using Figure 20-1 as a guide, draw one 179 by 179 square with a red fill and 3.25-point dark purple stroke. Position it on the left side of the stage. On the right side of the stage, using the same colors and stroke, draw two 140 by 140 rectangles, placing one above the other. Above the large rectangle using a 24-point bold dark purple Verdana font, type "Scroll Pane City". Place the labels Up, Resize, and Down beneath the large rectangle using a bold 16-point Verdana font. To the right of the top smaller rectangle, place the labels Right and Left. Next to the bottom small rectangle, type in the label Drag Contents. Lock the layer.

4. Select the Buttons layer. Use the Oval tool to create a circle with a 3.25-point stroke and a teal fill. Select the circle, press the F8 key to open the Convert To Symbol dialog box, using the name FireButton and selecting Button as the Behavior. Double-click the button to enter the Symbol Editing Mode, and place a keyframe in the Over and Down frames. Select the Over frame and change the fill color from teal to red. Return to the main timeline. Place a total of five buttons on the stage. One each should go above the Up, Resize, and Down labels, and one each next to the Right and Left labels. Use the following instance names for the buttons relative to the labels—Up: scrollU; Resize: resize; Down: scrollD; Right: scrollR; and Left: scrollL. (Except for the resize button, all of the others use instance names made up of "scroll" plus the first letter of the direction, U, D, R, and L.) Lock the layer.

5. Select the Pane layer and drag three FScrollPane UI components from the Components panel. Place one centered over each of the three red squares. Set the dimensions W = 150, H = 150 for the one over the large square. The two other scroll panes should retain the default dimensions of W = 100, H = 100. Assign the instance name viewer1 for the large scroll pane. The top smaller scroll pane is assigned the instance name viewer2 and the other viewer3. Lock the layer.

6. Select Insert | New Symbol to open the Create New Symbol dialog box. Select Movie Clip for Behavior and assign the name aFontMC. Click the Advanced button to open the Linkage section where you will type in **aFontx** for the Identifier. (If you see a Basic button and no Advanced button, you already have the Linkage area open.) Click Export For ActionScript, which will automatically select Export In First Frame. Click OK to enter the Symbol Editing Mode. Add a layer to the existing layer, and on the bottom layer, draw a rectangle with a teal fill and dark purple 3.25-point stroke, and the dimensions W = 210, H = 340. Lock the bottom layer. Using a 96-point yellow font of your choice, type **ABC**, and then below the A type **B** and below B, type **C**. Lock both layers and click the Scene1 icon to return to the main timeline.

7. Click the first frame of the Pane layer and enter the following script:

```
//Place scroll parameters in array
scroller = new Array(true, false, "auto");
```

```
//Assign scroll and style properties to Scroll Panes
for (x=0; x<scroller.length; x++) {
    setNow = eval("viewer"+(x+1));
    setNow.setVScroll(scroller[x]);
    setNow.setHScroll(scroller[x]);
    setNow.setStyleProperty("scrollTrack", 0xFFF270);
    setNow.setStyleProperty("arrow", 0x4FA6B0);
    setNow.setStyleProperty("face", 0x02453);
}
//Load the Scroll Panes with content
viewer1.setScrollContent("aFontX");
viewer2.loadScrollContent("cFont.swf");
viewer3.loadScrollContent("bFont.swf");
viewer3.setDragContent(true);
//Scroll Methods
scrollR.onPress = function() {
    moverH -= 5;
    viewer2.setScrollPosition(moverH, 0);
};
scrollL.onPress = function() {
    moverH += 5;
    viewer2.setScrollPosition(moverH, 0);
};
scrollD.onPress = function() {
    moverV += 5;
    viewer1.setScrollPosition(0, moverV);
};
scrollU.onPress = function() {
    moverV -= 5;
    viewer1.setScrollPosition(0, moverV);
};
//Expand the width of the content in viewer1
resize.onPress = function() {
    var viewBloom = viewer1.getScrollContent();
    viewBloom._width = 350;
    viewBloom._height = 350;
    viewer1.refreshPane();
};
```

When you test the movie, you will see images in each of the three scroll panes as shown in Figure 20-2. The large pane will scroll the image inside up and down using the buttons, but it will scroll left and right by dragging the scroll bar thumb. If you click the Resize button, the contents of the pane enlarge, but the pane stays the same size. In the top smaller pane, you will see no scroll bars, but using the buttons you can scroll

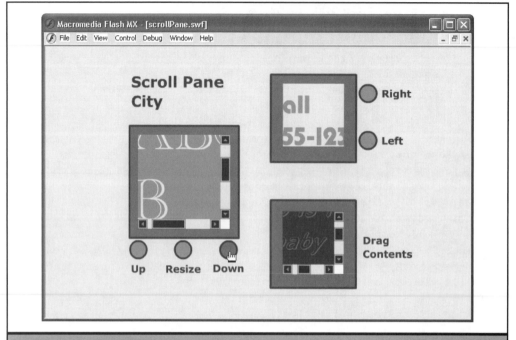

Figure 20-2.   *The three scroll panes have been configured in three different ways by the ActionScript, with two having scroll bars and the third without any scroll bars.*

the image inside to the left and right. Finally, the bottom small pane has contents that you can drag. Click on the inside of the pane and holding down the mouse button drag the contents inside in any direction you want.

getPaneHeight
FScrollPane.getPaneHeight(): Method

The getPaneHeight() method returns the vertical height of the scroll pane view. If you set the pane height dynamically using the _width and _height properties, this method will not work. It only operates if the FScrollPane.setSize() method is invoked or the scroll pane dimensions are set using the W and H values in the Properties or Info panels. The method returns an integer with the height in pixels. Add the following to the end of your script:

```
trace(viewer1.getPaneHeight());
trace(viewer2.getPaneHeight());
trace(viewer3.getPaneHeight());
```

The Output window shows 150, 100, and 100, indicating the same values you set in the H value window in the Properties panel.

getPaneWidth
FScrollPane.getPaneWidth(): Method

The getPaneWidth() method returns the horizontal width of the scroll pane view. If you set the pane width dynamically using the _width and _height properties, this method will not work. It only operates if the FScrollPane.setSize() method is invoked or the scroll pane dimensions are set using the W and H values in the Properties or Info panels. The method returns an integer with the width in pixels. Add the following to the end of your script:

```
trace(viewer1.getPaneWidth());
trace(viewer2.getPaneWidth());
trace(viewer3.getPaneWidth());
```

The Output window shows 150, 100, and 100, indicating the same values you set in the W value window in the Properties panel. (Because square shapes were used, the values from getPaneWidth() are the same as those found using getPaneHeight() in the sample movie.)

getScrollContent
FScrollPane.getScrollContent(): Method

Because the getScrollContent() method returns the full path and reference name of the content, you can use it to address the content within the pane. However, the reference name will not be the identifier of the symbol used. For example, place the following line at the end of your movie:

```
trace(viewer1.getScrollContent());
```

The Output window shows:

```
_level0.viewer1.tmo_mc
```

No matter how many different movie clips you use, the path name always results in tmp_mc, indicating a temporary name used while the MC is content in the scroll pane. In the sample movie, the method was used to get a reference to the content in the scroll pane with the instance name viewer1. The following lines placed the reference to the content into an object named viewBloom and then used it to change the size of the content stored in the scroll pane:

```
//Expand the width of the content in viewer1
resize.onPress = function() {
```

ACTIONSCRIPT USER INTERFACE COMPONENTS

```
var viewBloom = new Object();
viewBloom = viewer1.getScrollContent();
viewBloom._width = 350;
viewBloom._height = 350;
viewer1.refreshPane();
};
```

The setSize() method was not used because it sets the size of the scroll pane, not the contents of the scroll pane.

getScrollPosition
FScrollPane.getScrollPosition(): Method

The getScrollPosition() method returns an object with the current position values of a scroll pane. The object has the properties x and y that contain the current horizontal and vertical position of the scroll in a given pane.

For example, if you add the following code to the end of the sample movie, it first sets the scroll position at x = 2 and y = 3. Using an Object object named where, the getScrollPosition() method assigns the x and y values of the scroll pane to the object where:

```
viewer1.setScrollPosition(2, 3);
var where = new Object();
where = viewer1.getScrollPosition();
trace(where.x);
trace(where.y);
```

When you test the movie, the Output window shows 2 and 3 as the correct scroll position values. Had you set no scroll position, the output would have shown 0 and 0, the default start scroll positions of all scroll panes.

loadScrollContent
FScrollPane.loadScrollContent(URL [, funcName, location]): Method

The loadScrollContent() method loads either an SWF or JPEG file into a scroll pane. Optionally, you can include a reference to a function that fires when the file loads. In the sample movie, the method was used twice, once each for the two SWF files loaded:

```
viewer2.loadScrollContent("cFont.swf");
viewer3.loadScrollContent("bFont.swf");
```

If you want, you can add a function in the parameters. For example, add the following changes to kick in when a SWF file has been loaded:

```
viewer3.loadScrollContent("bFont.swf", "tilt");
function tilt() {
    viewer1._rotation = 80;
}
```

The function tilts the big scroll pane on its side, demonstrating how a function can be invoked by the loading of an external file into the scroll pane.

refreshPane
FScrollPane.refreshPane(): Method

Once you change the height or width of content in a scroll panel, you need to use the refreshPane() method to resize the scroll bars of the scroll pane. In the sample movie, one of the buttons was named Resize, and when clicked, it changed the content of viewer1 by changing the _width and _height property values. The following script shows how the method is used in context to refresh the scroll pane after its contents have changed:

```
resize.onPress = function() {
    var viewBloom = viewer1.getScrollContent();
    viewBloom._width = 350;
    viewBloom._height = 350;
    viewer1.refreshPane();
};
```

registerSkinElement
FScrollPane.registerSkinElement(element, styleProperty): Method

The registerSkinElement() method has two arguments. The element parameter refers to the movie clip instance that provides the skin for the component, and the styleProperty argument is the name of the FStyleFormat property. The method registers the skin element to a style property specified. The following example shows a movie clip with the instance name bigArrow_mc that replaces the default arrow styleProperty. See the section "FStyleFormat Properties" for a full range of style properties.

```
viewer2.registerSkinElement(bigArrow_mc, "arrow");
```

setDragContent
FScrollPane.setDragContent(drag): Method

Applying the setDragContent() method sets the ability to drag the content within a scroll pane. The drag parameter accepts a Boolean argument, with true enabling drag and false disabling it. In the sample movie, only a single scroll pane has dragable content. The following script uses the method to set the content in the viewer3 scroll pane to dragable in the sample movie:

```
viewer3.setDragContent(true);
```

setHScroll
FScrollPane.setHScroll(display): Method

The setHScroll() method has three values for the display parameter: true, false, and "auto". The first two choices are Boolean values, and the third is a string. When set to Boolean true, the scroll pane always displays the horizontal scroll bar, and if set to Boolean false, it never displays the scroll bars. The "auto" parameter only shows the horizontal scroll bars if the pane's content is too wide to display without a horizontal scroll bar. In the sample movie, all three values were used.

To set the parameters, an array with the three different parameter values gave different values to the three scroll panes. The following script segment shows how the setHScroll() method was employed:

```
//Place scroll parameters in array
scroller = new Array(true, false, "auto");
//Assign scroll and style properties to Scroll Panes
for (x=0; x<scroller.length; x++) {
    setNow = eval("viewer"+(x+1));
    setNow.setVScroll(scroller[x]);
    setNow.setHScroll(scroller[x]);
....
```

setScrollContent
FScrollPane.setScrollContent(target): Method

The most important step to keep in mind when using the setScrollContent() method is setting the linkage to the target. The target parameter is the movie clip's identifier, not its instance name. Generally, when you place an MC in the movie into a scroll pane, the MC will be in the Library panel and not on the stage. However, to load a target from the library, the symbol in the library must have an identifier that is set in the Linkage Properties dialog box. (To set the linkage, just select the symbol in the Library panel, right-click the mouse to open the context menu, and select Linkage.) You also need to select the Linkage options in the Linkage Properties dialog box: Export For ActionScript and Export In First Frame.

The following example specifies the movie clip instance aFontX as the target for viewer1:

```
viewer1.setScrollContent("aFontX");
```

setScrollPosition
FScrollPane.setScrollPosition(x, y): Method

The setScrollPosition() method can be used with any scroll pane, including those that have no scroll bars. The two arguments are values to move horizontally (x) and vertically (y) the indicated number of pixels. The arguments can be negative or positive. Negative values move up or to the right, while positive values move to the left or down. All movement applies to the content of scroll panes and has no affect on the pane's position on the stage. Finally, all movement is relative to the content's current position in the pane and not the stage. The position is a scroll position where the upper-left corner of the pane is the 0,0 position. As the pane scrolls in one direction, the content moves in the opposite, so it can be a little confusing when setting the values. For example, as you drag one of the scroll bar thumbs downward, the text scrolls upward.

In the sample movie, four buttons used the setScrollPosition() method to move objects vertically and horizontally. The following script is labeled "Right" on the stage:

```
//Scroll Methods
scrollR.onPress = function() {
    moverH -= 5;
    viewer2.setScrollPosition(moverH, 0);
};
```

setSize
FScrollPane.setSize(width, height): Method

The setSize() method sets the width and height of the scroll pane in pixels. Both parameters expect integers. In the sample movie, this method was not employed. Instead, the pane sizes were established by setting the width and height in the Properties panel. However, the same settings could be made using the setSize() method. To see how the methods can be applied, add the following line to the end of the sample movie:

```
viewer3.setSize(300,150);
```

The bottom-right scroll pane no longer encompasses the width of its content, and because it has been assigned "auto" scroll bars, the horizontal scroll bar disappears.

setStyleProperty
FScrollPane.setStyleProperty(styleProperty, value): Method

The setStyleProperty() method has two parameters. The styleProperty is an FStyleFormat property that can be used with components in general with a subset that can be used for only certain components. For example, the arrow style property is used with scroll bars but not with check boxes. (See the table in the next section for all of the FStyleFormats.)

The second parameter is the color or some other parameter of the styleProperty. Use the format 0xRRGGBB where RR (0–FF) is red, GG (0–FF) is green, and BB (0–FF) is blue. For example, 0x00ff00 is pure green. The color only applies to the specified styleProperty and not other properties that may make up the component.

In the sample movie, the changes to the arrow, scroll track and face are made so that their colors fit in with the color palette. The following script made the settings:

```
setNow.setStyleProperty("scrollTrack", 0xFFF270);
setNow.setStyleProperty("arrow", 0x4FA6B0);
setNow.setStyleProperty("face", 0x02453);
```

setVScroll
FScrollPane.setVScroll(display): Method

The setVScroll() method has three values for the display parameter: true, false, and "auto". The first two choices are Boolean values, and the third is a string. When set to Boolean true, the scroll pane always displays the horizontal scroll bar, and if set to Boolean false, it never displays the scroll bars. The "auto" parameter only shows the horizontal scroll bars if the pane's content is too wide to display without a horizontal scroll bar. In the sample movie, all three values were used.

To set the parameters, an array with the three different parameter values gave different values to the three scroll panes. The following script segment shows how the setVScroll method was employed:

```
//Place scroll parameters in array
scroller = new Array(true, false, "auto");
//Assign scroll and style properties to Scroll Panes
for (x=0; x<scroller.length; x++) {
    setNow = eval("viewer"+(x+1));
    setNow.setVScroll(scroller[x]);
....
```

FStyleFormat Properties

The following table contains the different FStyleFormat properties and their descriptions. Use these properties with the setStyleProperty() and registerSkinElement() methods.

Property	Description
arrow	Color of arrow (scroll bars and drop-down lists only)
background	Background color of a component
backgroundDisabled	Background color of a disabled component
check	Check mark color in check box
darkshadow	Inner border or darker shadow portion color of a component
face	Main color of the component
foregroundDisabled	Foreground color of a disabled component
highlight	Inner border or darker shadow portion color of a selected component
highlight3D	Outer border or light shadow portion color of a selected component
radioDot	Dot color in a selected scroll bar
scrollTrack	Track color in a scroll bar
selection	Selection bar color highlighting a list item in a component
selectionDisabled	Selection bar color that highlights a list item in a disabled component
selectionUnfocused	Selection bar color when of a component without keyboard focus
shadow	Outer border or light shadow portion color of a component
textAlign	Left, right, or center alignment for text displayed in or on a component
textBold	Boolean true value assigns bold style to text
textColor	All components assigned this default text color to the style format
textDisabled	Text color in a disabled component
textFont	Font name
textIndent	First indentation

Property	Description
textItalic	Boolean true value assigns italic style to text
textLeftMargin	Left paragraph margin in pixels for text
textRightMargin	Right paragraph margin in pixels for text
textSelected	Selected list color item in a component
textSize	Size of text in points
textUnderline	Boolean true value assigns underline style to text

Conclusion

The scroll pane is the last of the UI components. It contains a number of surprises because it is unique in scrolling, changing, and revealing external JPEG and SWF files as well as internal movie clips within the confines of a pane on the stage. Several panes placed on a single stage and in a single eye span can present graphics or even animated movie clips all contained within scrollable panes.

The next chapter is an exposition of the FStyleFormat. At the end of each of the UI component chapters, you found a table identical to Table 20-2. The table was available so that you could see a complete list of the style properties for UI components and make any changes in addition to those made in the sample movie in the component chapters. You will now be able to see all of them explained and applied, and yes, the table will be available again for a quick summary but with some additional elements as well.

The Complete Reference

ActionScript

Chapter 21

FStyleFormat

In the previous chapters on components, the emphasis has been on the components' methods and properties. This chapter focuses on style formats that can be applied to one or more components on the stage. By making changes to a single property, you will be able to make changes to that property in all of the different components used in your movie. For example, if you style the arrow and scrollTrack properties to be consistent with your overall design pattern, you can apply the changes to all of your components that have arrows and scroll tracks, not just a single component.

FStyleFormat Properties

As you have seen in a slightly different form in all of the component chapters, Table 21-1 contains the different FStyleFormat properties and their descriptions. These properties can be set using the style format objects and the global style formatting

Property	Description
arrow	Color of arrow (scroll bars and drop-down lists only)
background	Background color of a component
backgroundDisabled	Background color of a disabled component
check	Check mark color in check box
darkshadow	Inner border or darker shadow portion color of a component
embedFonts	Boolean value where false selects device fonts
face	Main color of the component
focusRectInner	A component's inner focus rectangle stroke
focusRectOuter	A component's outer focus rectangle stroke
foregroundDisabled	Foreground color of a disabled component
highlight	Inner border or darker shadow portion color of a selected component
highlight3D	Outer border or light shadow portion color of a selected component
radioDot	Dot color in a selected scroll bar
scrollTrack	Track color in a scroll bar

Table 21-1.   *Style Properties*

Property	Description
selection	Selection bar color highlighting a list item in a component
selectionDisabled	Selection bar color that highlights a list item in a disabled component
selectionUnfocused	Selection bar color when of a component without keyboard focus
shadow	Outer border or light shadow portion color of a component
textAlign	Left, right, or center alignment for text displayed in or on a component
textBold	Boolean true value assigns bold style to text
textColor	All components assigned this default text color to the style format
textDisabled	Text color in a disabled component
textFont	Font name
textIndent	First indentation
textItalic	Boolean true value assigns italic style to text
textLeftMargin	Left paragraph margin in pixels for text
textRightMargin	Right paragraph margin in pixels for text
textSelected	Selected list color item in a component
textSize	Size of text in points
textUnderline	Boolean true value assigns underline style to text

Table 21-1. *Style Properties* (continued)

GlobalStyleFormat

globalStyleFormat.styleProperty: Object instance

The globalStyleFormat is an object instance that provides a way to redefine style formats for all instances of components on the stage at one time. For instance, suppose you have ten different list boxes on your stage at one time, and you want to change all of the arrow properties to red. Rather than using the instance names of all ten list boxes, the following statement will change all ten for you in a single statement:

```
globalStyleFormat.arrow = 0xFF0000;
```

For use with a color palette or any other globally applied property, the globalStyleFormat saves a good deal of time.

You can globally define as many properties as you want. However, you do need at least one component on the stage, and you need to use the applyChanges() method once you have finished your assignments. For example, the following globally assigns values to three different properties and then applies the changes to any component on the stage:

```
globalStyleFormat.face = 0xFFE631;
globalStyleFormat.shadow= 0xF6EFDF;
globalStyleFormat.textFont="Verdana";
globalStyleFormat.applyChanges();
```

The following shows push button components on the stage in their default configurations:

All of the components have the same look after the changes from the globalStyleFormat is applied. The following shows the buttons (with labels applied) with the common style applied to them:

new FStyleFormat

FStyleFormat(): Constructor

The FStyleFormat() constructor creates a style object. Different properties can be attached to the object and assigned values. All of the properties and their values can then be used by components by assigning a listener to the object and assigning component instances to the parameter list of the listener. As convoluted as that may sound, the process is quite simple as you will see in the remaining examples in the chapter. The constructor works very much like other constructor objects in Flash MX ActionScript as shown in the following example:

```
doStyle = new FStyleFormat();
```

Methods

Only three methods are associated with the FStyleFormat object, and they are all uniquely fitted for work with formatting style elements to components. You will find that most of the work you do involves the addListener() method because with it you specify all the instances to which style changes apply. The addListener() method, though, is not like others you have seen that listen for events. This one simply includes in its parameters the instances that are styled.

addListener
styleFormatObject.addListener(component1 [,...componentN]): Method

Using the addListener() method is part of a process that allows you to make your style definitions within a StyleFormat object and then apply all of the defined styles to one or more of your components. When you want to have the same style set with more than a single component, you can define them in a StyleFormat object, and then assign a listener using the addListener() method. For example, suppose you have ten push buttons on the stage. You want half of them to have one color configuration and the other half to have another. You cannot use the global format style assignment (globalStyleFormat) because you have two different styles, but you do not want to have to assign each and every button the same set of styles individually using the setStyleProperty() method. By first creating a StyleFormat object for the two sets of buttons with different styles, you assign the styles to different properties. Then using the addListener() method you assign each instance a style set by including the instance names in the parameters. The following example illustrates the process:

```
doStyle = new FStyleFormat();
doStyle.face= 0x7B7284;
doStyle.arrow = 0xFFE631;
doStyle.addListener(pshBtn, comBx, listBx);
```

The instances pshBtn, comBx, and listBx now have all of the style characteristics defined by the doStyle object. You can have as many or few instances in the arguments as you want.

applyChanges
styleFormatObject.applyChanges([propertyName1, ...propertyNameN]):Method
styleFormatObject.applyChanges(): Method

The applyChanges() method is used to "set" the changes made in property assignments or to update any changes that have been made. The method is used in two different ways. One way is to update a single specific property and the other is to update all properties. First, the following globally assigns values to the face, shadow, and textFont properties, but only the face property is updated using the applyChanges() method:

```
globalStyleFormat.face = 0xFFE631;
globalStyleFormat.shadow= 0xF6EFDF;
```

```
globalStyleFormat.textFont="Verdana";
globalStyleFormat.applyChanges("face");
```

Because the first use of the method requires a property string as an argument, it only updates the properties named in the method's parameters. However, to update all changes, the method can be used with no properties placed in the arguments as the following shows:

```
globalStyleFormat.face = 0xFFE631;
globalStyleFormat.shadow= 0xF6EFDF;
globalStyleFormat.textFont="Verdana";
globalStyleFormat.applyChanges();
```

removeListener()
styleFormatObject.removeListener(component): Method

The removeListener() method has the effect of removing the style format that was assigned using the addListener() method. When a component is removed as a listener, a global style format replaces whatever style the component is assigned. If no global style is associated with a component, it reverts to its original (default) configuration and skin.

For example, the first line of the following script adds the doStyle FStyleFormat to the component instances comBx and listBx. The second line removes the doStyle style from the comBx instance only. If comBx has no global assignments, it simply reverts to its default style.

```
doStyle.addListener(comBx, listBx);
doStyle.removeListener(comBx);
```

Properties

You will find most of the properties to be the same ones introduced when discussing each of the components individually. However, in this context, the properties are part of an FStyleFormat object and the different properties are applied to more than a single component and single type of component. Table 21-1 shows all of the properties with a brief description of each. In this section, you will find examples generated in a Flash movie with push button, combo box, check box, radio button, and list box components. The scroll bar and scroll pane would be redundant as far as showing the different properties, but the same scripts would apply to them as well. Table 21-2 shows the components and the instance names employed:

Component	Instance Name
Push button	pBtn
Combo box	comBx
List box	listBx
Check box	ckBx
Radio button	radBtn

Table 21-2. *Components and Instance Names in Sample Scripts*

The particular variety of components were employed so that all of the different kinds of properties could be displayed. To work your way through the different properties, just place the five components on a new Flash MX stage and give each the indicated instance name.

arrow

styleFormatObject.arrow: Property

The arrow property is the small triangle found in scroll bars and drop-down lists. Its color can be changed using the format 0xRRGGBB where RR (0–FF) is red, GG (0–FF) is green, and BB (0–FF) is blue. For example, 0x00ff00 is pure green. If you dynamically change or update the color from one to another in a script, you need to use the applyChanges() method. The following places a yellow arrow on a darker colored face on the sample list and combo boxes:

```
doStyle = new FStyleFormat();
doStyle.face= 0x7B7284;
doStyle.arrow = 0xFFE631;
doStyle.addListener(comBx, listBx);
```

As a general rule, consider the face color whenever you change the arrow color so that you have the desired contrast in colors. (A white arrow against a white face will not show up too well.) The following shows the above-scripted changes (noting that push button components have no arrow property).

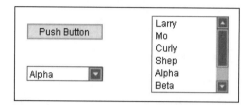

background
styleFormatObject.background: Property

The background property varies with different components. Its color can be changed using the format 0xRRGGBB where RR (0–FF) is red, GG (0–FF) is green, and BB (0–FF) is blue. For example, 0x00ff00 is pure green. If you dynamically change or update the color from one to another in a script, you need to use the applyChanges() method.

```
doStyle = new FStyleFormat();
doStyle.background = 0xFFE631;
doStyle.addListener(comBx, listBx, pBtn, ckBx, radBtn);
```

The different backgrounds can be seen in the following; note that the push button does not have a background property:

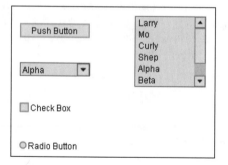

backgroundDisabled
styleFormatObject.backgroundDisabled: Property

The backgroundDisabled property applies only to disabled components. The disabled component's background color can be changed using the format 0xRRGGBB where RR (0–FF) is red, GG (0–FF) is green, and BB (0–FF) is blue. For example, 0x00ff00 is pure green. If you dynamically change or update the color from one to another in a script, you need to use the applyChanges() method.

In this following example, the listBx component instance is first disabled before the style is applied. Otherwise, the backgroundDisabled property could not be seen.

```
listBx.setEnabled(false);
doStyle = new FStyleFormat();
doStyle.backgroundDisabled = 0xF6EFDF;
doStyle.addListener(listBx);
```

check

styleFormatObject.check: Property

Not surprisingly, the check property only applies to FCheckBox UI components. The check mark's color can be changed using the format 0xRRGGBB where RR (0–FF) is red, GG (0–FF) is green, and BB (0–FF) is blue. For example, 0x00ff00 is pure green. If you dynamically change or update the color from one to another in a script, you need to use the applyChanges() method. The following script shows a contrasting change in color between the check box's background color and check mark color:

```
doStyle = new FStyleFormat();
doStyle.background = 0x7B7284;
doStyle.check = 0xFFE631;
doStyle.addListener(ckBx);
```

In the case of the check mark, you want to make certain that the background contrasts correctly with the check mark. The following shows this contrast:

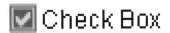

darkshadow

styleFormatObject.darkshadow: Property

The dark shadow is nothing sinister. It is the darker of two shadow elements found in components, and its color can be changed using the format 0xRRGGBB where RR (0–FF) is red, GG (0–FF) is green, and BB (0–FF) is blue. For example, 0x00ff00 is pure green. If you dynamically change or update the color from one to another in a script, you need to use the applyChanges() method. The following script generates contrasting colors between the darkshadow and background colors:

```
doStyle = new FStyleFormat();
doStyle.darkshadow = 0xFFE631;
doStyle.addListener(pBtn, comBx, rad, Btn, listBx, ckBx);
```

As you can see, all of the components in the set have dark shadows.

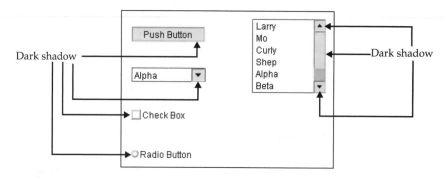

embedFonts
FstyleFormat.embedFonts: Property

The default condition for fonts in component instances is that their fonts are embedded. The embedFonts property can be set to Boolean true (embed fonts) or false (use device fonts.) To select device fonts, you would use the following script:

```
doStyle = new FStyleFormat();
doStyle.embedFonts = false;
```

face
styleFormatObject.face: Property

The face property is found on push buttons, and in the area surrounding arrow properties and the slider thumbs. The face's color can be changed using the format 0xRRGGBB where RR (0–FF) is red, GG (0–FF) is green, and BB (0–FF) is blue. For example, 0x00ff00 is pure green. If you dynamically change or update the color from one to another in a script, you need to use the applyChanges() method. The following script shows what aspects of the components are colored as faces:

```
doStyle = new FStyleFormat();
doStyle.face = 0xFFE631;
doStyle.addListener(pBtn, comBx, listBx);
```

As you can see in the following, the face property is in different places depending on the component:

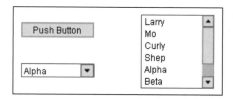

focusRectInner
styleFormatObject.focusRectInner: Property

The focusRectInner property is a component's inner focus rectangle stroke. The inner focus rectangle stroke color can be changed using the format 0xRRGGBB where RR (0–FF) is red, GG (0–FF) is green, and BB (0–FF) is blue. For example, 0x00ff00 is pure green. If you dynamically change or update the color from one to another in a script, you need to use the applyChanges() method. The following applies a yellow color to the inner focus rectangle stroke:

```
doStyle = new FStyleFormat();
doStyle.focusRectInner = 0xFFE631;
doStyle.addListener(pBtn, comBx, listBx);
```

focusRectOuter
styleFormatObject.focusRectOuter: Property

The focusRectOuter property is a component's outer focus rectangle stroke. The outer focus rectangle stroke color can be changed using the format 0xRRGGBB where RR (0–FF) is red, GG (0–FF) is green, and BB (0–FF) is blue. For example, 0x00ff00 is pure green. If you dynamically change or update the color from one to another in a script, you need to use the applyChanges() method. The following applies a yellow color to the outer focus rectangle stroke:

```
doStyle = new FStyleFormat();
doStyle.focusRectOuter = 0xFFE631;
doStyle.addListener(pBtn, comBx, listBx);
```

foregroundDisabled
styleFormatObject.foregroundDisabled: Property

The foregroundDisabled property applies only to disabled components. The disabled component's foreground color can be changed using the format 0xRRGGBB where RR (0–FF) is red, GG (0–FF) is green, and BB (0–FF) is blue. For example, 0x00ff00 is pure green. If you dynamically change or update the color from one to another in a script, you need to use the applyChanges() method.

In this following example, the listBx component instance is first disabled before the style is applied. Otherwise, the foregroundDisabled property could not be seen.

```
listBx.setEnabled(false);
doStyle = new FStyleFormat();
doStyle.backgroundDisabled = 0xFFE631;
doStyle.foregroundDisabled = 0xFF3333;
doStyle.addListener(listBx);
```

highlight
styleFormatObject.highlight: Property

The highlight is a component's darker shadow or inner border. The highlight rectangle stroke color can be changed using the format 0xRRGGBB where RR (0–FF) is red, GG (0–FF) is green, and BB (0–FF) is blue. For example, 0x00ff00 is pure green. If you dynamically change or update the color from one to another in a script, you need to use the applyChanges() method. The following applies a yellow color to the highlight property of different components:

```
doStyle = new FStyleFormat();
doStyle.highlight = 0xFFE631;
doStyle.addListener(pBtn, comBx, radBtn, listBx, ckBx);
```

The position of the highlight varies with different components as the following shows:

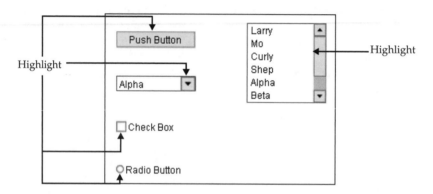

highlight3D
styleFormatObject.highlight3D: Property

The highlight3D property is a component's lighter shadow or outer border. The highlight3D rectangle stroke color can be changed using the format 0xRRGGBB where RR (0–FF) is red, GG (0–FF) is green, and BB (0–FF) is blue. For example, 0x00ff00 is pure green. If you dynamically change or update the color from one to another in a script, you need to use the applyChanges() method. The following applies a green color to the highlight3D and red to the highlight property to different components:

```
doStyle = new FStyleFormat();
doStyle.highlight=0xff0000;
doStyle.highlight3D=0x00ff00;
doStyle.addListener(pBtn, comBx, listBx, radBtn, ckBx);
```

The difference between highlight and highlight3D is sometimes a subtle one, but you should be able to clearly see the difference because the highlight is red and the highlight3D is green:

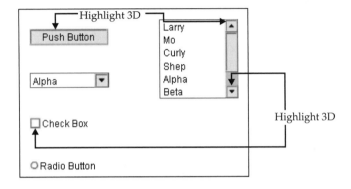

radioDot

styleFormatObject.radioDot: Property

To no one's amazement, the radioDot property only applies to FRadioButton UI components. The little dot inside the radio button can have different colors. Its color can be changed using the format 0xRRGGBB where RR (0–FF) is red, GG (0–FF) is green, and BB (0–FF) is blue. For example, 0x00ff00 is pure green. If you dynamically change or update the color from one to another in a script, you need to use the applyChanges() method. The following script shows a red dot inside the radio button:

```
doStyle = new FStyleFormat();
doStyle.radioDot = 0xFF1111;
doStyle.addListener(radBtn);
```

scrollTrack

styleFormatObject.scrollTrack: Property

The track across which the slider bar (thumb) runs is the scroll track. The FScrollPane, FListBox, and FComboBox UI components all use the scroll track. The scroll track's color can be changed using the format 0xRRGGBB where RR (0–FF) is red, GG (0–FF) is green, and BB (0–FF) is blue. For example, 0x00ff00 is pure green. If you dynamically change or update the color from one to another in a script, you need to use the applyChanges() method.

```
doStyle = new FStyleFormat();
doStyle.scrollTrack = 0xFFE631;
doStyle.addListener(listBx);
```

Be careful that the scrollTrack color contrasts well with the face property color because the two are adjacent. The default gray face contrasts well with the yellow scroll track color.

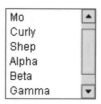

selection

styleFormatObject.selection: Property

Components like the combo box and list box have items that can be selected. When selected, they change colors. The color the selected items change to can be assigned using the format 0xRRGGBB where RR (0–FF) is red, GG (0–FF) is green, and BB (0–FF) is blue. For example, 0x00ff00 is pure green. If you dynamically change or update the color from one to another in a script, you need to use the applyChanges() method. The following changes the selection background to a dark gray that contrasts well with the white text that selected items display:

```
doStyle = new FStyleFormat();
doStyle.selection = 0x7B7284;
doStyle.addListener(comBx, listBx);
```

When you select an item, it changes to the selection property color, but if you select another item in a different component, the selection of the first one becomes unfocused and turns to the color of an unfocused selection. The selection in the combo box is the darker color of the selection while a lighter color appears in the list box because its selection is unfocused (the focus is on the combo box item).

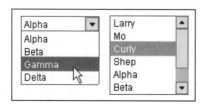

selectionDisabled

styleFormatObject.selectionDisabled: Property

This is a somewhat strange property. In order for an item to be selected, the component must be enabled. So how are you going to have a selected disabled item? The trick is to use your script to first select the item, and then more script to disable the component with the selected item. Components like the combo box and list box have items that can be selected. When selected, they change colors. The color the selected items change to can be assigned using the format 0xRRGGBB where RR (0–FF) is red, GG (0–FF) is green, and BB (0–FF) is blue. For example, 0x00ff00 is pure green. If you dynamically change or update the color from one to another in a script, you need to use the applyChanges() method. The following script first selects an item in the list box, then it disables the list box. Then it adds the style for disabled selected items. (Right off the top of my head, I do not know where this would be applied, but when you do need it, you will know how to use it.)

```
listBx.setSelectedIndex(3);
listBx.setEnabled(false);
doStyle = new FStyleFormat();
doStyle.selectionDisabled = 0xFFE631;
doStyle.addListener(listBx);
```

The following shows the disabled list box gamely displaying its selected item:

selectionUnfocused
styleFormatObject.selectionUnfocused: Property

When more than a single component with selectable items are on the screen at the same time, and you select one item in one component instance and then select another in another component, the one first selected becomes unfocused but still selected. The selectionUnfocused property allows you to select the color of unfocused selected items. Components like the combo box and list box have items that can be selected. When selected, they change colors. The color the selected items change to can be assigned using the format 0xRRGGBB where RR (0–FF) is red, GG (0–FF) is green, and BB (0–FF) is blue. For example, 0x00ff00 is pure green. If you dynamically change or update the color from one to another in a script, you need to use the applyChanges() method. The following script first requires that you have two component instances on the stage at the same time. Select one item, and then select another in a different component instance, and you will see the color change in the one first selected:

```
doStyle = new FStyleFormat();
doStyle.selectionUnfocused = 0x663333;
doStyle.addListener(listBx);
```

As you can see in the following, the shading on the selections is different.

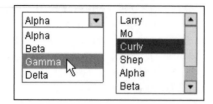

shadow
styleFormatObject.shadow: Property

The shadow property is the outer border or light shadow portion of a component. The color of the shadow area can be changed using the format 0xRRGGBB where RR (0–FF) is red, GG (0–FF) is green, and BB (0–FF) is blue. For example, 0x00ff00 is pure green. If you dynamically change or update the color from one to another in a script, you need to use the applyChanges() method. The following script displays the shadow properties in red and the darkshadow properties in green so that you can more easily distinguish one from the other:

```
doStyle = new FStyleFormat();
doStyle.shadow=0xff0000;
doStyle.darkshadow=0x00ff00;
doStyle.addListener(pBtn, comBx, listBx, radBtn, ckBx);
```

In the illustration, you can see the different shadow areas:

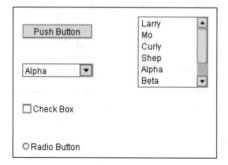

textAlign
styleFormatObject.textAlign: Property

The textAlign property has three values, left, right, and center. The following script right-aligns the text in the different components on the stage:

```
doStyle = new FStyleFormat();
doStyle.textAlign = "right";
doStyle.addListener(pBtn, comBx, listBx, radBtn, ckBx);
```

The right-aligned text moves the text away from the check box and radio button, and right-aligns it on the other components:

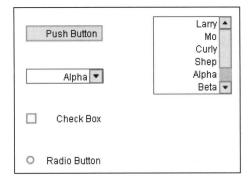

textBold
styleFormatObject.textBold: Property

The textBold property expects a Boolean value. The default is false, and by setting the textBold to true, the text in the components becomes bold as shown in the following script:

```
doStyle = new FStyleFormat();
doStyle.textBold = true;
doStyle.addListener(pBtn, comBx, listBx, radBtn, ckBx);
```

The following shows how the bold font looks on the different components:

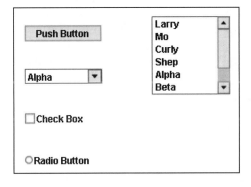

textColor
styleFormatObject.textColor: Property

The textColor property is simply the color of the text in the components. The color of the text property can be changed using the format 0xRRGGBB where RR (0–FF) is red, GG (0–FF) is green, and BB (0–FF) is blue. For example, 0x00ff00 is pure green. If you dynamically change or update the color from one to another in a script, you need to use the applyChanges() method.

```
doStyle = new FStyleFormat();
doStyle.textColor = 0x7B7284;
doStyle.addListener(pBtn, comBx, listBx, radBtn, ckBx);
```

The text was colored a medium light gray, giving it a nice unobtrusive look:

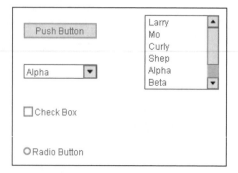

textDisabled
styleFormatObject.textDisabled: Property

The textDisabled property is the color of the text in the components when the component is disabled. The color of the text in a disabled component can be changed using the format 0xRRGGBB where RR (0–FF) is red, GG (0–FF) is green, and BB (0–FF) is blue. For example, 0x00ff00 is pure green. If you dynamically change or update the color from one to another in a script, you need to use the applyChanges() method. The following script disables the components and then sets the color of the text to a dark red:

```
pBtn.setEnabled(false);
comBx.setEnabled(false);
listBx.setEnabled(false);
radBtn.setEnabled(false);
ckBx.setEnabled(false);
doStyle = new FStyleFormat();
doStyle.textDisabled = 0xAA3333;
doStyle.addListener(pBtn, comBx, listBx, radBtn, ckBx);
```

You can see in the following illustration that selection items are unaffected by this property change:

textFont

styleFormatObject.textFont: Property

The textFont property accepts a string containing the name of the font to be used in the component style. Unless otherwise indicated, the font style is embedded in the SWF file and so whatever font you use will be available to the viewer. The following example uses the Comic Sans MS font. Use the name of the font exactly as it appears in your font list.

```
doStyle = new FStyleFormat();
doStyle.textFont = "Comic Sans MS";
doStyle.addListener(pBtn, comBx, listBx, radBtn, ckBx);
```

The Comic Sans font gives the components an informal look:

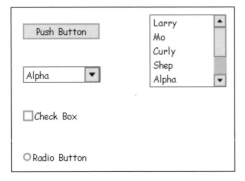

textIndent

styleFormatObject.textIndent: Property

The textIndent property can be set to any value you want to indent the text. The value assigned to the property is the number of pixels to indent the text from the left. If the text is center or right aligned, the indent is ignored.

```
doStyle = new FStyleFormat();
doStyle.textIndent = 7
doStyle.addListener(pBtn, comBx, listBx, radBtn, ckBx);
```

Note how the indent affects all of the components:

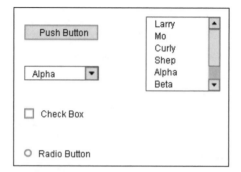

textItalic

styleFormatObject.textItalic: Property

The textItalic property expects a Boolean value. The default is false, and by setting the textItalic to true, the text in the components becomes italic as shown in the following script:

```
doStyle = new FStyleFormat();
doStyle.textItalic = true;
doStyle.addListener(pBtn, comBx, listBx, radBtn, ckBx);
```

Be careful using italic text because it often looks aliased:

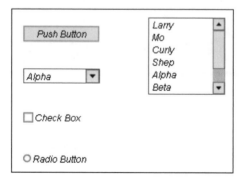

textLeftMargin
styleFormatObject.textLeftMargin: Property

The textLeftMargin property can be set to any value you want to set the margin of paragraphs on the left in components. The value assigned to the property is the number of pixels to indent the text block from the left.

```
doStyle = new FStyleFormat();
doStyle.textLeftMargin = 5;
doStyle.addListener(pBtn, comBx, listBx, radBtn, ckBx);
```

In most cases the textLeftMargin is indistinguishable from textIndent because the components generally lack text blocks. The text tends to be labels of the components or items. Compare the following with the textIndent and you will see they look very much alike:

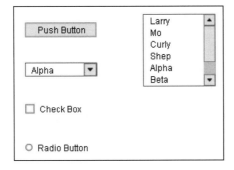

textRightMargin
styleFormatObject.textRightMargin: Property

The textRightMargin can be used as an "indent" for right-justified text. The property value sets the margin in pixels from the right side of the component. The following sets the margin on the right to 2:

```
doStyle = new FStyleFormat();
doStyle.textAlign = "right";
doStyle.textRightMargin = 2;
doStyle.addListener(pBtn, comBx, listBx, radBtn, ckBx);
```

textSelected

styleFormatObject.textSelected: Property

The textSelected property will accept a color value to assign to all selected items in a list box or combo box. The color of the selected item (text) in a component is changed using the format 0xRRGGBB where RR (0–FF) is red, GG (0–FF) is green, and BB (0–FF) is blue. For example, 0x00ff00 is pure green. If you dynamically change or update the color from one to another in a script, you need to use the applyChanges() method. In the following, the selected text is highlighted in yellow.

```
doStyle = new FStyleFormat();
doStyle.textSelected = 0xFFE631;
doStyle.addListener(comBx, listBx);
```

textSize

styleFormatObject.textSize: Property

One of the more fortunate choices in property units of measurement is that of the textSize property. The font sizes are measured in points (just like real fonts) instead of pixels. The following sets the fonts to 24 points:

```
doStyle = new FStyleFormat();
doStyle.textSize = 24;
doStyle.addListener(pBtn, comBx, listBx, radBtn, ckBx);
```

As you can see, you have to be judicious in choosing the text size or it will outgrow the component:

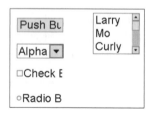

textUnderline

styleFormatObject.textUnderline: Property

The textUnderline property expects a Boolean value. The default is false, and by setting the textUnderline to true, the text in the components becomes underlined as shown in the following script:

```
uglyStyle = new FStyleFormat();
uglyStyle.textUnderline=true;
uglyStyle.addListener(pBtn, comBx, listBx, radBtn, ckBx);
```

The following shows the underlining in all of its retro glory:

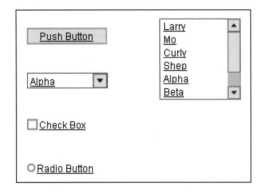

Conclusion

Flash MX gives developers more power to control more aspects of a Flash movie than all previous versions combined. The UI components are a useful set of tools for creating clear usability in a Flash-based Web site. However, unless the developer and designer have control over how the components are going to look in the overall scheme of the Flash site, components may lose both their aesthetic appeal as well as their usability. Fortunately, with the wide range of choices for component formatting, components can be adapted to just about any style the developer and designer select and provide good usability to boot.

The

Complete
Reference

ActionScript

Appendix A

Deprecated Terms
in ActionScript

615

Deprecated terms have been placed in this appendix for your possible use for targeting older Flash players, notably ones before Flash 5. It is also designed to help you filter out older Flash terms and replace them with the newer ones. If you are familiar with Flash ActionScript from previous versions, this appendix provides you with a quick look-up of terms that you may have used in the past and would like to replace with the Flash MX ActionScript. To avoid confusion, these terms were not introduced in the various chapters. In most cases, you will find that the newer terms are easier to use and read in scripts. Also, using the replacement terms will prepare scripts for future versions of Flash.

If your scripts need to conform to Flash 5 standards (for example, writing scripts for devices), you will find that all of the suggested replacements except for the three properties will work in Flash 5. If, for example, you are using scroll properties in Flash 5, use the deprecated terms because the new terms will not work with Flash 5.

Deprecated Term	Suggested Replacement
Actions	
ifFrameLoaded(scene,frame)	MovieClip._framesloaded
tellTarget("target")	MovieClip.action() Use dot style format with instance name, for example, myCar.gotoAndPlay("startRace")
toggleHighQuality()	_quality
Functions	
chr(n)	String.fromCharCode()
int(n)	Math.round()
length(exp), length(var)	String.length
mbchr(n)	String.fromCharCode()
mblength(string)	String(object)
mbord(char)	String.charCodeAt()
mbsubstring(val, index, count)	String.substr()
ord(char)	String(object)
random(val)	Math.random()
substring("string", index, count)	String.substr()

Deprecated Term	Suggested Replacement
Operators	
<>	!=
add	+
and	&&
eq	==
ge	>=
gt	>
le	<=
lt	<
ne	!=
not	!
or	||
Properties	
_highquality	_quality
maxscroll	TextField.maxscroll
scroll	TextField.scroll

Index

G

M

S

INTERNATIONAL CONTACT INFORMATION

AUSTRALIA
McGraw-Hill Book Company Australia Pty. Ltd.
TEL +61-2-9900-1800
FAX +61-2-9878-8881
http://www.mcgraw-hill.com.au
books-it_sydney@mcgraw-hill.com

CANADA
McGraw-Hill Ryerson Ltd.
TEL +905-430-5000
FAX +905-430-5020
http://www.mcgraw-hill.ca

GREECE, MIDDLE EAST, & AFRICA
(Excluding South Africa)
McGraw-Hill Hellas
TEL +30-1-656-0990-3-4
FAX +30-1-654-5525

MEXICO (Also serving Latin America)
McGraw-Hill Interamericana Editores S.A. de C.V.
TEL +525-117-1583
FAX +525-117-1589
http://www.mcgraw-hill.com.mx
fernando_castellanos@mcgraw-hill.com

SINGAPORE (Serving Asia)
McGraw-Hill Book Company
TEL +65-863-1580
FAX +65-862-3354
http://www.mcgraw-hill.com.sg
mghasia@mcgraw-hill.com

SOUTH AFRICA
McGraw-Hill South Africa
TEL +27-11-622-7512
FAX +27-11-622-9045
robyn_swanepoel@mcgraw-hill.com

SPAIN
McGraw-Hill/Interamericana de España, S.A.U.
TEL +34-91-180-3000
FAX +34-91-372-8513
http://www.mcgraw-hill.es
professional@mcgraw-hill.es

UNITED KINGDOM, NORTHERN,
EASTERN, & CENTRAL EUROPE
McGraw-Hill Education Europe
TEL +44-1-628-502500
FAX +44-1-628-770224
http://www.mcgraw-hill.co.uk
computing_neurope@mcgraw-hill.com

ALL OTHER INQUIRIES Contact:
Osborne/McGraw-Hill
TEL +1-510-549-6600
FAX +1-510-883-7600
http://www.osborne.com
omg_international@mcgraw-hill.com